THE FLETCHER JONES FOUNDATION
HUMANITIES IMPRINT

The Fletcher Jones Foundation has endowed this imprint to foster innovative and enduring scholarship in the humanities.

The publisher and the University of California Press Foundation gratefully acknowledge the generous support of the Fletcher Jones Foundation Imprint in Humanities.

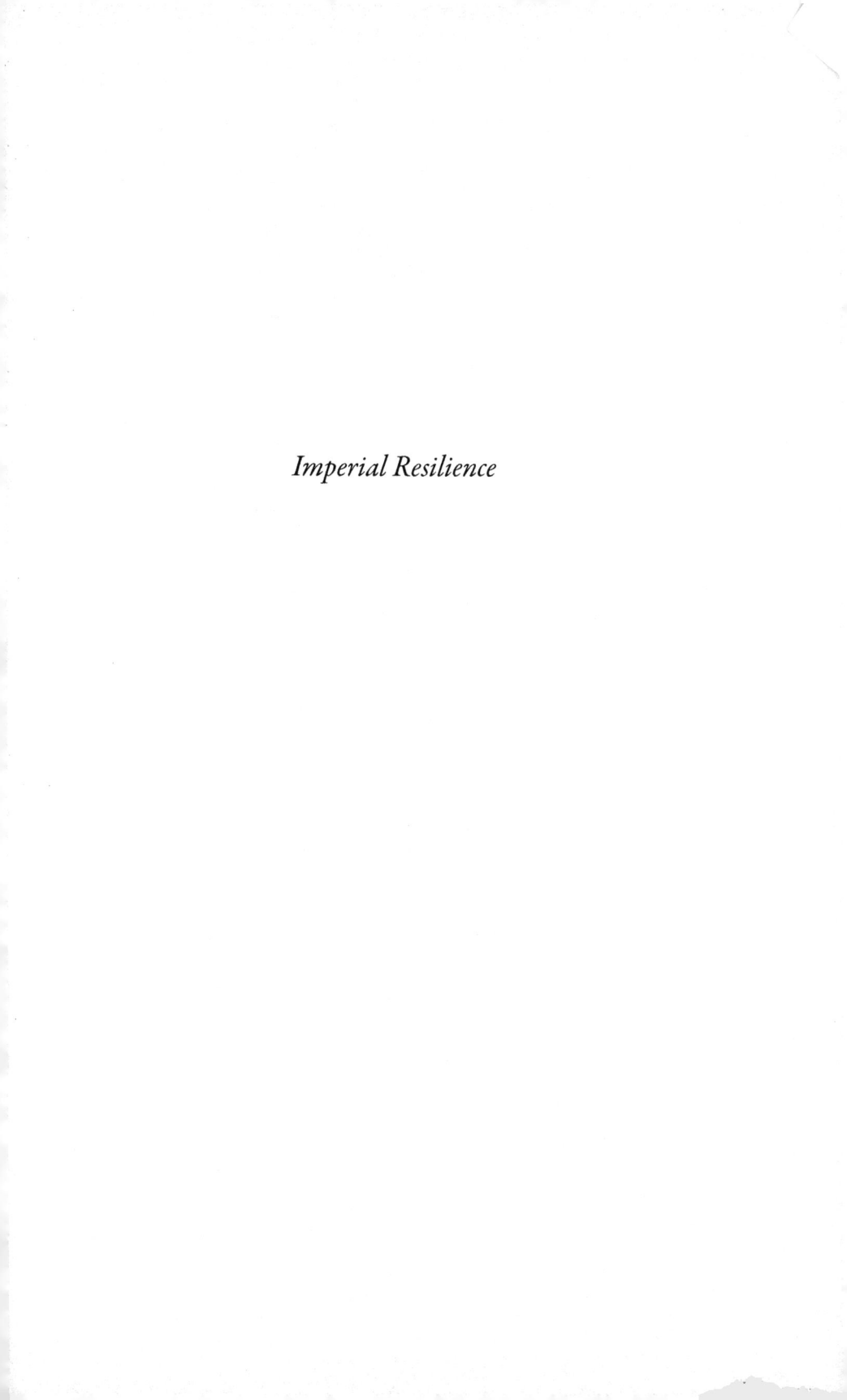

Imperial Resilience

Imperial Resilience

THE GREAT WAR'S END, OTTOMAN LONGEVITY,
AND INCIDENTAL NATIONS

Hasan Kayalı

UNIVERSITY OF CALIFORNIA PRESS

University of California Press
Oakland, California

© 2021 by Hasan Kayalı

Library of Congress Cataloging-in-Publication Data

Names: Kayalı, Hasan, author.
Title: Imperial resilience : the Great War's end, Ottoman longevity, and incidental nations / Hasan Kayalı.
Description: Oakland, California : University of California Press, [2021] | Includes bibliographical references and index.
Identifiers: LCCN 2021014322 (print) | LCCN 2021014323 (ebook) | ISBN 9780520343696 (cloth) | ISBN 9780520343702 (paperback) | ISBN 9780520975101 (epub)
Subjects: LCSH: Turkey—History—Mehmed VI, 1918–1922. | Turkey—History—1918–1960.
Classification: LCC DR589 .K355 2021 (print) | LCC DR589 (ebook) | DDC 956.1/023—dc23
LC record available at https://lccn.loc.gov/2021014322
LC ebook record available at https://lccn.loc.gov/2021014323

Manufactured in the United States of America

30 29 28 27 26 25 24 23 22 21
10 9 8 7 6 5 4 3 2 1

*Dedicated to the memory of my parents,
Mihriver and Reşid Kayalı*

CONTENTS

List of Maps ix
Acknowledgments xi
Preface xv

Introduction: Empire-to-Nation Transition
and Historical Representations 1

1 · Unfolding of an Ottoman Project in the Age of Nation:
The Quest to Preserve the Ottoman State 21

2 · Reversals of Fortune and Resilience:
The Last Year of the Great War 54

3 · Anti-colonial Resistance and the Search
for Self-Determination 86

4 · State Transformations: Anatolian Movement
and the Fertile Crescent, 1920–1922 116

5 · Struggle for Redemption and Imperial Dissolution 145

Conclusion 174

Notes 183
Bibliography 213
Index 231

MAPS

1. The Ottoman Empire after the Balkan Wars (1913) *xii*
2. Arab provinces of the Ottoman Empire *15*
3. Armistice of Mudros (October 30, 1918) *77*
4. Contours of territory demarcated for defense by the Anatolian movement (December 1919) *120*
5. Treaty of Sèvres (August 10, 1920) *137*
6. Border making and peace settlement *144*

ACKNOWLEDGMENTS

I owe a special debt to Kathy Hodges and Peter Thomas for making this book possible. To them and colleagues in the History Department at UC San Diego and beyond I thank for their amity, interest in my work, and support, among them Abdul-Rahim Abu-Husayn, Feroz Ahmad, Frank Biess, Bill Blair, Bob Edelman, Leila Fawaz, Ali Gheissari, Ryan Gingeras, Rachel Klein, Philip Khoury, the late John Marino, Uli Strasser, and Bob Westman. Michael Provence extended assistance and moral support at every stage.

I thank the staffs of Geisel Library, especially Interlibrary Loan, the ATASE Military Archives (Ankara), the British National Archives (Kew Gardens), the Prime Ministry Archives (Istanbul), and the French Ministry of Defense Archives (Vincennes). I have been the beneficiary of research grants from the UC San Diego Academic Senate and the Institute of Arts and Humanities and the University of California President's Research Fellowship in the Humanities.

Niels Hooper, executive editor at the University of California Press, deftly shepherded this book. I thank him and his staff, especially Enrique Ochoa-Kaup. Bill Nelson produced the maps. Wolf-Dieter Lemke generously shared the cover images from his private archive. Gary Hamel copyedited the manuscript.

I am deeply grateful to Ayşe for her unfailing kindness and selfless patience in all my endeavors, and to Murat and Nihal for their steady wisdom and filial devotion.

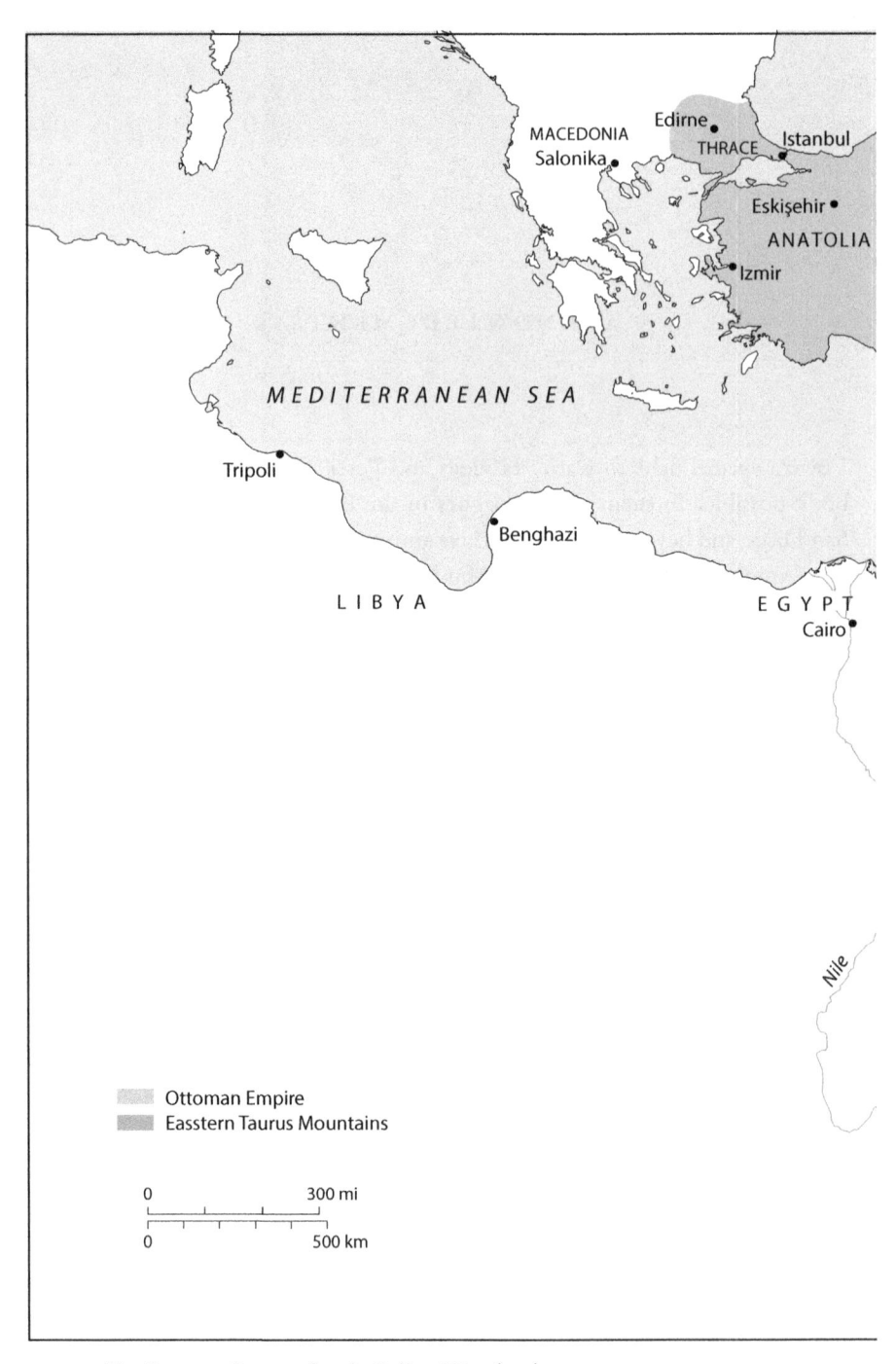

MAP 1. The Ottoman Empire after the Balkan Wars (1913)

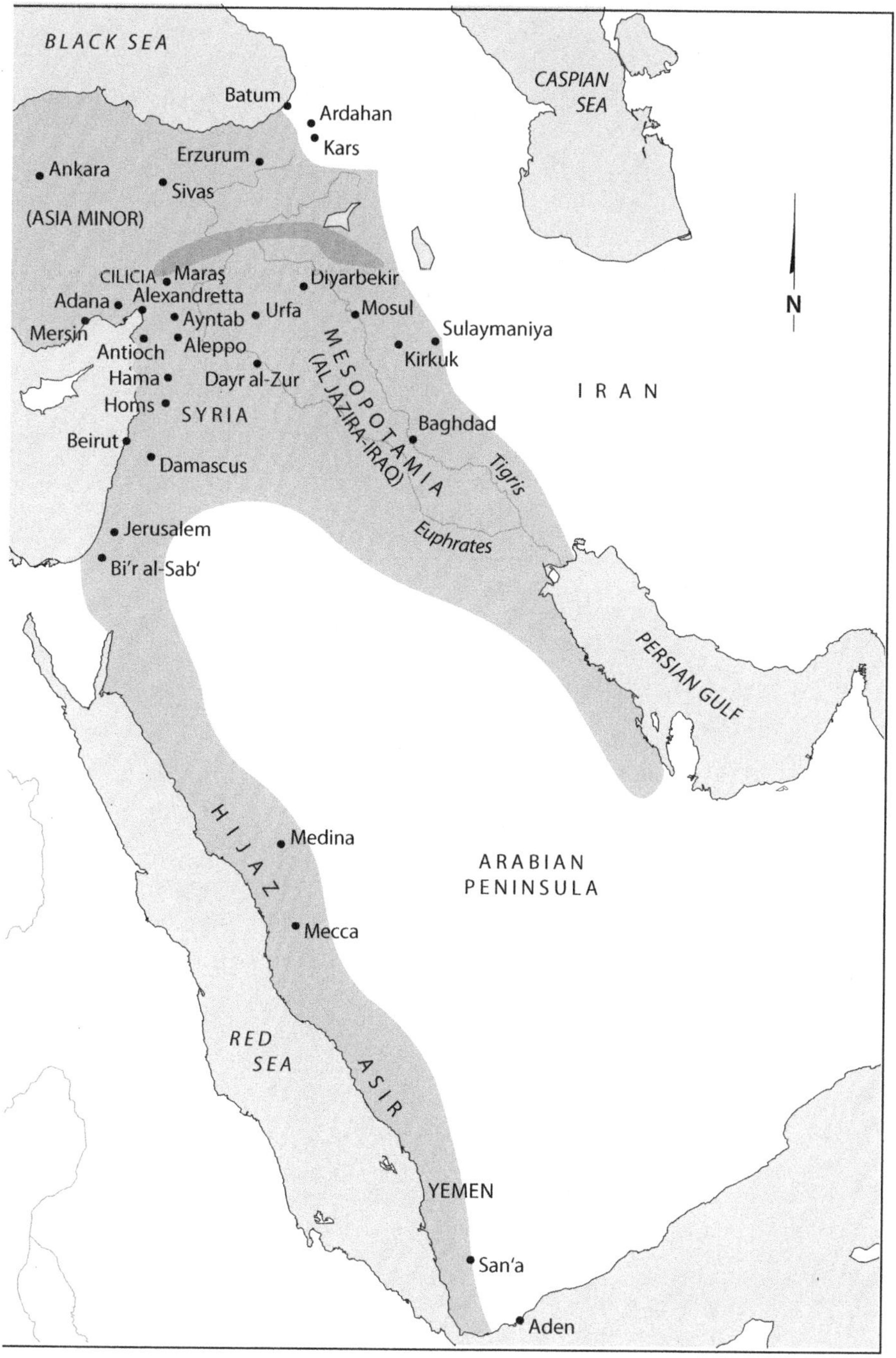

BLACK SEA
CASPIAN SEA
Batum
Ardahan
Kars
Erzurum
Ankara
Sivas
(ASIA MINOR)
CILICIA
Maraş
Diyarbekir
Adana
Alexandretta
Mersin
Ayntab
Urfa
Mosul
Sulaymaniya
Antioch
Aleppo
Kirkuk
MESOPOTAMIA
(AL JAZIRA-IRAQ)
Hama
Dayr al-Zur
IRAN
Homs
SYRIA
Beirut
Baghdad
Damascus
Tigris
Jerusalem
Euphrates
Bi'r al-Sab'
PERSIAN GULF
HIJAZ
Medina
ARABIAN PENINSULA
Mecca
RED SEA
ASIR
YEMEN
San'a
Aden
N

PREFACE

The beginnings of this project go back to a time when its geographical focus at the convergence of Turkey, Syria, and Iraq was remote from public consciousness. The region has become more recently a staple of international news owing to conflagrations of civil and military conflict, especially in relation to the civil war in Syria and the rise and expansion of the "Islamic State" political enterprise. The study's substantive concern and chronological focus are removed from the region's recent predicaments. It investigates the northern tier of the Ottoman Middle East one hundred years ago. Even as the events of the twenty-first century, many shaped by transnational actors and ideologies, have destabilized the entrenched certainties of nations and nationalism, nation-centric assumptions color the portrayals of the region over the last century. Histories have tended to presuppose nationness in this period and read it back to World War I and its immediate aftermath, notwithstanding deep ambiguities and competing allegiances, identities, and political projects. The book attempts an alternative reading of the history of this epoch, with a focus on Turco-Arab disengagement within the framework of the drawn-out exit of the Ottoman Empire from the historical stage.

As objects of intense scrutiny and deconstruction, nation and nationalism have been divested of their certitudes in recent decades. Deconstructing nationalist narratives does not displace the entrenched formulations, which intellectual and political elites of the twentieth century produced in particular contexts. They remain well and alive in day-to-day practice, school textbooks, the popular press, and political discourse, especially in those Middle Eastern countries where the social composition of the elites and state institutions have remained stable. Middle East scholars have brought nuance and clarity to the understandings of the political community in the region, including the nation. In a previous study, I attempted to situate the Arab provinces and Arab sociopolitical currents in the Ottoman Empire following the Young Turk Revolution of 1908 and the establishment of constitutional monarchy.[1] Examining the Arab provinces from the vantage of the imperial government in Istanbul, I argued that nationalism did not become the defining political current at the state level or the predominant collective identity of the empire's non-Christian constituent groups.

There has been less scrutiny, however, of the empire's twilight years, particularly the tumultuous interlude from 1918 to 1923, outside the nation-state paradigm, which presumes that ethno-regional nationalism emerged in Middle Eastern societies by default upon the debacle of Ottoman defeat in the Great War. The aim of this study is to explore the tortuous path toward the advent of nation-states in the northern tier of the empire against the background of continued armed conflict from the end of World War I into the 1920s and, in particular, the alternative concomitant political projects and collective identities that presented themselves from within the region.

Ottoman state legitimacy and institutions, including boundaries, were severely tested and undermined under the duress of wars that afflicted the Ottoman Middle East from 1911 to 1922. The book focuses on the second half of this period in a liminal region that may be defined for the contemporary reader as corresponding to southeastern Turkey, northern Syria, and northern Iraq, regions that meld into one another in terms of physical and human geography and that were sites of contestation among foreign and indigenous actors. The momentous course and processes of World War I and its aftermath in this region shaped the contours of the newly emerging states and mental and emotional maps along with political ones.

The following pages will be partial to terminology that eschews nation-state-centric designations, since the book's purpose is to bring to light the flux and contestation that surrounded the crystallization of the familiar political entities and to undermine the notion of compartmentalization along alleged natural boundaries. The region of focus corresponds to the territories within the upper arc of the "Fertile Crescent," a clumsy but useful term that connotes the lands stretching northward along the eastern Mediterranean coast, reaching the foothills of the eastern Tauruses in Asia Minor, and down south again to the river basins of the Euphrates and Tigris. Before the formation of states by the same names, Syria (customarily referred to as "Greater Syria" to distinguish it from the Ottoman province of Suriye) and Iraq signified geographical entities. Geographic Syria encompasses Palestine, Transjordan (Jordan), and the territories of the contemporary states of Lebanon and Syria. From a strictly topographical point of view, the lowlands of Syria extend toward the Tauruses in the north. Similarly, Iraq, synonymous with Mesopotamia, stretches in the same direction flanked by the Euphrates and the Tigris Rivers.[2] "Turkey," long used in Western accounts to refer to the Ottoman state, also denoted the geographical region corresponding to peninsular Asia Minor and its eastward extension toward the Caucasus and the mountain system flanking the Iranian plateau along its western rim. This "geographical Turkey" in Asia will be referred to as Anatolia.

Investigating the political and social dynamics that prevailed in the not readily differentiated regions of southeastern Anatolia, northern Syria, and Mesopotamia allows us to interrogate some of the fundamental premises of Middle Eastern states' official histories, which tend to couple putatively timeless national feeling with recently consummated foreordained geopolitical circumstance. Nationness is deemed to have always been present as destiny, even though the historical perceptions of the nation and its latter-day inculcations were inchoate. In northern Fertile Crescent, boundaries between Turkish-, Arabic-, and Kurdish-speaking communities were fluid and intraregional communications robust. Subsequent Turkish-Arab alienation and the Kurdish quest for self-determination have skewed the historical accounts of these regions and consigned the anti-colonial resistance of the post–World War I years to separate nationalist narratives. While no borders had existed in this territory since the Ottoman conquest of the Mamluk state in the early sixteenth century, it became an arena of negotiation and a mirror of the contingencies produced by war.

The post–World War I conflicts in Anatolia, Syria, and Mesopotamia reflected social and political communities' multifarious struggles to reclaim agency and autonomy and to protect economic resources, not the mobilization of simmering national feeling sweeping over the region. Foreign invasion and threat of hegemony spurred these movements. Official histories recognize the local militia activities only as side theaters of national consolidation and depict them from a dualistic vantage that appropriates and glorifies some and expunges others or denounces them as traitorous. Throughout this most active arena of Ottoman peoples' continued post–World War I conflict with France and Britain, local initiative, effort, and collaboration influenced the course of events. Just as this study moves away from an anachronistic territorial/geopolitical compartmentalization of the northern arc of the Fertile Crescent, it argues for the chronological desegmentation of the decade of warfare that started in 1911 and its examination as a continuum rather than in separate silos. The violence that lasted through 1922 had an incremental but also relational and cumulative impact on society, politics, and ideology.

The general observation that the continental empires of Europe entered the world war intact and left it obliterated conceals the unicity of the Ottoman experience. The Great War was sealed in the Ottoman Empire, as elsewhere, with an armistice agreement in the fall of 1918. Unlike in the European theaters, warfare in the Ottoman lands continued for another four years until the conclusion of a peace treaty. Even though the Great War's victors proposed a peace plan in the Treaty of Sèvres almost two years after the armistice and prevailed upon the sultan's government to sign it, the anti-colonial resistance in Anatolia, which had mobilized against the punitive violations of the armistice agreement in the interim, rejected the proposed treaty. The movement capitalized on successes against occupying foreign forces in Anatolia to proclaim sovereignty. It abolished the institution of the sultanate in November 1922 to position itself as party to the peace talks, the Lausanne Conference. The military and diplomatic events of the half decade from 1918 and 1923 are well known. This study aims to bring to life the vicissitudes of the anti-colonial struggle in the Anatolia-Syria-Mesopotamia nexus that the nation-centric framings of the narrative tend to obscure. Informed by valuable yet disparate micro-studies, it seeks to present a relational account of the last years of the empire in this geography, as it examines the consolidation of Muslim identity as a locus of solidarity under the circumstances of the war and the resilience of empire-thinking in the post–World War I period. A sharpened sense of Muslim grievances motivated combat on the battlefields and violence against Ottoman Christians on the home front during the Great War, solidifying a religiously monochromic understanding of the political community during the half decade of conflict that followed the war.

Note on spelling and transliteration:
In the study of a liminal period when identities were fluid, the rendering of proper names entails a hermeneutical quandary. The conventional renderings of many personal names that occur in this book derive from the very nation-centric accounts that the study interrogates. The historian's representations of personal names may prejudge and shape their analysis and incur the danger of violating the self-view of historical actors they study. Even as I maintain that

Ottoman subjects held multiple communal and cultural identities, which they did not define, sort out, or prioritize unless forced by circumstance, I cannot avoid ascribing to historical figures identities by rendering their names in a certain way (or by situating them within existing scholarship that does so) and thus projecting their evolved and crystallized self-views into the past.

A similar problem pertains to place names. Orthographic differences in the Arabic and Ottoman Turkish rendering of place names are minimal but amplify in the phonetic Latin script that Turkey adopted in 1928. The nationalization of place names later in the century poses an added complication. The author must make choices that do not violate the historical context but also do not entirely obfuscate current usage. I have opted, for instance, for the Arabic "Bi'r al-Sab'" in rendering the southern Palestinian town over the Turkish "Birüssebi" or current "Beersheva," but for the current usage "Cizre" (Kurdish town in Turkey) over Arabic "Jazirat ibn 'Umar" or Kurdish "Cizir." I cannot claim consistency in my choices. More central to the study are conceptual shifts and variations over time and space in the meaning of key terms and concepts, as will be probed where relevant.

The simplified transliteration of Arabic and Ottoman words does not do justice to the unique elements of the Arabic language and script. Ottoman transliterations are flattened to modern Turkish, while the diacritical marks are avoided in Arabic words, except the *hamza* (') and the letter *'ayn* (').

Words that have entered the English language occur in their familiar forms, for example, "jihad" or "ulama." Another such word, "pasha" is an Ottoman title that was used for officers at the rank of general in the military as well as for statesmen at the highest ranks of the officialdom and provincial governors. The last names adopted per the Surname Law of 1934 by Ottomans who became citizens of Turkey are indicated in parentheses.

Introduction

EMPIRE-TO-NATION TRANSITION
AND HISTORICAL REPRESENTATIONS

THE DISSOLUTION OF EMPIRES and their replacement by political formations recognized as nation-states is the paramount transformation of the modern history of the world. The chronological determination of an empire's end appears straightforward in retrospect, especially if an event with far-reaching repercussions, such as a revolution, military occupation, or defeat in war, is deemed to have marked its exit from the stage of history. Identifying such a landmark inevitably suggests a clear breaking point and concomitant transformation of empire into novel sovereign or sovereignty-seeking entities. This assumption of a clean break from empire to nation-states obscures the dynamics of imperial dissolution, the uncertainties that accompany it, and the alternative paths that present themselves.

Empires forfeit their vitality and possessions and vanish after they are reduced to remains in which time-honored practices of rule and social organization lose efficacy and relevance. Both the parts that splinter off and any remaining rump may then reenvision or reconstitute themselves in a different political form, as new or existing leadership cadres within the fragments rechannel ideological, human, and economic resources to internal consolidation. Imperial fragmentation bringing forth nation-states is a familiar process that followed the demise of Europe's land empires at the beginning of the twentieth century. Secession and shrinkage are not intrinsically sufficient conditions for empire's devolution or transmutation into nation-states. Nor is significant geopolitical rupture or territorial loss necessary for empire-to-nation transformation, as the modern experience of the "ancient empires" of Iran and China has demonstrated.[1]

Imperial institutions, habits, and practices of governance may persist or modify only gradually for a period of indeterminate length. In Russia, fragmentation occurred after the 1917 Revolution, but the resulting state entities did not crystallize as independent nations until several decades later, notwithstanding the Kremlin's official rhetoric of "sovereign republics" throughout the Soviet period.

The metamorphosis of an imperial vestige—an offshoot or the rump—into a nation-state is thus not foreordained, nor does it occur by default. The precise shape of the geopolitical mosaic that supplants empire is the result of contestation and contingency. The use or threat of military force, diplomacy, geography, economic ties, new conceptions of political community and identity, and foreign hegemony may produce novel political processes and geopolitical and demographic outcomes. Alternative paths of state rebuilding present themselves, as diverse choices are made by or for the peoples. If and when novel entities result from these processes, each creates structures to assert a self-contained existence and frequently myths of nationhood reaching back to "times immemorial."[2] For instance Hittite, Pharaonic, Phoenician, and Babylonian roots of Turkish, Egyptian, Lebanese, and Iraqi nations have become prominent strands in the respective national narratives.[3]

Official histories identify key dates, sanctify lines drawn in the sand, and glorify or discredit personalities, often retrospectively, in the construction of teleological narratives. Boundaries created thus, whether chronological, geographical, ideological, or primordial, tend to obscure uncertainties, fluidities, and contestations. Histories of the new states in the Middle East accept the termination of the Great War's hostilities in 1918 as marking the end of empire and the liberation of nations, obscuring the intricacies of collective consciousness in each area as well as the persistence of shared allegiances and cognitive maps formed within the Ottoman imperial system. They depict empire as a structure that confined and suppressed the nation, emancipating it only at the fateful hour of empire's departure from history. In these narratives, bonds formed by time-honored commonalities and shared histories within the imperial framework and operative in the post–World War I half decade fade away, as does the subsequent deliberate, tangled, and often violent construction of the nations within newly determined borders.

Segmented national narratives of Ottoman successor states have obscured the salience of imperial dynamics and practices in the early twentieth-century Middle East.[4] Popular and most elite allegiances did not transform, nor did extant identities "surface," abruptly. Memories and myths of national indignities under the empire distort the portrayal of the political and social vicissitudes of the immediate post–World War I period. The abiding premise of these narratives is that a decaying Ottoman Empire was swept away during World War I, and military defeat and the breakdown of wartime government released latent and clashing ethnonationalisms, as the perfidy of war's victorious powers endeavored to quash national aspirations.

The dominant trends of historical and related social science scholarship have reinforced fragmented nation-centric historical outlooks. The paradigm of Western modernity, which long dominated the writing of the recent history of the non-Western world, upheld the nation as an intrinsic feature, indeed the agent, of modernization. The modernization theory's critics privileged Marxist perspectives to explain the stunted development of Middle Eastern and other non-Western states as the result of economic dependency on the West, though generally without questioning the primacy, if not inevitability, of the nation-state.[5] In the prolific theoretical work on nationalism since the 1980s, the hegemony of the nation in historical studies and social sciences in general has been duly recognized.[6] The efforts of historians and social scientists to upend the conventional, primordially biased understandings of nations and nationalism have dovetailed with a cognate concern in postcolonial and cultural studies to decenter the European model of the nation.[7]

While globalization and regional integration have undermined the nation's hegemony, the dissolution of the Soviet system has demonstrated that the nation is far from being an obsolescent or retrograde form. Conflicts waged in the name of the nation have not abated. Nation and nation-state remain in the Middle East as the predominant sociopolitical frame, despite challenges from supranational and particularistic movements. Correspondingly, the near hegemony of the nation has prevailed not only in the study of the contemporary Middle East but also in the histories of the late World War I and the postwar interlude, which the present study investigates. In Ron Suny's words, "The historiography of the end of the Ottoman Empire, much of it genuinely scholarly but too much of it polemical and propagandistic, has been shaped by contemporary politics framed within the legitimizing limits of nationalist normality."[8]

The premise of this study is that the retrospective projection of the certainty of the nation and the nation-state to the 1910s and early 1920s has obfuscated the history of this period of upheaval. In recent decades, the emergence of overarching Islamic political projects, quests for broad regional unity, vibrant faith-based solidarity groups, and ethnic/sectarian realignments have contested the primacy of the nation in the region and loosened its strictures as analytical prism. The different ideologies, allegiances, and notions of political organization inherent in these currents have roots coeval with nationalism. They vied with the nation and with one another at the time of imperial dissolution.

PERIODIZATION

If the presupposed "normality" of the nation has been a straitjacket in the investigation of the Middle East in the late 1910s and early 1920s, conventional periodization has posed a concomitant constraint. The end of the world war in November 1918 accompanied by the collapse of Europe's imperial regimes led to the splintering of their domains into nation-states and a proliferation of sovereign states unmatched until European decolonization in the post–World War II period. In the Middle East, however, the transition from empire to nation-states can be understood best by distancing oneself from 1918 as the watershed it was for the European states. Such an approach will highlight the differences in the Ottoman war experience from that of other belligerents and offer a more apposite framework to analyze the Middle Eastern transformations in the 1910s and the early 1920s.

Continual warfare marked the period from 1911 to 1922 in the Middle East, with only brief periods of respite. Embroiled in a defensive war in North Africa in 1911 upon the Italian occupation of Libya, the Ottoman government had to vie for peace (Treaty of Ouchy on October 18, 1912) in order to be able to confront a more vital threat from an alliance of Balkan states ("Balkan League") of Serbia, Montenegro, Bulgaria, and Greece, all former Ottoman possessions that had become independent by 1908. In 1912 and 1913, the Ottoman Empire fought their armies, which overran Ottoman territories in Macedonia and Thrace; captured the empire's former capital, Edirne; and threatened the contemporary capital, Istanbul. In the ensuing peace treaty signed on May 30, 1913 (Treaty of London), Istanbul conceded all the empire's European possessions except eastern Thrace, the hinterland of Istanbul, which included Edirne. The following year, the Ottoman state entered World War I and left it in defeat in 1918. The wartime British occupation of the empire's southern ("Arab") provinces, followed by French and Greek seizure of Ottoman territories galvanized an anti-colonial resistance, protracting the hostilities with Britain, France and Greece until the end of 1922.[9]

From the viewpoint of diplomatic and military history, the division of the decade-long warfare into distinct phases (the Libyan War, the Balkan Wars,

World War I, and the War of Independence) has an apparent rationale. Yet this periodization misinforms the investigation of the overall effect of warfare on politics, society, and the shaping of ideology. For the masses that faced mobilization, requisitioning, famine, relocation, and other economic and social deprivations and hardships connected with the war, the decade of warfare was less fragmentary than the conventional periodization suggests. Political identities and allegiances of both elites and popular groups unfolded over time against the cumulative political, demographic, territorial, and socioeconomic dislocations that accompanied the wars. This "Long War" witnessed a quest to refashion imperial ideology and a redefinition of collective identity, which nation-centric histories elide in pointing to nationalisms as undermining the empire before 1918 and quickly supplanting it after the Ottoman military surrender. Thus, in this representation, 1918 separates not only two distinctive periods of armed conflict, but also the imperial era from the national era. Histories selectively harness the experience of the last decade of the empire's existence to ideological ends and the needs of national narratives. The long-war view subverts this misconstruction by restoring the fluidity and ambiguities of the interlude in its own right. It allows us to explore the intrinsic possibilities, opportunities, and aspirations in this period frequently erased in teleological accounts, which reflexively appropriate the period between the end of the war and the peace settlement in 1923 for the nation(s).

The liminality of the 1918–1923 period is inherent in the ways in which it is referred to. One of the common designations, the "Armistice Period," foregrounds the vantage of the imperial government. It encompasses the four years from the miscarried Armistice of Mudros, signed between the Entente powers and the Ottoman government on October 30, 1918, to a second truce, the Armistice of Mudanya, in October 1922.[10] All belligerent parties of World War I, known as the Great War or the European War at the time, understood the armistices of Fall 1918 in Europe and the Middle East as the beginning of negotiations that would lead to peace treaties. The Ottomans' distinctive experience was that such a treaty would not be settled for four years. Therefore, the protracted "Armistice Period" epitomizes the singular failure to agree on peace terms between the Ottoman Empire and the Allies, with all its political, diplomatic, and military repercussions.

In historical national narratives, the same general period is rendered under different rubrics. Turkey, Syria, and Iraq have characterized the anti-colonial movement against European occupation as struggles for independence, albeit as distinct Turkish, Syrian, and Iraqi movements, obscuring interconnections at a time of ambivalent political agendas.[11] Indeed, the participants in the resistance referred to their quest in terms of devotion to the native land (*al-haraka al-wataniya* [patriotic movement] in Arabic) or the political community (*Milli Mücadele* [popular struggle] in Turkish). The terms *watani* and *milli* both later evolved to be associated semantically with the nation-state.[12] War of Independence (İstiklal Harbi) is rendered in modern Turkish, with some flourish, as the War of Salvation (*Kurtuluş Savaşı*). The seemingly contradictory designations of "armistice" period on the one hand and "war" of independence/salvation on the other reflect the ambiguities and paradoxes of the interlude. The two terms are also indicative of the emergent duality in political authority. From the point of view of the sultan and his government, who sought to preserve his throne and caliphal authority as hostage to the British and French occupation forces in Istanbul, this was the Armistice Period. For the popular forces that opposed occupation, it was a liberation struggle.

Fall 1918 did not signify for the Middle East a closure similar to the experience of the other land empires of Europe. Russia had effectively left the war with the Bolshevik Revolution in November 1917. Within about a year of the armistices, the defeated Central Powers, except for the Ottoman state, signed peace treaties which legitimized new regimes. War and revolution revamped the political geography of eastern and central Europe and consigned the Habsburg and Romanov empires to history. The expiration and replacement of imperial monarchies and formal consummation of international accords notwithstanding, the sociopolitical transformations were far from being seamless. Historians have recently proposed the "extended war" approach as intrinsically relevant to central and eastern Europe as well. The Great War accompanied such momentous dislocations and destruction as to engender renewed and sustained violence "from Baltic States through Russia and Ukraine, Poland, Austria, Hungary and Germany all the way through the Balkans," as an editorial titled "War in Peace" observed in Austria.[13] The postrevolutionary civil war convulsed Russia's European territories and eastern European countries under its influence.

In the Ottoman Empire, the absence of a peace agreement perpetuated intrigue, violence, and warfare, as local and external actors jockeyed for advantage. The events of the immediate post–World War I period left a heavy imprint on imperial governance and sovereignty and, ultimately, the Middle East's map; but far from precipitating national states, postwar outcomes stymied the state-seeking projects (e.g., in Syria, the Hijaz, and

Armenia). There is, therefore, merit in stripping this period of the deterministic vantage of national narratives and examining it as the continuation of the beleaguered and truncated empire rather than the gestational period of foreordained nation-states. The assumption of a sharp break between empire and the nation-state along the fault line of 1918 has privileged the utilization of such terminology as "national struggle," which affirms the teleology of nationness in the Middle East. It ignores the flux and anguish of a search for political identity at a crucial juncture in the region's history, as it excises the Ottoman backdrop from the narratives of the nation-states that came of age in the interwar period.

NORMALITY OF NATION AND THE OTTOMAN PAST: HISTORIOGRAPHY AND SOURCES

The approach of official and national histories to the Ottoman past of the region is problematic not only in their nation-centric outlook on the World War I years and the immediate aftermath but also in their tendency to delegitimize the Ottoman reign as alien and/or stiflingly oppressive.[14] A corollary of this assessment, the view of the Ottoman state as the prison of the nation, if not as colonizer, is a retrospective and anachronistic characterization. Arab histories have tended to expunge the four centuries of Ottoman rule by leaping from the glory of the Arab states in the medieval period directly to the beginnings of Arab national consciousness or "Arab awakening" in the late nineteenth or early twentieth century.[15] Accordingly, conventional histories of the Arab lands during the long Ottoman era treated political, social, and cultural processes in isolation, with scant attention to ties to Istanbul or the rest of the Empire. By disowning the legacy of Ottoman governance, they dispensed with commonalities with other Ottoman peoples, reaching into history only to identify the strands of long-standing but woefully suppressed nationhood.[16]

A parallel, albeit distinctively schizophrenic, approach long characterized the Turkish Republican approach to Ottoman history. Early Turkish national narratives labored to set apart Republican history from Ottoman precedents in sharp strokes, positing an alterity between the Ottoman and the new Turk. The elision of the Ottoman "other" from Republican Turkish history fit the logic of the deliberate cultural and institutional disconnect with Ottoman precursors, as effected by measures such as the "clothing reforms" and the 1928 switch from the Arabic alphabet to the Roman script. Next to this compartmentalization between Republican and Ottoman history, however, there was a contradictory dimension in the relationship to the Ottoman precedents, namely the selective harvesting of history in the service of a useable past.[17] This effort appropriated the high achievements of the Ottoman Empire as evidence of the Turks' genius and prowess, stemming from a distant mythical past and becoming cyclically manifest in the evolution of the consummate nation. While in Arab narratives the Ottoman past came to signify Turkish domination and a rude intrusion into the course of Arab history from which there is nothing to redeem, Turkish Republican historiography reinforced this vantage with its exclusion of the Ottoman state's non-Turkish-speaking majority from Turkey's origin history. It regards the latter-day failures of empire as having been set aright by the Turkish nation and its leading light Mustafa Kemal (Atatürk) in the new Republic. Also reinforcing nation-centric approaches are the secular biases of the Kemalist period that associate a maligned Islamic torpor with Arabdom; the Arab histories' assessment of the Ottoman state as a precursor of colonial rule; and structural attributes of Middle East scholarship (particularly linguistic and methodological specialization in area studies research).

The enduring commonalities between the Arabs and Turks as the main constituent groups within the Ottoman imperium and the tortuous parting of the ways have received scant attention not only in national(ist) histories but also the broader scholarship. Pioneering scholars of Turkey analyzed the Republican transformation as the culmination of a long-standing modernizing process.[18] They confined their close treatment of the Ottoman struggle to keep pace with modernity to the Turkish element and implicitly acknowledged the nation, a salient concomitant of modernity, as having already taken form in the dwindling empire. The appropriation of the Ottoman past for the Turks has elided Arab and other groups' sociopolitical and cultural experiences from the narrative. Modernity thus emerged as the preserve of the Turks in the linear narrative culminating in Republican Turkey. More recently, scholars have found the opportunity for cross-fertilization with a willingness to move away from a nationalist perspective in history writing and a readiness to investigate the broad canvas of the ecumenical Ottoman backdrop. Yet attention to contact, impact, and overlap between ideological, cultural, and political trends in Istanbul/Anatolia and the Arab provinces, including during and after World War I, has remained outside the mainstream of historical research.[19]

A productive debate on the revolutionary claims of the Kemalist movement and historiography has partially eroded the dissociation of "imperial" and "national" historiographies. Insisting on an absolute break, albeit revolutionary in magnitude, without due appraisal of long-term incremental transformations can be facile. Erik Zürcher has made a compelling and sustained case for organic continuity in political organization, institutions, and leadership from the Young Turk period to the war of independence and into the Republic.[20] Others, among them the preeminent historian of the era immediately preceding the Republic, Feroz Ahmad, are partial to a significant break in the 1920s as manifested in substantive institutional and ideological transformations.[21] Reşat Kasaba takes the side of rupture in approaching the subject from the vantage of transmutations in collective identities and sociopolitical visions against the background of the Long War's upheavals.[22] The debate's virtue lies in that neither position can be defended without scrutiny of oft-dismissed Ottoman precedents.

Yet other historians point to alternative junctures as the breaking point. Aykut Kansu privileges the 1908 Revolution, which he sees as having ensued from socioeconomic upheaval in the eastern Anatolian provinces, over the "Kemalist Revolution."[23] Scholars who argue for pivotal demographic transformations and accompanying coercive population policies accept 1913, the denouement of the Balkan Wars, as the beginning of an era when the Ottoman political leadership starts "seeing like a nation-state."[24] Their works dovetail with those that examine the violent decade of the Long War within the paradigm of genocide studies, which underscores abiding state responsibility and accountability and thus privileges robust organic linkages over time to the detriment of contingency and transmutation.[25]

By scripting the postwar half decade into fragmented national histories, mainstream scholarship has been complicit in the proverbial "exaggeration of the death" of empire. Even the historian with whom nationalism or secularism has little purchase has not seen merit in studying a period that has subsequently come to be associated with the fraying of time-honored institutions and ushered in the indignities of foreign overbearance. The political and social processes as well as ideological formulations that accompanied this period of upheaval and deep uncertainty remain in relative obscurity. Yet nation-state-oriented thinking and presumption of imminent and inevitable imperial demise alone do not explain the misrepresentation or neglect of the immediate postwar years. The nature and limited availability of historical sources from the transition period have reinforced the neglect. After 1918, military collapse, foreign occupation, attenuation of resources, breaks in parliamentary proceedings, curtailment of diplomatic representation, and fragmentation of political authority took a further toll on the production of official records. In the Ottoman documentary evidence of the post–World War I years, the same stoical disposition prevails as in past transition periods marked by territorial loss, such as in the aftermath of the Berlin Treaty (1878) or the Balkan Wars (1912–13). The mere fact that the Istanbul governments generated and dispensed documents until 1922 (simply crossing out the names of provinces where Ottoman officials ceded authority to occupation forces) attests to the endurance of empire and the self-view of the Ottoman state cadres.

In the reconstruction of social and political processes in areas where foreign occupation obviated the Ottoman administrative structure, diplomatic archives and registers of popular movements gain especial importance. Retrospective ego documents, particularly memoirs, throw light on the postwar interlude but tend to read back in time the virtues of the nation and indulge in self-vindication and self-promotion, distorting an accurate appraisal of political inclinations and worldviews during the historical window of the immediate postwar years. They must be read with more than the customary caution for such sources. Those written during the authoritarian presidency of Mustafa Kemal (1923–1938), in particular, were open to opprobrium, if not sanction, and displayed a tendency for ingratiation and self-promotion.[26]

One retrospective source stands out in its aura and extraordinary impact on the historiography, and in particular, on the production of "correct" national history in Turkey, and therefore the shaping of a modern collective self-view: Mustafa Kemal's *Nutuk* (or Speech), an oration he delivered in 1927 before the congress of the Republican People's Party for six consecutive days.[27] It is an account of Kemal's role in the struggle for independence after he arrived in the Black Sea town of Samsun on May 19, 1919, and proceeded to join the resistance in defiance of his assigned duties as military inspector. The speech is memoir, diary, documentary evidence, historical vindication, and ideological manifesto all at once.[28] *Nutuk* remains as the basis of textbook accounts of these years in "Turkish Revolution" classes, mandatory for all university students in Turkey, and has been internalized by generations of historians. In the words of one such influential historian, "With Atatürk's speech, the history of this [national] struggle found its authentic expression from its official and most authoritative spokesperson."[29] Delivered and written soon after the repression of a major rebellion in Kurdish territories, but before the full formulation and inculcation of an ethno-racial Turkish identity, *Nutuk* excises the Arab peoples from the history of the empire's twilight.

Hegemonic national narratives obscure local organizational initiatives and leadership instrumental in the shaping of the Great War's aftermath, especially in the Anatolian-Syrian-Mesopotamian frontier. Local histories are a valuable source but tend to exhibit the same nation-centric bias as the memoirs. The autobiographical or biographical element is preponderant in some of these accounts, which typically belabor the role of a town, region, or local hero in the national project, with self-congratulatory glorification and often an agenda of one-upmanship.[30] Generally drafted by amateur historians, these accounts tout and vindicate "patriotism based on locality."[31] Yet, far from interrogating the broad strokes of national histories, these sources strive to plug local and regional struggles into the master narrative of the nation and thus take for granted the framework and teleology of the nation as they strive for validation of contribution toward its success. Local histories have not adequately insinuated themselves into general accounts, in part because of their obscure publishers and poor circulation. Read between the lines, these books offer valuable information for a more nuanced understanding of the period and reveal dynamics that cannot be restricted to the hegemonic framework of the nation. The customary emphasis on the Anatolian resistance as personified by Mustafa Kemal and the government he presided over in Ankara after April 1920 not only subverts the decentralized struggles but also reinforces the foregone conclusion of the empire's bankruptcy.

Anti-colonial resistance and the struggle for independence have received considerably more attention from the historians of Turkey than the inglorious World War I.[32] Many studies that address aspects of the postwar half decade (e.g., social and political organizations, local uprisings, the press, etc.) follow closely the outline and presuppositions of official history. Even those works that question such premises of the historical canon as the secular thrust of the struggle for independence view the communal framework of the nation and the physical framework of the nation-state as settled.[33] The contingencies of the Long War recede against the certainties of national redemption and the inevitability and finality of the empire's demise. The retrospective Kemalist vision of the nation and the Wilsonian schema reinforce each other in both Turkish and Western historiography in presuming a match between territory and the essential nation. The Long War perspective proposed in this study highlights continuities that the Kemalist paradigm subverts.[34] This book seeks to expand the history of the empire-to-nation transition chronologically as well as geographically by restoring the linkages in the Anatolia-Syria-Mesopotamia nexus overlooked in histories of national development.

The division of the Fertile Crescent into multiple states controlled by Britain and France engendered disjointed struggles and accommodations with the colonial powers to forge new nations accompanied by myths of long-standing distinctiveness and cohesion. The short-lived Arab government set up in Damascus (1918–1920) has attracted scholarly attention in its own right as the precursor of the Syrian state.[35] Scholars who are cognizant of Syria's emplacement in the Ottoman ambit have of late written about interactions within the broader region in diachronic studies. This book benefits from this strand in the scholarship that emphasizes continuity and interregional dynamics and seeks to build upon them.[36]

TERMINOLOGY AND ITS PITFALLS

Ambiguities in evolving and differential meanings of concepts across time, geography, linguistic domains, and self-views present challenges that defy resolution by way of a simple terminological excursus outlining established usage or a template that guides the reader with authorial definitions. The connotations of certain key analytical terms may intersect in different regional and cultural idioms without complete overlap against a wide definitional range. Even when vocabulary is shared, associated concepts have often evolved differentially, as novel understandings have inflected earlier ones. Further, terms rarely translate to other languages (in our case, Turkish and Arabic to English) with their original valences intact. In the present study these challenges are palpable. I address some of the terminological issues and their conceptual implications at apposite junctures in the book.[37]

A paramount example related to the quandary of shifting meanings is the term *millet* with its conceptual range and variations across time, geography, and languages.[38] Within the Ottoman system *millet* referred to religio-sectarian communities to which the state accorded a degree of autonomy.[39] In Ottoman history (and the Ottoman language), *millet* was occasionally used to signify the Muslim community as well. Later in the nineteenth century, especially in the pen of intellectual-bureaucratic reformist authors, *millet* gained currency in reference to the political community of the Ottoman Empire and totality of its people, namely an overarching Ottoman millet, the strong Islamic resonances in the thought of some of these authors notwithstanding. The adjective *milli* accordingly suggested "popular" or "native to the empire." The term *hakimiyet-i milliye* (popular sovereignty), for instance, entered political parlance with the constitutional revolution in 1908.[40] The demographic preponderance of Muslims in the territorially shrinking empire and the concomitant emphasis on Islam in the imperial self-view and ideology increasingly associated both *millet* and *milli* with the community of Muslims.[41] At the same time, groups with nationality claims within or outside the empire, whether sovereign or not, were referred to as millets. Thus, in Ottoman Turkish *millet* came to refer to multiple forms of community, for example, the Muslim or Jewish millet, the Ottoman millet, the Albanian or Arab millet, and so on. A word of Arabic origin, *millet* maintained its meaning as "religious group" in the Arabic language, as Arab political discourse secularized the Islamic concept of *ummah* (religious community) or encumbered the tribal term *qawm* (kinship group) in referring to "nation" or "nationality." Any one of these terms in the early twentieth century carried an inherent ambiguity, reflecting ambivalent collective self-views. Their adjectival forms, for example, *milli* (from *millet*) and *qawmi* (from *qawm*), added further valences and ambiguity. Historians have tended to ascribe to these terms their latter-day connotations, which skews our understanding of their usage in the past. The Turkish word *milli* could mean "popular" or "mass," "local," "native," "national," or "imperial" at any given point during the period under study here.[42] Similar equivocality attended increasingly politicized notions such as *ırk* (race)[43] and *vatan* (homeland).

As the fluidity of the words *millet*, *ummah*, and *qawm*, also suggests, Ottoman subjects adhered to multiple overlapping communal and cultural identities, which they did not define, tease apart, or prioritize unless driven by circumstance or emergent hegemonic discourses, such as Wilsonianism, which privileged nationality as repository of political rights. In the post-Ottoman era, Middle Easterners projected their evolved and crystallized self-views into the past, guided by literati and men of politics acting on their own positionality and ambitions shaped within opportunity spaces often removed from popular experiences and aspirations. Prejudging the identity of individuals, especially those being drawn into the social and physical mobility of an expanding modernity, is as presumptuous as it is challenging, but it surfaces as an unavoidable exercise in a study that takes as its subject—in the absence of a more familiar handle—Turco-Arab relations in portraying the resilience of empire.

The term *Arab provinces* conjures up those regions of the empire where a preponderance of the inhabitants communicated in a dialect of the Arabic language regardless of whether they harbored a notion of distinctiveness by virtue of doing so. The Ottoman system foregrounded religious affiliation and modes of livelihood (peasants, merchants and manufacturers generally organized in guilds, and nomadic pastoralists) in its administrative practice and took little interest in the ethnic identity of its Muslim subjects. The "Arab provinces" reflected the legacy of historical configurations of political power and adaptations to geography and local/regional economic flows. They had changing administrative borders not drawn according to ethnic criteria. Thus, large numbers of non-Arabic speakers lived in a province like Aleppo, which extended in the north to the border of the central Anatolian province of Sivas. (See Map 2.) One can only surmise based on observational accounts about what proportion of the province's population spoke Arabic or identified as Arabs. Ottoman Mosul, another "Arab province," almost certainly did not have an Arabic-speaking majority. Cultural geography was a poor guide to delineate and spatially categorize peoples along the Anatolia-Syria-Mesopotamia frontier.

Generally juxtaposed against the Arab provinces, Anatolia, like many other geographical designations (e.g., Near East, Syria, Arabia, Levant), was not a well-defined entity, particularly in its eastern reaches not demarcated by the peninsular coastline. Greek in origin, *Anatolia* denotes "the eastern lands" vis-à-vis Greece. It is separated from Iran to the east with steep mountains. In the southeast, the most plausible limits of Anatolia from a geographical point of view are the Taurus Mountains. The Ottoman intellectual Şemseddin Sami Fraşeri (1850–1904), an early Albanian proponent of Ottoman imperial identity as well as promoter of both Turkish and Albanian cultural consciousness, portrays Anatolia (Anadolu) in his magnum opus *Kamus-ül Alam*, an annotated historical, geographical, and biographical encyclopedic dictionary.[44] While stating that the eastern delimitations of Anatolia are ill-defined, he describes the region as comprising the lands to the west of a line drawn from the Caucasus mountain range in the northeast to the south of the Gulf of Alexandretta "bordering Syria, Cezire, and Kurdistan." Anatolia thus defined in physical terms is one and the same in Fraşeri's view with a cultural geography of Turkish-speaking majorities, composed of the mixture of denizens with age-old roots in the region and Turkic and Circassian peoples who entered it with Seljukid and Ottoman conquests. He describes the latter as "linguistic conquerors" who were "physiognomically vanquished" (*lisanca fatihlerden*

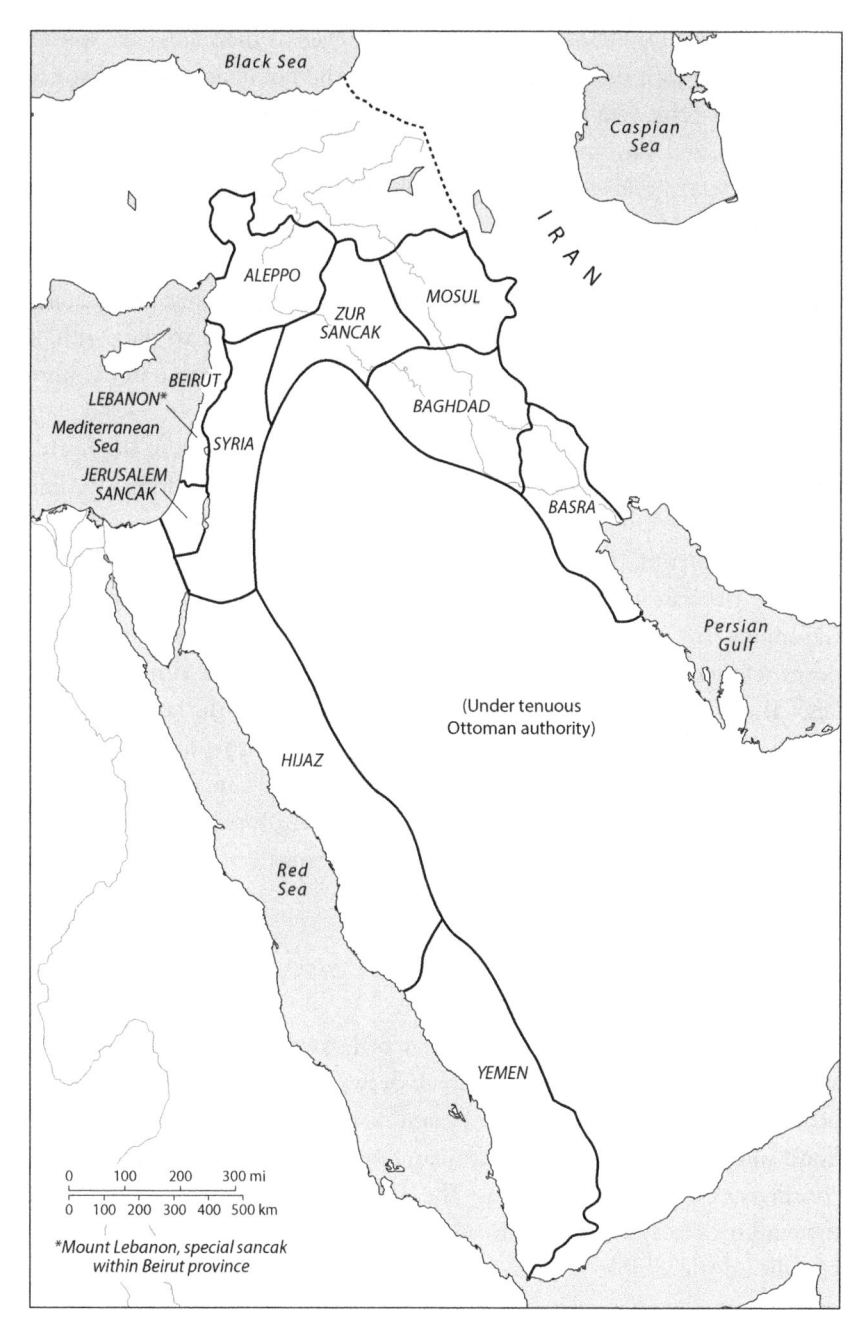

MAP 2. Arab provinces of the Ottoman Empire. Cartography by Bill Nelson

simaca akvam-ı mağlubeden), suggesting that even as their language spread after blending with the local populations, they did not maintain any distinctive physical traits. Şemseddin Sami's definition leaves the provinces of Diyarbekir, Bitlis, and Van, and the entire Aleppo province with the exception of the Maraş *sancak* outside of geographical Anatolia.[45] In the postwar political and military landscape and in the idiom of local and external actors, Anatolia referred to a broader perceived, albeit still indistinct, geography. This study will accordingly adopt the label southeastern Anatolia to refer to the lands that skirt the foothills of the eastern Tauruses and extend to the south, a region that topographically is an extension of the Syrian plateau in the west and Mesopotamia in the east.

Geographical concepts in the Middle East, as in other parts of the world, have been defined variably with historically contingent connotations.[46] After the twentieth-century establishment of the state of Turkey, the received and revived memory of Turkic presence in Anatolia/Asia Minor has concretized Turkey's association with Anatolia in ways that have obscured the multiple transmutations and adumbrations of "Turkey" as a historical construct. Europeans referred to the Ottoman state, and frequently to Asia Minor, as "Turkey." The Ottomans employed this external ascription in the last decades of the empire in diplomatic discourse, as the term seeped into sporadic common usage. The conceptual similitude of "Turkey" to the Ottoman Empire along with its abrupt disassociation from it has muddled historical analysis in ways that this study will endeavor to identify and interrogate.

CHAPTER OUTLINE

The book is organized chronologically. In order to place postwar fragmentation and the fraught notion of a break between empire and nation into a broader historical context, chapter 1 examines the alternative paths to nationhood and statehood in the late Ottoman Empire and foregrounds the role of contingency in national assertions: The separation of "national" groups from the empire as early as the first decades of the nineteenth century responded to political and socioeconomic circumstances that favored regional independence touted by politically ambitious individuals or groups. Predominantly Christian-populated parts of the empire achieved independence first, often with the support of Great Powers. The secessions engendered the elaboration of the idea of an Ottoman political community for Muslims, which resonated with ever-changing geopolitical circumstances and gained further strength during and in the immediate aftermath of World War I. The chapter offers an appraisal of Ottoman wartime policy in the Arab provinces, specifically in Greater Syria, as an integral part of the effort to preserve the imperial state by foregrounding Muslim communality. It argues that the measures that the policies the Ottoman government implemented in Syria demonstrate its policy to achieve closer integration of the Arab provinces into the imperial nexus. The government engaged in patriotic propaganda and delivered public services in Syria during World War I in tandem with strategic-military infrastructural projects. Ottoman policy evinced the leadership's continued commitment to preserving Arab lands within the empire even in the face of increasingly unfavorable military circumstances.

Chapter 2 appraises the implications for the empire of seminal military and external developments that unraveled starting in the fall of 1917 and reassesses the path to the relinquishment of hostilities within one year. In November 1917, Russian withdrawal from the war created openings and optimism for the survival of the Ottoman state. Even as the British army defeated Ottoman forces in Palestine and occupied Jerusalem in December, President Woodrow Wilson's denunciation of secret treaties gave renewed hope to the maintenance of Ottoman territorial integrity. During the relative lull in the war fronts in the first half of 1918, the Ottoman government successfully argued for Russia's restitution of former Ottoman Caucasian territories. The United States and Britain's ostensible support for self-determination, even if without explicit endorsement of the principle for the Ottoman Empire or its peoples, emboldened Ottoman claims for sovereignty. The respite in 1918 ended with German setbacks in Europe and the British armies' renewed advance in September to Damascus and farther north. The crushing defeats on the battlefront did not result in the downfall of the Ottoman regime. Upon the resignation of the discredited wartime cabinet, a new government had to negotiate for a cease-fire, which came with heavy terms: the Mudros Armistice left most of Syria-Mesopotamia under British occupation and required the surrender of the Ottoman army units in these territories and the Arabian Peninsula. In Syria, the British left Sharif Faysal, wartime ally and son of Grand Sharif of Mecca Husayn, who had risen in revolt against the Istanbul government in June 1916, at the head of the administration they set up in Damascus.[47] After the formal conclusion of the hostilities, the sultan's government cooperated with Allied authorities in Istanbul, as the Ottoman parliament continued its sessions.

Chapter 3 addresses the local, regional, and inter-regional dynamics within the vanquished empire in the context of the victors' projects as debated at the Paris Peace Conference in 1919. It focuses on the claims and agendas of new sociopolitical formations that crystallized in the Middle East within the crucial year that followed the armistice, particularly popular militia groups intercommunicating across southeastern Anatolia and northern Syria. Almost immediately after the armistice, removed from the loci of political authority in Istanbul and Damascus recognized by the Allies, pockets of popular resistance emerged motivated by local patriotism, religious solidarity, and concern to protect social capital and economic assets, some that had accrued from the expropriation of Christians. In the capital, too, newly founded associations took an anti-colonialist stance by espousing Wilsonian language as a rhetorical and strategic resource against European occupation, Armenian revanchism, or Greek territorial designs. Both the imperial government and the resistance groups invoked President Wilson's Fourteen Points in advocating for rights premised on historically constituted religious commonality, especially after the Greek invasion of western Anatolia in May 1919.

The congresses that the Anatolian defense organizations convened aimed at repulsing Allied occupations. They outlined a set of goals, which included, in addition to a reversal of Allied aggression since the armistice, an acknowledgment of the right of self-determination of peoples under British occupation at the war's end. The Peace Conference rejected the Istanbul government's appeal to respect Ottoman territorial integrity within a federative structure, while the exigency of forestalling European aggression galvanized both the Anatolian and the Syrian resistance. Anatolian and Syrian groups communicated and deliberated in their search for a viable framework of coexistence. Contacts between Anatolian, Iraqi, and Syrian groups, including agents of Faysal's government, revived the idea of a confederative arrangement, which staunch advocates of Ottoman decentralization had sporadically articulated since the turn of the century. These groups deployed anti-colonial appeals in an Islamic idiom of religious struggle against a common enemy.

Chapter 4 takes up the mired Ottoman peace settlement and the exploration of paths and opportunity spaces for geopolitical survival. The deferment of a peace agreement between the Ottoman Empire and the Allied powers granted to the imperial government the latitude to reinstate regular governance. To local actors, including popular militias, it gave an opportunity to define goals, formulate strategies of resistance, and forge new alliances. The Ottoman Empire held new elections at the end of 1919 in a seeming restoration of the political order and an assertion of self-determination. As an emergent leader of the Anatolian anti-colonialist resistance, Mustafa Kemal pronounced the outlines of a program in an idiom that reflected the movement's vision for the Ottoman state under the postwar circumstances.

One of the first acts of the new parliament was to approve a manifesto for independence (*misak-ı milli*, or popular accord, known as the National Pact), which declared the status of parts of the empire under occupation and populated by an Arab majority as contingent on a plebiscite. The Peace Conference reconvened in the spring of 1920 to deliberate on the Ottoman settlement around the agenda of establishing mandates, which revitalized anti-colonial sentiment in the broader region and opened the way for renewed cooperation between Anatolian, Syrian, and Iraqi groups for a federative reorganization. When the Allies landed troops in Istanbul and forced the closure of the parliament in March 1920, the Anatolian movement arrogated to itself executive and legislative powers by forming an elected assembly in Ankara, removed from direct foreign interference. In Damascus, Faysal responded to the mandate scheme with the accomplished fact of having the Syrian Congress declare him as King of Syria. The chapter examines multiple manifestations and dimensions of collaboration between militia forces and their relations with Ankara and Damascus. In the summer of 1920, France moved militarily against the Faysal government and ousted the king, as the Istanbul government was forced to give its consent to the punitive Treaty of Sèvres, which confirmed a French mandate in Syria and British mandates in Iraq and Palestine and carved out the greater part of Asia Minor among the Allies and their proxies. The Ankara government's rejection of the Treaty of Sèvres exacerbated the split with the sultan's government and emboldened its independent actions, including a bilateral agreement with French authorities specifying a boundary between the area France earmarked as its Syria mandate and the Ottoman rump, where the Anatolian resistance was striving to consolidate its authority. Similarly, Faysal's failure in Damascus to preclude French control over Syria intensified the Syrian groups' quest for joint anti-colonial action in the broader region.

The last chapter (chapter 5) investigates the reshaping of military and political objectives toward redeeming as large a part of the empire as possible against the background of continued occupation of Ottoman territories and the renewed activity in international forums toward an Ottoman settlement. After the territorial compromise with France in southeastern Anatolia and northern Syria, the Ankara government directed its attention to northern

Iraq to the extent allowed by the more existential threat that the Greek army posed in western Anatolia. Ankara organized, equipped, and funded militia bands and dispatched them to northern Iraq to carry out propaganda among local groups in order to fortify tribal resistance against British occupation. An Egyptian officer of Circassian background who had entered Ottoman service during World War I, 'Ali Shafiq al-Misri, known as Özdemir, led a sustained campaign in northern Iraq.

A decisive victory by the army of the Ankara government against the Greek forces in August 1922 and their subsequent evacuation of Anatolia triggered significant shifts in the military, political, and diplomatic arenas. The Allies consented to a new armistice by negotiation with the Ankara government. Strengthened by the military victory and the diplomatic recognition, Mustafa Kemal maneuvered the deposition of Sultan Vahideddin (or Mehmed VI, r. 1918–1922) in November 1922. The Ankara government entered the new round of peace negotiations held at Lausanne over the patrimony of the Ottoman Empire. In return for the international validation of recent military gains, Ankara compromised on the territorial objectives of the anti-colonial movement. Fierce opposition in the Ankara assembly to territorial concessions in the Arab provinces stalled the signing of the treaty, as combat in northern Iraq continued during the deliberations. The final text of the Treaty of Lausanne, the founding charter of modern Turkey, left the status of the northern Mesopotamian province of Mosul to future negotiations and arbitration. This chapter includes an analysis of the struggle over Mosul, which lasted until the region's eventual inclusion into the Iraq mandate by the League of Nations in 1926. The discussion anticipates Turkey's lingering geopolitical interest in the Arab regions and calls into question the conventional discourse of a westward looking Turkey that extricated itself from the Middle East and its imperial past as early as 1919.[48]

ONE

Unfolding of an Ottoman Project in the Age of Nation

THE QUEST TO PRESERVE
THE OTTOMAN STATE

THE OTTOMAN EMPIRE, long in possession of wide territories in southwest Asia, northern Africa, and eastern Europe, was relinquishing regions in its outer frontiers to neighboring land empires in the eighteenth century. Within another century, pieces of its European territories started to splinter off as self-contained entities, primed by decentralist and autonomist forces within the Ottoman administrative system, and increasingly under the protection of the Great Powers of Europe. Successor states came into existence out of the territories of the Ottoman Empire along diverse trajectories, which came to be inscribed in these states' histories as movements nurtured by patriotic sentiment and fulfilling suppressed visions of the nation.[1] The Ottoman statesmen strove to preserve the empire from unraveling by deploying the center's military, administrative, political, and diplomatic resources, as well as by fostering a collective identity commensurate with the communal makeup of the diminished territories. They sought to solidify sovereignty over the imperial domain even as warfare increased the threats to the state's territorial integrity.

EARLY PATHS TO STATEHOOD AND NATIONHOOD

At the turn of the nineteenth century, autonomist movements strengthened not only in the empire's outlying regions in Europe but also in Egypt and central Arabia. Secessionism had its earliest successes in the largely Christian-populated Balkan Peninsula. Greek independence, which ensued in 1831 from a decade-long armed struggle against the Ottoman central government, was the prototype of nationalist secession in Europe. Diverse ideological and social forces, institutional legacies, and exogenous and endogenous influences were at play in the "Greek Revolution" that culminated in the formation of an independent state on the Peloponnese Peninsula.[2] Among them were the autonomous organization of the non-Muslim communities (*millets*); the precedent of self-rule by a strong Ottoman governor in northwestern Greece; the vanguard role of the European Greek diaspora inspired by the Enlightenment and enriched by maritime trade; the Philhellenic enthusiasm of intellectuals and statesmen in Europe; and, most crucially, the alliance of Russia, Britain, and France to transcend their rivalries and extend military support to the rebels. The European allies agreed to install a German prince as head of the independent state, which aspired to bring under its jurisdiction the Greek Orthodox populations of the Ottoman Empire, if not the entirety of the Ottoman domains for a revival of the Byzantine Empire. In 1831, neither the new state's political structure and ideological underpinnings nor its vision and ambitions resembled those of a nation-state, which was still a concept foreign to popular consciousness in many parts of Europe.

Other Balkan territories of the Ottoman Empire inhabited by Serbian, Bosnian, Bulgarian, and Romanian peoples were riven by socioeconomic conflicts that found expression in ethno-religious terms. Groups among them challenged the authority of Muslim local elites as well the cultural preponderance of the ecumenical Orthodox Church and the privileging of Greek as the language of liturgy and culture. Their middle classes and intellectuals embraced regionalist identities and religio-cultural vernacularism. In Serbia, these tensions preceded the Greek Revolt, continued through most of the nineteenth century, and crystallized in partial autonomy. The idiom of Muslim oppression of Christians animated insurgency among the Balkan peoples, inflaming religious animosity and thereby exposing the Muslims remaining in the newly independent areas to persecution. At the same time, Muslim suspicion and persecution of non-Muslims residing within Ottoman borders increased. Serbia, Romania, and Montenegro became independent states, and Bulgaria effectively so, at the Berlin Congress held in 1878 under the auspices of European states. The congress revamped the Concert of Europe in a partition of large portions of the Ottoman territories after the empire's near mortal defeat against Russia in 1877 and its relinquishment of territories to its northern neighbor, including the Caucasian districts of Kars, Ardahan, and Batum in the east, known as the "Three Provinces" (*Elviye-i Selase*). The secessions and detachments in Europe decided in Berlin left within the Ottoman Empire only Macedonia and Thrace with their mélange of ethnic communities. These territories became the Balkan states' object of irredentism and resulted in their splintering and partitioning in the Balkan Wars of 1912–1913 at the expense of the Ottoman state.

At the start of the Great War, the Ottoman Empire was still in possession of districts with Christian pluralities in such regions as western Anatolia (Greek Orthodox), eastern Anatolia (Armenian and Assyrian), or Mount Lebanon (Maronite and Greek Orthodox). The non-Muslim communities generally lived next to Muslim settlements within Muslim-majority provinces. Wars, mass killings, and demographic engineering thwarted these Christian groups' ambitions for political autonomy and attenuated, and ultimately eliminated, the chances of nationalist assertion or separation from the empire, if not their very existence.[3] Thus, by the 1920s, the empire devolved into demographically Muslim-dominated fragments, in which Islam occupied a prominent place in cultural and social identification.[4]

If secession and independence marked nation-state formation along the empire's European periphery inhabited by preponderantly Christian populations, colonialism engendered fragmentation and dismemberment in the Muslim-majority African periphery. France colonized Algeria as early as the 1830s, removing it from the Ottoman geopolitical sphere. Colonial acquisition further parceled out Ottoman North Africa with the French occupation of Tunisia in 1881 and the British invasion of Egypt in 1882. Egypt retained a nominal connection to the Ottoman Empire until Britain declared it a formal protectorate following the Ottomans' entry into World War I in alliance with the Central Powers. By 1912, Italy had colonized the Mediterranean littoral of Libya from west of Tripoli to east of Benghazi and extended its control in the last remaining Ottoman province in Africa, Trablusgarp (Tripolitania). An indigenous resistance in the Libyan interior mobilized by the leader of the dominant Sanussiya religious order, Ahmad Sharif al-Sanussi, and actively aided by Ottoman officers continued into World War I. Even as the North African peoples did not repudiate their connections to the Ottoman state, their quest for independence from colonial rule defined the regionalist contours of their nationalist movements, which reached political consummation only in the middle of the twentieth century.

OTTOMAN RESPONSES

The fissiparous trend in the Balkans and North Africa motivated the Ottoman government to cultivate state loyalty and patriotism. In the classical system of the Ottoman Empire, the elite identity of the ruling group and administrative cadres was known as *Osmanlılık*, or "Ottomanness." The ruling elite and the learned were socialized in a form of Turkish infused with Arabic and Persian vocabulary and syntactic elements, known by the dynastic designation of "Ottoman" language (*lisan-ı Osmani*). This idiom was the distinguishing mark of an aristocratic *ethnie*, a ruling group that was ethnically and, to a limited extent, religiously diverse yet "incorporated bureaucratically" into a distinctive culture.[5] The devolution of central power over time diminished the cultural exclusivity of the Ottoman elite in terms of training for service, undermined the sultans' absolute powers, and empowered the military and local elites throughout the realm. Such diffusion of power accompanied a diversification and a degree of democratization of politics. The incorporation of vernacular elements into imperial politics from outside the trained officialdom as early as the seventeenth century marked the beginnings of early modernity in the Ottoman Empire.[6]

The internal decentering against the backdrop of novel forms of political negotiation with vested interest groups like the janissary units and provincial notability coincided with the external consolidation of a continental state system premised on precise delimitations of territory. As frontiers devolved into boundaries, territory emerged as an integral dimension of the imperial self-view against the constant contestation of lands on the battlefield. In the nineteenth century, loss of territory in warfare or as a result of autonomist secessions energized by a discourse of nationality compelled the cultivation and dissemination of the idea of loyalty not only to the ruler but also to the imperial patrimony. This allegiance ultimately engendered the notion of identification with the collectivity inhabiting the territory, with an eye to integrate larger segments of imperial subjects and foster their stake in the vigor of the state. Coupled with inducements and pressures from European powers, which sought to streamline their economic expansion into the Middle East by obtaining privileged status in trade and investment, the Ottoman government engaged in the restructuring of its legal and political institutions.[7]

During the nineteenth century, the Ottoman Empire became the site of an experiment with a modernizing civic project implemented to ensure the survival of a state vulnerable to predation amid international power struggles and domestic insubordination. The Ottoman state was not alone in this endeavor: the empires of eastern Europe, as well as the Iranian and semi-autonomous Egyptian governments, engaged in similar restructuring by accommodating to their local circumstances some of the institutions and practices more typical of post-Enlightenment Western European states. The package of reforms collectively known as the *Tanzimat* ("reorganization") gave a new lease on life to the militarily weakening Ottoman state.[8] The reprieve owed as much to the intrinsic efficacy of restructuring as to Western Europe's support for the centralization policies of Ottoman governments in the process of the empire's immersion into the capitalist world economy and financial dependence on Europe.

Ottoman intellectuals, along with some statesmen, responded to the fundamental transformations of the nineteenth century by recognizing that Ottoman strength could be restored only with the creation of a community that had a material or ideological stake in the state institutions. The recognition of individual rights, limits placed on the exercise of arbitrary authority by the sultan and his government, and the commitment to equality between religious groups, as articulated in seminal royal charters and upheld by legal changes, constituted the basis for the creation of a more inclusive political community and the progressive transformation of the subjects into imperial citizens.[9] Commitment to legal equality, representative government, and constitutional ideas, accompanied by the rapid improvement of communications, buttressed integrative currents and expanded the meaning and scope of Ottomanness. *Ottoman* transformed from signifying an attribute of a small group—those holding state office and educated and socialized in the idiom of the ruling elite, namely, Ottoman Turkish—to the designation of subjects inhabiting the territory under the sultan's jurisdiction. In the second half of the nineteenth century, Ottomanness, as conceived by Ottoman bureaucrat-intellectuals, thus signified a broad-based positive affective relation of subjects equal before the law to the state, its monarch, and its territorial domain.[10] The Law of Nationality promulgated in 1869 posited Ottomanness also as a legal identification of nationality.[11]

The common translation of *Ottomanness* as "Ottomanism," however, couches it primarily as a sociopolitical current. If *Ottomanness* suggested a relationship with the state, *Ottomanism* situated such a self-view within a set of allegiances and commitments that overlapped but also competed with one another, such as those to the imperial patrimony, ethno-religious group, one's own immediate locality or social environment (family, clan, village), and social status (peasant, pastoralist, artisan). While Ottomanism fostered the bonds of an increasingly self-conscious and broadening community with the state, the various segments of the society internalized it to different degrees. Such groups as pastoral communities outside the reach of the state or non-Muslim stakeholders with de facto immunities (e.g., from conscription) were ambivalent about the obligations that attended embracing Ottomanism.

Ottoman patriotism and a consciousness of legal citizenship bonds among Ottomans, as well as a contractual relationship between the ruler and the ruled, came to fruition with the promulgation of the Constitution of 1876. The constitution incorporated principles and stipulations that were progressive for its time (including governmental accountability, representative government, and nominal separation of powers) and introduced a parliament based on universal male suffrage with a tax caveat. The Constitution of 1876 survived until 1924, though Sultan Abdulhamid II (r. 1876–1909) quickly prorogued the parliament in 1878 and effectively suspended the constitution until 1908.[12] Abdulhamid's Islamic and populist policies and personal rule spread over four decades. Departing from secular bureaucratic Tanzimat Ottomanism, Sultan Abdulhamid revived the majority Muslims' sense of the primacy of an Ottoman-Muslim community. He appropriated the heretofore tenuous Ottoman claim to the Muslim caliphate with the goal of garnering domestic and pan-Islamic support and utilizing it as a locus for anti-imperialist mobilization. The strong association of Ottomanism with the family and person of the sultan, acting as the foremost champion of Islam, enhanced its resonance with Muslims. These transformations gave justification to the sultan's adoption of extraordinary powers couched in the language of the defense of the Muslim state against the (Christian) imperialist onslaught. Many non-Muslims viewed Abdulhamid's Ottomanism with apprehension and as exclusionary, even as it professed to foster bonds between all elements of society.

The "Hamidian period," the common designation of the 1878–1908 era, was transformative in the unfolding of the Ottoman state's self-view and the concepts of political community and political identity. After the Berlin Congress, the ratio of the empire's Muslim inhabitants to non-Muslims increased drastically owing to contraction in Europe and the flight or expulsion of the new states' Muslim inhabitants. Displaced Muslims became refugees within the new boundaries of the empire. The demographic upheaval was a precursor of developments in the last decade of the empire, when the proportion of predominantly Muslim areas within the truncated empire further increased upon the secession and dismemberment of large Christian-majority Balkan regions and displacement and extermination of Anatolian Christians. The junctures of 1878 and 1918, forty years apart, bear strong parallels: defeat in war, foreign occupation, loss of vast territories, dramatic demographic transformations, and a recalibration of ideological and organizational strategies aimed at stemming imperialist subjugation of the Ottoman state.

As self-proclaimed caliph and the ruler of the strongest Islamic state, which the Ottoman Empire represented despite its territorial retrenchment and financial woes, Abdulhamid was well positioned to tap into, politicize, and mobilize Islamic sentiment. When the New Imperialism of the post–Berlin Congress era brought Muslim-populated areas in Africa and Asia under European control, Islamic ideologies emerged as the focus of resistance. Against a European assault on Muslim-populated lands, the caliphate stood as a vehicle that could be wielded to serve both domestic and foreign policy exigencies. The sultan was not alone in advancing Islamic counteraction: local and transnational activists (e.g., Jamal al-Din al-Afghani) and regional leaders, some leading a mystical or millenarian movement (e.g., al-Sanussiya in Tripolitania and al-Mahdiyya in the Sudan), sought to rally populations against European colonialism around the symbols of Islam.

By undermining the liberal political reforms that had culminated in the parliament and constitution, Sultan Abdulhamid arrested the institutional advancement toward the creation of an Ottoman citizenry. Liberal-minded Ottomans opposed Abdulhamid's regime and called for a return to constitutional monarchy. In 1908, army officers of modest social background and modern education led several local uprisings to persuade the sultan to restore the constitution and the parliament in what is known as the Young Turk Revolution. If "revolution" overstates the restitution of the constitutional monarchy, "Young Turk," a European designation at first, belies the agency of diverse ethno-religious communities in the movement and the opening of politics and civil society to social groups empire wide. The revision of the Ottoman constitution in 1909 laid the ground for the political transformations of the subsequent Young Turk era. It revoked Abdulhamid's prerogative to annul the parliament as stipulated in the 1876 Constitution and invoked by him in 1878. Other amendments provided for expanded freedoms of speech and association.

The very pioneers of these political changes found that the revolutionary euphoria gradually subsided. The main group within the Young Turk movement, the Committee of Union and Progress (CUP), dominated the restored political process and resorted to strong-arm tactics against the background of multi-party contestation of elections, military entanglements, local revolts, secessions, and annexations. The Committee's clumsy stewardship of governance and imperious proclivities compromised its moral authority. In one desperate effort after another, the CUP revoked or diluted the very principles and guarantees that it had championed against the autocracy of the palace. The predominantly pro-CUP opinion in the 1908 parliament broke down amid increasingly more vocal expressions of sectional (e.g., ethnic, religious, and provincial) interests as well as vigorous opposition from the conservative branch of the Young Turks, the *Hürriyet ve İtilaf* (Liberty and Entente) Party. Liberty and Entente advocated decentralization and enhanced provincial authority, which clashed with the CUP's centralist policies for saving the empire amid international warfare and domestic revolts.[13]

In the aftermath of their secession, the peoples of the European territories formerly belonging to the Ottoman Empire solidified their self-view as nations. By 1912, Greece, Serbia, Montenegro, and Bulgaria, which had declared its full independence as accomplished fact in the turmoil of the 1908 Revolution, were dispatching conscripted armies against the Ottomans and vying for the incorporation of co-ethnic populations in the ethnically and religiously mixed territories of Macedonia and Thrace still under Ottoman rule. The forces of the Balkan alliance captured all the European provinces of the Ottoman Empire except the narrow hinterland of the capital. If the Ottomans were able to redeem eastern Thrace, they owed it to the enemy states' turning against one another in contesting the territories the Ottomans had been forced to relinquish. Borders were drawn at the end of the fighting in 1913, and from the conflict ensued the inevitable uprooting and relocation of ethno-religious groups.

MUSLIM GROUPS AND COLLECTIVE IDENTITY

The privileging of Islam as the main basis of imperial collective identity did not preclude the growth of ethno-cultural awareness among the Muslim groups, or even the construction of alterity between one ethno-linguistic Muslim group and others. The literary and intellectual elites formulated ideas and programs that further stimulated ethno-cultural identities. In view of the absence of clear, popular, and sovereignty-seeking political agendas in these formulations, which coexisted with imperial allegiance and a strong sense of Muslim commonality, scholars have characterized them as pre-national or proto-national. It is customary to refer to evolving conceptions of communal distinctness and the consciousness of meso-level identities and bonds of belonging within the hitherto inchoate cultural-linguistic communities as

"Arabism," "Albanianism," "Turkism," and so on. These serve as useful analytical categories in examining the development of the sense of nationality among the Muslim groups, who were largely self-contained as regional majorities within the Ottoman realm. In Syria, for instance, a literary revival and linguistic pride produced the *nahda*, or cultural awakening, in the second half of the nineteenth century. The Turkish-speaking intellectuals in Istanbul embraced the findings of European Turcology and the cultural sensibilities of Russian Turks and developed the sense of belonging to a distinctive social category transcending the borders of the empire. Albanian and Kurdish intellectuals and middle-class elements increasingly gave expression to cultural consciousness more as members of distinct communities. Vital threats to the empire energized political movements or novel geopolitical visions among segments of these populations.

Albania declared independence in November 1912, the first Muslim-majority Ottoman territory to do so, in order to forestall the spill-over of the Balkan states' expansionist thrust to the west of Macedonia into Albanian-populated territory. The Balkan Wars and the Balkan states' scramble for the remnants of the Ottomans' European provinces (1912–13) choked the Albanian provinces' connection with the rest of the empire and exposed them to attacks from Serbia and Montenegro.[14] Albanian cultural and ethnolinguistic consciousness cutting across differences of religion and dialect had matured in the preceding decades. Uprisings against Istanbul had portended autonomist aspirations in Albania as early as 1910. The Ottoman government adopted measures aimed at accommodating Albanianism within the imperial framework. Imperial loyalty and diverse local allegiances in the western Balkans coexisted with a growing consciousness of ethno-cultural identity. The perceived vital threat of irredentism at play in the Balkan wars, the fear of political subjugation, and the demonstration effect of "emerging neighboring states that were harnessing the potential of their citizens via the army, the police and schools" sealed Albanian secession.[15] Some of the leaders of Albanian nationalism had held high positions in the Ottoman state as late as 1912.[16] Many other Albanians, especially those domiciled outside of the western Balkans, preserved pro-Ottoman loyalties; some became preeminent actors in the Ottoman political and cultural spheres into the 1920s.[17]

The Albanian predicament was emblematic of the ethno-national vs. imperial-statist tendencies that would percolate among the diverse ethno-religious groups within the empire in the next decade in response to changing political circumstances. All ethno-linguistic and religious communities in the empire comprised groups with sectional interests and sociopolitical outlooks, which they negotiated with other groups within and outside their communities as well as with the Ottoman state. Even when they advanced claims based on ethnic identity, they adhered to multiple other identities that could ebb and flow or realign in different constellations, depending on the exigencies of the interests they pursued.

Glimmerings of ethno-cultural consciousness had also emerged among the subjects that spoke a dialect of the Kurdish language and inhabited the mostly mountainous eastern periphery. Tribal chieftains or men of politics episodically invoked Kurdism to cultivate social cohesion, and the literati touted the use of Kurdish in print.[18] The Entente powers, first Russia and subsequently Britain, fomented Kurdish uprisings in order to coopt local allies into their geopolitical designs and military effort.[19] Sociopolitical differentiation in a fragmented and topographically and climatically hostile environment thwarted the diffusion of a broad Kurdish collective identity. Synergies between Kurdish public figures and their organizations in Istanbul or Europe and local communities remained weak, even if many of the former derived from chieftains' families. During the postwar half decade, however, the Kurds of the Middle East would be thrust to the center of political schemes concocted in Wilsonian terms.

Among the Muslim peoples of the Ottoman Empire, the emergence of a sense of nationality associated with the genesis of modern nationhood can be traced furthest back in the case of the Arabs. The different strands of Arabism and its diffusion from intellectual formulations to cultural and sociopolitical platforms have received a great deal of scholarly attention.[20] The social formation of ethno-linguistic-regional identities and their articulation with politics has been delineated in the case of the Arab-speaking peoples of the Ottoman Empire with a robust interrogation of retrospective nationalist-minded vantages that privilege essentialized ruptures.[21] Arabism responded to the Ottoman government's domestic and external problems and found a niche in the decentralist platform arrayed against CUP's centralist policies, as it became manifest in organizational activity by reformist groups from Cairo to Basra to the Arab Congress of 1913 in Paris. Elaborations on the sense of Arab distinctiveness found expression in political proposals for confederative organization of the empire.[22] The disproportionate attention to the roots of Arab nationalism arises from the aura of the 1916 "Arab Revolt," which acquired impeccable nationalist credentials in historical lore, and from the concern with the post-imperial predicaments of Arab peoples in their quest for unity. In most histories, the events of the Great War and Istanbul's concomitant abnegation of its accommodationist stance toward decentralist demands eclipse its efforts to uphold the multi-ethnic empire.

IMMIGRATION, MUSLIM NATIONALISM, TURKISM

The Balkan Wars brought to a culmination the large-scale flight of Muslims leaving the territories that separated from the Ottoman state. The influx of hundreds of thousands of destitute Muslim immigrants into the empire's truncated territories posed more than a humanitarian, social, and economic problem. It hardened the attitudes of both immigrants and their hosts against the Balkan nations and their Great Power protectors, whom Muslim Ottomans viewed as persecutors of their coreligionists. By significantly increasing the number of Muslims in the empire, immigration further skewed the demographic balances already much altered by the secession of predominantly Christian-populated Balkan territories in the previous decades. The drastic proportional rise of the empire's Muslim population, the rancorous wars with Christian states that had been former dominions, and the perceived diplomatic isolation of the Ottoman state accelerated the rethinking of the basis of the Ottoman state as a multireligious polity. The displacement of entire Greek communities from western Anatolia to Greece in 1913–14 signified more than a practical measure of accommodating the influx of Muslim immigrants or retaliation to similar policies that the Balkan countries carried out. It put the place of non-Muslims in the Ottoman community in question, with disastrous results for Ottoman Christians in the following years of the Great War.

The Balkan crisis ushered in the authoritarian rule of the CUP in 1913 after a brazen power grab in the fog of war. The conclusion of the Balkan Wars coincided with the entrenchment of illiberal CUP rule. The Committee's top cadres included staunch adherents of Turkism who, it has been argued, imputed the success of the Balkan states to their having forged ethnolinguistic nations.[23] They responded to the losses with "a grand design for Turkish nationalism by intense Turkification at home as well as a purposeful orientation toward the Turkic groups in Asia."[24] The proposition that the CUP switched to an ethnically theorized Turkish nationalist program as the bedrock of the polity, begetting ethnonationalist responses from other Ottoman groups and thus undermining not only the multireligious but also the multiethnic framework of the empire, warrants critical scrutiny.[25] The imperative to salvage the state and its extant domains remained central to the political elite's choices.

If the Great War reinforced a national sentiment, the absence of which the Ottoman leadership held responsible for the humiliating defeat against the coalition of formerly subject Christian states, it derived from a sharpened consciousness of the common destiny of the empire's Muslims. A collective Ottoman identity congealed under the state aegis as integral Muslim nationalism.[26] Muslim nationalism foregrounded identity rather than an ideological essence or legal order derived from Islamic precepts.[27] Ottomanist ideology that came to find expression as an inchoate Muslim nationalism defies the characterization as instrumentalist "Turkish nationalism supported by Islamic elements."[28] Turkism sparked the imagination of segments of the literati, some of whom had connections with the state cadres, yet it did not reverberate with the Turcophone population at large, who held fast to the Muslim self-view.[29]

Halide Edib (Adıvar), a pioneering and prolific author, who attained visibility in the early years of the Young Turk period and subsequent fame as one of the leading female intellectuals of the Middle East, wrote in venues associated with the Turkist movement before the war. Her post-1920 activism and literary-intellectual output garnered her a place in the pantheon of Turkish nationalism, even though she fell out with Mustafa Kemal in the 1920s. In a series of lectures she delivered in India in 1935, Halide Edib referred to "Ottoman" as a "state of mind in state-building."[30] It had its roots in the effort to create a "ruling caste" but became analogous to more recent projects of "fabricating nations wholesale."[31] Halide Edib's Turkist affinities did not conflict with her Ottoman communitarian sensibility or political commitment for the multinational empire during the war years. As Ronald Suny writes, "The CUP elite was not so much engaged in creating a homogenous ethnic nation as it was searching unsuccessfully, flailing around to find ways to maintain its empire."[32]

One strand of the argument for the Turkish-nationalist turn in the aftermath of the Balkan Wars emphasizes the growing salience of Anatolianism in the discourse of elites in Istanbul.[33] In the aftermath of the Balkan Wars and loss of vital provinces, a subset of the intellectuals and political figures turned their gaze to Anatolia as the wellspring of the material and spiritual revitalization of the empire. Only a segment of this cadre had ancestral connections to the region. Intellectual and emotional appeals to Anatolian identity found expression under the auspices of CUP clubs and publications. The movement's subsequent close association with a Turkish ethnonational turn is influenced by the reincarnation and popularization of Anatolianism in Turkish Republican state nationalism, which manufactured myths about Turkic origins of ancient civilizations in Asia Minor. The contemporary concomitance of Anatolia with the state of Turkey, too, misconstrues the Anatolia discourse in the 1910s, two decades before it became co-opted into a racialized Turkish nationalism by the Republic's "Turkish History Thesis."

Anatolia acquired political and cultural prominence within the logic of the empire's geopolitical transformation. By 1913, the Ottomans had lost almost the entirety of their European territories. Such was the threat of foreign invasion of Istanbul that shifting the imperial center to Anatolia was contemplated.[34] While strategic and military circumstances dictated this consideration, Anatolia assumed a new importance from a psychological standpoint as well. A disproportionately large segment of the Ottoman military and political leadership came from either the Balkan provinces, now lost, or western Anatolia, a region commercially and culturally more closely linked to the Aegean basin and the former Ottoman possessions in Europe than to the hinterland in Asia.[35] As the physical center of gravity of the empire moved east, so did the emotive mooring of segments of the political and intellectual elite. The emphasis on Anatolia that this geopolitical shift in focus engendered differed from the Anatolianism of the Republican period, which was constructed to impart an identity to the vestige of the empire cut off from its long-held territories in Syria, Mesopotamia, and Arabia during the Long War and to reimagine it as the site of the authentic and primordial essence of the new state.

Falih Rıfkı (Atay), famed Turkish author and a fixture of the entourage of leading Ottoman and Turkish Republican statesmen, expressed the disorienting effect of the shift of attention to an ill-defined Anatolia in the 1910s:

> In the past, the Turkish millet would be associated with Rumelia. The extent of the Turkish millet would perhaps extend to Bursa and Eskişehir [both towns in northwestern Asia Minor], but Anatolia would not evoke a sense of wholeness. Regional dialects were mutually unintelligible. Those from Konya [central province], Trabzon [eastern Black Sea coast] and Bitlis [eastern mountains] could not feel at one with each other like the Turks of Üsküp, Manastır [Skopje and Monastir in northern Macedonia] and Salonika [Greek Macedonia]. We thought of Anatolia as a place of exile or [a place of recruitment] if we needed to waste tens of thousands of lives in Yemen or Albania.[36]

Falih Rıfkı asserts that Anatolians did not have a "sense of uniqueness" associated with nationalist movements, even as geography textbooks identified Anatolia, excluding the eastern reaches of Asia Minor, as the homeland of the Turks.[37] The post–Balkan War foregrounding of Anatolia did not engender policies that undermined the commitment to preserve the empire. Nor did it signify the adoption of a Turkish nationalism that militated against the accommodation of non-Turkish-speaking groups within the empire. Confronted with geopolitical and demographic transformations, however, Istanbul calibrated its policies to emphasize bonds among Muslims. The trauma of defeat at the hands of former Christian subject peoples provided a psychological impetus for this outlook. The ideological shift compromised the sociopolitical status of non-Muslim subjects within the Ottomanist framework and paved the way toward the displacement and destruction of entire communities.

The Great War accelerated the ideological—and eventually geopolitical and demographic—transformations engendered by the Balkan Wars. The war's uncertainties, insecurities, and suffering aroused religious sentiment, both in soldiers, who were socialized/indoctrinated to see death as martyrdom for religion, and the civilians, who sought solace in faith in the face of hardships. "The use of Islamic themes for mobilizing purposes evoked an imagined community among Ottoman Muslims."[38] The Islamic appeals reflected the political elites' embrace of religious patriotism in the face of renewed conflict with European powers.[39] With full commitment to the empire's defense and the jihad, the Ottoman government sent its armies to distant fronts from Basra and Yemen to the Balkans. The surge of Islamic sentiment within a discourse of holy war; a long legacy of European predation cloaked at times as defense of coreligionists; and Ottoman Christian complicity—real, perceived, and manufactured—underpinned acts of both organized and indiscriminate violence against Christian minorities, most radically against Armenians.[40] The purge of Christian populations enhanced Muslim demographic preponderance. Conversion to Islam allowed some Christians to escape the worst of the physical violence.[41] These transformations of World War I prefigured the ideological premises and social foundations of the anti-colonial resistance in the Great War's aftermath.

The Ottomanist agenda underwent several permutations since it was first conceived in the mid-nineteenth century to assume a dimension exclusionary of non-Muslims during the Long War. Ottoman statesmen embraced the imperative to preserve the integrity of the imperial state. The primacy of state survival became ever more intertwined with the governing cadres' professional socialization in state institutions and their collective and individual self-views, especially for those who came from a military background. A corollary of state-preservation was the need for a sound administrative infrastructure. In contradistinction to Tanzimat's bureaucratic centralization and Hamidian palace patronage, in the immediate post-1908 period, integration within the framework of an idealized form of contractual state-society relationship commensurate with modern citizenship came to the fore as the assured way to sustain the administrative order, even as the government confronted and had to address demands for expanded local and communal prerogatives.[42] The CUP's leadership cadres believed that such integration would marshal the empire's resources effectively and forestall military and economic pressure from European countries.

Continued military reverses and economic subjugation coupled with increasingly authoritarian misgovernment militated against the accommodation of ethno-religious and sectional interests and reinforced decentralist proclivities, including in the Arab provinces. During World War I, Istanbul resorted to an agenda of integration that would draw strength from the Muslims' loyalty and commitment to the state and from Muslim imperial collective identity, supplant the politics of nationality, and impart a new lease on life to the state's integrity at a time of war and internal insubordination, especially in the empire's periphery. Reverses during the Great War would lead to a recalibration of the integrationist policies for the sake of salvaging the empire, but not before the genocide of the large non-Muslim Ottoman community of Armenians.

WAR AND OTTOMAN INTEGRATION: SYRIA AS MICROCOSM

The outbreak of the Great War brought home the challenge of preserving the empire's lands coveted by European powers and the necessity of closer integration of the provinces. It also provided latitude in justifying and implementing extraordinary measures to ensure these objectives. The exigencies of legitimating the state, solidifying central authority, and organizing defense against foreign encroachments and internal subordination rendered Syria the prime object of a concerted effort to preserve the territorial integrity of the empire. Syria carried vital importance for Istanbul because of its critical location at the intersection of Anatolia, Mesopotamia, and Arabia and its Mediterranean coastline, which was vulnerable to attacks from the Entente navies. It was at the junction of the empire's Red Sea provinces and the Sinai Peninsula, the crossing point to British-controlled Egypt, that served as a critical site for Britain's overall war operations, Ottoman claims of legal possession of the territory notwithstanding. The outbreak of an uprising in the Hijaz in 1916 enhanced Syria's significance for the revolt's containment. Germany devoted extraordinary logistical and personnel resources to Syria owing to its strategic importance, making it the preeminent site of sustained operational collaboration between the two Central Powers. In the major towns of Greater Syria, Damascus, Beirut, and Jerusalem, Arab consciousness and Arabist organizational and intellectual activity had grown during the previous decades. Istanbul sought to defuse the autonomist and potentially separatist currents by forging a new governmental relation with the Syrian provinces and implementing measures that would strengthen their ties to the state while the Ottoman army waged war in the region.

The government established the Fourth Army Corps for its operations in Syria and assigned the minister of the Navy, Cemal Pasha, to its command.[43] Cemal was the CUP's point man regularly appointed to critical military-administrative posts, in which his aura as one of the top CUP leaders provided him effective liberty to implement extraordinary, and frequently extralegal, actions in restoring order and executing state policy.[44] He arrived in Syria at the end of 1914 with emergency powers as army commander and the governor-general of the Syrian provinces. During his three-year tenure in Syria, Cemal Pasha directed two failed offensive campaigns against the Suez Canal, the first in early 1915 and the second in the summer of 1916. The British forces repulsed both attacks inflicting humiliating losses on the Ottoman forces. In 1917, a reorganization of the Ottoman army formations and their command amounted to a demotion of Cemal Pasha. It enhanced the role of the German military mission and unified the southern armies under the command of General Erich von Falkenhayn, released from his post as the chief of the general staff of the German army the previous year. In December 1917, a British counteroffensive would succeed in capturing Jerusalem, as Cemal left his post and returned to Istanbul.

The severe defeats that the Ottomans suffered under Cemal's watch in the Sinai and Palestine fronts defined his tenure in Syria and the balance sheet of his military career. His arbitrary and authoritarian rule as the top administrator in Greater Syria left an enduring and tarnished legacy. Arab national histories appropriated the war years as the touchstone of the injustices and the physical and psychic oppression that the Syrians suffered before nationalism's redemptive power unshackled them. Cemal Pasha's erratic and autocratic acts compounded the brunt of hitherto unimaginable horrors of war in Syria, including large-scale combatant and civilian losses of life, starvation, disease, and displacement. The aura of Cemal's oppression has long obscured a set of undertakings extraordinary in their articulation during wartime, which were executed to expand the Ottoman state's integrative capacities in Syria and beyond. Viewed from the perspective of state consolidation and legitimation and within the context of the Long War, these policies render to an assessment that foregrounds the logic of empire rather than its moral and political bankruptcy.

Greater Syria stands out as a Great War theater, the home front experiences of which have been amply written about in historical narratives and cultivated in Syrian and Lebanese collective memory.[45] Popular lore has associated the Ottoman word for military mobilization, *seferberlik*, with the entirety of the war experience. Subsumed in *seferberlik* is the totality of wartime losses, suffering, and indignities: mass conscription, the severe food shortages and starvation arising from military requisitioning, forced labor, the agricultural calamity of a locust invasion, enemy blockades, profiteering and other supply problems; inflation and economic destitution; execution and deportation of community leaders on trumped-up charges of treason; and sickness and epidemics. Cemal Pasha's figure was central to the societal collapse in coastal Syria and its historical representations, which have kept alive and embellished upon the war's centrifugal impact. The poignancy of Syria's war experience is matched by the intensity of the Ottoman state's efforts to reassert itself in the region. It is possible to view what has come to be recognized as one man's ill-guided policies within the context of the centripetal forces that the Ottoman governing elite strived to foster as its integrative vision for the Ottoman state.

JANUS FACE OF OTTOMAN STATE PRACTICES

Wartime Syria became the site of rigorous and deliberate application of state processes. This effort carried the imprint of the extraordinary war powers assumed both at the center, where ad hoc ministerial decisions rather than the deliberative parliamentary process shaped policy, and at the provincial level, where Cemal Pasha's writ superseded administrative provincial and municipal authority. An extraordinary court-martial set up in the town of Aleyh tried prominent Syrians, whom documents confiscated in the vacated French consulates implicated with foreign sympathies and separatist collaboration with the Entente powers. The state enacted judicial powers in the trial of well-known community leaders, intellectuals, politicians, and notables with trumped-up charges. More than thirty sentenced to death were executed by hanging in Beirut and Damascus in August 1915 and May 1916 in the two cities' main squares, each later named Martyrs' Square and solemnized with monuments commemorating those who gave their lives for the nation.[46] Hundreds of others were sent into exile in Anatolia, often summarily.[47] An extensive tract published under Cemal's auspices in Arabic, Turkish, and French defended the actions that echoed his tactics against the CUP's political opponents and those suspected of breaking the public order in his prior posts in the capital and the provinces.[48] Cemal remarked, "We are tired of the government falling in a position of weakness. We decided to punish the criminals in the severest way and without mercy no matter what their social standing. Thus, we think that henceforth their like will act appropriately."[49] The executions elicited a visceral outrage from the public and compounded the indignities and suffering it had to endure due to the war.

Compulsory enlistment into military service intruded into and disrupted the lives of individuals, families, and communities. The Ottoman state had conscripted soldiers from the Syrian provinces before, but their large-scale deployment in combat during the Great War was unprecedented. Estimates of the number of Arab soldiers in the Ottoman army vary by hundreds of thousands.[50] Since registration and conscription were relatively spotty in the Mesopotamian and Arabian provinces, the majority of these soldiers are likely to have been Syrian, not all of whom were native Arabophone. Estimates of Arab, Kurdish, or Turkish soldiers from mixed provinces are observational or speculative, as the Ottoman official records did not ordinarily document ethno-linguistic affiliation of Muslims. Uniform conscription and military service, a litmus test of modern citizenship, was generally dreaded and, if possible, evaded. Local military service had emerged as a principal demand of the decentralist reform committees in Syria before the war. During wartime, military and civilian authorities assigned many Syrian units to regiments deployed in diverse and often remote fronts. Even if the government projected military service as a form of patriotic allegiance to the state and religion, most soldiers regarded it as coercive imposition in the category of requisitioning and exile, if not a death sentence.[51]

Cemal Pasha led efforts to insinuate the state into the lives of Syrians and the landscape of Syria in disciplinary strategies besides trials, scaffolds, exile, and the draft.[52] He staged spectacles of state power, such as military parades with abundant display of the Ottoman flag in streets lined with residences and businesses. The public rituals had a strong coercive dimension, even as they were choreographed to garner legitimacy for the state. Grandiose urban construction projects enhanced the state's presence visually, among them avenues that cut through the town centers, especially the wide boulevards in Damascus and Jaffa. These arteries became venues for parades and similar processional rituals and performances of power that served as reminders of the proximate state and imperial grandeur.[53] Cemal revived the Hamidian project of creating highly visible structures as signs of governmental prowess and authority.

Next to punitive, coercive, and state-magnifying undertakings, Cemal sponsored projects that signaled state capacities and a commitment to improve conditions of life in stark contrast to the ravages of the war. Indeed, he promoted measures to blunt opposition to state authority and manufacture popular assent, such as sanitation and the creation of tranquil spaces like parks and gardens aimed at enhancing the health and welfare of the urban population while providing tame forms of leisure.[54] Cinemas opened in Damascus and Bi'r al-Sab' (Birüssebi/Beersheva).[55] In addition to providing a venue for leisure, the cinema served the screening of propaganda films to large audiences and venues for patriotic public lectures.[56]

The government efforts benefited from research and publication initiatives aimed at enhancing the social and physical legibility of Syria and facilitating the exercise of patronage over the region's present and past. Prior to Cemal's arrival, the governor of Beirut, Azmi Bey, had commissioned two bureaucrat-intellectuals, Muhammad Bahjat and Rafiq al-Tamimi, to undertake a comprehensive survey of social and cultural life in the province. Al-Tamimi exhibited the hybrid affiliations and allegiances of many Arabs within the same social and professional circles. Before the war, he held jobs in the provincial civil service, belonged to the Committee of Union and Progress, and acted as one of the founders of the Arabist society, al-Fatat.[57] The authors published their two-volume compendium in 1916, the result of painstaking ethnographic work that took them to towns, villages, and Beduin encampments throughout western and southern Syria.[58] Cemal approved another compendium on Lebanon as late as December 1917, the brainchild of former Aleppo governor Hüseyin Kazım, who was domiciled in Beirut during the war.[59]

The Ottomans cultivated knowledge on history for identity production and ideological needs.[60] According to Zeynep Çelik,

> Attention to Islamic culture was as central to late-Ottoman thinking as the desire to compete with Europe for a reputation for modernity. A 1914 document encapsulated the growing focus of Ottoman authorities and cultural leaders on Islamic heritage. Intended to provide a comprehensive record, it announced the establishment of a special committee to build a collection of plans, drawings, and photographs of the "old Islamic monuments in Ottoman lands."... The resulting collection was to be used in schools to raise consciousness of the value of the Islamic past through its architectural landmarks.[61]

Cemal Pasha engaged in a program of preserving, renovating, and publicizing historical monuments in Syria. He did not confine this work to Islamic sites but to a broader shared heritage. Christian and Jewish sites received attention, not just because these communities were demographically well represented in coastal areas and larger cities, especially among the literati and merchant classes, but also because posturing as their guardians gave preemptory signals to the Entente powers, whose protectorship of the non-Muslim communities had customarily provided justification for intervention and bellicosity. This effort reached back into the ancient period to indulge what Benedict Anderson has referred to in the context of the museum as "profane ecumenical genealogizing."[62] It sought to establish the lineage of the Ottoman state as the last of a series of great states and civilizations that historically had molded Syria.

Ottoman state consolidation strategies dovetailed with Germany's cognate efforts to pair knowledge with power in the Middle East and to rival Britain and France not just on the battlefield but also in the cultural domain. German officers and advisors closely cooperated in the cataloging and publicizing of historical sites, structures, and artifacts. The wartime alignment of camps imparted German Orientalists and archaeologists primacy in the study of both biblical lands and Islamic culture and history. Germany had the opportunity to compete with imperialist rivals France and Britain for the patronage of the Orient. In the tradition of time-honored practices of Orientalist scholarship, German scholarly work was connected to policies and aspirations of the German government. In September 1917, Berlin solicited a report on new scientific initiatives and projects pertaining to "Turkey" and appraised which of these policies would align with German state interests and should be incentivized.[63]

The agendas of the Ottoman and German governments are embodied in the person and work of the German scholar Theodor Wiegand, a director of the Berlin Museum and previously the head of the German Archaeological Institute in Istanbul. Enlisted as an officer in the German army and assigned to Syria as general inspector of antiquities in Syria and Arabia, Wiegand joined Cemal's entourage in an advising capacity.[64] He oversaw the establishment of an agency for the protection of Syrian antiquities, the *Denkmalschutzkommando*, which produced and published an album with one hundred exquisite plates of ancient, medieval, and early modern sites in Syria, from the Wailing Wall and the Church of the Nativity in Bethlehem to the Umayyad Mosque and the Salimiya Mosque.[65] In the foreword, Cemal, under whose name the album was published, welcomes the opportunity "to study the needs of this valuable part of my country and to contemplate the preservation and proper administration of its old monuments." Cemal presents to Ottoman citizens ("patriots") the treasures of their country. *Alte Denkmäler* differed from Wiegand's other publications, as he explains in the introduction to one of his scientific contributions.[66] Its purpose was to depict the Ottoman state as the natural guardian of Syria's historical greatness and impart legitimacy to the Ottoman order. The scholarly detail that has been left out in *Alte Denkmäler* is presented in this later publication, which illustrates aerial views of ancient sites.[67]

Despite the war, the Ottoman state redoubled its modernizing efforts in Syria. According to Salim Tamari, "The war transformed [Palestine] into one major construction site. [Work battalions were] mobilized by the Ottoman Corps of Army Engineers to substantially modernize the communication and transportation system.... Many features of Palestine's modernity attributed to the British colonial administration seem to have been initiated by the Ottomans in this period." Tamari cites a source that he characterizes as "the first work on modern history of Palestine in the new century,"[68] that attests to "the major changes brought about by the technological exigencies of war. Water wells were drilled all over the country and linked through pipes to major urban centers. Railroads linked the north of the country to the southern front; a network of telegraph and telephone lines connected the country to the outside world. Post offices . . . were unified and foreign post services replaced by Ottoman postal service; roads were expanded to allow the operation of military traffic and mechanized cars."[69]

The establishment of Bi'r al-Sab' as a modern town is emblematic of war-related development. A small settlement before the war in the Bedouin-populated Negev desert, Bi'r al-Sab' was the village-size center of a district by the same name connected administratively to the Jerusalem *sancak* (district).[70] Military exigencies provided the impetus behind the development of the town, specifically the construction of a branch from the Hijaz Railway into the town to connect with the railway to the Sinai, christened as the Hijaz Railway Egypt Branch (*Hicaz Demiryolu Mısır Şubesi*).[71] The project was directed by the architect of the Hijaz Railway Meissner Pasha.[72] In the ceremony held to mark the completion of the line, Cemal Pasha had the honor of tightening the last sleeper screw with a silver wrench.[73] Bi'r al-Sabʻ thus stood as a site for the performance of modernity, having both a cinema and a local newspaper, *Musavver Çöl Gazetesi* (Illustrated Desert Gazette), published in Arabic and Turkish.[74] Its development impressed one German observer as progressing "with American speed."[75] Another wrote that the war "was more creative here than decades of full and lethargic peace."[76]

Management of wartime pestilence and disease required the implementation of measures that enhanced the state's control over the bodies of citizens in Syria. Epidemics festered among soldiers as well as the civilian population ravaged by famine. The government built new hospitals and administered most of the existing ones.[77] The physical health of the populace had to be protected by the provision of clean water, as implemented in Aleppo after the typhoid epidemic in 1915.[78] Cemal Pasha had leverage over resources that could be mobilized to supplement government efforts. He commissioned the directors of the Zionist agricultural research center near Haifa, the Aaronsohn brothers, to address the eradication of the locust, an effort that was stymied by the unavailability of the necessary supplies due to the Entente blockade of the Syrian ports.[79]

The Ottoman state embraced the role of educator by expanding instruction at all levels and in competition with foreign and missionary schools.[80] In Syria, when the war crippled schools connected with the Entente powers, Cemal Pasha diversified schooling with an eye to raise informed and skilled citizens from different walks of life. He opened girls' schools with the assistance of Halide Edib, whom he invited to Syria.[81] He established or embarked on the building of industrial schools (Beirut, Bi'r al-Sabʻ), an agricultural school (Baka'a), and a teacher's college (Aleppo).[82] He set up boarding elementary schools to distance students from disruptions related to the war emergency. The provision of schooling aimed at legitimating the existing order and instilling the values of the state.[83]

If the promotion of secular schools reflected one dimension of the educational policy, the launching of an Islamic higher academy in Jerusalem was indicative of another. The academy was named *al-Kulliya al-Salahiya* after Salah al-Din al-Ayyubi (Saladin), the Muslim ruler of the Cairo-based dynasty famed for having recovered the Crusader stronghold in Palestine in the twelfth century. The school taught a curriculum in the Islamic sciences in both Turkish and Arabic to students mostly hailing from Anatolia and Syria.[84] In December 1917, when the British commander Allenby captured Jerusalem, the very town once liberated by Salah al-Din, al-Salahiya moved to Damascus, where it petered out at the end of the world war.[85] Another project conceived in the spirit of revitalizing the Islamic heritage and strengthening Islamic sensibilities, the reorganization of Damascus's Islamic library, faltered as enemy forces advanced north.[86]

MOBILIZING SUPPORT AMID WAR'S VIOLENCE

As the lynchpin of the policy to mobilize support for the state and the war effort in Syria, Istanbul managed the popular press. The government did not rely on punishment and censorship alone, cognizant that journalists had come to play a role in voicing oppositional ideas, frequently in an Arabist idiom.[87] Instead, it implemented a systematic policy of taming the press and co-opting it in support of government objectives. In Syria, this effort entailed cultivating a press that would reinforce the ideological goals of maintaining and promoting Islamic solidarity by keeping the discourse of holy war alive, while incentivizing compliance with government authority and fostering the virtue of loyalty to the state.

The formulation of a comprehensive Islamic propaganda campaign received attention first in the spring of 1915. A memorandum that Deputy Commander-in-Chief Enver Pasha sent to Cemal Pasha detailed the purposes behind the foundation of a propaganda organ and broached ideas about the manner of its organization.[88] A newspaper published in Syria would strive for the enlightenment of Muslims inside and outside of the empire to parallel similar publications in the capital.[89] Damascus was an appropriate site for the publication and distribution of such a propaganda organ owing to the city's status as a hallowed center of the first Islamic empire and its central location on crossroads, including the pilgrimage route, which connected the southern provinces both with one another and the imperial center.

The memorandum recommended the cultivation of journals currently in circulation in Syria, until such time as an official newspaper was founded, by allocating monthly subventions and ensuring the provision of the necessary paper, a rare commodity during the war, to be obtained from Germany. The newspapers, including *Ra'y al-'Am*, *Ittihad al-Islam*, *al-Balagh*, and *al-Iqbal*, were to provide war news and "useful" summaries from the capital's papers on domestic and foreign affairs. Contributions from distinguished Syrian men of letters would be compensated. The memorandum proposed Shakib Arslan, deputy in the Ottoman parliament and Ottomanist activist and thinker known for his intimacy with Enver Pasha, as the appropriate person to take charge of this propaganda operation in Syria. He would be expected to review the contents of the papers and commission articles to Syrian authors.

Cemal welcomed the initiative and replied that he had already engaged in the kind of relationship suggested in the memorandum with some Syrian papers. He urged that *al-Muqtabas* and *al-Mufid*, the two leading opposition papers of Damascus and Beirut, should also be co-opted. Cemal succeeded in inducing the owners of the papers *al-Muqtabas*, *al-Balagh*, *al-Ra'y al-'Am*, *al-Iqbal*, and *Ittihad al-Islam* to sign an agreement with the offer of a subsidy—and also intimidation. He calibrated the monthly subventions to the newspapers according to the perceived influence of each paper and its editor(s).[90] He reported that the agreement with *al-Mufid* became void when the "Arab government trial" sentenced its owner, 'Abd al-Ghani al-'Uraysi, to death and closed down the paper.[91] Muhammad Kurd 'Ali, influential Damascene intellectual, proponent of decentralization before the war, and editor of *al-Muqtabas*, escaped persecution at the Aleyh trials and embraced the integrationist agenda of the Ottoman government. When the propaganda organ that Istanbul sponsored in Damascus to promote the jihad started to appear as *al-Sharq*, Kurd 'Ali played a leading role in the publication.[92]

Muhammad Kurd 'Ali's activities as public intellectual point to the transformed intellectual landscape in Syria during the war years. Kurd 'Ali had been influenced by the turn-of-the century Arab reformist intellectual tradition, the *salafi* movement, which had arisen from within the religious establishment as a modernist critique of the conservative ulama (religious scholars). The latter, as well as the first generation of Islamic modernists writing in Cairo during the Hamidian period, like Muhammad 'Abduh and his disciples, stood behind Islamic universalism and the Ottoman state mission. The students of the salafis, though, derived from diverse walks of middle-class society in Syria and "espoused ethnic interests against centralist policies" in an Arabist idiom.[93] Some advanced the vision of a federated Ottoman state.[94] Muhammad Kurd 'Ali supported the Arab Congress held in Paris in 1913, a meeting of delegates from different Arab provinces and diaspora representative of religious/sectarian groups, whose demands the Ottoman government sought to allay by pledging the implementation of decentralist measures. Once the Great War broke out, Istanbul fell back on integration cum centralization. Kurd 'Ali advanced this cause in Syria by partnering with the conservative Syrian notables who supported Cemal's integrationist agenda. His compromise with the Ottoman authorities bears the signs of opportunism, for which he has been judged harshly in retrospect.[95] In a more charitable appraisal, Salim Tamari associates him with the view that upheld "Arabs and Turks as the essential core and last remaining bulwark of Ottomanism" and "bilingualism as a means of enhancing Ottoman citizenship in the Empire."[96]

Another facet of the modern methods of propaganda used to create and expand a public opinion supportive of the war effort and of the Ottomanist platform comprised managed transmission of war news from the Syrian front to the capital. Leading Istanbul-based authors who would later attain further fame in the Turkish Republic accompanied Cemal during his tenure or visited for extended periods, including Falih Rıfkı and Halide Edib.[97] Cemal relied on them to vindicate his policy and to further the public consciousness of the empire-wide war effort. Falih Rıfkı authored the justificatory tract published after the court-martial proceedings at Aleyh. Ahmet Rasim, whom Talat Pasha tasked with intelligence, later reminisced about the vagaries of war reporting and the control Cemal exercised by withholding or distorting information.[98] Mehmed Akif (Ersoy), a renowned poet and the future author of Turkey's national anthem, who published the preeminent Islamist journal *Sebilürreşad*, visited Cemal Pasha as a member of a mission to promote the jihad in the Arab provinces for the Ottoman intelligence service, the *Teşkilat-ı Mahsusa*.[99]

WAR AND MOBILITY

The war intensified the circulation of people within Syria and between Syria and other regions of the empire. The Ottoman government compelled, facilitated, or controlled these movements, as elsewhere in the empire. Mobility dictated by different circumstances had the intended or unintended consequence of creating linkages that fostered self-consciousness as imperial citizens, even when accompanied by disaffection. Thousands of young Syrians left their villages and towns for the first time to be transported to distant fronts. Far-flung military service had a practical and ideological rationale. Desertion, the single most important logistical problem that the Ottoman armies confronted everywhere, posed a greater threat in a familiar setting proximate to home.[100] More important, as the experience of the best known Syrian regiment that fought far away from home suggests, the Ottoman state saw empire-wide utilization of troops from a specific locality, in this case Aleppo, as a strategy of integration and a symbol of imperial solidarity by way of patriotic fraternization with ethno-linguistic others.

The government showcased the Aleppo regiment as the locus of a set of performances in the service of collective welfare. A welcoming ceremony in Gallipoli featured fanfare and orations in Arabic and Turkish. A delegation of Syrian men of religion and authors followed the regiment to the capital and then to Gallipoli in the fall of 1915.[101] The contingent included Syrian journalists and scholars like Muhammad Kurd 'Ali, whom Cemal Pasha had enlisted to the defense of the empire and the government.[102] He commissioned them to write articles for Syrian newspapers about the valor and successes of the Ottoman armies. On the occasion of this contingent's arrival in Istanbul, the speaker of the Ottoman parliament announced that the delegation requested him to transmit greetings to the "Chamber of Deputies which is the foremost manifestation of all Ottomans uniting in the service of the country."[103] A reciprocal and even more symbolically laden visitation followed the journey of the Syrian men of letters to Istanbul and Gallipoli. In February 1916, the effective commander-in-chief of the Ottoman armies, Enver Pasha, toured Syria with an entourage of religious officials and other dignitaries. The trip culminated in a visit to the Prophet's Mosque in Medina in the company of Cemal and Faysal in an act that was choreographed to refurbish Islamic-Ottomanist allegiances.[104] Kurd 'Ali and his associates authored commemorative books on both the Gallipoli and Medina trips.

The construction and repair of land arteries within Syria and between Anatolia and Syria strengthened physical intra-empire communications and facilitated circulation. The staging of campaigns necessitated the overhaul of transportation networks and public works, and the resources allocated to the war effort made possible the expansion of roads and railroads. Newly built arteries facilitated communications for the army and the civilians alike. No uninterrupted railway connection existed across the Taurus range connecting Anatolia with Syria as late as the end of the war, but travel and shipments had become less arduous with road and tunnel improvements.[105] Intramural connections also developed significantly as new roads were cut within the cities, including the majestic boulevards in Damascus and Jaffa, and public transportation assumed renewed attention. More effective distribution of electricity in Aleppo, for instance, allowed the launching of plans for an electric tramway.[106] The Entente countries were forced to abandon their economic concerns and concessions, such as in railways and postal services, leading to their standardization and integration into imperial networks.

The CUP implemented radical measures during the war that targeted entire populations, most notably the Armenians in 1915–1916. Large numbers of Armenian deportees entered the northern region of Cemal's command in Syria. Cemal had served as minister in the Unionist cabinet (i.e., affiliated with the CUP) that displaced Ottoman Greeks and Bulgarians from their western Anatolian homelands in 1913 and 1914 on grounds of security concerns and with revanchist motives.[107] But he had left Istanbul for Syria prior to the Armenian deportations and massacres in Anatolia. His policies vis-à-vis the Armenians stood apart from those of the CUP central committee overseen by Minister of the Interior Talat Pasha. In the memoirs he penned just before he was assassinated by Armenian militants in 1922, Cemal provides a long-winded defense of what he portrayed as humane and charitable acts in destitute Armenian communities, including the facilitation of the Armenians' relocation away from the death camps of the desert, the social and educational facilities he set up, and his interventions with regional authorities in an effort to mitigate the carnage. Recent research has demonstrated that aspects of his apologia deserve merit.[108] However, they do not absolve Cemal of complicity and culpability in genocide for assimilating resettled Armenian children into Islamic culture, in particular in the 'Ayn Tura orphanage under the supervision of Halide Edib.[109] What gained Cemal the sobriquet "Butcher" (*saffah*) were his harsh measures against real or perceived Syrian opponents, which did not single out Christian Arabs.

BALANCE SHEET IN SYRIA

Writing in 1917, American-educated sociologist and journalist Ahmed Emin wrote, perhaps with the consciousness of writing for a German-speaking audience, that the war saved for "Turkey" its southern provinces including Syria. According to Ahmed Emin, with French propaganda and incitement becoming more and more vigorous in Syria before the war, it was only a matter of time before this territory would be torn asunder. "Through judicious work in the last years of the war, Turkey has re-conquered Syria and made a strong attempt to win it culturally."[110] Cemal implemented policies within the logic of the evolved conception of Ottomanism, one refurbished with an emphasis on Muslim identity. In his canonical work on Arab nationalism, George Antonius, a vehement critic of the CUP and Cemal's oppressive acts and executions in Syria, wrote that Cemal "professed, not without sincerity, a belief in the virtues and the future of an Ottoman nationalism based on Moslem solidarity."[111] The Ottoman state exhibited a set of disciplinary capacities in Syria. Regulatory and legitimizing policies in the sphere of physical and social communications, urban renewal, or the appropriation of the symbols of the past complemented such punitive measures as executions and exile. Once the war was concluded with Ottoman defeat and British occupation of Syria, Cemal's policies, which were meant to preserve Syria for the empire, would be viewed as a fool's errand.

Syria experienced a confluence of the seminal processes of the war, which arguably influenced and transformed it more than any other region of the empire. The constellation of war contingencies induced Istanbul to institute an extraordinary military-administrative regime in the Syrian provinces. The memory of the war has remained potent in the countries that emerged out of Greater Syria and has influenced and augmented both scholarly and popular accounts of the war. Syria hence presents an apposite site for studying war, society, and politics—and, centrally for the present study, for appraising the imperial policy of Ottoman governments in the Arab provinces.

Positing a wartime Syrian exceptionalism, however, may misrepresent both the Syrian and the broader Ottoman war experience. Many of the circumstances, processes, and policies examined in this chapter were not unique to Syria. The imperial, indeed, global, context of the war cannot be appraised properly without divesting from the unicity that official histories and collective memory construct for the Syrian provinces, even if one recognizes that the confluence of distinctive factors inflected and amplified Syria's war experience and demanded Istanbul's inordinate attention. The larger-than-life persona and wartime tenure of Cemal Pasha bears similarities to that of other wartime provincial governors. The governor of the Aegean province of Aydın Rahmi Bey (Evrenoszade) was known for his independent actions and his infrastructure modernization program.[112] In addition, he notably gave wide latitude to German advisers, including in bringing epidemics under control.[113] Independently minded Diyarbekir governor Mehmed Reşid (Şahingiray) inflicted overzealous violence on Christian populations in eastern Anatolia without having to account for his actions.[114] The devastations of the war, including requisitioning, famine, disease, and even the locust plague, encapsulated in the *seferberlik* ethos in Syria, permeated huge parts of the imperial geography and society. In eastern Anatolia, in particular, the Russian invasion, hostile terrain, and harsh winters aggravated the suffering of both the soldiers and the civilians.[115] Memories tend to fade when not embraced and extoled by a narrative specific to the region and suited for subsequent mythmaking.

Practices of modernity accompany total wars. They are collateral to the military effort but not merely as they pertain to military prowess and efficiency. War provides "fertile soil" for an "authoritarian state that is willing and able to use the full weight of its coercive power to bring . . . high-modernist designs into being, especially in the presence of a prostrate civil society that lacks the capacity to resist these plans."[116] The Ottoman government sought legitimacy as a modernizer throughout the empire. Quoting Bernard Lewis that "the Young Turks may have failed to give Turkey constitutional government [but] they did . . . give Istanbul its drains," Sibel Bozdoğan remarks that they also "initiated important urban, modernization, sanitation, and transportation projects in the hope of reviving the empire" and "mobilized architecture for identity construction and nation-building."[117] Thus, the urban renewal projects in Syria fit into a broader pattern, as do the efforts to preserve and publicize historical monuments and sites. As Zeynep Çelik argues, "In order to craft a new and dynamic imperial image that enhanced cultural wealth and diversity, the Ottomans . . . highlighted *asar-ı antika* (relics) of all periods with great pride."[118]

OTTOMAN WAR EFFORT IN ARAB PROVINCES BEYOND SYRIA

The Ottoman war effort encompassed all Arab provinces, even though the multifaceted campaign, alongside military operations, with its social, cultural, and infrastructural dimensions was centered in Syria. The second main theater of confrontation was Mesopotamia.[119] The British army gained a foothold in Basra without significant Ottoman resistance as early as November 1914 and made its earliest advances into Ottoman territories from the Persian Gulf. The British occupation of Baghdad, however, was stymied by the resistance of Ottoman forces, which won a decisive battle at the end of 1915 just southeast of Baghdad, laid siege to the British garrison farther south in

Kut al-Amara, and in April 1916 managed to take the British troops prisoner together with their commander, General Townshend. A renewed offensive by the British army, bolstered with troops from India under General Maude, occupied Baghdad in March 1917. The Ottoman-German military command formed a new army corps based in Aleppo in order to stem the British advance, named the Yıldırım (Thunderbolt) Army under the command of General Erich von Falkenhayn, who had served as minister of war in Berlin, and, at the beginning of the Great War, as chief of the staff of German armies. Yıldırım was reassigned to Palestine to halt the British incursion into Syria.

Yıldırım incorporated the Fourth Army and displaced Cemal Pasha from the command position, an event that would soon lead to Cemal's departure from Syria. In an apparent compromise, Cemal was named commander of the operations in the coastal Arabian provinces of the Hijaz and Asir (to the north of Yemen) that had been under his purview as commander of the Fourth Army. Ottoman military presence along the Red Sea had been negligible before the war. The outbreak of hostilities with the Entente and subsequently the Arab Revolt necessitated the diversion of troops and resources to Arabia. After the completion of the Hijaz Railway to Medina in 1908, the Ottomans had established the town as a forward base in Arabia.[120] Cemal's infrastructural policies in Syria spilled over to Medina, where he built roads and brought to the town amenities including electricity.[121]

The loss of prestige caused by the abandonment of Mecca to Sharif Husayn led to a spirited defense of Medina, the second holy city of Islam. Even after Medina could no longer be defended and had to be evacuated, Ottoman troops commanded by Fahreddin Pasha (Türkkan) resisted the siege of the Medina fort. This resistance, carried out under circumstances of great deprivation, depended on the personal valor and convictions of Fahreddin but was also emblematic of the ideological commitment to Islam and the empire. The commander of the German military mission, Otto Liman von Sanders, criticized the stubborn defense of Medina in his memoirs with the incongruous remark that it "can be explained only by the Turkish national point of view."[122] According to Liman, "Nothing but the political and religious interests of Turkey caused Enver to call attention again and again to the great importance of Medina and of the communication with the city," even as it became impracticable to defend the town after the country south and west of Dead Sea had fallen into enemy hands.[123]

In Yemen, the government had formally recognized in 1911 the Zaydi Shiite leader Imam Yahya Hamid al-Din and granted a degree of autonomy in return for allegiance to the sultan. Imam Yahya supported the Ottoman war effort by embracing the call for jihad and mobilized forces against the British with the help of two Ottoman divisions, as the Ottoman effort in the Hijaz focused on the defense of Medina in the aftermath of Husayn's revolt.[124] An officer who served in the British colonial administration in Aden would later point to the irony of the wartime collaboration between Yemen's ordinarily intractable Imam Yahya and Istanbul, while the Ottoman forces fought the traditional Ottoman ally, Grand Sharif of Mecca, in the Hijaz.[125]

The Ottoman war aims included the recovery of Arab-populated former provinces of the empire or the augmentation of the bonds with regions that had attained various degrees of autonomy. Şükrü Hanioğlu, who has documented in his work the Turkish nationalist proclivities of CUP leaders, writes that their "self-imposed task of empire-saving" prevented the Unionists "from unleashing their Turkism as a policy."[126] Rather, they hoped "that full Ottoman control would be reestablished over the various autonomous regions of the empire. The Ottoman abolition of the self-governing status of Mount Lebanon in July 1915 provided a hint as to what lay in store for many such regions in the event of victory. The Ottoman Foreign Ministry conducted extensive preparatory work on the history and legal circumstances of autonomous regions such as Kuwait, Qatar, Najd, Bahrein, and even Hadramawt and Oman."[127] In the case of Egypt, the widely held proposition that the Suez campaigns were a German stratagem aimed solely at tying up British troops rather than a sanguine endeavor to bring Egypt back to the Ottoman fold discredits the Ottoman effort and reinforces the trope that German preponderance in the alliance denied the Ottoman state agency during the war.[128] The Suez campaigns were complex operations in which the government invested large numbers of combatants, but especially labor and infrastructural resources unparalleled in any other Ottoman front. The goal of fomenting internal revolts in Egypt when Britain's prime focus was the war in Europe made the Suez campaigns a calculated gambit and put Syria at the center of the logistical execution of these plans.

To the west of Egypt, Ottoman missions operated in Libya. The region's powerful tribal mystical order under the leadership of Ahmad al-Sharif al-Sanussi had staged the resistance against the Italian occupation and managed to restrict Italian control to the Mediterranean coast. The Sanussi order remained loyal to Istanbul despite a sense of abandonment in battling the Italian invasion after the withdrawal of Ottoman logistical support in 1912.[129] The network extended its influence to northern Sudan and posed a two-sided threat to British Egypt from the south and the west. When Italy joined the Triple Entente in May 1915, the Ottomans resumed active cooperation with Ahmad al-Sharif. The Sanussis' dogged anti-colonial resistance, their commercial and religious influence along the Sahara-Mediterranean nexus, and their origins in the Hijaz conferred prestige on them far and wide, which could be harnessed to the jihad.[130] Enver Pasha sent his half-brother Nuri to Libya at the head of an Ottoman military mission. The Libyan forces strove to penetrate Egypt from the west, though their actions remained limited to harassment attacks against the British. Later in the war, Prince Osman Fuad, the grandson of Sultan Murad V, r. May–August 1876 and grandnephew of the reigning Sultan Reşad, or Mehmed V, r. 1909–1918 took over the command of the Ottoman Africa Groups. Osman Fuad's participation galvanized the pro-Ottoman movement in North Africa.[131]

War became the stimulant for changes in Ottoman state and society as well as in collective self-views. On the eve of Ottoman entry into the Great War, Islam had emerged as the basis of commonality in the search for a collective identity. Under Abdulhamid II, Islam's political role emanated from royal (and caliphal) patronage. Abdulhamid and his ideologues effectively mobilized Islam as an anti-imperial ideology and a defensive proto-nationalism. In the post-1908 period, Islam as culture, as faith, as system of morality, and as basis of solidarity entered the wider intellectual debates. The main positions in these debates, schematically described as Westernist, Turkist, Arabist, or Islamist, all addressed religion. The Islamists came to terms with and strove to achieve syntheses with the other currents. The prominence of the ruler and the ulama receded in public deliberations pertaining to religion. If the person of the sultan mediated the Islamic identity of Ottomans before, the religio-cultural communality of a preponderantly Muslim population now became the anchor, as Ottoman statesmen and intellectuals became preoccupied with the survival of the Ottoman state and the integrity of its domains.

On the eve of World War I, in 1913, the CUP had wrested power with a high-handed coup d'état in what was the most blatant breach of the constitutional order established in 1908. The audacity of the act surpassed previous arrogations of power, such as the manipulation of the elections in 1912 in the Committee's favor. At a time when the empire was suffering humiliating defeats in the Balkan Wars, the CUP could rationalize the legitimacy of the coup. The halt of military losses in the Balkans and the Ottoman recovery of some, however, owed less to the policies and actions of the new CUP government than to internecine conflict in the Balkans. The CUP neutralized or eliminated the leaders of the main opposition party before the empire moved into new elections at the end of 1914.

After the colossal losses in the Balkans, the CUP was more willing to heed the localist sentiment in the Arab provinces, which included the vision of a Turco-Arab federative reorganization along the model of Austria-Hungary.[132] Its accommodating response to demands from the provincial reform societies and the Arab Congress of 1913 is well-documented.[133] The outbreak of the world war made these schemes moot and, from Istanbul's point of view, dangerous after the discovery of France's subversive contacts with leaders in coastal Syria and the outbreak of a separatist revolt in Mecca.

One of the most important figures of the Anatolian independence movement in its early stages, Kazım Karabekir Pasha, reminisced in the 1930s with typical nation-state-oriented retrospection, that he had advised as early as 1909 to relinquish the Arab provinces to their fate.[134] He claims to have urged the strongmen of the Committee of Union and Progress to give preferential treatment to Turkish-populated areas in infrastructural projects and not waste resources in the Arab provinces. Karabekir laments in his book that no one heeded his advice. The CUP government that led the empire during the war was committed to the defense, retention, integration, and even recovery of relinquished Arab provinces. The majority of Muslim Arabs supported these efforts.[135] War pressed the urgency of solidifying central control over the provinces and consolidating a monolithic state to secure the empire's survival and longevity until it compelled a recalibration of this vision by 1918, as will be discussed in the next chapter.

TWO

Reversals of Fortune and Resilience

THE LAST YEAR OF THE GREAT WAR

THE EUROPEAN STATES went to war in 1914 self-assuredly and expecting a short and contained war. Three years later the conflagration had spread far beyond the European continent with no end in sight and uncertain prospects of victory for either alliance, as the warfare's undiscriminating devastation at the battlefront and home front alike rendered moot the notion of victory. Only in retrospect would it be known that the Great War was entering its final year in November 1917, a pivotal month in the conflict. After having declared war against Germany in April, the United States became enmeshed in front warfare in Europe by the end of October. The revolutionary resurgence in Russia brought to power the Bolshevik government ("October Revolution," November 7), which denounced the war as a colonial stratagem, putting the Entente alliance into military uncertainty and diplomatic imbroglio. The British government's pledge to the Zionists for a national home in Palestine (Balfour Declaration, November 2) complicated conflicting war aims in Syria.

In Middle Eastern combat, a British offensive by General Allenby's Egyptian Expeditionary Force into southern Palestine captured Bi'r al-Sab' and defeated the Ottoman armies in the Third Battle of Gaza (November 7). The British would continue the offensive to capture Jerusalem at the end of the year. The loss of this prized possession, perennially coveted by the European powers and a source of religious prestige for the Ottomans, epitomized the profound impact of the war. With the defeats in Palestine and Mesopotamia, the Ottoman army was gravely weakened due to casualties on the battlefield, illness, desertion, and captivity. On the Ottoman home front, the war footing had disrupted civilian society with violence and crippling deprivation. The economy had broken down amid inflation and profiteering. During the early months of 1918, however, the actual theaters of the war saw a respite, even reversals of previous setbacks, to dissipate the sense of imperial doom.

THE FATEFUL NOVEMBER 1917

The revolutionary ferment that began in St. Petersburg in March 1917 had portended uncertain Russian commitment to the Entente war effort. It culminated in the Bolshevik takeover and Russian withdrawal from the hostilities, which would have an indelible impact on the course of the war. The American military engagement on the side of the Triple Entente would compensate for the Russian withdrawal in terms of the military balances between the Allies and the Central Powers in the overall war. For the Ottomans, however, Russia's withdrawal carried immediate and immense military and geopolitical significance. The vital direct threat to the empire's existence disappeared with the Bolshevik government's abandonment of claims on Istanbul and the Straits of Bosporus and Dardanelles. The Ottoman command could now pursue the war effort largely unencumbered by its endemically vulnerable eastern front, where against Russia it had suffered its worst defeats. Russia had captured wide swaths of eastern Anatolia following the debacle in Sarıkamış (December 1914), the earliest and most devastatingly bungled of the war's campaigns for the Ottomans, adding to Russia's 1878 annexation of the Caucasian districts of Kars, Ardahan, and Batum.

Equally consequential was Russia's post-revolutionary ideological denunciation of territorial conquest. On November 8, Lenin issued his "Decree on Peace," calling for a just peace without "seizure of foreign lands." The declaration stated that "[T]he government considers it the greatest of crimes against humanity to continue this war over the issue of how to divide among the strong and rich nations the weak nationalities they have conquered."[1] This amounted to a condemnation of the Triple Entente's wartime agreements to divide up Ottoman territories, especially the Sykes-Picot secret accord, which had specified the apportionment of the Fertile Crescent between Britain and France while conceding Istanbul and eastern Anatolia to Russia.[2] Finally, the decree underscored and elevated "voluntarily expressed consent and wish of nations," a principle that would enable the Allies to scramble for the moral high ground even as they pursued predatory war aims.

The advance of the British army into Palestine, coinciding with the Foreign Office's pledge to the British Zionist leadership to acknowledge the region as a Jewish national home, opened the door for Cemal Pasha to seek negotiations with the Hashemite family for a reconciliation.[3] Toward the end of November, the new Russian government affirmed Lenin's lofty declaration with concrete actions. Having renounced the tsarist government's war aims, the Bolsheviks repudiated the Allies as colonialists and released the terms of the Sykes-Picot agreement, which negated Hashemite ambitions, exposed the guile of the British promises in regard to their realization, and raised the scepter of colonization. The unraveling of the Entente alliance with Russia's revelation of the terms of the secret treaty enhanced Istanbul's hope to bring back the Hashemites and their sympathizers into the fold. Soon after the Bolsheviks published (November 23) and disseminated the Sykes-Picot document, Cemal famously announced it to local leaders at a dinner in Beirut on December 6, on the eve of his return to Istanbul, and informed his audience of a peace offer to Sharif Husayn.[4] The leaders of the revolt had not been oblivious to the Entente scheme, but the publication and circulation of its lurid details, Cemal expected, would appeal to the Hashemites' ambivalent following.[5] It would thus offer an opportunity to sway public opinion in favor of the government.

Cemal Pasha arranged for the Arabic translation of the Sykes-Picot documents to be printed in Syrian papers and distributed widely. He offered amnesty to those who had joined the revolt and had Syrian ulama write conciliatory letters to Sharif Husayn as intermediaries.[6] Cemal dispatched an emissary to Faisal with his offer of peace in the interest of Islam with extensive autonomy for the Arab provinces. The emissary arrived in Faysal's headquarters in Aqaba bearing also a letter addressed to Ja'far al-'Askari, Faysal's effective chief of staff. Al-'Askari was an Ottoman officer who had been close to the government circles in Istanbul and rendered distinguished service for the Ottoman army before he threw in his lot with Sharif Husayn.[7] Faysal conveyed Cemal's proposal to his father by telegram. Husayn reportedly responded to his son on December 17 that it is too late for an understanding.[8] It was also too late for Cemal to follow up on his initiative; he left Syria as Palestine was being captured by the British army. His successor and namesake Mersinli Cemal Pasha and the governor of the Syria Province Tahsin continued contacts with Faysal sporadically, including the dispatch of an emissary in February 1918.

It appears that Faysal and Husayn responded to the Ottoman initiatives differently. Talha Çiçek has established that Faysal did not send a formal response to the Ottoman peace proposal until January 26, 1918. Departing from the outright rejection he received from his father the previous month, Faysal declared his family's allegiance to the Ottoman sultan and held out reconciliation in the spirit of Islamic unity and acting together if Arab autonomy were to be assured within the empire. While Husayn communicated the Ottoman government's peace offer to his British allies, Faysal may not have kept the British liaisons in his camp abreast of his contacts with the Ottoman authorities.[9] Who knew what at what point remains murky, but it could be surmised that Faysal started to assume a stance independent of Sharif Husayn at this juncture. Contacts between the Ottoman leaders in Syria and Faysal continued.

VISIONS OF HONORABLE PEACE

As the Ottoman command in Syria was probing the possibility of an understanding with the Hashemites following Moscow's disclosures, Foreign Minister Ahmed Nesimi brought the Russian armistice proposal to the floor of the parliament on December 3, 1917.[10] The proposal met with an exuberant reception and accompanied a moment of reflection and deliberation about where the Ottoman state stood in the war effort. The discussion revealed the attitudes of Ottoman statesmen toward the Arab provinces amid differences about the appropriate Ottoman stance vis-à-vis a possible peace agreement. Even as he presented the Russian proposal and spoke in support of the ceasefire with Russia, the foreign minister indicated commitment to continued struggle on the battlefront for the redemption of wartime territorial losses and restitution of the status quo ante. Others favored a reassessment of the war aims at this juncture and urged commitment to peace rather than war. A deputy representing Istanbul, Salah Cimcoz, asserted that the war was fundamentally changing the world, and the Ottoman state, too, should prepare for a new form of governance. He pointed not only to revolutionary Russia but also to the "mighty Germany in the West," which was in the process of "changing its form of government even before the war's end and grounding it on democratic foundations." This apparent call for compromise on geopolitical objectives was at the same time casting doubt on the fortitude of the monarchy.

The remarks elicited a protest from another deputy, Veli of the Aydın Province, who denounced Cimcoz's words for amounting to unconditional peace independent of the wartime allies. Veli argued that peace should ensure the attainment of war aims by preserving the Ottomans' dignity, political unity, integrity, and independence. He implored that the Ottoman state should seek to preserve its unalienable rights in such occupied provinces as Baghdad just as Germany defends its rights in Alsace-Lorraine.[11] As for the Hijaz, he added, it is ten times more valuable than Alsace-Lorraine. Veli declared, "We entered the war to preserve our political unity and independence" adding, without a hint of irony, "and not *pour le Roi de Prusse*."[12]

Yet a third member of parliament, deputy for the Black Sea town of Sinop, Hasan Fehmi, voiced his conviction that relations with the new Russia would lead to peace. He offered a favorable assessment of the revolutionary changes in that country, imputing to the defunct tsarist regime the ambition to "bring the world under its monopoly." He emphatically endorsed the revolutionary government's desire to stop the spilling of blood in a war that was costly for all parties. Hasan Fehmi further commended the new government in Russia for its plan to divide the lands under the tsar's monopoly by granting liberty to all peoples in the imperial domains "whose civilization, history, language, and literature warrant it." Questioning the received logic of empire, Fehmi added that "even if such a government may appear to be weak, in fact it is the strongest government of the world."

Ottoman wartime policy was made not in parliament but in the councils of the Committee of Union Progress. The parliamentary proceedings, however, reflected perceptions of what the ongoing war revealed and portended for the empire. Some saw the realignment in the Entente camp, namely the Russian withdrawal and American entry into the hostilities without declaring war against Istanbul, as an opportunity to strive for an honorable peace that would cut the Ottoman losses. Others viewed the shifts as providing an opportunity to restore occupied Ottoman territories. For yet others, the integrity, even the survival, of the state called for a revamped political organization premised on decentralization and greater regional/communal autonomy. All agreed that a peace agreement with Russia would obviate the vital threat of Russian ambitions to obtain Istanbul and the Straits.

On December 15, the Central Powers signed a cease-fire agreement with Soviet Russia at Brest-Litovsk. Russian withdrawal from the war dramatically altered the military and the geopolitical calculus in Russian-occupied eastern Anatolia and opened the way for the restoration of territories not just in Anatolia (lost since 1914) but also the "Three Provinces," Kars, Ardahan, and Batum, in the Caucasus region previously annexed by Russia. It further released troops and materiel to be moved to other fronts.

VYING FOR THE HIGH ROAD: LENIN, LLOYD GEORGE, WILSON AND THE OTTOMAN EMPIRE

As the upheaval in Russia altered the course of the war, it generated propagandistic reconceptualizations of a postwar world order. The promulgation of Vladimir Lenin's Decree on Peace prompted the British and American statesmen to spell out their governments' vision and postulates to restore peace. Impelled by the requisites of meeting the Bolsheviks on the moral high ground in the ostensible defense of democracy, peace, and peoples' fundamental rights, Prime Minister David Lloyd George and President Woodrow Wilson issued grandiose proclamations to secure Allied war aims, including, in the case of Britain, thinly disguised colonial ambitions in the Middle East. Lloyd George's statement on British war aims on January 5, 1918, and Wilson's declaration of the Fourteen Points three days later obfuscated as much as clarified the two governments' intentions and positions with regard to the Middle East, as the statements were notably ambiguous in their pronouncements pertaining to the Ottoman Empire.[13]

Lloyd George distinguished between the homelands of the "Turkish race" and other parts of the empire to which he ascribed "separate national conditions," specifically Arabia, Armenia, Mesopotamia, Syria, and Palestine. Averring that Britain acknowledged the continued existence of a "Turkish Empire" consisting of Thrace and Asia Minor, the statement left open the nature of the recognition Britain envisaged for each one of the enumerated constituent parts with "separate national conditions," which could not be "restored to their former sovereignty." It laid out parallel stipulations for the Austro-Hungarian Empire. The explicit disavowal of the goal of dismantling Austria-Hungary, however, contrasted with the scheme proffered for the Ottoman Empire. While arguing for "self-government" for Habsburg "nationalities who have long desired it," the proclamation was silent on this prerogative for the peoples of the Ottoman Empire. Lloyd George deemed self-government for the nationalities within the Habsburg domain as necessary to eliminate unrest in Europe and to ensure peace, whereas the absence of symmetry in the stipulations for the two empires betrayed self-serving and, if not clearly enunciated, colonial objectives in the Middle East. The classification of the Ottoman realm in geographical terms reflected the primacy of strategic and economic considerations underlying the mutual agreements within the Entente camp as well as wartime transactions with, and commitments to, local or exogenous claimants. Yet, the proclamation envisaged separation of Arabs and Turks as the principal criterion in the partitioning of Ottoman imperial territories, affirming the British war aim to stimulate, reify, and politicize ethnic identity in the Ottoman Empire. Lloyd George's blueprint was silent on the Kurdish ethnic element and its preponderance in parts of the designated territories marked by ethnic confluence and heterogeneity (especially, Mesopotamia). In the coming years, British authorities would assiduously cultivate Kurdish identity in their pursuit to secure geostrategic objectives at the expense of the Ottoman state and promote an ethnonational and colonial carving up of Asia Minor and Thrace, territories that the proclamation aggregated in "racial" terms (Turkish) and stipulated as the confines of a truncated Ottoman state.

President Woodrow Wilson was the last to proclaim a vision of a new international order. His Fourteen Points would resonate more widely and commandingly around the globe than Lenin's or Lloyd George's statements.[14] The Fourteen Points took shape during the fall of 1917 on the basis of the deliberations of a committee ("Inquiry") led by White House adviser Col. Edward House and largely composed of scholars of history and law.[15] The committee's recommendations for the Middle East bore strong resemblance to Lloyd George's declaration: "It is necessary to free the subject races of the Turkish Empire from oppression and misrule. This implies at the very least autonomy for Armenia and the protection of Palestine, Syria, Mesopotamia and Arabia by the civilized nations. Turkey proper must be justly treated and freed from economic and political bondage." The Inquiry report did not provide a definition of "Turkey proper" or explicate the nature or extent of the "political bondage." Indeed, the committee's language about the Middle East would appear in the actual text of the Fourteen Points with even further ambiguity.

Wilson's formal announcement on January 8, 1918, did not patently support British and French war aims. Echoing the Russian revolutionary denunciation of annexations, the Wilsonian manifesto appeared to discredit colonial claims: the very first article of the Fourteen Points denounced secret treaties.[16] At the same time, this proposition also looked ahead to the peace talks with Russia rather than to the exploits of the past, as Wilson stated in the preamble.[17] The Sykes-Picot Treaty, the paramount secretly drawn treaty, now revealed, stood as the formidable threat to the Ottoman Empire's territorial integrity in 1918, particularly as the British forces had started to create the conditions to realize its terms with their occupation of territories in Palestine and Mesopotamia during the previous months.

Even though the Russian disclosure of the Sykes-Picot Treaty starkly exposed Franco-British claims on Ottoman territories, Article 12 of the Fourteen Points addressed Middle Eastern affairs with no apparent acknowledgment of the wartime schemes or the ongoing occupation of Ottoman territory by America's allies, but with nods to both state sovereignty and the nationality principle: "The Turkish portion of the present Ottoman Empire should be assured a secure sovereignty, but the other nationalities which are now under Turkish rule should be assured an undoubted security of life and an absolutely unmolested opportunity of autonomous development." The Fourteen Points did not repudiate the legitimacy of the Austro-Hungarian (Article 10) or Ottoman imperial states. The insistence on the "autonomous development" of the two empires' peoples implied the consent of the governed with no explicit support or anticipation of secession. The document invoked a congruence of nationality and territorial sovereignty only in its rejection of Vienna's suzerainty over Italian-speaking Habsburg territories.[18] Article 12 thus presumed, with vague caveats, the continued existence of the Ottoman state. The ambiguities in its phrasing have allowed the invocation of the clause by various parties at different times to promote conflicting objectives. In view of the explicit emphasis on nationality rights in the proclamation's preamble and elsewhere, the presumption of Turkish sovereignty in imperial domains inhabited by peoples belonging to "other nationalities" placed Article 12 at odds with the general tenor of the manifesto. Like Lloyd George's declaration, Wilson's Article 12 was far less explicit about political rights and divisions envisaged for the peoples within the Ottoman imperium compared with the more specific recommendations pertaining to Europe.

It may be argued that American economic and strategic interests in the Middle East concerned the policy makers only to a limited extent, and therefore Article 12, the only clause relating to the Middle East in Wilson's declaration, was understandably unnuanced and should not be parsed fastidiously. From the vantage of Washington, the Middle East was a side theater, and the United States never declared war against the Ottoman state. The Wilsonian position on the Middle East would be reinterpreted with greater specificity as the United States became involved further in the overall war effort and in the quest to bring an end to the hostilities in order to arrive at a settlement. Yet Wilson's January 1918 manifesto acquired iconic status both in its letter and spirit, even after the United States distanced itself from the president's declared aims in 1920. Countless actors invested in the resolution of the global conflict referred to Wilson's January 8, 1918, statement and invoked it in whole or in part. Its implications for the Ottoman war and peace, therefore, warrant scrutiny.

The declaration employed the designations "Ottoman Empire" and "Turkish Empire" interchangeably, obscuring the meaning of the "Turkish portion of the present Ottoman Empire," a phrase that is analogous to the relevant language in Lloyd's George statement, where the reference is to a territory inhabited by a vaguely delineated ethnicity, the "Turkish race." "The present Ottoman Empire" conjures up territories still under the control of the Istanbul government and its army, which at the time of Wilson's proclamation in January 1918 had extended south to Palestine and Baghdad if not, from the standpoint of international law, the entirety of the Ottoman domains as they existed in 1914. While explicit about the advocacy of peoples' or nationalities' rights, the Fourteen Points does not invoke specific national groups except for the reference to Italy mentioned above and a more general reference to the "lines of allegiance and nationality" in the Balkans. Indeed, there is no conflation of political allegiance with nationality, and, as in the cases of the United States, Russia, Austria-Hungary and others, the text foregrounds "peoples" of states rather than "nationalities." The declaration includes no reference to Arabs, Turks, or any other Middle Eastern groups as nationality, political community, or in connection with a geographical entity, even though the prior "Inquiry" had mentioned Palestine, Syria, Mesopotamia, and Arabia in recommending their protection by the "civilized nations." The ambiguity in the language of the declaration is compounded when one considers that "Turkish" was commonly used by Westerners as a synonym for "Muslim," in which case the contradistinction of "Turkish" and "other nationalities" would imply that the nationalities referred to in the text were the non-Muslims of the empire. This is a reasonable inference in view of the fact that the persecuted Armenian population of the Ottoman Empire was paramount in the mental map of the American statesmen and public owing to the vast resonance of the Armenian suffering and decimation in the United States during the war.[19]

The Fourteen Points, like Lenin and Lloyd George's proclamations, aimed at seizing the opportunity to end the war in the wake of the momentous political changes in Russia. Its preamble speaks to the German stance in the Brest-Litovsk talks that were in progress. Wilson criticizes German negotiators for their hard line in making concessions to Russian sovereignty and to the wishes of the peoples in occupied Russian territories. Articles 5 and 6 address these concerns, calling for "an evacuation of all Russian territory"

(Article 6) and the determination of all questions of sovereignty with due consideration of the "interests of the populations concerned" (Article 5). The president calls for the restoration of the "invaded portions" of France and the evacuation and restoration of Belgium. There is no similar appeal to the United States' British ally in the case of the Ottoman Empire, whose territories were under British occupation, unless the phrase "sovereignty of the present Ottoman Empire" is interpreted as referring to the legal geopolitical entity that was the Ottoman state under existing international law. But it is evident from the assurances of sovereignty for the "Turkish portion" that the drafter couched Article 12 with calibrated ambiguity to accommodate the declared or evolving political interests and designs of America's allies in the Middle East. These designs had begun to be implemented militarily by way of occupation of Ottoman territories and toward the implementation of the secret Sykes-Picot accord. Wilson's statement does not reject or contravene Lloyd George's assertion that "it would be impossible to restore [Arabia, Armenia, Mesopotamia, Syria and Palestine] to their former [i.e., Ottoman] sovereignty," but it does not posit the breakup of the Ottoman Empire as accomplished fact or a geopolitical or military objective. On the contrary, the president's denunciation of secret treaties undermines the very Sykes-Picot blueprint that partitioned the empire. Wilson ostensibly had such disdain for Sykes-Picot as to remark that the name of the treaty "sounded like the name of a tea; 'a fine example of old diplomacy.'"[20]

The Ottoman statesmen would construe the Wilsonian manifesto as an endorsement of the state's sovereignty. The specific clause that pertained to the Ottoman Empire, Article 12, was equivocal in the affirmation of the broad principles the manifesto laid out; yet it did not uphold the British and French territorial war aims that had been incorporated, albeit in sanitized and general terms, into Lloyd George's declaration. The general and ambivalent language of the Fourteen Points made the principles open to interpretation. The spirit of the entirety of Wilson's pronouncement did not negate imperial sovereign rights. The Wilsonian emphasis on autonomous development of peoples and nationalities fit into the logic of solutions that Ottoman statesmen were independently exploring to secure the empire's longevity, as demonstrated by Cemal's proposal to the Hashemites with regard to autonomy for the Arab provinces.

As the talks at Brest-Litovsk between the Central Powers and Russia, which had started with the cease-fire negotiations in December, moved in February 1918 toward establishing a territorial settlement of German-occupied territories, Wilson issued a supplement to his Fourteen Points under the rubric "Four Principles," conceived as guidance in the talks between Germany and Russia.[21] Article 4 of the Principles asserted, "All well defined national aspirations shall be accorded the utmost satisfaction that can be accorded them," a proposition that called into question the very essence of empire. Yet, the existential threat that Istanbul confronted at this juncture was not vibrant national or autonomist movements but the Entente occupation of southern Mesopotamia and Palestine. The genocide of the Armenian population had eviscerated the likelihood of subversive Armenian national assertion. In the Arab provinces, the revealed secret agreements, and the British support for the establishment of a national home for Jews in Palestine had led to disappointment and resentment and, among many, strengthened pro-government proclivities and Ottomanist allegiances. Further, Article 2 of the Four Principles, which stated that "Peoples and provinces are not to be bartered about from sovereignty to sovereignty as if they were mere chattels and pawns in a game ... of the balance of power" upheld the Ottoman position that rejected occupation and partition. The Four Principles gave further reason to Ottoman statesmen to embrace the Wilsonian vision as an anti-colonial platform during the Brest-Litovsk talks and beyond.

RESPITE, RECOVERY, AND RECONCILIATION

In the early months of 1918, Ottoman wartime fortunes recovered on both the diplomatic and military fronts. Even before the conclusion of the peace talks with Russia, the Ottoman army mobilized in eastern Anatolia to recuperate its war losses. Together with the other Central Powers, the Ottoman Empire signed the Brest-Litovsk Treaty with Russia on March 3, 1918, which secured gains in eastern Anatolia that would have been unimaginable a few months earlier and would not be matched at any other Ottoman war front. In addition, the Treaty restored Kars, Ardahan, and Batum, which Istanbul had ceded to czarist Russia in 1878. A local resistance coordinated by a joint Armenian-Georgian-Azerbaijani administration rejected the restitution of these areas to the Ottoman Empire. The resistance coalesced to proclaim the Transcaucasian Democratic Federative Republic on April 22, by which time the Ottoman armies had advanced into the Russian-occupied region up to the 1914 borders, and within a few days took Kars.[22] The Federation was unable to preserve its unity against the Ottoman advance and broke up into

Georgian, Armenian, and Azerbaijani Republics in May. Istanbul signed separate agreements with the new states that ratified the return of the Three Provinces lost more than three decades earlier.[23] Azerbaijan's subsequent decision to throw in its lot with the Central Powers against the Entente in an anticipated scramble for the Baku oil fields strengthened the Ottoman position in the Caucasus and resulted in the dispatch of Ottoman troops to Baku.

The spring of 1918 heralded auspicious developments for the Central Powers in Europe. Relieved on the eastern fronts, the German armies moved against the Entente forces in western Europe, disrupted the communications of the French and British armies, and approached the French capital (Spring Offensive).[24] The course of events in the Caucasus and the semblance of a turnaround in the war in favor of the Central Powers gave the Ottomans the opportunity to consolidate their military position in the east. Minister of War Enver Pasha, the effective commander-in-chief of the Ottoman army, entrusted the Azerbaijan campaign to his brother Nuri Pasha, who led a newly constituted "Islamic Caucasus Army" to defend Azerbaijan and extend assistance to the self-proclaimed Northern Caucasus Republic in Circassia. This campaign did not signify a realignment of Ottoman war aims or the beginning of an Ottoman thrust into the Turkic Caucasus and Central Asia as the consummation of a long-standing pan-Turkist agenda. Enver's postwar personal adventure in Central Asia organizing Turkic resistance forces against the Bolshevik army has reinforced the tendency to view him as the influential wartime Ottoman statesman who envisaged reframing the ideological, demographic, and geopolitical basis of the Ottoman state.[25] His proclivities should be seen in the context of the overall imperial strategies to disrupt Entente gains and ambitions, in this case in the oil-rich Caucasus, and to mobilize Muslim opinion behind the Ottoman state around an anti-imperialist platform. As Michael Reynolds has convincingly argued, "The Ottomans' goal was not unification with their ethnic or religious brethren. Rather, their overriding objective was more straightforward and far less romantic: to weaken Russian power by splitting apart the Russian Empire and to put a buffer between their borders and Russia's."[26]

The Brest-Litovsk Treaty, negotiated in the spirit of Lenin's Decree ("peace without annexations") and Wilson's Fifth Principle ("all questions of sovereignty be determined in the interests of the populations involved"), left it to the populations of Kars, Ardahan, and Batum to "reorganize their national and international relations in agreement with the neighboring

States, especially with Turkey."[27] Wilson continued to elaborate on the Fourteen Points and Four Principles by promulgating on July 4 his "Four Ends," which exhorted "the settlement of every question, whether of territory, of sovereignty, of economic arrangement, or of political relationship, upon the basis of the free acceptance of that settlement by the people immediately concerned."[28] The Ottoman government agreed to make provisions for a referendum in the three districts.[29] Far from seeing the bases of the Ottoman imperium shaken by emerging democratic norms of a changing world order, the Ottomans became an early executor and ultimately beneficiary of the plebiscitary principle in the Wilsonian era. Carried out by teams sent from Istanbul following separate agreements with the three Caucasian republics, the July 1918 plebiscite resulted, as anticipated, in favor of remaining within the Ottoman Empire.[30] A law officially confirmed this settlement the following month.[31] The Georgian government unsuccessfully objected to the referendum results in Batum, where the Muslims, who were more predisposed toward the reunion, did not constitute a clear majority.[32]

Ottoman political gains and military advances on the Caucasian frontier continued into the late summer. The notion of a Turkist resurgence and pursuit of novel geopolitical objectives in Turkic regions suggests yet another turn in the one-dimensional interpretations of Ottoman policy as Turkism/pan-Turkism, Islamism, or Ottomanism and indicates a detachment from, if not abandonment of, the Arab regions. Throughout the spring of 1918, however, the Ottomans held off enemy advance in the south. A British attempt to break out of Jerusalem and take Nablus in March 1918 failed at the battle of Turmus 'Ayya south of Nablus. Liman von Sanders, who had taken over the command of the Yıldırım army from General von Falkenhayn, made forays against Allenby's forces in May 1918. Liman later wrote, "This success (even *The Times* called it a British reverse) had a certain repercussion on the disposition of the Arabs."[33] In Mesopotamia, the British forces entered Kirkuk in May 1918 but were unable to hold on to the town.[34] The shift from a defensive posture on the southern fronts to an offensive one in the east obliged a reshuffling of military command and units. At the end of June, Enver transferred Halil Pasha, his accomplished uncle who had dealt the British army the crushing defeat at Kut in 1916, from the command of the Sixth Army in Mosul to that of the Eastern Army Group tasked with the Caucasian campaign.[35] The mobilization of Ottoman forces, including from units stationed near Mosul, to the Caucasus diluted the Ottoman defensive positions in the Mesopotamian front but did not compromise the efforts to defend the southern provinces. The Syria and Iraq fronts remained in relative stasis through the end of the summer. The dispatch of Prince Osman Fuad in May to collaborate with the local forces resisting the Italian occupation in Libya bolstered Istanbul's propaganda effort.[36]

The Ottoman government capitalized on the favorable turn of events and took measures of reconciliation, appeasement, and relaxation of state controls.[37] An amnesty in late spring allowed Syrian and Hijazi exiles, except some twenty who had been convicted by Cemal Pasha's court-martial, to return to their lands.[38] The contacts between Ottoman authorities and Sharif Faysal that had sputtered on since November acquired a new lease on life. In May, the top military and civilian authorities in Syria, Mersinli Cemal Pasha and Governor Tahsin, made further overtures to Faysal. In a letter he sent on June 10, Faysal communicated detailed terms as the basis of an understanding with the government: withdrawal of Ottoman troops south of Amman, the return of Arab soldiers and troops to Syria for service under an Arab command in any joint war operations, and Syria to enter in a relationship with Istanbul on the model of Bavaria-Germany or Austria-Hungary. Ali Allawi, Faysal's authoritative biographer, argues convincingly that Faysal tried to keep his talks secret both from his British allies and his father. His letter displayed "a willingness to conceive of the empire as a confederation of states inside which Arab aspirations could be met."[39] The British authorities intercepted Faysal's communication. In order to keep him in the fold, they pledged him expanded authority in Transjordan. The Ottoman leadership looked on the confederative organization of the empire favorably. None other than Ziya Gökalp, a sociologist of mixed Turkish-Kurdish lineage known as the ideologue of Turkish nationalism and influential CUP Central Committee member, had described the Ottoman Empire as "the progressive America of the East" as early as in 1909.[40] He characterized the empire as a Muslim state based on the Turkish and Arab elements and proposed a Turco-Arab federative empire in 1914 and 1918.[41]

British military campaigns had come to a standstill by the summer of 1918, with no significant new gains to assuage the Syrian sympathizers of independence. In order to counteract what appeared to be flagging support, a group of Syrian leaders based in Egypt pleaded with the British authorities to confirm and clarify the pledges made to the Arabs. London obliged on June 16, possibly now cognizant of ongoing negotiations between Faysal and the Ottoman authorities, with a policy statement labeled "Declaration to the Seven."[42] In reference to areas that were "formerly under Ottoman dominion" and now had come under the control of Allied forces (corresponding from the Sinai to Jerusalem in Syria and from the Persian Gulf to the northern boundaries of the Baghdad province in Mesopotamia), the declaration gave assurances for "future government... based upon the principle of the consent of the governed." For areas still under "Turkish control," the British government pledged to "continue to labour" for the freedom and independence of "the oppressed peoples of these areas."[43] The British rhetoric notwithstanding, the relative calm in the southern fronts continued through the summer, with the exception of an unsuccessful yet inconsequential German-Ottoman raid on a British garrison near Jericho (Abu Tulul).[44]

The course of events in the first half of 1918 eased some of the Arab doubts about the Ottoman government's fortitude against the adversities of the war and its ability to defend the realm. This salutary shift was reflected in the thinking, sentiments, and allegiances of such prominent individuals as 'Ali Rida Pasha al-Rikabi under the strains and uncertainties of war. Al-Rikabi, a high-level functionary born and raised in Damascus, who embodied the mobility that the Ottoman system provided to well-positioned provincial citizens, attended the military academy in the imperial capital and held his administrative-military posts primarily in the Arab provinces. He had served as the governor of the *muhafızlık* of Medina, a new administrative unit carved out of the province of the Hijaz in 1910 with the purpose of projecting Ottoman power into the Hijaz and the rest of the Arabian Peninsula, and later as mayor of Damascus under Cemal Pasha. Al-Rikabi is reported to have been approached by T. E. Lawrence in 1917 to agitate on behalf of the Arab Revolt.[45] In June 1918, an Arabist opponent of CUP from coastal Syria who had joined Sharif Husayn's government and liaised with the British authorities, Fu'ad al-Khatib, reported, in the words of his interlocutor Col. G. E. Symes, on "ominous" rumors about an initiative by Rida Pasha al-Rikabi to work with neutral countries toward "a settlement of the Syrian question on Devolution lines" because "there was great doubt and heart-burning amongst Syrians on the Allied side."[46] Symes related intelligence from another informant that "it was possible that a section of the Syrians, discouraged by the recent course of the War, was turning its thoughts again to the old 'decentralization' programme, subject to adequate guarantee of local autonomy." Any initiative for negotiations is likely to have been aborted by the rapid deterioration of the Central Powers' war effort in the fall of 1918. Al-Rikabi was appointed commander of Ottoman forces stationed in Tiberias at the interface with the British units in Palestine.[47]

FALL 1918: OTTOMAN DEBACLE IN SYRIA, PURSUIT OF CEASEFIRE, AND NEW GOVERNMENT

In the second half of the summer, the Entente armies checked the German advances to gain the upper hand on the European fronts with critical consequences for the Central Powers' overall war effort. Even as the Ottoman push into Azerbaijan continued and the forces of the Central Powers repelled British units dispatched to Baku, General Allenby broke through the Ottoman defensive lines in Syria on September 19.[48] The British forces overcame the Ottoman armies, most decisively at the battle of Nablus (Megiddo) in northern Palestine and forced their retreat. The expansion of the British occupation in Syria paralleled an equally decisive Entente offensive in the Balkans. The Bulgarian line collapsed, severing the communications between the Ottoman Empire and its allies. Bulgaria sued for and obtained an armistice, concluded on September 30 (Armistice of Salonica).

The steady advance of British forces toward Damascus after the battle of Nablus led to commotion and power struggles in the provincial capital. Local notables under the leadership of Saʿid al-Jazaʾiri, who conceded the failure of his mediation attempts between Mersinli Cemal Pasha and Faysal, formed a provisional government to claim control amid the power vacuum. General Allenby made sure Faysal entered the city ahead of the British units before setting up an occupation administration. Within three days of Ottoman military evacuation, on October 3, Faysal and his retinue made an easy entry into Damascus, with Allenby's Egyptian Expeditionary Force close on the wings. Almost immediately, Faysal was in a power struggle with the local leadership. He prevailed with the crucial British support and proceeded to form an administration under his auspices in the name of his father. He appointed ʿAli Rida Pasha al-Rikabi military governor. The extension of the authority of the Faysali state to coastal Syria fell in contention very soon, due to French objections. Nor did the withdrawal of Ottoman administration signify the abandonment of Ottoman claims in Syria.[49]

As the fortunes of war turned against the Ottomans in September, Sultan Vahideddin, who had ascended the throne upon his brother Sultan Reşad's death in July, appealed to Britain in defiance of the CUP leadership in order to end the hostilities. Vahideddin relied on the intermediacy of Ottoman Armenians who lobbied for Armenian national rights in Paris (Armenian National Delegation), including the son of former prime minister Nubar Pasha of Egypt, Boghos Nubar. The Armenian delegates deemed the sultan's circumvention of the CUP leaders and his plea coming from a position of weakness potentially advantageous in order to secure concessions for the Armenians. They obliged by approaching the British ambassador in Switzerland, Horace Rumbold, days after Allenby entered Damascus, with a proposal to grant autonomy to the Hijaz, Syria, Palestine and Mesopotamia, regions that would remain under Ottoman rule within an arrangement akin to the prewar status of Egypt.[50] This was an unconvincing proposal for the British, when their army had acquired strategic advantage on the battlefront along its advance positions and was poised to secure the broader Entente geopolitical war aims.

On September 28, 1918, as the Ottomans were suffering their most decisive defeat of the entire war in Syria, President Wilson made a speech in New York emphatically declaring that "peoples be ruled ... by their own will and choice" and not by "the right of force" wielded by "strong nations or group of nations." He characterized "the interest of the weakest ... as sacred as the interest of the strongest."[51] The United States' critical mobilization of its resources for the Entente war effort had imparted moral authority to President Wilson. Istanbul and Washington had not declared war against one another, which in the eyes of the Ottoman statesmen made Wilson potentially a benevolent broker. The Ottoman government turned to the United States in pursuit of an armistice that would preserve the empire's independence and Ottoman suzerainty over the occupied provinces. The Ottomans' allies were similarly posturing in an effort to move to a cease-fire with the most favorable terms possible, signaling readiness to subscribe to the Wilsonian principles as the basis of an armistice.[52] During the weeks in October that led to the armistices, the Wilsonian premise became the basis of understanding with Germany and Austria-Hungary ("pre-Armistice Agreement") and offered a lifeline to the defeated states. Despite the state of non-belligerence between the United States and the Ottoman Empire, the two countries did not have direct diplomatic channels of communication. The Ottoman appeal to the United States for its intercession, communicated first via Spain and one week later via Switzerland, did not elicit a response from Washington.[53] American prevarication notwithstanding, the Ottoman government continued to sue for armistice talks with the Entente Powers premised on the Wilsonian principles.

On October 13, 1918, the CUP government led by Talat Pasha resigned. Sultan Vahideddin appointed as grand vizier Ahmed İzzet Pasha, an Albanian general who had been at odds with the Unionists and thus had been removed from Istanbul for service in Yemen prior to the war. In his inaugural speech in the parliament, İzzet Pasha declared his government's readiness to conclude peace in accordance with the Wilsonian principles.[54] He invoked and quoted from the president's July 4, 1918, "Four Ends" speech advocating for the will of "the people immediately concerned" and rejecting the settlement of issues "upon the basis of the material interest or advantage of any other nation or people which may desire a different settlement for the sake of its own exterior influence or mastery." The Ottomans interpreted Wilson's words as a repudiation of the Sykes-Picot Agreement and the privileging of popular will.[55]

İzzet Pasha was painfully aware of the compromised position of the Ottoman presence in the Arab provinces when he took office. Allenby was setting up an "Occupied Enemy Territory Administration" (OETA), which divided western Greater Syria into three administrative regions, South, West, and East. OETA-West incorporated areas of direct control pledged to France (the "Blue Zone") in the Sykes-Picot agreement, apart from the territory to the north of Aleppo, which the Ottoman army continued to defend.[56] As the British forces moved northward from Damascus, General Liman von Sanders, in his last days as the commander of the Yıldırım group of forces before the command's transfer to Mustafa Kemal, ordered territories should not be relinquished "without good reason," and, in the event of failure, that troops should be concentrated in the heights to the north of Aleppo—a strategic decision to avail of the advantage that the hilly ground would provide in combat.[57] In tandem with the advance in Syria, the British army resumed its first major offensive in Iraq since April 1917. Under the command of General Alexander Cobbe, the British forces quickly moved north from Baghdad during the last week of October and forced the Ottoman Sixth Army to withdraw to the outskirts of Mosul.

Upon his unanticipated appointment to the grand vizierate, İzzet Pasha deemed that addressing two exigencies would ensure to his government the standing to negotiate the future of the Ottoman state: endorsement of the Wilsonian principles and disavowal of the wartime CUP government. During the days before his government's resignation, Talat Pasha had conceded that the circumstances of the war demanded a revision of the centralist administrative policies implemented in the preceding years.[58] İzzet pledged to resolve the status of the Arab provinces by granting autonomy on condition of continued allegiance to the sultanate and the caliphate. Within two days of coming to office, he sent a letter to Faysal in which he admitted the gross misdeeds that the previous government had committed everywhere, including in Arabia. Invoking his "purest sentiments about the Arab nation (*kavm-ı Arab*) well-known to [Faysal] and [his] esteemed father," he stated that he considers extending "the hand of unity and friendship" as a religious duty in order to ensure the future of the Ottoman state which has served Islam for ages.[59]

An elaboration of Wilson's evolving credo for peace issued at the end of October, however, stymied the grand vizier's vision. Colonel House, the architect of the "Inquiry" that paved the road to the Fourteen Points, authored a document titled "Commentary" in the light of the decisive developments of the nine months since the promulgation of the Fourteen Points.[60] It brought only limited clarification to the text of the Twelfth Point:

Anatolia should be reserved for the Turks. The coast lands, where Greeks predominate, should be under special international control, perhaps with Greece as mandatory.

Armenia must be given a port on the Mediterranean, and a protecting power established. France may claim it, but the Armenians would prefer Great Britain.

Britain is clearly the best mandatory for Palestine, Mesopotamia, and Arabia.

A general code of guarantees binding on all mandatories in Asia Minor should be written into the treaty of Peace.

The text reveals that the expectation that Armenians and Greeks in Asia Minor would receive a separate and tutelary political status under a mandatory arrangement had crystallized before the conclusion of the armistice. The Commentary referred to the British role for Palestine, Iraq, and an undefined "Arabia" without bringing clarity to the status of the occupied Arab provinces, especially Syria (except for Palestine), a silence that in effect deferred the status of Syria to allies Britain and France unconditionally.

İzzet Pasha recalled in his memoirs his thinking at this juncture about the prospective political and administrative framework of the southern territories no longer under Ottoman control. Invoking once again the Austria-Hungary model, he foresaw for Iraq and Syria a relationship of administrative autonomy within the Ottoman state analogous to Hungary in the Habsburg domains. For the Hijaz, he conceded a Hashemite monarchical state within the provincial administrative boundaries of the Hijaz, provided that the kingdom would recognize the caliphal prerogatives of the Ottoman sultan.

This was tantamount to recognizing the independence of the Hijaz while denying Sharif Husayn any caliphal aspirations and authority over the Fertile Crescent. In İzzet Pasha's geopolitical vision, Yemen's Zaydi region in the mountainous interior, where Imam Yahya's sovereignty was all but assured as early as 1911, would have independence, but coastal Yemen would remain under Ottoman suzerainty.[61]

MUDROS: THE ARMISTICE THAT WASN'T

Before a framework for peace and a geopolitical reconfiguration could be negotiated, military operations had to be terminated with a cease-fire. Istanbul continued to scramble to find an interlocutor, even as armistice talks progressed between Germany and the Allies through the month of October. In the absence of a response from the United States to his initiative aimed at securing American mediation to end the hostilities, İzzet Pasha placed his hopes about obtaining a palatable armistice on the differences emerging between the Allies. He approached the commander of French forces in Salonica, General Franchet d'Espèrey, through the intermediacy of the former French consul in Damascus and director of the Ottoman Bank, Marcel Savoie.[62] Suspicious that an agreement between the French and the Ottomans would be untoward to British interests and hard-fought gains, London reconciled to negotiating an armistice, prodded by the proactive intercession of General Townshend, a captive of the Ottomans since the Kut battle in 1916. The British government tasked Vice Admiral Somerset Gough-Calthorpe to open talks, and Istanbul appointed Minister of the Navy Rauf (Orbay) as chief negotiator.

The talks began on October 26 on a British navy ship anchored at Mudros on the Aegean island of Lemnos. Faced with the threat of further advances into Ottoman territory, the Ottoman delegates had little choice but to submit to Allied dictates and consent to an agreement that was premised on the cessation of hostilities and the preservation of the existing military status quo. The terms included the immediate demobilization of the Ottoman army (Article 5) and open-ended clauses giving the Entente powers the right to occupy "important strategic points," should their security be threatened (Article 7), as well as the right to occupy the six eastern ("Armenian," in the English text) provinces in the event of disturbances (Article 24).[63] In Syria, Iraq, the Hijaz, Asir, and Yemen, the agreement stipulated unconditional surrender of Ottoman troops to the nearest Entente command; and in Cilicia, it called for the withdrawal of the Ottoman army from the region, leaving only limited forces necessary to ensure public order (Article 16). Separate clauses governed the conflict in Libya, where Ottoman officers assisted with the coordination of the local resistance against Italian occupation forces. They were to capitulate to the closest Italian garrison, and, failing their compliance, the Ottoman government would cut all communication with them (Article 17). Thus, the Mudros agreement called for the elimination of Ottoman military presence in the empire's occupied southern provinces while also bringing limitations to Ottoman troops in areas adjoining the occupied regions.

Compared with the cognate accords that set the other belligerent states on a course from the cessation of hostilities to peace settlements, the Mudros agreement displayed peculiarities in its conception, implementation, and interpretation. An armistice's rationale is to suspend military operations and achieve a mutually agreed framework for disengagement until such time when a permanent political compact can be negotiated. At the time of the signing, British forces were in occupation of areas within the Mosul, Aleppo, and Syria provinces, which Britain and other Entente Powers had acknowledged in previous accords as falling under French influence or control. The Ottoman armies confronted primarily British forces in the active fronts of the war in these provinces, but France and other European adversaries would be bound by the armistice agreement's terms. The protracted renegotiation of the wartime understandings pertaining to the Middle East among the Allied powers and between them and the local actors advancing their own claims would complicate and ultimately frustrate the transition from the armistice to a settlement, setting the Ottoman postwar experience markedly apart from that of the other defeated powers.

Ambiguities in the wording of the Mudros agreement and the wide latitude of discretion conceded to the victors in its key clauses generated endemic controversy and set hurdles to the prospects for the peace settlement. The hastily drawn-up agreement referred to regions with vague delimitations rather than specific boundaries, a matter left to the peace talks. Cilicia, the plains cut by the Amanos Mountains, which extend north from the west of Antioch and are linked to the Taurus Mountain system, was an ill-defined historical-geographical expression with no place in Ottoman usage, though the Ottoman delegates signed on to Mudros's stipulation of troop evacuation pertaining to "Kilikya." Some of the agreement's geographical references invoked the names of Ottoman provinces, for example, Syria, Hijaz, and

Yemen, yet provincial administrative units did not correspond precisely to geographical conceptions. Such discrepancy was most apparent in the case of Syria, which as a geographical entity encompassed the provinces of Syria, Aleppo, and Beirut, as well as the separate administrative units of Mount Lebanon, Jerusalem, and Dayr al-Zur.

The zones of military disengagement subsequently became nodal points in boundary negotiation and delineation, as stakeholders encumbered them with novel meaning and conjured them up as natural and/or negotiated borders. Lines imagined to connect cease-fire positions of opposing armies did not correspond to clearly identifiable cultural, demographic, or topographical boundaries as templates for new geopolitical formations, nor did the sides conceive of any such lines as stable demarcations of the kind ordinarily arbitrated in a treaty.[64] Subsequent projects of nation-building appropriated, elaborated, and even sacralized these constructs. The failure to follow up the Mudros agreement with a comprehensive treaty imparted a degree of stability to boundaries thus conjured up and defended. The permanent boundaries of the successor states, and in particular the border between the new Turkey and the Syria mandate, did settle in time near the cease-fire positions of opposing armies, but the seesaw of military and diplomatic conflicts that ensued after October 1918 accompanied multiple boundary renegotiations in the next few years and contestations that have endured until our day. By virtue of belonging to a contractual agreement, Mudros's vague territorial references and delimitations served to impart legitimacy to efforts of state preservation and state building with the presumption that they embodied distinct social and geographical essences.

The most notable latter-day reification of the cease-fire positions links Mudros to the vision of a post-empire Turkish state in its natural borders. The underlying assumption is that the troops fighting the British forces pulled back in October 1918 to ensconce themselves in the Turks' homelands, which they then defended valiantly. Imbued with Turkish national feeling, a sense of patriotism grounded in a well-defined piece of territory, and availing of the requisite ethnic, administrative, and infrastructural cohesion, the Turks successfully defied and averted foreign encroachments into their homeland. The view that the Turkish-speaking and other peoples of the Ottoman Empire emerged from the war geographically compartmentalized into historically legitimated ethno-national units obscures the processes and contingencies of the late war and postwar period. Nation-building and state-building muddled through a myriad of uncertainties in the region during the next several years.[65]

The notion that the armistice lines represented an Arab-Turkish disentanglement owing to a putative commitment on the part of the Ottoman army to defend and preserve the "Turkish parts" goes in tandem with the proposition that the British-Arab army made a deliberate push to effect such a separation.[66] The pursuit of strategic and diplomatic objectives through patronage of ethno-religious groups was a venerable tradition in European countries' relations with the Ottoman Empire and stood to command a modicum of legitimacy at the Wilsonian juncture. The British troops' haste to advance to Aleppo before the signing of an armistice, however, is more indicative of the objective to situate British authorities as the arbiters between the Arab and French allies and to assert control over a critical stretch of the Berlin-Baghdad Railway than a drive to pair the military advance with an ethnographic border. The towns of Damascus, Homs, Hama, and Aleppo, aligned from the south to the north near the eastern Mediterranean coast, were at the crux of Britain's conflicting commitments to its French and Hashemite allies. In October 1918, the British forces made a last-ditch effort to gain control over them.

The epistolary negotiations between the grand sharif of Mecca and the British high commissioner in Egypt (the Sharif Husayn–McMahon correspondence, July 1915-January 1916) had included the four major towns in the promised region of Arab independence. The future status of the coastal strip to the west of the line, however, had remained in abeyance with the spurious ethno-national caveat that this region could not be considered "purely Arab."[67] Britain subsequently acknowledged this district as belonging to the French strategic and economic sphere in the Sykes-Picot Treaty. The tier to the south of the designated coastal strip was thrice promised: to the Arabs, the French, and the Zionists. Britain retained control over the south-to-north Damascus-Aleppo axis and the lands to its south along the Eastern Mediterranean with strategic and diplomatic motives but legitimated such control within an ostensible ethnographic rationale. The same was true for the west-to-east "Mudros line" construed to connect battle positions.

The argument partial to a deliberate ethnic disentanglement as a war aim and as the premise of the cease-fire assumes that the advancing British-Arab units could have pressed on to the north against the active defense of the Ottoman forces, had their objective not been to reach a line that separated Arabs and Turks. In fact, effective British units had diminished in size, in large part due to illness; Aleppo could be penetrated only with difficulty by the combined British and Hashemite troops and with crucial assistance of irregular tribal units. Faysal's troops pushed farther north but could advance

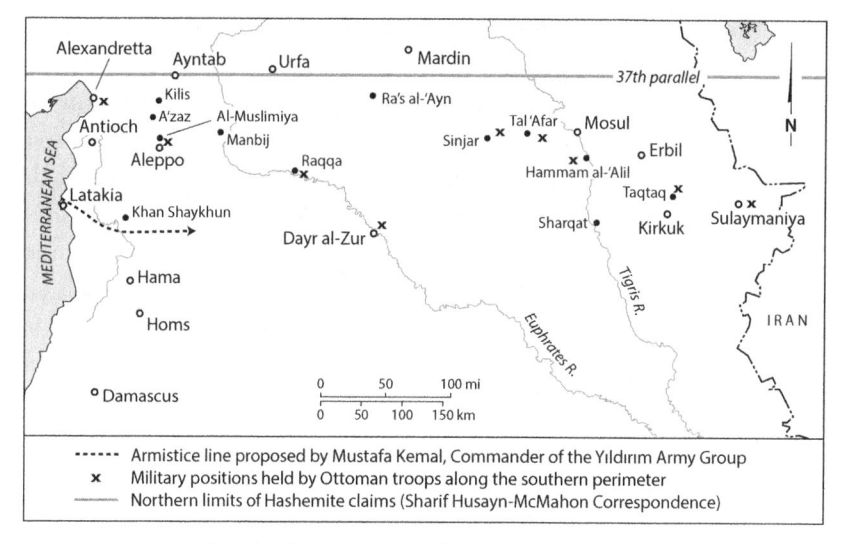

MAP 3. Armistice of Mudros (October 30, 1918). Cartography by Bill Nelson

only up to al-Muslimiya just to the north of Aleppo.[68] During the peace talks in 1919, Faysal would claim for the Syrian state he aspired for territories far beyond those conquered by the British in cooperation with his tribal forces.[69]

A combination of logistical and military factors rather than the quest to secure ethnic or linguistic compartmentalization determined the contours of the Mudros agreement. No clear ethno-linguistic lines on the ground divided interwoven communities who had lived together within the same Ottoman polity, intermarried, engaged in economic activity, or seasonally migrated in the broader region.[70] The exigency to secure an end to armed conflict eclipsed any effort to engineer an ethno-linguistic division of Arab, Turkish, Kurdish, or other communities. As it would become clear no sooner than the conclusion of the armistice, the British considered territories to the north of the cease-fire positions well within the ultimate Allied war aims. Indeed, Britain and France pursued this goal in defiance of the armistice agreement after it went into effect on October 31, 1918, and Ottoman resistance was broken.

The vagueness of the territorial references in the Mudros agreement served its central purpose of securing a quick cease-fire, while also leaving space for interpretation and, consequently, freedom of action for the victors. First to come to terms with the practical implications of the ambiguity were the Ottoman units facing the British army, led by Mustafa Kemal Pasha. Mustafa Kemal had left his command of the Seventh Army in December 1917, resentful of his subordination to General Falkenhayn, under whose charge the Ottoman armies in the region had coalesced as the Yıldırım Army Group, but he was recommissioned in the summer of 1918. As soon as the government communicated the armistice terms to the army command, Mustafa Kemal instructed his army groups that the limits of "Syria," where, according to the armistice agreement, Ottoman troops were subject to surrender to the Allied command, should be regarded as the northern boundary of the province of Syria. In contrast to the future reinterpretation of the Mudros delimitations in the different imaginings and articulations of boundaries contingent on changing military circumstances and diplomatic exigencies, he identified the northern boundary of the Syria Province as the line from the immediate north of Latakia to the east via Khan Shaykhun, one hundred kilometers to the south of the city of Aleppo.[71]

In an attempt to resolve ambiguities in territorial designations to strategic advantage and stem loss of territory, Mustafa Kemal reinforced the Ottoman claim for the entirety of the Aleppo Province with a specious ethnonational argument that marshaled Wilsonian legitimation. Writing from the battle lines, he identified Alexandretta and Antioch to the west of the city of Aleppo, Jabal Sam'an to its south, and Qatma and Kilis to its north as "inhabited by Turks" and asserted that three-fourths of the "population of Aleppo," presumably Aleppo City, consisted of "Arabic speaking Turks." When Mustafa Kemal cabled the grand vizier inquiring about the definition of the territorial boundaries of "Syria" and "Kilikya," he received a reply that evaded ethno-territorial criteria. The focal concern of the armistice was the surrender of the Ottoman troops, of which none were now remaining in the Syria Province or the southern half of the Aleppo Province. As for Cilicia, where Ottoman military presence to secure public order was recognized in the agreement, the precise extent of this unoccupied region, according to Istanbul, "would be decided, if needed." In sum, the Armistice did not have the aim or result of inscribing the lines of an Arab-Turkish separation. At a time when armistice talks in Europe were progressing with appeals to the Wilsonian principles, however, Middle Eastern actors sought to buttress geopolitical, strategic, and military objectives by drawing from and appealing to the ascendant Wilsonian discourse, even though President Wilson had not sanctioned an Ottoman armistice based on his declared principles, which would have compromised British and French war aims.

The Allies understood the Armistice of Mudros as binding only for the vanquished. After Mudros imposed restrictions on the Ottomans, including the demobilization of the armies, Britain continued to pursue geopolitical objectives with military action and forced Istanbul to surrender further territories. Within days after the armistice came into effect, British forces advanced claims beyond the city of Aleppo for Alexandretta on the eastern Mediterranean coast. Simultaneously, British units in Iraq moved to Mosul in northern Mesopotamia beyond positions held by the Ottoman Sixth Army from Raqqa and Dayr al-Zur to Sinjar, Tal 'Afar, Hammam al-'Alil (some twenty kilometers directly to the south of Mosul on the Tigris), Taqtaq, and Sulaymaniya. (See Map 3.)[72] Britain aspired to bring Mosul, being on riverine and overland crossroads and the hub of a grain-producing region with oil deposits, under direct control. Sykes-Picot had allotted Mosul to the region of French indirect influence as an extension of the Syrian interior, while Sharif Husayn considered Mosul as belonging to the territories he had negotiated with McMahon. Husayn also had demanded Alexandretta, but the town, with its strategically and commercially valuable harbor in the northwestern corner of the Mediterranean, had been left outside the area promised to him.[73]

In October 1918, the British had reasons directly related to their imperial interests, commitments to allies, and leverage derived from their prominent role in the Middle Eastern theater of the war to strive to capture Mosul and Alexandretta. The attainment of this objective after the armistice went into effect was regarded as a technicality. Mudros's stipulation concerning the imposition of control over ports and railways and other sites "in the event of a situation arising which threatens the security of the Allies" (Article 7) provided the justification for expanding the occupation.[74] The entry of British forces into Mosul three days after the signing of the armistice was the first of several acts that contravened the terms of Mudros. The commander of the Ottoman Sixth Army, Ali İhsan (Sabis) Pasha, did not offer resistance, under orders from Istanbul, and within several days vacated the town. Some ten days after the signing at Mudros, a British detachment landed in Alexandretta.[75] Mosul and Alexandretta remained as contested zones between the Ottomans and the Allies.

At the signing of the armistice, Aleppo, an important crossroads for commerce and the terminus of the railway from Beirut via Rayak, was in contention between the opposing sides. Despite his declared intent to retain Aleppo and its outskirts to the south, Mustafa Kemal had been forced to pull his army to the north of the city. Large parts of the region comprising the northern and western parts of the Aleppo Province, remained on the Ottoman side. To the east of Aleppo, particularly in the sparsely populated region between the Euphrates and the Tigris, there was no significant military contact except to the south of Mosul, where in Sharqat the Ottoman army had suffered its last defeat in the war (October 30), and thus the armistice was of little use in providing a cohesive boundary. The stretch of lands that remained in Ottoman hands from the north of Aleppo to the south of Mosul included the interior of northern Syria. King Husayn had wanted the British "to push on beyond Aleppo." According to British sources in Cairo, "In this event he did not think any Turkish or Kurd or any Moslem of Anatolia would fire a single shot at them as all would realise that the Allied armies came as deliverers from C.U.P. even as they had delivered the Arabs. . . . He considered Feisal's presence with the Allies would be of considerable use to the other."[76] Husayn's remarks demonstrate his continued interest in pressing the demands he had articulated at the beginning of his contacts with McMahon for incorporating into the Sharifian state the areas up to the 37th parallel, stretching ninety kilometers to the north of Aleppo and including Urfa, Ayntab, Alexandretta, Adana, and Mersin, even as he recognized concentrations of Turks and Kurds in this region.

While the British forces violated the armistice agreement with further conquests, the Ottomans were not able to comply fully with the terms of the agreement owing to the rogue, but symbolically laden, actions of their forces stationed in the Hijaz. Instead of surrendering to the nearest Allied commander, as the agreement stipulated, Ottoman forces in Medina under the command of Fahreddin Pasha persevered in the defense of the town.[77] After Sharif Husayn's revolt, the Ottomans could no longer defend Mecca, but they held on to Medina, the site of the Prophet's tomb and the capital of the first Islamic state in the seventh century. Since the Hijaz Railway reached the Medina terminus in 1908, the town had served as a military outpost with favorable communications. The Medina garrison continued its dogged resistance months beyond the armistice. Medina's defense is symbolic of the significance of Islamic legitimation for the Ottomans. Even though the Istanbul government was forced to order the end of the siege, Fahreddin's defiance would continue into 1919, when delegations sent from Istanbul, British pressure in the Red Sea, and the depletion of his resources convinced him to surrender.

PUTTING EMPIRE BACK TOGETHER AGAIN?

No sooner had hostilities formally ceased at the end of October 1918 than contacts exploring the relinking of the Ottoman domains' political destiny resumed. Nuri al-Saʿid, a former Ottoman officer who had joined the Hashemite ranks and marched with the Sharifian forces to Aleppo, established contact from the British headquarters in Qatma in northern Syria with Major Ömer Halis (Bıyıktay), commander of an army regiment, and delivered a proposal for an Arab-Turkish federative arrangement.[78] Halis was a classmate from the Ottoman military academy, who had served in al-Saʿid's native Iraq during the war.[79] Nuri al-Saʿid's proposal was not a repentant initiative meant to restore the status quo ante. Rather, he acted as a representative of the political movement seeking to form an administration in Damascus. He decried, for instance, the lowering of the Arab flag by an Ottoman military unit in the district of Antioch, arguing that Antioch had been occupied before the Armistice, and was therefore within the jurisdiction of the Syrian government.[80] Nor was this private initiative a subversive conspiracy against the British or the other Allies. Al-Saʿid indicated the wish to work with the British government, no doubt to secure Arab autonomy under Allied aegis.

Nuri al-Saʿid's purpose was to open the door for communication with the Ottoman government and relay a confidential letter from Sharif Faysal to Grand Vizier İzzet Pasha. He declared the loyalty of the Arabs to the Ottoman government with the reproach that "you would not have suffered this disaster, if proposals made several years ago had been accepted. . . . We want Arabia to be to the Ottoman state what Bavaria is to Germany." This desire for a federation was accompanied by an assurance that Sharif Husayn was not interested in the office of the caliphate, "even though this is what Britain wishes." He stated that the Arab government wanted to be subject to the Ottoman sultan, gave assurances that it would prevent tribal incursions into the north ("the shaykhs are hostage to us"), and asked for cooperation such that "we can be more effective in the peace conference." He asked for a short letter addressed to Faysal if negotiations along these lines were desirable.[81] İzzet Pasha had sent precisely such a letter some two weeks prior.[82] In the interim, the armistice had been signed. Istanbul now rebuffed the initiative and advised the provincial authorities that any talks should be with the British directly, and not through Faysal's delegates, thus rejecting Faysal's presumption of political authority in Damascus.[83] Ali Fuad (Cebesoy), who commanded the Twentieth Army Corps as it withdrew from Syria at the time of the armistice, mentions in his memoirs reports of contacts in early November between officers across the armistice line toward a federative political arrangement, even as he dismisses Nuri al-Saʿid's initiative as a British ploy.[84]

The idea of a federative Ottoman state had a long pedigree. According to Bernard Lewis, the leader of the decentralist faction within the anti-Hamidian Young Turk opposition, Prince Sabahaddin, a disaffected member of the Ottoman royal house, promoted the "idea of a federalized, decentralized Ottoman state," influenced by the work of Edmond Demolins circa 1900.[85] It had been advanced by Arab proponents of decentralization inspired by the Austro-Hungarian model as early as the turn of the century.[86] The government shunned the federation proposition as broached in the immediate aftermath of the armistice not because of loss of faith in preserving the Arab provinces or diminished interest in geopolitical formulas that would maintain the empire's integrity, but because of doubts about the Hashemite sharif's authority in Damascus as an outsider. In his attempt to garner legitimacy outside of Damascus, Faysal made a trip to Aleppo in order to defend his family's insubordination and to demand the Aleppines' loyalty, justifying the Arab Revolt as a response to Turks' violation of Islam.[87] Ten days later, the Ottoman government released the Beirut lawyer Tawfik and Baalbek's Yusuf Sulayman, who had been sentenced by the Aleyh court-martial for striving to set up an Arab government and exiled to Çorum in Central Anatolia.[88] Istanbul appeared to be in search of the right allies and interlocutors in the Arab provinces to deliberate on a new imperial order. On the eve of the peace talks in Europe, these contacts, and the gradual crystallization of an opposition to occupation across the region, demonstrated the will to resist the empire's dismemberment.

A parallel effort aimed to restore the empire's political institutions and practices. In the days leading to the armistice, the Ottoman parliament, the same body that had started its work in 1914 after the third elections of the Second Constitutional Period, reconvened after a six-month recess. Throughout the war, the parliament held sessions in short annual terms. The decisions of the council of ministers supplanted parliament's prerogative to legislate owing to the war emergency. New elections had been due at the end of 1917 but postponed due to the war emergency. In the spring of 1918, before going on recess, the parliament extended its term for another year instead of going to elections that had been rescheduled for the fall of 1918. During the heady days of the Great War's end, approximately one hundred, or one-third, of the deputies did not or could not attend the sessions.[89] Many of the absentees were the representatives of the Arab provinces under Allied occupation, though other deputies from the occupied districts who remained in Istanbul continued to participate in the sessions.

The workings of the Ottoman parliament in the fall of 1918 are emblematic of both the indelible ruptures that the Great War inflicted on the state and society and of the Ottoman state's resilience at the war's end. The absence of three serving Armenian members displaced and killed in 1915–16 was the starkest reminder of the war's violence. Many other deputies were absent because they were displaced from the capital by circumstance, or they were restricted in their movements owing to foreign occupation of imperial territories. For others, the state had squandered its authority and legitimacy, rendering representation meaningless. The capitulatory terms of the armistice opened the way for Allied superintendence in the capital and influence over all the branches of the Ottoman government. The collapse of the wartime CUP government, however, emboldened debate. When a group of Greek deputies demanded an investigation of the CUP government's wartime policies, the draft resolution mentioned injustices committed against not only Armenians and Greeks but also Arabs. These references met with the protest of some Arab deputies. 'Ali Haydar, deputy for the Red Sea independent sancak of Asir, asked for their deletion from the record.[90]

The difficulty of keeping the 1914 parliament alive in the post-armistice period under the drastically changed circumstances and the strains of the Allied squeeze in Istanbul soon became apparent. On December 21, 1918, Grand Vizier Tevfik Pasha dissolved this third parliament of the Second Constitutional Era. The closure came before the expiration of the one-year extension mandated the previous year. Deadlocks over legislation, the return of war-displaced populations, and the unresolved status of the territories under occupation provided the ostensible reasons for disbanding parliament. More likely, the sultan and the British were leery of continued Unionist influence in parliament. With this concern, in November the sultan had replaced the İzzet Pasha government with a new cabinet headed by Tevfik Pasha. The CUP leadership might have left, but the majority of the serving deputies had been elected on the CUP ticket. The Allies' fear of a functioning and potentially strident parliament muddying the waters, as they strove to gain further influence over the Istanbul government by landing and stationing troops in the capital and anchoring their fleets in the Bosporus, far surpassed any public image advantage from appearing to countenance the mechanisms of democratic government. As wartime regimes were collapsing in all the defeated countries, a functioning parliament in the Ottoman capital seemed like an anomaly. In closing it, the new government dispensed with the constitutional requirement to announce new elections within four months of the closure.[91] The annulment of the legislature gave the Ottoman political leadership greater latitude in attending to the requisites of the armistice agreement and making terms with the accomplished facts that ensued from it.

For many, the agreement's punitive terms and the nonchalance with which the victors flouted them made marking time until the conclusion of a peace treaty untenable. In the hope of countering Mudros's sanctions and mitigating the consequences of noncompliance to Allied dictates, Ottoman officers, politicians, and intellectuals gravitated toward the deployment of the idiom of nationality as a framework around which the Wilsonian credo could be concretized and its prevalent moral authority harnessed. If Mudros threatened the integrity of the empire, the people of its unoccupied parts could be rallied with the expectation of the "secure sovereignty" enunciated in Article 12 of Wilson's manifesto. Such an effort would bring results if accompanied by legitimizing strategies that the new geopolitical and military calculus presented, including rallying around the nation discourse.

In 1913, after the devastating defeats of the Balkan wars and the consequent territorial losses, the Ottomans were able to summon an effort to take advantage of emerging differences among the Balkan allies and to preserve the state. Against the loss of its predominantly Christian Balkan provinces and the increasingly perilous erosion of legitimation based on state sovereignty, Istanbul resorted to an identitarian mobilization that elevated Islamic sentiment, which later became the mobilizational strategy of the Great War. The ultimate objective was to save the state and protect, to the extent possible, imperial territorial integrity. In 1918, national rights and self-determination were the ascendant legitimizing tropes, to which the elites in Istanbul and Anatolia would resort in the quest to preserve/redeem the state.

In stark contrast to its European wartime allies and the Romanov Empire, the end of the war did not upend the imperial structures of the Ottoman state. The cessation of the hostilities revived political practices and institutions that had lapsed under the declared war emergency. The CUP's unchecked dominance justified by the war emergency had enfeebled Sultan Reşad's authority, already circumscribed since his ascendance to the throne in 1909 as the constitutional monarch. The validity of the sultanate as an institution remained, however, and was buttressed by the caliphal prerogatives that wartime propaganda had promoted. Sultan Reşad died in July 1918. No sooner had his brother Vahideddin risen to the throne than the tide of the war definitively turned against the Central Powers in the European theaters, followed by critical Ottoman defeats in Syria. The reverses undercut the CUP government's authority, and within weeks of an armistice agreement with heavy terms, forced the wartime top leadership to take flight. The empire was weakened militarily and diplomatically, but Sultan Vahideddin appointed a compliant government to restore his authority. The state did not face outbreaks of pent-up social and political dissent at the Great War's end, allowing the sultan to maintain his throne and government through the armistice and beyond. In contrast, in Berlin and Vienna the monarchs succumbed to insurrections and popular backlash, and the new regimes would expeditiously sign peace treaties with the victors consigning the imperial monarchies to history and erecting new nation-states. When the victors of the Great War put forward peace plans, they denied self-determination to Ottoman constituencies, fostering anti-colonial resistance and reimaginings of the imperial state, as armed hostilities continued. Alternative views of the collective self developed gradually in the turmoil of the post–World War I years in the crucible of a popular liberation struggle, military resistance, and diplomatic negotiations.

THREE

Anti-colonial Resistance and the Search for Self-Determination

THE CIRCUMSTANCES OF OTTOMAN DEFEAT and foreign occupation elicited divergent responses from political elites and emergent popular groups. In Istanbul, Sultan Vahideddin saw the best chance for the Ottoman state's survival and the recognition of his symbolic prerogatives as caliph in cooperating with the Allied powers, who imposed effective control over the capital. In Syria, Faysal's dependence on British financial, political, and military support continued after he formed his government in Damascus under British auspices and as a relative newcomer to Syrian politics. In Iraq, a British civil administration governed under the influence of the government of India without the semblance of incorporating meaningful participation of indigenous elements.

The Ottoman armies, demobilized in compliance with the armistice agreement and ravaged by the depredations of prolonged combat, shortage of food and supplies, and harsh climate and terrain, gradually formed scattered clusters of resistance throughout the region. The discharged troops coalesced with deserters, irregular bands, and tribal contingents to form self-defense units motivated by communal solidarity, religious imperative, and local patriotism. The Allies' occupation of large territories and their hold over the imperial government galvanized clusters of volunteers in the provinces independent of central direction. The loci of armed resistance in Anatolia became more coordinated upon the Greek occupation of the Aegean coast starting in May 1919, and in Syria upon the British decision to evacuate in favor of France in Fall 1919. The immediate threat that foreign intrusion posed to established sociopolitical relations and to cultural and economic assets in the countryside impelled local chieftains to organize and lead the resistance to occupation. While the remnants of the CUP organizational framework and bureaucracy facilitated this provincial mobilization, local notables, including men of religion, and their retinues played a prominent role.[1]

Unionist organizations and networks were entrenched in the fabric of the social and political life of the provinces, where the Committee's organizational structure and influence had progressively increased since 1908. In Anatolia, the first local organizations of the resistance, the "defense-of-rights" and "rejection-of-annexation" societies, were outgrowths of the CUP branches or linked to them.[2] The Committee may have been discredited and banned in Istanbul but its cadres beneath the top leadership and its empire-wide organization and networks survived to leave a deep imprint on the course of postwar events. As early as the beginning of the Long War, the CUP had begun to act on the menace of insurrection and foreign invasion to bolster its provincial network. It established the *Teşkilat-ı Mahsusa* (Special Organization), an intelligence and propaganda network as a shadowy arm of the government. With its extensive reach into the empire's periphery, the Teşkilat became complicit in the genocidal displacement of the Armenian population. It also employed Arab operatives to monitor dissent and carry out propaganda in the Arab provinces. During the last years of the war, Teşkilat-ı Mahsusa changed its name to *Umur-u Şarkiye Dairesi* (Office of Eastern Affairs), foregrounded Muslim solidarity, and remained active, including in the Arab provinces, beyond the end of the war. In October 1918, right before the CUP relinquished power, Enver Pasha proposed the grandiose moniker *Umum Alem-i İslam İhtilal Teşkilatı* (Revolutionary Organization of the Islamic World) for the same organization. The provincial networks took on a life of their own after the armistice.[3]

THE WRONG PATH TO PEACE:
CONTINUED OCCUPATION AND RESISTANCE

In the fall of 1918, the belligerent powers in Europe laid down their arms contingent on the endorsement of the general spirit of the formulas President Wilson enunciated. In contrast to the German and Austro-Hungarian armistices, the Mudros agreement was not premised explicitly on the Wilsonian credo elaborated by the Fourteen Points and its addenda (Four Principles and Four Ends). Britain and France continued to pursue their aims with the force of arms while touting the Wilsonian principles. One week after the armistice went into effect, they issued a joint declaration promising indigenous administrations and self-determination in "liberated" areas in Syria and Mesopotamia.[4] This statement reinforced Faysal's claim to lead an Arab state proclaimed two days after he entered Damascus in a declaration widely distributed as leaflets.[5] However, his legitimacy remained precarious as long as occupation continued. France rejected Faysal's authority in coastal Syria, and many Syrians including pro-Ottoman loyalists and Arabists were wary of his British ties and his resolve to withstand French demands.

In the weeks following the armistice, as the Allied powers prepared for a peace conference that would secure a permanent settlement, it became apparent that the post-Mudros Allied territorial objectives were not limited to the unfinished business of occupying Mosul and Alexandretta. During the winter of 1918–1919, Allied forces occupied additional regions that had remained under Ottoman control at war's end in order to secure geopolitical advantage before any forthcoming peace talks. British troops captured the remaining portions of the Aleppo Province, including Kilis (December 6), Ayntab (January 1), Maraş (February 22), and Urfa (March 7), while France landed forces in Adana and Mersin in December. Thus, to the east and the south of the arc of the Taurus Mountains, Britain had occupied the very same areas in which it had, with conflicting agreements, recognized the claims of its allies. The contestation over Allied territorial claims from northern Iraq and Syria to western Anatolia defined the course of the post-Mudros war in the Middle East.

The Muslim Ottoman majority in Anatolia perceived the Entente powers as favoring the interests and political desires of Christian groups in the empire. The Great Powers had had an abiding interest in these groups and historical affinities with them for cultural, economic, humanitarian, and strategic considerations. The thinking of volunteer paramilitaries throughout the Long War was "informed in part by the experience of Muslims as victims of foreign, Christian expansionism or independence movements."[6] The fear that displaced and dispossessed Christians (mostly Armenians and Greeks) would return under Allied protection to reclaim their abandoned lands and property mobilized to action those who had benefitted from what the deportees left behind during their displacement. The determination to forestall Armenian restitution and resettlement was the paramount impetus in organizational activity in the eastern provinces and the crystallization of militia resistance. Armenian refugees and diaspora Armenians fought alongside the French army as the Armenian Legion (first organized as the *Légion d'Orient* in 1916) and supported French occupation forces.[7] In the early days of the armistice, the parliament deliberated on the repatriation of Ottomans who had had to leave their homes during the war and the restitution of their property.[8] This was meant to appease the Allies and preclude the invocation of Article 7 of the Mudros agreement, which gave the Allies the right to intervene in the Armenian provinces. From the vantage of the beneficiaries of dispossession, the parliamentary discussion had the alarming effect of affording legitimacy to the Armenian demands for repossession, even in the absence of ratified policy.

The heavy terms of the Mudros agreement thus sparked agitation, especially in areas with concentrations of Christian populations. Local initiative spawned groups under a plethora of designations and gradually raised popular forces representing broad segments of the population. In Izmir, within one week of the signing of the armistice, a group that called itself the Society for the Defense of Ottoman Rights (*İzmir Müdafaa-ı Hukuk-u Osmaniye Cemiyeti*) constituted itself officially and filed documents with the provincial authorities.[9] The violations of the armistice agreement further energized local groups in the newly occupied and neighboring regions. As early as December 1918, defense groups in Adana mounted resistance against invading French forces and the Armenian Legion.[10] Across the zones of British and French occupation in southeastern Anatolia and northern Syria, the popular organizations would actively cooperate militarily and politically in the name of Islamic unity until the end of the Long War.

In areas that remained outside effective occupation but under imminent threat, many of the popular organizations styled themselves as defense-of-rights groups and often coalesced to form congresses. For instance, as soon as the armistice was signed, the people of Kars constituted the Kars Muslims' Congress (*Kars İslam Şurası*). The Ottoman inroads into the Caucasus in Spring 1918 had met with British efforts to concentrate troops in the region. The armistice agreement stipulated not only the demobilization of the Ottoman forces but also the surrender of the Three Provinces. The Kars Congress rallied local forces to preempt the capture of the town and formed a regional government under the rubric of Provisional Government of the Southwestern Caucasus, arrogating to itself authority over the Muslim areas of Kars and its vicinity. In the empire's European territories, the Ottoman Council for the Defense of Thrace (*Trakya-Paşaeli Müdafaa Heyet-i Osmaniyesi*) also espoused the irredentist aim of regaining Muslim-populated western Thrace ceded to Greece in 1913.[11] These organizations would acquire a degree of coordination within one year of the armistice and play a crucial role in the anti-colonial resistance in all parts of the rump empire, including in the creation of a new political authority and military organization in Ankara.

The Wilsonian principles became constitutive of anti-colonial movements as a legitimating crutch in the quest for independence.[12] Like the resistance groups and the Faysal administration, the imperial government and literati in Istanbul couched their objectives in Wilsonian terms, with the conviction that political demands presented in the language of self-determination and respect for sovereignty would command moral persuasion during the course of the peace settlement. They belabored the case that Muslims constituted ethno-national majorities in all provinces of the empire in order to delegitimize the geopolitical aspirations of Christian populations and Allied intervention on their behalf. At the same time, in their defense of state sovereignty, which the Wilsonian principles privileged in tandem with minority rights, they acknowledged Muslim ethno-national differences and heterogeneity as a feature of the empire's legitimacy and argued that Muslim groups harbored allegiance to the Ottoman imperial framework.

In order to negate territorial claims based in Arab nationality rights, Grand Vizier Tevfik Pasha called for the urgent formation of a committee in November 1918 to investigate the historical presence of Turks in the provinces of Syria and Aleppo as well as the Iraqi provinces.[13] He instructed the compilation of historical and statistical documents and their close examination as well as the publication and dissemination of brochures based on them. He urged that this research elicit sufficient information on the Kurds in these regions and, in order to ensure this, that two members belonging to the Kurdish "element" be included in the committee. Large Kurdish communities inhabited the contested armistice frontier, where the British army was expanding to capture new territories. Thus, Istanbul moved away from the Turkish-Arab ethnic dichotomy inherent in the depictions of the region's demography, in the policies pursued by the Allies aimed at division among Ottomans, and in the rhetoric of the administration in Damascus that styled itself as Arab nationalist. The very strategies, however, entailed purposive engagement in the language of ethnicity in novel terms, even as they were meant to counter the reification and politicization of ethnic difference.

The Wilsonian imperative inspired the formulation of rhetorical and statistical strategies and as such the validation or remolding of identities in the effort to counter enemy inroads. In November 1918, the Izmir daily *Anadolu* (Anatolia) wrote that the Wilsonian principles provided for "an imaginary promised land" (*arz-ı mevud-i muhayyel*) to every people (*kavim [qawm]*).[14]

Imparting reality to the imaginary emerged as the obvious task in order to achieve redemption. The same month, another Izmir daily, *Köylü* (Peasant), belabored statistics to document the Turkishness of the Aydın Province on the Aegean coast against Greek claims.[15] Before parliament's closure in December, deputies representing the province of Adana and the five other provinces inhabited by Armenians joined together to form the "Eastern Provinces group," an explicit purpose of which was to compile and propagate population statistics.[16] These efforts would intensify against the background of the peace talks in Paris, to which the Ottoman Empire and the other Central Powers were not invited.

The Ottoman government expected that the Mudros agreement would be central to the peace negotiations pertaining to the empire. During the days prior to the opening of the conference, Istanbul made a renewed effort to bring defiant officers in the Hijaz and Yemen into compliance with the Mudros terms and surrender to an Allied commander. The government finally prevailed over Fahreddin Pasha to end his resistance in Medina. At the beginning of 1919, Fahreddin was still holed up within the fortress of Medina defending the Prophet's Mosque against the forces of Sharif Abdullah, Husayn's son and Faysal's older brother, who commanded the Arabian operations of the Arab Revolt.[17] Faced with the increasingly dire circumstances of the siege, Fahreddin complied but refused to surrender to Sharif Abdullah, whom he did not recognize as a bona fide Allied commander. He was whisked to the British authorities in Aqaba, who exiled him to Malta. Non-Hijazi Arab soldiers under Fahreddin's command wanted to return home after their arduous stint under the siege. Abdullah recruited them to his own forces, warning them that the alternative was that they would be treated as prisoners of war.[18]

The Ottoman government's protestations that the Allies were violating the armistice with continued land grabs since October 31 met with similar recrimination from the British authorities. Even after the surrender of Medina on January 10, on the opening day of the Peace Conference (January 18, 1919) Admiral Calthorpe, British commissioner in Istanbul, reported that he would not "accept criticism or complaints of the manner in which terms of armistice are being carried out" as long as the Ottomans neglected "in a most glaring way to carry out [their] obligations." He claimed that Ottoman troops were dragging their feet in evacuating the Caucasus with the feeble excuse that winter was making withdrawal difficult, and he did not know yet if the units in Yemen had relinquished their arms.[19]

PARIS PEACE CONFERENCE

The Peace Conference convened in Paris with wide international participation but excluded the Central Powers. In his opening speech, President Poincaré counted "the Syrians, the Lebanese, the Arabs" as "captive nationalities" who "turned towards us, as their natural defenders."[20] Four powers, the United States, Britain, France, and Italy, represented with two delegates each, dominated the proceedings, and together with Japan's delegates, constituted the "Council of Ten," where most decisions were taken. The conference took up Syria, Palestine, Mesopotamia, and Turkey as separate entities in the deliberations. Faysal, standing in for Sharif Husayn, was given the opportunity to present the case for Arab independence. The council also heard pro-French expatriate Chekri Ghanem, who favored Syrian statehood under French guidance.[21]

With respect to Syria, Palestine, and Mesopotamia, the deliberations revolved around the template that had emerged from the Entente powers' wartime agreements. The negotiation of claims with an eye to apportion the region by establishing mandates constituted the conference's main agenda as far as the Middle East was concerned. The mandate arrangement, first formulated in concrete terms in relation to the political future of German colonies in Africa, signified the assumption of responsibility by an Allied power to lead an enemy territory to independent existence. The international association that was proposed in the Fourteen Points (Article 14), the creation of which as "The League of Nations" the Peace Conference approved within days of its opening, would exercise oversight over the mandates. While the conferees acknowledged that the occupied Ottoman territories differed from the German colonies in the degree of institutional development, the Peace Conference favored a prospective mandate regime in the Middle East with President Wilson's blessing.[22]

Faysal took exception to this regime, as it compromised the extensive realm of Arab independence promised to his father. Invoking the Wilsonian principles, he pleaded that "the Arabic-speaking peoples of Asia, from the line Alexandretta-Diarbekr southward to the Indian Ocean, be recognized as independent sovereign peoples, under the guarantee of the League of Nations."[23] This maximalist demand contravened both British and French designs and was certain to be ignored. The northern boundary that Faysal put forth for Arab independence was extraordinary in that it exceeded the desiderata Husayn had articulated in his correspondence with McMahon.

It pushed the borders from the Birecik-Urfa-Mardin line (the 37th parallel) up to Diyarbekir some seventy-five kilometers to the north. Faysal argued that this geographically and economically unified territory corresponded to natural frontiers inhabited 99 percent by Arabic speakers of "Semitic stock."[24] The rationalization of desired geopolitical outcomes based on ethnological/demographic claims was not new, but it gained paramountcy as a new international system was forged in Paris that ostensibly privileged majorities and second-guessed their political will.

Even as President Wilson advocated for the mandates, he supported a formal assessment of the political desires of the region's denizens. The conference approved of the dispatch of a fact-finding commission to Syria. The delegates addressed the question of whether Turkey and/or Armenia should be constituted as mandates contingent on a similar process of inquiry to be arranged under US auspices. The conference proceeded under the assumption of a drastic curtailment of Ottoman sovereignty, yet with no disposition to consider self-government for the peoples of the empire. France opposed the idea of canvassing public opinion from the beginning. When Britain too withdrew its support, the commission had to be constituted as an American delegation (King-Crane Commission), which was dispatched to Syria in June.

Particularly consequential for the Ottoman state in the Paris Conference were the claims of the Kingdom of Greece, a late entrant into the war on the side of the victorious Allies. Greek prime minister Eleftherios Venizelos asked in February 1919 for Greece's annexation of western Asia Minor (Aydın Province and parts of Bursa Province) and the Aegean islands, inhabited by large Greek Orthodox populations, to be exact "1,188,359 Greeks and 1,042,050 Mohammedans."[25] The territorial demands were vast and compelling in their detailed ethnographic justification consistent with the spirit of the Wilsonian principles, if not in their precision. The Tevfik Pasha government submitted a memorandum to the Allied high commissioners in Istanbul affirming adherence to the Wilsonian principles but rebutting the Greek and Armenian claims by arguing that Thrace and Anatolia were home to an overwhelming majority of Turks. Tevfik Pasha expressed the view that the Wilsonian principles could not be applicable to the Arab peoples, who, he argued, were inseparable from the Ottoman state, but could be granted broad autonomy.[26]

The Ottoman government and public received the deliberations in Paris around Greece's claims and a possible Armenia mandate in Anatolia with existential trepidation. General Allenby's visit to Istanbul in February 1919 brought home and exacerbated the fears. Allenby declared that he would facilitate the return of Armenians who had been deported but escaped death. He demanded the restitution of their property and the government's assistance to ensure this. The general further informed the Ottoman ministers that he would be dispatching officers to the Armenian districts to appraise the damage to Armenian property and asked for the facilitation of their work.[27] The deliberations in Paris, from which the Ottoman government was excluded, and ultimatums by Allied officials in the region spurred civic organizational activity to repudiate the demands the government was powerless to reject.

APPROPRIATING WILSONIANISM

In Istanbul, the *Milli Kongre* ("National Congress"), a platform composed of members from a multitude of civic associations, took upon itself the task of reinforcing the legitimacy and integrity of the rump empire in conformity with the Wilsonian conception, in particular the reference in Article 12 to the "Turkish parts" of the empire and the recognition of their sovereignty. The congress found it imperative to gather the testimony of European scholars, literati, and travelers about Turkey as a political entity inhabited by a Turkish majority, in order to make a case about sovereign independence. Its circular dated February 19 enjoined members to search for such references in books and bring them back to the leadership for use in advocating for the legitimacy and right to sovereignty of the besieged empire.[28] Foreign epistemological imprimatur became central to asserting a legitimate right to independent existence and to forestalling further division. Even as the anti-colonial opposition deployed in its arsenal nationality rooted in ethno-linguistic criteria, it advanced the other, and at times contradictory, interpretation of the Wilsonian doctrine, which upheld state sovereignty, administrative unity, or historical allegiance.[29]

The Muslim populations of provinces where Christian groups harbored territorial claims felt especially poignantly the imperative to demonstrate historical and statistical evidence of their provinces' integral belonging to the Ottoman state. Confronted with a project of carving out a Turkey limited to central Anatolia, which they perceived as emerging in the Paris Conference, they touted the Turkishness of their respective provinces, conflating "Turkish," "Ottoman," and "Muslim." The propaganda effort targeted Greek claims in western and northeastern Anatolia and Armenian claims in eastern

Anatolia and Cilicia. A deputy from Adana, a town now under French occupation, coauthored an article on the historical rights of the "Turks" in Adana and insisted on the implementation of the Wilsonian principles.[30] Nearby Tarsus resisted French occupation by advancing rights not in ethnic terms but the district's historic bonds with and allegiance to the Ottoman state. "We submitted to the Ottoman community 400 years ago under our leader Ramazanoğlu.... We want to stay Ottoman forever."[31] The Trabzon Society for the Protection of National Rights (*Trabzon Muhafaza-ı Hukuk-u Milliye Cemiyeti*) resolved to mount a defense for the affiliation of Trabzon with the Ottoman state on the basis of scientific evidence and to compile "social and political documents and statistics" to be presented as memoranda to the Allied governments.[32]

The public appeals did not signify a latent Turkish nationalism revealing itself with Ottoman defeat or a spontaneous generation of ethnonational consciousness so much as an attempt to tailor the political goal of ensuring the survival of the state to fit the Wilsonian template. A delegate at a consultative assembly that the sultan convened (*Saltanat Şurası*) opined that "a new Turkey will seek to ensure administrative and national unity according to the text and spirit of Wilson's principles."[33] Substantiating political demands in reference to the Wilsonian points was judged to be a good strategy against the background of the ongoing Paris Peace Conference, launched with an acclamation of Wilson's aims. The relevance and applicability of the Fourteen Points to the Ottoman peace settlement, however, was contested from the beginning. The Allies had not agreed prior to the armistice to uphold an Ottoman settlement premised on the Wilsonian principles, unlike in the case of Germany and Austria-Hungary.[34] Even as Poincaré delivered his inaugural oration at the conference, his government was at loggerheads with Faysal about French presence in Syria. Paris was more inclined to proceed with an implementation of the Sykes-Picot arrangement than to adhere to the lofty principles of self-determination, nationality, or restoration of invaded territories.

The conference focused in its first six months on the establishment of the League of Nations and securing a consensus about the settlement pertaining to Germany (finalized with the drafting of the Treaty of Versailles in June 1919). Almost from the very outset, Woodrow Wilson was preoccupied with election-year politics at home and absented himself from the talks for a long period. Without an imperative to reconcile Allied occupation of vast Ottoman territories with the Wilsonian credo, the Ottoman settlement remained precarious. The United States had not fought the Ottoman Empire during the war, and therefore had meager standing in the determination of the status of Ottoman territories.[35] British and French aspirations and wartime commitments in the region outweighed America's. In Washington, treaties with the Ottomans' wartime allies took precedence over the settlement for the Middle East. Indeed, the Allied powers continued military operations in Ottoman territories throughout spring 1919 in order to gain further advantage before a settlement. British forces occupied southeastern Anatolian towns of Maraş in February and Urfa in March. Italy landed forces in Antalya on the Mediterranean coast in March. The Allies tightened their control over the capital. Greece's occupation of Izmir and environs in May 1919 with British carte blanche further complicated the settlement pertaining to the Ottoman state, not only because it introduced another military conflict in the midst of the peace talks but also because it galvanized anti-colonial resistance in Anatolia.

The lack of progress in achieving the fundamentals of an Ottoman peace settlement revitalized local resistance and the related "congress movement." In view of the distinct threat of expanding occupation by Greece, Muslim popular groups in western Anatolia and the eastern Black Sea region, both areas with large historic Greek Orthodox communities and the objects of the Greek Kingdom's annexationist *megali idea* (great idea), convened congresses in Trabzon (February 1919 and May 1919) and Izmir (March 1919).[36] These conferences arrogated representative authority to make decisions about the future of the respective regions and to establish the requisite political and militia organizational structures for the realization of these decisions.

After months of expectation of a commitment by the Peace Conference for a semblance of independence for Syria, Faysal witnessed the conference agree on a Covenant for the League of Nations, which stipulated mandates in Syria and Mesopotamia under the League's auspices. He returned home at the end of April and immediately called for a Syrian Congress (*al-mu'tamar al-suri*), akin to the congresses in Anatolia.[37] The Syrian Congress would consist of elected and invited members from all parts of Syria and present a unified position in front of the King-Crane commission of inquiry scheduled to make their fact-finding journey within weeks. The secondary voters, who had been elected by primary voters in 1914 in the two-tier Ottoman elections, acted as electors for the eighty-five members of the congress. The process produced a socially diverse cohort of multiple political tendencies and affiliations, including Ottoman loyalists Muhammad Fawzi al-'Azm and 'Abd al-Rahman al-Yusuf, who temporarily acted as president and vice-president, respectively.[38]

Within a month after Faysal's return, the Allied powers allowed Istanbul a one-time representation before the Council of Ten. The Ottoman government had remained as a distant bystander to the proceedings of the Paris Conference. Before sending a delegation, a new Ottoman government led by Damad Ferid Pasha issued a statement to the council. Ferid was a leader of the opposition to the CUP and a pro-British statesman married to the Sultan's sister.[39] The occupation of Izmir by Greece on May 15, about two weeks earlier, put its mark on this statement couched in the language of national rights. It invoked the necessity for Izmir to "remain Turkish in the light of the requirements of the latest civilizational era with regard to rights and justice." The statement described the occupation as futile and temporary and referred to the government's determination to render it null and void in the councils of the Peace Conference based on documentation. It characterized "our homeland (vatan)" as the home of Turks by a large majority and a site of Turkishness since centuries ago.[40] Confronted with the Greek occupation sanctioned by the Allies, the imperial government appealed to historically constituted rights and the will of the Turkish majority in the region by adopting the language of nationality.

Istanbul resorted to validations of Turkish and Muslim identity circumstantially in defending imperial sovereignty and territorial integrity. Damad Ferid Pasha led the Ottoman delegation to Paris and made his appearance before the council on June 17, where he expounded on a broader vision and agenda for the empire with a Wilsonian justification to defend its independence as it existed before the war. With little regard to the geopolitical and diplomatic realities of the moment, Ferid argued that the Ottoman government had asked for an armistice in agreement with the Wilsonian principles and with the expectation that the proper application of these principles would restore world peace. He made a case for sovereignty and territorial integrity by invoking rights premised on Islamic identity and historically constituted religious commonality. The grand vizier rejected claims advanced in the language of Arab nationality rights over the territories ringed by the Tauruses, describing the mountains as nothing but a natural rugged range constituted at the time of the creation of earth, not a line that divides Turks and Arabs. He granted, though, that in most areas beyond the Tauruses, from the Mediterranean to the Arabian Peninsula, "a different language" is spoken next to Turkish. Ferid Pasha argued that "these territories are united and inseparably bound to Istanbul by sentiments stronger than nationality. . . . The same hopes and purpose, the same beliefs, the same spiritual and material interests have blended to such an extent that the splintering of this dense body may violate the peace and welfare of the entire East." Discrediting the premise behind the imminent dispatch of commissions of investigation to appraise local circumstances and popular will, he maintained that "resorting to the opinion of the people of these lands would be futile, as their fate cannot be separated from that of the exalted and important interests of 300 million Muslims."[41] With these bold remarks, the grand vizier was rejecting occupation in the empire's southern territories, physical determinism based on topography dividing peoples apart, and disparities of collective purpose and identity among the Muslims of the empire. He argued for the existence of strong religious bonds as well as allegiance to the Ottoman state and wielded the veiled threat of a worldwide Muslim reaction to any disruptive schemes. This uncompromising last-ditch plea for the continuance of centralist governance and for the restoration of the status quo before the war was woefully at odds with the prevailing circumstances and Istanbul's position of weakness and vulnerability. His interlocutors derided the grand vizier and his remarks, deemed so detached from reality as to be of no use in advancing meaningful negotiation.

Six days after the grand vizier's presentation to the Council of Ten, the Ottoman delegation submitted a written memorandum. The tenor of this written note as deposited in the British archives was different, especially with regard to the Arab provinces. It proposed a confederative structure for the empire:

> The Arab provinces lying to the south of the Turkish countries, and including Syria, Palestine, the Hedjaz, the Asyr, the Yemen, Irak, and all the other regions which were recognized as forming an integral part of the Ottoman Empire before the war, would have a large measure of administrative autonomy, under the sovereignty of His Imperial Majesty the Sultan....
>
> ... The Governor of each autonomous province shall be appointed by His Imperial Majesty the Sultan, except in the Hedjaz, to which may be granted a special organization in agreement with the Power most directly interested in it. In all the Arab countries the Ottoman flag shall fly on the territory of the *emaret* (principality) or autonomous province. Justice shall be done in the name of His Imperial Majesty, the Sultan, and the coinage shall bear his name, Tughra.[42]

A more detailed statement that the government made public elaborated in justificatory tone on the proposed administrative reorganization.[43] In conciliatory language, it sought to exonerate the Ottoman state for entering the war and for its wartime policies. The facile renunciation of war responsibility was consistent with the smug tenor of the earlier oral presentation. Nevertheless, the memorandum substantiated the vision for the reorganization of the empire. The Istanbul government was not only acknowledging the Wilsonian tenets as the "principles of the future," but also laying down the contours of a geopolitical framework, albeit in the most general terms, with reference to the Fourteen Points. The proposal was informed by the language of nationality that saturated the peace talks, where forceful arguments had been heard for Arab independence, whether limited to Syria or more broadly, and for Turkish majoritarian rights in Asia Minor to counter Armenian and Greek territorial demands. The memorandum called for an independent homeland for Turks and broad administrative autonomy for Syria, Elcezire (al-Jazira, or Mesopotamia), the Hijaz, and Yemen. Modulating the grand vizier's previous remarks about ethno-linguistic heterogeneity in the region, it subscribed to a "national dividing line" which extended from Kirkuk to the north of Latakia on the Mediterranean coast via Mosul, Ra's al-'Ayn, and Aleppo, between the independent Turkish lands and the regions of Arab autonomy. Significantly, it insisted on the sultan-caliph's political sovereignty in a confederated state in the empire's prewar domains. The government would welcome assistance from the League of Nations as long as it did not violate the stipulated independence. This caveat suggested an opening to Britain and France to pursue interests in the areas that they had brought under their occupation or influence during the war. The crude demands that the delegation enunciated in its oral presentation to the council were now revised, ostensibly to align with the text of the Wilsonian principles.

The dividing line that Ferid Pasha posited bore little similarity to demarcations of regions identified as comprising Arab lands in previous schemes of division, most recently the ones presented by Faysal to the Peace Conference (Alexandretta-Diyarbekir line). Instead, Ferid Pasha put forth an approximation of the limits of territories controlled by the Ottomans at the time of the Armistice of October 1918, without regard to the fluidity, heterogeneity, and scattered distribution of ethno-linguistic communities across a wide zone. The ascription of ethnic identities with respect to an imagined dividing line did not account for the Kurdish population within the proposed federative structure, even though the Kurds arguably represented the largest ethno-linguistic population in the broader region of northern Syria, northern Mesopotamia, and southeastern Anatolia. What made the areas to the north of the designated line "Turkish" was not the ethnicity or spoken language of their inhabitants, but the unconditional territorial claims of the Ottoman government aligned with the armistice status quo.

ENTER MUSTAFA KEMAL

The Greek navy's landing in Izmir with the blessings (and naval support) of the Allies in May 1919 significantly ruptured the post-armistice status quo. Far from being a continuation of diplomacy with other means, the unprovoked belligerence of former imperial subjects found new adherents to the resistance in Anatolia, among them Mustafa Kemal, who happened to leave Istanbul for the Black Sea coast on official duty as military inspector the day of the Greek landing in Izmir (May 15). Almost immediately, Mustafa Kemal abandoned his assigned mission, and soon after, his military uniform, and joined the resistance efforts marshalled by former Unionists. He collaborated with such fellow commanders as Ali Fuad (Cebesoy) and Kazım Karabekir Pashas, who had organized the extant troops of the Ottoman army to resist the expansion of British occupation in their respective regions of command in central and eastern Anatolia. Mustafa Kemal supported strengthening linkages between the nodes of resistance. By the end of summer 1919 he emerged as the principal organizer of a broad movement. His role would be extolled by histories and authors of history textbooks to the effacement of other actors, signifying the conception and construction of a Turkish nation in Kemal's image from the moment he joined the movement. This view is consistent with, indeed derives from, Kemal's own interpretation and narration promulgated in his *Speech* in 1927.[44]

The two predominant themes in the *Speech* are the primacy of Mustafa Kemal's agency in the movement and the teleology of a nationalist vision. The arrogation is not surprising in the autobiographical account of a leader who had consolidated near absolute political power at the time he constructed and dictated the narrative. Taking their cue from Mustafa Kemal's account, many, including historians, have subscribed to the notion that Kemal singlehandedly inspired and organized the resistance movement with a clear blueprint for the creation of a sovereign nation-state for Turks. According to them, if Mustafa Kemal did not articulate every piece of his grand plan at each juncture of the movement, it was because he was hedging against conflicting sensibilities or lurking threats to his vision. It has thus become established wisdom, for instance, that "he could not yet announce [his] views publicly... [because he] could not afford to antagonize [conservative Turkish opinion] until his victories ended the crisis of foreign intervention."[45] There is no question that Mustafa Kemal played the paramount role in the military and political events of the postwar years. It is also reasonable to assume that he held some of his plans, feelings, and convictions close to his chest when he deemed this necessary. The master narrative of nation building, however, should be scrutinized for a more nuanced and less deterministic appraisal of the sociopolitical, military, and diplomatic processes, which considers context, precedent, and contingency within not just the realm of the future Turkish state but more broadly in the contested lands of the Ottoman state after World War I.

As he joined and organized the resistance movement, Mustafa Kemal endorsed an unequivocal indictment of the Istanbul government for abdicating the responsibility to defend the land. The Ottoman government was just as helpless against the Greek occupation of Izmir as it had been against the British and French capture of wide territories within the Taurus arc and since the armistice. Sultan Vahideddin, especially the government of Damad Ferid Pasha, prevaricated by subscribing to a policy of appeasing Britain and France, whose benevolence was essential for any pretense of retention of power and legitimacy. The memorandum Mustafa Kemal cosigned with other high-ranking officers on June 22, 1919, articulated the responsibility and right of the people (*millet*) to take the defense of the land into their own hands. The officers sent the memorandum to provincial authorities and urged the dispatch of three delegates "who have earned the respect of the people" to a new congress to convene in the eastern Anatolian city of Sivas.[46]

Kemal's proposed congress was in the mold of meetings held in different parts of the empire since the armistice to address foreign occupation or threat of occupation. Notables who styled themselves as resistance leaders in the eastern provinces had already scheduled a congress in the town of Erzurum before Kemal's active involvement in the Anatolian movement. It was held in July 1919 as a regional initiative in response to the presence of British occupation forces in the Caucasus as sanctioned by the Mudros agreement (Article 15). Apprehensions about the establishment of an Armenian state with Allied backing and the revival of the project for a Greek Pontic state on the eastern Black Sea coast ("not backed by Venizelos nor supported by statistics," according to Arnold Toynbee[47]) galvanized the organizational activity in the east. Mustafa Kemal participated in the Erzurum Congress, attended by representatives from five eastern provinces, as an outside delegate and chair.

The congress declared that the eastern Black Sea and eastern Anatolian provinces are an indivisible whole that cannot be separated from one another or the Ottoman community (Article 1 of the congress resolutions).[48] Its regional scope notwithstanding, the congress embodied and articulated the important underlying themes of the growing resistance more broadly. It condemned violations of the Mudros cease-fire, linking the ostensibly opportunistic Greek and Armenian designs to "annihilate Islam" to the aggression of the foreign powers.[49] It formulated its resolutions as the defense of the state and religion. Apprehension about the return of Armenians to their homes under Allied auspices to reclaim personal and communal properties and businesses impelled the provincial notability to action.[50]

The canard of Christians as internal enemies working hand in glove with imperialist aggressors, which had been instrumental in the violent wartime ostracization of non-Muslims from the Ottoman community, persisted after the armistice. Consistent with the identification of the Ottoman political community with Muslims in the preceding years, the Erzurum resolutions portrayed the eastern provinces as inhabited by a predominantly Muslim population "like all other districts that remained within our boundaries at the signing of the armistice" (Article 6). It characterized the Muslim elements in the region as true brothers who possess a sentiment of sacrifice with respect to one another and are respectful of each other's ethnic/cultural/racial and social circumstances (Article 1). The strong emphasis on the concept of popular/national will (*milli irade*) in the Erzurum documents became emblematic of the discourse of the resistance. The retrospective appraisal that the Erzurum Congress "reformulated the Kemalist drive towards a specifically Turkish nation-state," however, is not borne out by its agenda or discourse, which were as inclusive of Muslim groups as they were exclusive of non-Muslims.[51]

The tenor of the Erzurum Congress resolutions as they pertained to Christian elements contrasted with the inclusive aura of the Syrian Congress in Damascus. Interconfessional differences in Greater Syria, particularly in Lebanon, came into sharper relief at the war's end owing to Allied dispensation for the political preferences of non-Muslim groups, especially France's guardianship of the Maronite community. While the Syrian Christians were not alone in having reservations about the political ascendance of Faysal in Damascus as an outsider, they also had reason to be circumspect about his leadership as a scion of the religiously conservative Hashemite family. Therefore, from the very days he arrived in Damascus, Faysal deliberately reached out to the Christian communities with an inclusionary discourse.[52] Faysal's inclusion of Christians in his cabinet and in the Syrian Congress broadened his base, affirmed his Syrianist credentials after the Peace Conference thrust aside broader Arab independence, and garnered him legitimacy in his transactions and negotiations with the British and French authorities.

At the same time, successive British and French occupation of Syria and popular perceptions of their favor for non-Muslims reinforced Muslim communal identification and allegiances. The programmatic emphasis on Muslim commonality would reverberate in the inter-communal discourse and dynamics within the Anatolia-Syria convergence zone. The Islamic rhetoric of anti-colonial mobilization in Anatolia resonated in Syria and buttressed religious solidarity in the broader region. These religious bonds fortified time-honored imperial connections in social and economic life and provided for a commonality of purpose and action, nurturing political agendas that reimagined the imperial polity and collectivity in the face of postwar realities.

THE SPECTER OF ANATOLIAN-SYRIAN COLLABORATION RISES

In the summer of 1919, reports alleging initiatives for cooperation between leadership cadres in Syria and Anatolia circulated in the councils of European governments. Based on documents of disputed authenticity, these reports alleged an agreement between Faysal and Mustafa Kemal as early as June 1919 toward the creation of a federation modeled on the Austro-Hungarian Dual Monarchy, in which Sharif Husayn would obtain a unitary Arab state and declare his allegiance to the Sultan-caliph. Arthur Balfour, in Paris for the peace talks, transmitted to London in August "a copy of an alleged Treaty between the Emir Feisal and Mustapha Kemal communicated confidentially by Boghos Nubar Pasha," who lobbied at the Paris Peace conference for the redemption of an Armenian state in Anatolia.[53] The document may have been forged to reanimate sagging British military commitment to the Middle East and to plant mistrust among the British against Faysal and the Ottoman government just before Ferid Pasha's representation before the Council of Ten and during the King-Crane inquiry commission's visit in Syria. It was drafted in French with spelling errors and titled: "Secret Treaty between the Turkish and Arab Governments signed by Emir Fayçal et Moustafa Kemal, June 16, 1919, in Aleppo." Kemal was in Amasya on this date, far north of

Aleppo. The reports mention former district governor (*mutasarrıf*) of Karak (Transjordan) as the intermediary.

The alleged agreement noted the regret of the two parties, "the Turkish nation and the noble Arab nation," about the "division that exists at this point within the Muslim world and pledged "mutual assistance by unifying forces for the defense of religion and country (*Patrie*)" (Article 1). It called for a holy war in the event of the partition of Iraq, Palestine, Syria, and Asia Minor (Article 2). The Sharif would organize military units similar to those in Anatolia and tribal forces by agreement with shaykhs, which would be ready to participate in the holy war when called (Article 6). Neither party could accept the partitioning or occupation of "the Turkish Empire and Arabia" (Article 3). The agreement further stipulated the recognition by the Ottoman government of the formation of an Arab government under Sharif Husayn, which would include Greater Syria, Iraq, and Arabia, but would be connected to the Ottoman Empire and remain loyal to the caliphate (Article 4).

There are reasons to suspect that this document may have been forged or falsified.[54] It is unlikely that Mustafa Kemal would have been in a position to negotiate such an accord as early as June 1919, when he was just joining the resistance. On the other hand, Faysal's representatives may have contacted Kemal as an official of the Ottoman government, since he had not yet declared a break with Istanbul. Other reports suggest that Faysal had indirect communication with Sultan Vahideddin in July 1919 with the intermediacy of the same Esad Bey.[55] The Hashemite family and those around them were familiar with Mustafa Kemal as a commander in the Syrian fronts during the Great War and would have regarded him as an authoritative negotiating partner or intermediary. At a time when the Franco-British scramble for hegemony seemed to dim the prospects toward independence and the grand vizier was making a pitch at the Peace Conference for an Ottoman confederation, it is probable that Faysal would send out feelers to Ottoman officials with an eye to redefine his relationship with the imperial government and secure autonomy.

While tampering, accidents of transmission, and infelicities of translation should be taken into consideration in too close a parsing of the document, the reports of an agreement tapped into political sentiments existing in the region and would reverberate for months. Mustafa Kemal's stature within the movement rose in the second half of 1919, making the reports more alarming for the Allies. As late as December, French intelligence reported that "Arab and Turkish agents were seeking to create a xenophobic pan-Islamic movement."[56]

Subsequent contacts akin to the alleged June 1919 agreement are well substantiated, as will be shown in chapter 4. Because of the strong possibility that the scheme put forth in the document would have resonated with segments of the Syrian and Anatolian peoples, the Foreign Office paid keen attention to it, doubts about the authenticity of the agreement notwithstanding, and the King-Crane Commission took it under consideration in its work.[57]

The fate of the Faysal government was mired in Anglo-French frictions and the Paris peace talks, where Faysal in vain strove to take a more active role than he was afforded. Britain's will to prop up Faysal to gain influence in Syria against France's resolve to prevent it weakened during the summer of 1919, as had been foreshadowed by London's withdrawal from the commission of inquiry sanctioned by the peace conference in the spring (and constituted as the King-Crane commission) to travel to Syria. Short of independence, which seemed elusive at the conference, many Syrians favored a tutelary relationship with the United States, and failing that, Britain. London, however, reached an understanding with France to allow French authorities a free hand in Syria in return for French consent to British control of Palestine. Despite divisions about the future political status of Greater Syria among the many groups in the region, and within the Syrian Congress itself, the congress reached an agreement on demands to be communicated to the King-Crane Commission (Damascus Program). The manifesto called for the unity of Greater Syria, rejected French control, and left an opening for British mandatory control over the entirety of the occupied areas, thus opposing the Zionist program and a separate mandate for Palestine.[58]

The French threat to Syria and the British attempts to consolidate their rule between the upper reaches of the Euphrates and Tigris and to extend occupation farther north threw the entire region into a renewed colonial scramble and activated resistance on the ground and possibilities of cooperative action. As the country that bore the brunt of the Entente's Syrian and Mesopotamian operations during the war, Britain staked out a claim for Mosul, which Sykes-Picot had placed within the French sphere of indirect control. The British government sought to consolidate its hold on Iraq by backing a tutelary Arab government that would extend its influence into the disputed Mosul region and northward up to Diyarbekir.[59] The effort to consolidate a British hold on northern Mesopotamia, inhabited by a Kurdish majority, necessitated the forging of a more deliberate Kurdish policy. As a second congress convened in September 1919 in the east-central Anatolian town of Sivas under Mustafa Kemal's leadership with the purpose of broadening the scope of the resistance movement, the British authorities aimed at creating a cleavage between the consolidating anti-colonial resistance in the region and Kurdish leaders and groups.

THE SIVAS CONGRESS: THE COORDINATION OF THE ANATOLIAN MOVEMENT

As a landmark in the systematization of the resistance and an important juncture in Mustafa Kemal's career by virtue of confirming his leadership of the "congress movement," the Sivas Congress has come to be regarded retrospectively as a constitutive turning point in the execution of the Turkish national program, which is self-same with the personal history of the leader. An assessment of the congress in its immediate historical context lays bare ambiguities, even contradictions, which militate against this deterministic nation-centric conception and bring to light indeterminacies that prevailed at the time. Though Mustafa Kemal and his associates envisaged the Sivas Congress as a manifestation of the expansion and coordination of the resistance movement, fewer than forty delegates attended it. Nevertheless, an organizational structure to spearhead the resistance emerged out of the conference.

The Sivas Congress resolved the unification of all defense-of-rights groups under an overarching committee, the Anatolia and Rumelia Defense of Rights Society (*Anadolu ve Rumeli Müdafaa-ı Hukuk Cemiyeti*). Mustafa Kemal led its Representative Council (*Heyet-i Temsiliye*). Each provincial defense-of-rights committee was designated as a "central" committee not bound by the decisions of the Representative Council, which ensured the continued primacy of local initiative and prerogatives. The Sivas declaration, issued on September 11, 1919, incorporated some of the resolutions of the previous congress in Erzurum and echoed the Wilsonian principles in asserting the supremacy of the national/popular will. It declared the congress's main purpose as the continued existence of the Muslim caliphate and Ottoman sultanate (Article 2).[60] Its first article said: "The areas that remained within our boundaries at the time of the conclusion of the armistice with the Entente states on October 30, 1918, and inhabited at all points by an overwhelming Muslim majority united by religion, race, and origin cannot be separated from the Ottoman community in any manner." Article 9 indicated the constituency of the Anatolia and Rumelia Defense of Rights Society (ARDRS) as "all Muslim elements filled with mutual respect and sentiment of sacrifice towards one another" and proclaimed "all Muslim patriots" as natural members of the society (Article 4).

As in the Erzurum resolutions, Sivas foregrounded the rights of the Ottoman Muslim majority and spelled out the main objectives of the movement as resisting foreign encroachments and Armenian and Greek political projects. Article 4 acknowledged the protection of equal rights of non-Muslim elements ("with whom we have for long lived in the same country/fatherland"), while it rejected the bestowal of any special privileges that would violate "our political sovereignty or societal harmony." During the very days when the congress met in September, General Harbord was touring eastern Anatolia at the head of the second of the American fact-finding commissions in the Middle East ("American Military Mission to Armenia.") Harbord's charge was to appraise the feasibility of an Armenia mandate in Anatolia, which the Peace Conference was considering entrusting to the United States. Several days after the conclusion of the congress, Mustafa Kemal and other officials met with General Harbord in Sivas. They impressed on the general the prowess of their movement and convinced him that an Armenia mandate was impracticable.[61]

The elevation of Muslim identity projected a semblance of unity but did not address engrained sociopolitical divisions within the Ottoman society. In Anatolia, the stance of top provincial civil officials, large landlords, men of religion, and other communal leaders with respect to the developing duality in the power structure was an indicator of the level of provincial support for the resistance, particularly in the absence of a mediating representative body following the suspension of parliament in December 1918. Political entrepreneurs strengthened their power bases across diverse social groups. Some formed militias with appeals to local identity, which at times coincided with ethnic identity (e.g., Kurdish, Albanian, Circassian). These loci of provincial power could be coopted by the resistance, the Istanbul government, or the Allied powers.[62] The Damad Ferid government provoked Kurdish groups in the region against the organizational activity of the resistance. The loyalist governor of the neighboring Mamuret-ül-Aziz Province Ali Galib mobilized members of the Kurdish tribal family Bedirhan in an effort to sabotage the Sivas meeting and set afoot a broader rebellion. The British officer Major E. W. C. Noel, who had been forging alliances in and around upper Mesopotamia since April, helped incite the ultimately unsuccessful uprising against the Sivas "rebels."[63]

The Sivas resolutions foregrounded the reference to "our borders" as the boundaries that obtained on October 30, 1918 (Article 6). The imagining of a border from fluid and contested cease-fire positions offered flexibility to geopolitical claims. The authoritative reaffirmation of the movement's vision in January 1920, as will be discussed in chapter 4, explicitly called for the determination of the political will of the people inhabiting territories occupied before the armistice based on their free choice. The resistance leaders subscribed to the view that the letter and the spirit of Mudros as an interim agreement should be upheld until the negotiation of a peace treaty. They adhered to a strategy of identifying, developing, and defending the movement's program in accordance with the requisites of mutually agreed formal accords.

The implication of the congress resolutions for large numbers of Arab Muslim Ottomans inhabiting areas under European occupation remained ambivalent and subject to the vagaries of shifting political, diplomatic, and military circumstances. The spotty provincial representation at the congress did not include delegates from the areas under Allied occupation, including the districts extending from Mersin to Urfa and Mosul that had come to be occupied by Britain and/or France after the armistice. The network of defense-of-rights organizations, now under the aegis of ARDRS, did not extend to the south of the Tauruses, even though there were pockets of resistance to British and French occupation in these areas, and more would be formed with linkages to Sivas, and later, Ankara.

Just as Faysal received the King-Crane Commission in June–July 1919 with the trappings of a popular representative government embodied in the Syrian Congress, Mustafa Kemal and his associates met with General Harbord as the Representative Council anointed by the Sivas Congress. The Anatolians and the Syrians aimed at swaying the Allied delegates against tutelary arrangements. Both the Syrian Congress and the ARDRS hoped to prevail in the idiom of self-determination and popular will. In the face of the French resolve to assert control in Syria and southeastern Anatolia with Britain's acquiescence, the Syrians and the Anatolians confronted a common adversary in France. As the Anatolian resistance gained greater political unity after the congresses, the leadership of the ARDRS sought to expand the organization's influence, including to Syria. The earliest armed resistance against British and French occupation took place to the south of the Tauruses in southeastern Anatolia, staged by local militias, before the political unification of the defense groups accomplished military coordination. Even in the later stages of the Anatolian movement, when a regular army began to be formed under a central command, the war against the Greek armies in western Anatolia tied up these forces. The militias in southeastern Anatolia as well as in northern Syria and Iraq were largely left to their own devices during the postwar half decade.

THE FRENCH THREAT AND COLLABORATION IN THE ANATOLIA-SYRIA FRONTIER

In the quest to restore political order in the region, the leadership of the Anatolian movement emerged as viable interlocutors for Syrian and Iraqi popular groups. In the fall of 1919, diplomatic developments outside the control of the Middle Eastern actors transformed the regional political and military dynamics. First, the threat of French invasion and subsequently French occupation galvanized the scattered resistance groups and enhanced the opportunities for cooperation. Second, the American commitment to the postwar settlement started to erode unexpectedly. In September 1919, Britain and France had reached an agreement about their respective domains of control in the Middle East, which, with some modifications, followed the script of the Sykes-Picot Treaty. Britain pledged to withdraw its forces from Syria and southeastern Anatolia in favor of France. The agreement was a harbinger of European colonial control in the very spheres of influence agreed upon during the war.

Already hamstrung by President Wilson's illness, the moderating influence of the United States frittered away when in November the Senate rejected US membership in the League of Nations. The American divestment from the peace process complicated and opened the way for the implementation of French and British colonial designs in the form of mandates. The King-Crane Commission had concluded unequivocally that in Syria, with the exception of Mt. Lebanon and environs populated by Catholic Maronites, there was no support for French presence.[64] The broader shift in American foreign policy doomed the commission report to be ignored and jeopardized the prospects for self-rule in Syria. Britain and France would solidify their military presence to institute the regimes of domination they negotiated at the Peace Conference.

The French replacement of British forces in November 1919 set in motion militia activity that the British occupation, even where it violated the ceasefire agreement, had not. Unencumbered by strong local opposition, except from friendly Christian communities in coastal Syria, France sought to fulfill the colonial war aims it had long pursued. While many Arabs, including the

Faysal government, rejected French presumptive rights deriving from wartime agreements between the Entente states as illegitimate and a violation of self-determination, they had been prepared to cooperate with Britain in the determination of the political status of the Arab provinces. British armies had fought the Ottoman forces during the war, and after their victories they could profess right of conquest. The transition from British to French control, however, signified that Britain was honoring its commitments to France at the expense of those to the Hashemites and their Syrian followers. Hence, Faysal's reliance on British cooperation and goodwill waned as Britain extricated itself from Syria.

The agitation that prospective French occupation set afoot provided fertile ground for reconfiguring the resistance in the broader region. In October 1919, British reports indicated that Faysal's defense minister, Yusuf al-'Azma, was expected to arrive in Istanbul along with the former Hawran governor Jamal Nasser to engage in negotiations with the Ottoman government.[65] Yet the sultan's government did not have the ability or the will to shape the circumstances on the ground in its distant provinces, nor did it have freedom of action in Allied-controlled Istanbul. In contrast, the regional resistance groups, either cut off from or only tenuously connected to Istanbul or Damascus, sought ways of resisting further European penetration and colonial schemes.

In October 1919, Mustafa Kemal solicited reports from officers who held regional command of vestigial Ottoman troops in the Anatolian provinces in an effort that aimed at assessing military capacities but also at winning the commanders' allegiances. The commander of the independent Thirteenth Army Corps in Diyarbekir, Colonel Ahmad Jawdat, an Iraqi Arab officer and the most proximate Ottoman military authority to Syria, Iraq, and the occupied southeastern Anatolian towns of Maraş, Ayntab, and Urfa, commented on prevailing political attitudes in his region. Professing insight into the Arabs' inherent national/collective attributes (*tabayi-i kavmiye*) and political attitudes, Jawdat deemed it unlikely that "all parts of Arabia" could form a single government under Sharif Husayn. He expressed his conviction that a great majority of Arabs would opt to preserve their connection with the Ottoman government to the extent they are granted equality and freedoms. He pointed out the mobilization in Syria against occupation and attested to opposition to mandatory schemes. It would be possible for the peoples of Iraq, Syria, Hijaz, and the Arabian Peninsula, he maintained, to form separate Arab states with bonds to the caliphate as a form of confederation like the

United States. Jawdat proposed an emblem that would represent this union: a group of crescents on the Ottoman flag depicting the number of states in this arrangement, modeled after the stars on the American flag.[66]

Against the background of the Peace Conference's failure to deliver Arab self-determination and growing resentment of possible imposition of European mandates, the Allies followed the developments in Syria anxiously. The French government received reports about a "very distinct Turco-Arab rapprochement" and rumors of a general uprising as Britain relinquished OETA-East.[67] According to intelligence that reached London in November, "During the past three weeks general situation in Syria has undergone a slight change, as a result of [British] evacuation [in favor of France] which has now commenced, of increasing uncertainty regarding eventual settlement, and an active undisguised propaganda by Turks."[68] The report mentioned that the chief of the General Staff of Faysal's army, Yasin al-Hashimi, was among those communicating, indeed "conniving," with Mustafa Kemal.[69] As the British forces evacuated Syria, and French troops occupied the coastal regions in November 1919, François Georges-Picot, now France's high commissioner in Syria based in Beirut, referred to a document that he believed was "the first document that establishes in a precise way the existence of relations, indeed of a treaty, between the Turkish nationalists and Arab partisans of an absolute independence."[70] General Allenby claimed Yasin's actions, in particular his relations with Mustafa Kemal, were a danger to Allied troops, and he arrested him, eliciting protestations from Faysal.[71] It was apparent that the replacement of British occupation forces by those of France accompanied a climate of opinion in Syria that was favorable to the Anatolian movement.[72] Prime Minister Lloyd George was obliged to announce in London on November 8 that there was agreement in the peace conference that "Turkish rule" should end in the Arab provinces.[73] It was an assurance that hardly provided comfort to the Syrians, with French forces poised to occupy all of Syria.

The Anatolian movement lacked the military capability to respond to French occupation expanding from Adana to southeastern Anatolia and northern Syria upon British evacuation of this region. At the end of 1919, a political structure to direct the resistance had emerged, but only fragments of trained units existed, and a general mobilization to constitute a regular army was still a distant prospect. The ARDRS Representative Council rendered political support to the popular resistance in the occupied areas. As its president, for instance, Mustafa Kemal protested the French actions in Adana, captured after the armistice, particularly the hoisting of French flags in public places, their distribution to the population, and penalties exacted from those who did not properly display them. In doing so, he spoke in the name of "Ottoman national unity."[74]

A former Ottoman officer and director of the police in Aleppo, Lieutenant Colonel Shakir Ni'mat al-Sha'bani, led the logistical contacts in southeastern Anatolia and northern Syria. He may have been responsible for the dissemination of propaganda circulars obtained by the British in October calling for reconciliation "between the sons of one religion" and a petition to "point our arms towards the traitors who wish to tear up Islam." The leaflets attributed to Mustafa Kemal urged for cooperation "against treacherous parties who want to divide our country" and heralded that his *mujahids* (fighters for the faith) would soon join their Arab brothers against the enemy.[75] Ni'mat sought cooperation between the groups he led in Aleppo and the Anatolian movement. He approached Mustafa Kemal in December and offered to take the command of forces fighting the French take-over of Maraş, Ayntab, and Kilis. Reporting anti-French organizational activity in Aleppo, he argued that the forces in Aleppo could join the Anatolian resistance, were the French to be held back. Ni'mat favored the federative framework, in which Syria would have its independence but remain connected to the Ottoman sultanate.[76]

French intelligence observed in the fall of 1919 "an unusually numerous presence of Turks in Aleppo," referring to the envoys and agents from the north.[77] American sources reported that "Kemalist propaganda, which aims at a religious war, extends throughout the region."[78] The religious exhortations, according to Colonel Meinertzhagen, were strengthening anti-European and pan-Islamic feeling in all of Greater Syria.[79] A pan-Islamic society known as *al-Jam'iya al-Islamiya* (or *Islam Cemiyeti*), which had branches not only in Anatolia but also in other Muslim countries, carried out propaganda touting restored unity and broader collaboration with other Muslim peoples.[80]

The ties between resistance forces in the broader region were strengthened by the idiom of a religious struggle against the common European adversary. The political culture of the empire still carried the deep imprint of Islam. Islamist intellectual activity, which had become ever more diverse and accessible in the wake of the Young Turk Revolution of 1908, continued in the years after World War I. Islamist intellectuals published essays in popular Islamic journals like *Sebilürreşad*, the best known and most durable among them.[81] Around the time Mustafa Kemal landed in Samsun to join the Anatolian resistance, the journal relocated to neighboring Kastamonu on the shores of the Black Sea in order to escape censorship in the capital. The intellectual and celebrated poet of modernist Islamic convictions, Mehmed Akif, was *Sebilürreşad*'s leading light. In March 1921, the Ankara government would adopt one of Akif's poems as the Independence March—a poem that is suffused with Islamic exhortations ("independence is the right of my millet who worships God") and is distinctly anti-West in its thrust ("what you call civilization is a one-toothed monster"). The stark secularist programs of Turkish Republican governments in the 1920s and 1930s have obscured the religious aura of the anti-colonial movement and dismissed the Islamic discourse and symbols espoused by the resistance as cynical or opportunistic exploitation of religion, yet Akif's march remained as Turkey's national anthem.[82]

National histories subsume local movements and level their contingent circumstances, objectives, and ideological underpinnings within hegemonic narratives. Even as they celebrate local sacrifice and heroism, they cast local movements as belonging to an unequivocally nationalist vision or program. These movements may be interpreted as "Turkish nationalist," "Arab nationalist," "Syrian nationalist," or "Ottomanist," but it has been anathema to national(ist) history to acknowledge the commonalities and synergies with cognate resistance movements in neighboring areas that subsequently fell outside the borders of the nation-state, indeed came to belong to the entity that the nation-state has in time constructed as its "other."[83] Both in Anatolia and Syria local initiative and organization was paramount in the resistance against foreign encroachment. The movements' organizational structure, ideological thrust, and commonality of objectives call into question tidy compartmentalization. There is merit in parsing the resistance movements with circumspection about rigid ideological and identitarian categories.

The contacts between the occupied territories and the rump empire occurred along different axes. Faysal strove to secure a semblance of independence for Syria after backroom diplomacy's partitioning schemes jettisoned the Hashemite objective of unifying the Arab provinces under one rule. The Paris Peace Conference instead deliberated on setting up mandates in Ottoman territories, including Syria, in the same breath as tutelage arrangements for German colonies in Africa. The claims over Syria that France advanced resolutely at the Peace Conference posed real peril for Faysal's objectives. He could not assuredly repudiate restoring links to the Ottoman state or ignore the resistance that was galvanizing in Anatolia. When he went back to Europe in September 1919, he rebuked British Prime Minister Lloyd George for the "return to the unjust policy of colonialism" and declared that he did not go to war against the caliph to see the Arab country divided.[84]

Motivated by the threat of colonial subjugation, and increasingly emboldened by the successes of local resistance movements in southeastern Anatolia, popular groups in northern Syria collaborated in joint action. These forces rallied around such figures as Ibrahim Hananu, who personified the multiple identities and shifting political allegiances typical of the members of the late Ottoman bureaucratic elites and provincial notability. Hananu, a native of a rural town to the west of Aleppo, was the son of a notable family of Kurdish origin. He received his higher education in the Mülkiye (School of Civil Administration) in Istanbul and taught in the Harbiye (Military Academy). Hananu's insistence on armed resistance against French occupation of Syria led to a fallout with Faysal. He acted independently of the Sharifian government as the head of a militia and made common cause with similar local resistance groups that were mobilizing to repulse French occupation in southeastern Anatolia.[85]

Allied with Hananu, but independent in his activities, was the younger Saleh al-ʿAli. Al-ʿAli led a contingent of soldiers and engaged in guerrilla activity against the French forces. Based closer to the coast to the southwest of Aleppo in the Latakia mountains, his links with the Faysal administration were tenuous. Al-ʿAli's movement aimed at keeping the French out of the predominantly Alawite region.[86] To Latakia's north in the Antioch area, Subhi Barakat, who was loyal to Sharif Husayn, and, like Hananu, was a member of the Syrian Congress, led an autonomous resistance movement.[87] He cooperated with Hananu and al-ʿAli, until the French completed Syria's occupation in 1920.[88]

Even when local forces and societies touted their connections to the "Arab government," they acted with considerable independence as the fortunes of the Faysal government oscillated. Michael Provence suggests that Yasin al-Hashimi "convened a war council, probably against the wishes of Faysal and appointed [Ramadan] Shallash military governor of the district of Raqa and the Euphrates."[89] In cooperation with Ibrahim Hananu, Shallash defeated the British forces in occupation of Dayr al-Zur on the Euphrates at the confluence of the re-delineated spheres of control between Britain and France. When the "Arab government command" in Dayr al-Zur informed the governor of Mardin that it had ousted the British from the region and that "Mosul could be liberated with enough money and soldiers," the governor asked the Ministry of the Interior in Istanbul about the appropriate response. The advice was that assistance would not be possible due to the dire circumstances, but that "all Ottoman hearts along with the world of Islam" hoped for the al-Zur command's success.[90]

As the contours of postwar settlement in Europe crystallized in 1919, there was relative stasis in the Middle Eastern status quo. The armistice agreements that Germany, Austria-Hungary, and Bulgaria signed in October and November 1918 initiated the peace talks toward a territorial settlement. In the Middle East, British and French transgressions struck at the foundations of the Mudros agreement as a framework for a peace accord. The failure to follow up the armistice with a timely peace agreement allowed the Anatolian resistance, galvanized by the threats that Allied noncompliance posed, to forge a political program rooted in the legitimacy and basic premises of the armistice agreement. In the coming year, the Damascus government too would recalibrate its stance in the quest to attain independence, confronted with British and French infringement of agreements the Hashemite leadership had arrived at with British authorities. Local groups put up resistance to French occupation in the southeastern Anatolian-Syrian frontier with only tenuous links with the Damascus government and ARDRS, motivated by Islamic solidarity, and at times in the name of the Sultan-Caliph. In Iraq, the single-handed British military control similarly generated resistance. The sporadic and local anti-colonial resistance of the first year of armistice would subsequently expand to revolts and warfare. The military and human losses of the war, the bankruptcy of the wartime CUP government, large-scale foreign occupation, and crises of authority and legitimacy throughout the Ottoman domains impaired the social, political, and administrative structures of empire but did not put an end to them.

FOUR

State Transformations

ANATOLIAN MOVEMENT AND
THE FERTILE CRESCENT,
1920–1922

THE PARIS PEACE CONFERENCE concluded on January 21, 1920, one year after it first convened. It closed following the German ratification of the Versailles Treaty and the launching of the League of Nations (January 10), without having devised a settlement with the Ottoman government. The US Congress's failure to ratify American membership in the League of Nations, the core institution of the new world order championed by President Wilson, confirmed American disengagement and removed Washington's disciplining influence and its moral authority, exposing Britain's and France's neocolonial designs and mutual rivalries in the Middle East. The two powers had to reckon with the strengthening of the anti-colonial resistance in the occupied Ottoman territories and the growing assertion of power and authority by ascendant actors and movements, most significantly in Anatolia.

The goals, strategies, and ideological disposition of emergent political structures and local actors in the Ottoman realm responded to the contingencies of international relations dominated by the war's victors and to the failure to achieve a collective settlement for the Ottoman Empire. During 1920 and 1921, bilateral interactions increasingly shaped the transformations in the military, political, and ideological fields in the region. Against the backdrop of continued armed conflict, all actors invoked, reinterpreted, and attempted to render usable the norms that carried the day at the Great War's end as the basis of an evolving regional and international order. Imperial institutions remained resilient, albeit beset by crisis and the contestation of traditional Ottoman authority, and despite diplomatic agreements that aimed at reducing the empire to an unsustainable core

THE THIRD CONSTITUTIONAL PERIOD

The Ottoman Empire went to parliamentary elections at the end of 1919, some six months after the Allies agreed on treaty terms with Germany (June 28) and three months after the conclusion of the Austrian settlement with the Treaty of Saint-Germain (September 10). Bulgaria signed a treaty on November 27, at Neuilly-sur-Seine, when elections for the legislature were in progress in the Ottoman Empire, except in its occupied territories. The Ottomans went to the polls at the same time as Italy and France did in a semblance of returning to postwar political stability.[1] The British commissioner in Istanbul, Admiral Calthorpe, reported to Foreign Secretary George Curzon as early as July 1919 about strong public opinion in favor of elections and the opening of parliament. Curzon deemed this undesirable on the grounds that elections might revive the Committee of Union and Progress (CUP). Indeed, Britain had implicated Grand Vizier Tevfik Pasha for harboring Unionists and successfully pressured for the suspension of parliament the previous December. Yet Calthorpe opined that obstructing the elections would violate both the Wilsonian principles and the Ottoman constitution. Writing during the days of the Erzurum Congress, he commented with prescience that barring the parliament might lead to its being convened in the interior of Anatolia. He warned of an independent, possibly "fanatical," and anti-Europe administration that would reject Istanbul's authority.[2] In October 1919, though, a new government led by Ali Rıza Pasha replaced the Ferid Pasha cabinet. Concrete plans to hold elections followed from talks that Mustafa Kemal and other leaders of the Anatolian movement held with the ministers of the Ali Rıza Pasha government, which signified a convergence of purpose between the Ottoman government and the Anatolian movement.

In his authoritative account of the governmental structure and political dynamics in Istanbul during the years of the armistice, Sina Akşin characterized the period beginning with the grand vizierate of Ali Rıza Pasha as the "Last Constitutional Period," a designation that privileges a retrospective vantage, but also encapsulates the endurance of the Ottoman political order into the postwar period.[3] If the 1877–78 parliament was the First Constitutional Period of the Ottoman Empire, and the Young Turk Revolution in 1908 ushered in the Second Constitutional Period, new parliamentary elections at the end of 1919 heralded a third constitutional period, following the one-year post-armistice interlude, which Akşin dubs in his schema as the "Return to Absolutism." The cumulative effect of ruptures caused by defeat in war, territorial losses, collapse of wartime government, and the closure of parliament throughout 1919 signified a sufficiently sharp break that warrants this description.

The convening of the parliament entailed inherent difficulties and risks. Elections could not be held in areas occupied by foreign armies. A parliament in which several provinces would not have representation would have implied a tacit admission of the separation of large pieces of the empire. Representatives from some of the occupied provinces who happened to be in residence elsewhere, including former deputies from the 1914 parliament, stood as candidates and obtained seats. While the Aegean districts under Greek occupation and southern districts occupied subsequent to the ceasefire (such as Adana, Maraş, and Ayntab) received representation, the districts that were under occupation at the time of the Mudros agreement remained outside the scope of the elections.[4]

The composition of the new parliament reflected the unresolved geopolitical status of the empire and the growing strength of the resistance movement in Anatolia. The 1919 elections, held in accordance with the existing electoral law, brought 172 deputies to parliament, 73 fewer than in 1914.[5] The influence of ARDRS, wielded by its Representative Council, was evident in the campaign. The revived Liberty and Entente Party, the principal rival of the CUP before 1914 and now in opposition to the ARDRS slates, withdrew from the ballot in protest, ensuring a sweep of the ARDRS-endorsed candidates. For the first time, the Ottoman parliament poignantly included no Christian deputies. Large sections of the Christian population had perished or left the confines of the rump empire, but the absence of non-Muslims was not warranted based on population attrition alone.[6] The new parliament embodied the supremacy of Muslims in the political community.

In the run-up to the elections, toward the end of 1919, Mustafa Kemal and his associates relocated from Sivas to the more central Ankara. The capital, Istanbul, was under Allied supervision, and the work of the new assembly might have been obstructed directly or by way of Allied pressure on the sultan, as had been the case a year earlier. On the other hand, a parliament in session in the capital representing the popular will would strengthen forces favoring independence as a testament to the persistence of the state institutions and established political processes. In the end, there was agreement that parliament would continue to function in the imperial capital. Mustafa Kemal had been elected deputy, but fearing reprisals for his insubordination, would not go to Istanbul to take his seat.

A BLUEPRINT FOR LIBERATION

Upon his arrival in Ankara at the end of December, Kemal utilized the opportunity of a gathering with journalists to elaborate on and bring clarity to the resolutions and aims of the congresses held in the previous months.[7] He referred to a boundary in the Anatolia-Syria-Iraq frontier, mentioned but not delineated in the congress resolutions, as the line that extended "from the south of the Gulf of Alexandretta to Antioch, passes between the Qatma and Aleppo train stations to reach the Euphrates to the south of the Jarablus Bridge, and follows the Euphrates [south] to [include] Dayr al-Zur before it extends east to include Mosul, Kirkuk, and Sulaymaniya."[8] (See Map 4.) Mustafa Kemal's objective in this formulation was to seek the independence of territories south of the Tauruses including Alexandretta, which the Allies had not occupied by October 31, 1918, down to the immediate north of Aleppo town, where Ottoman and Allied forces had disengaged. He was also placing claims to Dayr al-Zur, deep into the Euphrates basin, and the Syrian-Iraqi borderlands, where the population was Kurdish or Arabic speaking. The chiefs of important Arab tribal groups in the broader region, Mash'al of the Shammar confederation and Muhammad and 'Ali Sultan of the Jubur tribe, had affirmed their imperial allegiances.[9] The territorial claims extended to northern Iraq and a large swath of Kurdish-populated land to the west of the border with Iran. Kemal insisted on the inseparability of the delineated territories from the "Ottoman community."[10] In the absence of formally negotiated borders, he thus broached a geopolitical claim premised upon an interpretation of the Mudros terms.

Kemal proceeded to reconcile Wilson's Twelfth Point with the Mudros agreement allowing himself an interpretation of the ambiguities of both texts. He subscribed to a broad appraisal of the "Turkish portion," alluded to but not specified in the Twelfth Point ("The Turkish portion of the present Ottoman Empire should be assured a secure sovereignty.") He equated this territory with the areas within the boundaries of the Armistice agreement, described in the congress declarations as areas "within our boundaries inhabited by an overwhelming Muslim majority" at the time of the signing of the cease-fire. He identified this majority, an integral part of the Ottoman community, as Turkish-Kurdish. Cognizant of Hashemite claims, partially underwritten by Britain, that the area extending to the Tauruses in the north was within the Arab sphere, Mustafa Kemal opined that Turks had inhabited this region for a millennium. He misrepresented Ferid Pasha's initial argument in Paris by

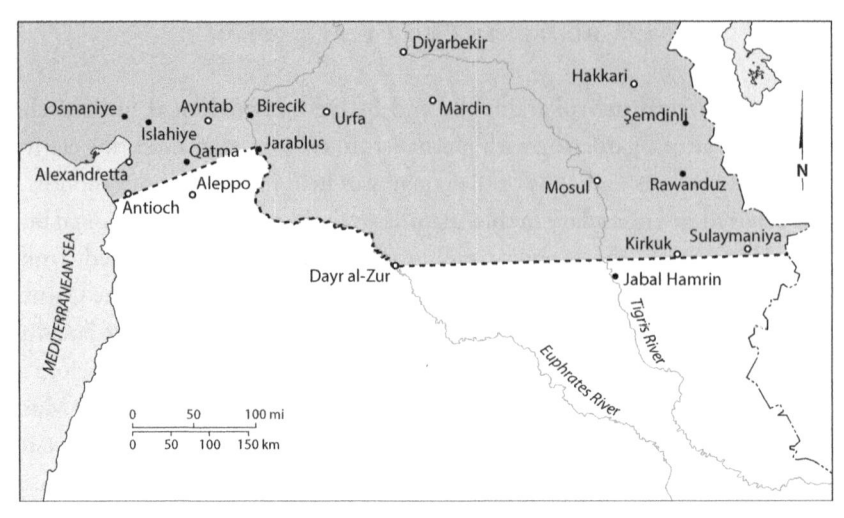

MAP 4. Contours of territory demarcated for defense by the Anatolian movement (December 1919). Cartography by Bill Nelson

alleging that the grand vizier construed the Tauruses as a boundary "because he thinks the language spoken to the south of the Tauruses is Arabic."[11]

In fact, the position Mustafa Kemal laid out was consistent with Ferid Pasha's final appeal to the Council of Ten, which articulated a similar dividing line within a confederative geopolitical framework. Kemal paid tribute to independence movements in other "territories of Islam," specifically citing Iraq, Syria, and Yemen, and added that their success would be a huge boon for the world of Islam. He described these areas lying to the south of the delineated border as inhabited by brethren, co-religionists, and longtime compatriots. The speech, published in newspapers supportive of the movement, was directed as much to a foreign audience as to the notables and literati in Ankara. On the eve of the opening of parliament in Istanbul under the watchful eyes of the Allied powers, Kemal was careful to present a moderate position. He opined that the assistance of another state would be welcome in rebuilding the land and elevating its people, an anathema to his future stance. Touching on accusations he repudiated as baseless, he defended the treatment of the non-Muslims within the Ottoman community.

In those parts of Greater Syria and Mesopotamia that Mustafa Kemal did not explicitly place within the territorial objectives of the movement, he and his associates continued to observe the circumstances on the ground, the openings for bringing into being a broader anti-colonial movement, local demands for the restoration of Ottoman political authority, or opportunities for a federative arrangement that would reconstitute the imperial state. The speech in Ankara provided a template for independence under the prevailing military circumstances and negotiated accords. It posited the Mudros agreement as the basis, indeed a surrogate, of a territorial treaty. Kemal undergirded this agenda by invoking Wilson's principles and alluding to its Twelfth Point in his own reading.

As the continued pursuit of colonial aspirations stalled a settlement regarding the Ottoman Empire at the Paris Peace Conference, this very failure of international diplomacy energized the drive to resist foreign encroachments and the quest for self-determination, buoying the hopes of the Anatolian movement and the pro-independence public in general. Political rallies were held in Istanbul and spread to Anatolia, the largest on January 13 in the hippodrome in the capital's Sultanahmet district. The French replacement of British troops in the occupied territories triggered local political protestations followed by armed resistance. When the commander of occupation forces, General Querette, entered Maraş on January 6 with his fifteen hundred men, some five hundred residents signed a letter of protest. The letter proclaimed that the military occupation aroused great excitement in the heart of the Muslim millet and warned Querette against interfering with the local government or the security forces.[12] It denounced the attempt to cut off a sancak "ninety percent Muslim" from the 650-year-old Ottoman state as a violation of Wilson's Twelfth Point and the terms of the armistice.

THE NATIONAL PACT

The parliament convened on January 12, 1920. Because not all deputies had been able to arrive in the capital to take their seats, it immediately went on recess for ten days.[13] In its eleventh session on February 17, the parliament approved the *misak-ı milli* (National Pact), a program that asserted Ottoman economic and territorial rights and independence. Harkening back to the resolutions of the Erzurum and Sivas Congresses, the declaration foregrounded the indivisibility of the Ottoman state's territories, which it characterized as inhabited by Muslim majorities. The state's territorial extent would be contingent on the free decision of the populations of its parts inhabited by Arab majorities and under enemy occupation on October 30, 1918. Similarly, the misak stipulated the affirmation, by plebiscite, if necessary, of the reincorporation of the Caucasian districts into the Ottoman state and called for the free vote of the people of western Thrace (contested between Greece and Bulgaria since 1913) for the determination of the region's legal status. The declaration insisted on the security of Istanbul, the center of the Islamic caliphate and Ottoman sultanate and government. It vouched for minority rights on the principle of reciprocity for Muslim minority rights in the neighboring countries. Finally, the misak called for both economic and political independence.

The misak-ı milli stands in Turkish nationalist lore as the blueprint that guided the war of liberation from its very beginnings until independence was secured at the Treaty of Lausanne in 1923, and thus as the foundational charter of the new Turkey. Turkish national history later sanctified the evolving credo that was christened as the misak-ı milli and readily associated it with the nation-state. The word *milli*, and its noun form *millet*, assumed the meaning "national" in this sense only after various transformations over time. The retrospective certainties associated with the term stand in stark contrast to the ambiguities surrounding it at the time of the early articulations of the resistance's objectives and their reformulation in January 1920.

The foundational significance of the misak-ı milli in the Turkish national narrative calls for an examination of the genesis and conjunctural iterations of the text as well as the shifts in the semantic overtones of its vocabulary. The document was issued with the following preamble: "The members of the Ottoman Chamber of Deputies acknowledge and affirm that the independence of the state and the future of the *millet* can be assured by complete adherence to the following principles, which represent the maximum of sacrifice that can be made toward the attainment of a just and lasting peace, and that the continued existence of a stable Ottoman sultanate and society is impossible outside of the said fundamentals."[14] The declaration's paramount article was the first one that outlined boundaries. Indeed, Article 1 has become synonymous with the entire document in future discourse:

> Inasmuch as it is necessary that the destinies of the portions of the Ottoman state which are populated exclusively by an Arab majority, and which on the conclusion of the armistice of the 30th of October, 1918, were in the occupation of enemy forces, should be determined in accordance with the votes which shall be freely given by the inhabitants, the totality of those parts whether within or outside the said armistice-line, which are inhabited by an Ottoman Muslim majority, united in religion, culture and in aim, imbued with sentiments of mutual respect for each other and of sacrifice, and wholly

respectful of each other's racial and social rights and surrounding conditions, form a whole which does not admit of division for any reason in fact or by fiat.

The text of Article 1 has been rendered in multiple ways and interpreted, reinterpreted, and regularly misquoted to make it conform to suitable visions of history in the subsequent decades. The multivalence derives as much from the varying uses with which the document has been encumbered as from the ambiguities inherent in its various renditions. The purpose here will not be to trace the dogmatic and creative ways in which the National Pact has been utilized in Turkish Republican history, but rather to examine what the misak signified for the resistance movement in the immediate context of its issuance. This compels closer scrutiny of Article 1.

The Erzurum and Sivas resolutions as well as the National Pact stressed the indivisibility of the Ottoman domains that had remained free of Allied occupation at the time of the armistice. All three documents appropriated this realm for the Muslims, asserting the presence of a clear Muslim majority in every region. The plan of action for liberation expanded and became more explicit in the iterations of these fundamentals. Erzurum was primarily concerned with the eastern provinces and possible Greek and Armenian projects to carve out territories along the Black Sea and in the "six provinces" with Allied backing. Sivas underscored the commitment to the defense of sovereignty to the entirety of the post-Mudros rump empire. The National Pact also addressed the political status of the Arab-populated areas occupied before the armistice and affirmed them as an integral part of the Ottoman political community contingent on the free vote of the population.

The resolutions should be examined with consideration of meanings associated with the prevalent idiom at the time of their drafting and with attention to the valences that some of the vocabulary has acquired subsequently, as new meanings were anachronistically attributed to the texts' original rendering. The Erzurum document posits the people as united by religion and "race" (*dindaş ve ırkdaş*), and all three documents refer to "racial rights" (*hukuk-u ırkiye*). The Arabic loan word translated as "race" (ırk/عرق) and carrying the general meaning of "root" suggested in Ottoman parlance long-standing commonality and was utilized in references to descent, culture, and/or religion. In the late twenties and thirties, Turkish nationalism came to be deeply influenced in its formative construction by the European milieu of racialist thought and politics. The word *ırk* acquired the connotations of race prevalent in this chauvinistic milieu of a belabored myth of an essential and superior Turkish phenotypic group inhabiting Anatolia since ancient times. State propaganda peddled race as the ultimate essence of Turkish identity.[15] In this ideological setting, a misreading of the texts of the resistance movement flourished. This flawed assessment as well as "translation" into contemporary Turkish have denied the multiplicity of ethno-linguistic identities and obscured alternative sociopolitical imaginings of the Ottoman collectivity and polity in an era of ferment. Thus, "unity by race" has been read into the National Pact of 1920, and its promulgaters have been credited with a prescient race-based nationalist self-discovery congruent with a political project molded by military and diplomatic exigencies.

Alternate renderings of key phrases in the text have arisen as the original documents produced in longhand were copied, or transcribed from Arabic to Latin script, with modifications conveying different—and based on the circumstances—expedient meanings. For instance, the document describes the Ottoman-Muslim majority as united by religion, culture, and aim (*dinen, irfanen, ve emelen*). However, "by culture" (عرفاناً) has consistently been rendered as "by race" (عرقاً) because of an apparent orthographic confusion.[16] Such may be justified by the simultaneity of orthographic *and* semantic similarity of the two words as used at the time of the document's conception. The uncritical and systematic persistence of the infelicity, coupled with other erroneous renderings, conjured up a commitment by the leaders of the resistance to a racialized Turkish identity, notwithstanding the ubiquitous references in the texts to Muslims and the Ottoman Muslim community. Similarly, it has become common to render "by aim" (*emelen* املاً) as "by origin" (*aslen* اصلاً owing to another plausible orthographic confusion. In successive renderings of the relevant clauses, the alternative readings have occurred interchangeably, until the Republican reading settled for ırk ("race") and *asl* ("origin"). School books and other publications, including scholarly monographs, have presented the National Pact as the fundamental credo of a primordial Turkish nation. The Grand National Assembly of Turkey published in 2015 the authoritative original facsimiles of the "national sovereignty" documents.[17] The volume includes Latin alphabet transcriptions and renderings in contemporary Turkish—that is, as cleansed of most Arabic and Persian terms and constructs. Even as the printed facsimile of the National Pact unmistakably shows the word *irfanen*, the transcription insists on *ırken*. The discrepancies reveal the willful or unconscious biases of nationalist strictures that inform historical analysis.

The Ottomans, and statesmen and literati in particular, were not naive about racialist ideologies and the race discourse of the nineteenth and early twentieth centuries, which informed ethno-national literary, cultural, and—albeit fringe—political agendas and nurtured the growing consciousness and expressions of nationality as accompaniment of modernity. The "Wilsonian moment" further validated and energized the formulation and projection of communal self-views as discreet nationalities.[18] Segments of communal leaders foregrounded ethno-national rights and/or geographical identity for political advantage or as vindication at an uncertain time, faced with changing international norms and discourses impinging on their lives. For those vested in the persistence of the state upon its time-honored juridical and communal foundations and its geopolitical domain, Muslim communality remained as the mainspring of the sociopolitical bonds that undergirded the polity. The National Pact acknowledged the self-determination of peoples, the arbiters of whose political fate were now the foreign powers. The assurances for "racial" rights (*hukuk-u ırkiye*) in all three documents point to the expediency of a decentralized administration in line with changing norms and expectations of the Wilsonian moment.[19]

While recognizing the right to self-determination of the Arab majorities in Ottoman territories occupied at the time of the signing of the armistice, the misak affirmed the indivisibility of territories "*within* or *outside* [emphasis added] the armistice line which are inhabited by an Ottoman Muslim majority." The statement did not allude to how Ottoman Muslims outside the armistice lines might give expression to self-determination. A recent model was the July 1918 plebiscite in Batum, Kars, and Ardahan, which had been conducted after the Brest-Litovsk Treaty conditionally ceded the districts to the Ottoman Empire. The misak's suggestion of a popular vote in the territories occupied by Britain and France conformed to Wilsonian norms but was certain to be ignored by the two powers. The fate of the findings of the King-Crane Commission had revealed the hazards of assessing the popular will.

As a manifesto of independence, the misak-ı milli document was critically influential at the time of its issuance; and, therefore, the seminal place it has come to occupy in the Turkish national narrative is unsurprising. Where it has most often been invoked, however—namely, as earmarking a hallowed space for independent nationhood for Turks one and the same with Turkey's present borders—it does not align with the geopolitical objectives articulated in the parliamentary resolution. National histories look through the framing of the postwar independent state to encompass all areas inhabited by a Muslim Ottoman majority and unoccupied in October 1918; they discount the possibility of a political solution (e.g., a federation) that includes the occupied areas. The document does not define the "whole which does not admit of division," but commits to the incorporation of territories as determined by plebiscitary process in the Arab-populated areas. The Anatolian movement extended beyond the upper reaches of the Tigris and Euphrates Rivers and maintained an active interest further south into Syria and Iraq. It consistently monitored political and military developments with an eye to extend its influence into these areas.

As the National Pact attained iconic status in the Turkish Republic as the fundamental charter of the founding of modern Turkey, official history invalidated its stipulation about the inseparability of Arab majority regions (per the vote of the inhabitants) that had fallen under European control before October 30, 1918, by expedient erasure of the clause from the text.[20] The omission was consistent with the image that the Republican regime projected for both domestic and foreign audiences, namely that of a non-irredentist modern secular nation-state free of Ottoman-era ties and looking to the West.[21] It went in tandem, first, with the cultivation of the notion of a homogenous ethno-linguistic nation, moving away from and suppressing the pluralist model; and, second, the construction of Turkish-Arab alterity, which demanded a version of the foundational document that would be usable in projecting the particular self-image. Histories have explained away the misak's references to the Arabs and Arab provinces as a circumstantial aberration.

The process by which the document was drafted, deliberated upon, and ratified in parliament is not well-known. As an item of first business, an internal committee deliberated upon a text that was first drawn up in Ankara, possibly by Mustafa Kemal himself. When the draft resolution came before the floor on February 17, the deputies approved and promulgated it by acclamation. The text bears similarities both in style and content to earlier congress resolutions and Mustafa Kemal's statement at his Ankara meeting several weeks before. The absence of the clause referring to the free vote of the Arab inhabitants in these earlier documents has led to the speculation that the particular clause was inserted as it moved from draft form to resolution.[22] The final form was approved unanimously and enthusiastically, demonstrating that the lawmakers aspired to and declared as their goal the retention of the imperial framework and the provinces that the Entente powers had captured during the war. This aim was consonant with the events of winter 1919–1920: the inconclusive end of the Peace Conference, Faysal's shrinking authority in Syria, the emergence of France as the common adversary in Anatolia and Syria, the continued invocation of a federative reorganization by diverse actors, growing ARDRS involvement in the militia warfare in the Anatolia-Syria nexus, and the initiatives for broader collaboration exactly at the very juncture of the opening of parliament.

FAYSAL'S SETBACK IN PARIS AND EXPANSION OF JOINT RESISTANCE BY POPULAR GROUPS

Two weeks before the peace conference closed on January 21, 1920, Faysal arrived in Beirut from his second trip to Paris within a year having failed to influence the Allies to agree to independence for Syria.[23] Faysal's inability to procure an agreement, which would have bolstered his position in Damascus, strengthened the tendency in Syria to seek greater cooperation with the Anatolian groups, whose resistance against French occupation achieved its first successes in Maraş in February 1920 and emboldened the anti-colonial forces.[24] The ARDRS leadership sent loyal young officers to the occupied provinces to assist in the coordination of local forces, among them Captains Kılıç Ali and Kamil Polat, who fought in the skirmishes that broke out in Maraş between the militias and the French troops amid destruction and hundreds of deaths and other casualties.[25] Groups in Syria explored joint defense with the Anatolian militias. Just before Faysal returned to Syria empty-handed, his deputy Amir Saʿid al-Jaza'iri had commissioned two Syrian notables to establish contact with the Anatolian resistance: Saʿid Haydar, a Lebanese who had studied law in Istanbul and possessed Arab nationalist credentials as a founding member of al-Fatat; and Badi' Bakdash, a former Ottoman officer from Syria with multiple family links by marriage to high Ottoman officials. The two emissaries met with associates of Mustafa Kemal in Istanbul and drafted an agreement that included the unification of military forces under a single command from southern Jordan to the Black Sea. "In the event of the successful outcome of their efforts against the West, the Arabs and the Turks will live side by side in two independent states but their relations will be nearly on the same lines as the relations of Austria and Hungary in the pre-War Austro-Hungarian Empire."[26] If such an agreement ever had a chance to be approved and implemented, the diplomatic push in Europe toward the establishment of mandates thwarted it during the drawn-out trip of the envoys, who returned to Damascus in April.

More spontaneous collaboration manifested itself on the ground between militia forces in southeastern Anatolia and northern Syria. A circular Mustafa Kemal sent to army commanders on January 24, 1920, made manifest the Anatolian movement's ties with Syria. Kemal indicated that a popular organization (*teşkilat-ı milliye*) had materialized in that part of the Aleppo *vilayet* claimed by the Arab government, which was making "every effort not to separate from the Ottoman community under any circumstance." Division commander Lieutenant Colonel (*Kaymakam*) Emin (Amin?) Bey, together with Shakir Ni'mat at the same rank, belonged to this organization. The circular recommended a pincer action against the French forces occupying Maraş and Pazarcık to its south to be executed by the Aleppines and a popular militia in the north yet to be constituted.[27] In a diplomatic initiative, Shakib Arslan, propagandist for Cemal Pasha during the Great War and now advisor to Faysal, wrote to a Russian diplomat purportedly in the name of Faysal, that "Faisul has learnt a bitter lesson in France.... All hatred against the Turk had been dispelled and all that was now wanted was mutual trust and combination in support of the common cause."[28]

A second circular Mustafa Kemal sent to army commanders working with ARDRS groups in the name of the Representative Council (February 15, 1920) reveals the extent of the regional connections. Kemal referred to multiple past contacts between the ARDRS and Syrian resistance groups, namely the presidency of the Aleppo National/Popular Organization (*Halep Teşkilat-ı Milliye Riyaseti*), the Ottoman Forces General Council Defending Syria and Palestine (*Suriye ve Filistin Müdafii Kuva-yı Osmaniye Heyet-i Umumiyesi*) headquartered in Damascus, and Shafiq al-Misri [Özdemir], the commander of the Cairo volunteer units and Amman Circassian detachment. Included in this circular was a summary of a communication previously sent to the Damascus and Aleppo groups.[29]

The document throws further light on existing proposals for political projects and tactical collaboration between the Anatolian and Syrian groups. Though he did not explicitly reference his December communication with Ni'mat and Emin, Mustafa Kemal mentioned a proposal made by his interlocutors for joint action in order to achieve independence for Iraq, Syria, and Turkey and work toward the establishment of "a confederation or other connection to be determined in the future." He wrote that the ARDRS had endorsed the proposed line of action and had sent detailed instructions toward its realization, but that a response had not yet been received. Turning to strategies immediately to be implemented, he proposed in the idiom of a unified resistance a series of actions, which included the defense of Damascus "with the utilization of our forces in the vicinity of Hawran, Baalbek, and Damascus" against all occupation forces; forestalling with the forces in Marji'yun and Amman (?) any advance of the enemy from Sidon and Beirut into the interior; inciting riots in Beirut and Tripoli toward the same end; and tasking the forces in Homs with countering a possible attack from the direction of coastal Tripoli, as well as with aiding in the defense of Damascus. As part of a comprehensive plan to ward off French occupation, ARDRS was taking upon itself the coordination of the resistance but lacked the resources to back it up.

Mustafa Kemal referred to the success of the resistance along the line from Osmaniye, situated some fifteen miles inland to the north of the Gulf of Alexandretta, northeast to Maraş and from there southeast to Urfa. He identified the defense of Islahiye, across the mountain range east of Osmaniye, as a bridgehead to control French advances and the provisioning of existing French troops to the town's north. He urged that the militias in Hama and Homs secure Hama and Aleppo and move expeditiously to the north and join forces with militia units there to eliminate the French and Armenian occupation forces that had inserted themselves "between the Arab and Turkish millets." Mustafa Kemal asked that similar instructions be forwarded via Maraş to Shakir Ni'mat in Aleppo, who had emerged as the critical intermediary between the two nodes of resistance separated by French military presence.[30]

Further support for unity came from diaspora Arabs and Arab peoples of colonized or occupied countries. Syrian expatriates in Europe, abreast of the vagaries of the peace conference and concerned about an outcome that would ignore the will of Middle Eastern actors, submitted a petition to the Ottoman consulate in Zurich for the restoration of Ottoman rule and administrative autonomy. Anticipating broad support for this outcome, they pressed for a plebiscite enunciated in step with the misak as proclaimed in Parliament.[31] In North African colonies, demonstrators demanded the protection of the caliph's rights, responding to the appeals of the resistance to external Muslims for moral and political support.[32] A segment of the political elite within Syria explored Ottomanist options in charting Syria's future, as demonstrated by Sa'id Haydar and Badi' Bakdash's aforementioned mission. Secretary of State for War and Air Winston Churchill remarked in March 1920 in Parliament that French occupation of Syria had led to a desire in British-occupied Iraq "to make common cause with the Turkish Nationalists, thus uniting two forces by whose division our policy has hitherto prospered."[33]

The Arab provinces remained under the tutelage of the mutually suspicious Entente allies France and Britain. The uncertainty in the political status of the Ottoman imperial vestiges lingered on. In Syria, while there were differences between the Hashemite leadership, segments of Syria's Arabists, and pro-Ottoman elements, sentiments for continued political, social, and economic ties with Anatolia remained strong, at times preponderant, especially in northern Syria. Opportunities to redeem the wartime losses prompted the Anatolian leadership to revive such linkages.

NEW SOVEREIGNTIES

The Paris Peace Conference had endorsed the plan to institute mandates in the Ottoman territories in the early stages of the talks. Bilateral talks between France and England at the end of 1919 moved the two countries closer to the mandatory division of the Fertile Crescent. After the conference suspended its sessions and Faysal returned home, Britain, France, and Italy moved away from the formal mechanisms of the Supreme Council in Versailles in favor of a tripartite meeting that started in London on February 12 (London Conference) without the participation of the United States, which was poised to pull out of the peace talks under domestic constraints. Political activity in Istanbul and Damascus and militia operations in the southeastern Anatolia–northern Syria nexus intensified during the London Conference, where talks pertaining to the Ottoman settlement lasted with interruptions until April. The conferees were profoundly aware of the resumption of parliamentary politics in Istanbul as well as the ferment in southeastern Anatolia/northern Syria and the resolve of militias to thwart occupation. The cooperation of the Istanbul government with an assertive parliament drove Britain and France to increasingly more intrusive measures. They pressured the sultan to dismiss the Ali Rıza Pasha government (March 3). *Le Petite Marseilles* reported that "Mustafa Kemal and his gangs . . . are warning us that we must return to them Thrace and Syria and Smyrna and Palestine."[34]

The diplomatic stalemate triggered political initiatives in Damascus aimed at ending unilaterally the indeterminate postwar political status of Syria. Faysal reconvened the Syrian Congress, which on March 8 declared independence with Faysal as king. The same day, Iraqi officers in Damascus proclaimed independence for Iraq under his brother, Abdullah.[35] The resolute political acts in Istanbul and Damascus occurred against the backdrop of militia engagement of French troops in northern Syria and southeastern Anatolia, most fiercely in Maraş and Ayntab.

Not appeased by the sultan's dismissal of the Ali Riza Pasha government, Allied occupation forces ascended the shores of Istanbul on March 16 and proceeded to seize parliament and arrest a group of deputies suspected of Unionist sympathies. They subsequently deported several to Malta along with prominent figures associated with the wartime CUP government. Sultan Vahideddin reappointed Ferid Pasha as grand vizier on April 5 and six days later formally dissolved the parliament, which had adjourned after the Allied raid. The failure of diplomacy and the crackdown in Istanbul energized the efforts to extend the organizational and political activity in the Anatolia-Syria nexus for more extensive and effective armed resistance.

The ARDRS Representative Council invited the deputies in the Ottoman parliament to reconvene in Ankara and called extraordinary elections to replace those who were not able or willing to comply. On April 23, 1920, joined by new members, mostly ARDRS loyalists nominated by its local branches rather than elected by popular vote, the deputies convened in Ankara as the *Büyük Millet Meclisi* (People's Supreme Assembly, better known as Grand National Assembly [GNA]).

The opening of the GNA took place during the course of the reconvened meeting of the Allied Supreme Council at San Remo (April 19–26). The Allies negotiated in secrecy and agreed on not speaking to the press beyond official daily summaries of the proceedings.[36] Their disposition would not have been a secret to either Istanbul or Ankara since the preceding London Conference, where peace terms pertaining to the Ottoman Empire had been discussed and taken shape. The Council resolved to grant mandates to Britain (in Mesopotamia, Palestine) and France (in Syria). It recommended a US mandate over Armenia with no American delegation present to acknowledge it.[37] Before the talks started, the Allies estimated that they would need a military force of three hundred thousand to implement peace terms for Asia Minor, but only Greece was ready to provide troops, which Britain and France feared would further strengthen the resistance.[38] Even though there was no conclusive agreement on the Ottoman territories other than the mandate assignments, a *New York Times* report dated April 25 wrote prematurely that the "Turkish Treaty" was now "officially called practically finished."[39]

In a closed session of the GNA as early as the second day of its opening (April 24), Mustafa Kemal addressed conditions in Syria and Mesopotamia and conveyed his assessment of where the Anatolian struggle stood in relation to developments regarding these regions.[40] He appraised the cooperation between the Anatolian movement and Arab resistance from the perspective of Islamic solidarity. Describing the forces arrayed against them as a crusader effort, he maintained that "the forces of the world of Islam have been the only source for salvation and success." Mustafa Kemal placed the onus of the evolving political destiny of Syria in the peace conference squarely on the shoulders of the Syrians: He opined that those Syrians who had harbored the desire for independence since before 1914 had attempted to attain their unrealistic goals on the coattails of enemies who had "resolved to destroy us all." He continued, "When they realized the error they had fallen in, they turned towards continued coexistence within the Islamic community. They understood that cooperation with the foreign countries would be tantamount to servitude." In relation to Iraq, Kemal alluded to British actions that caused the ire of the Muslim people, who, he maintained, proposed to remain as part of the Ottoman lands. His appeal to the Iraqis was to seek independence with their own means. Once independence was accomplished, there would be no obstacles for unity. Mustafa Kemal returned to the wish to see the world of Islam united materially and morally, admitting that a declared commitment to redeem the Arab provinces was beyond the means of the Anatolian movement. He proposed a federative or confederative arrangement, beyond an alliance, premised on the attainment of independence.

Mustafa Kemal brought further clarity to some of his remarks from April 24 one week later in an open session, as he reaffirmed the areas he had specified in his December speech in Ankara as inalienable from the Ottoman community. These "national boundaries" extended "from the south of Alexandretta eastward" and included Mosul, Sulaymaniya, and Kirkuk. The community inhabiting the areas demarcated by this line, he declared, was not "exclusively Turkish, exclusively Kurdish, exclusively Circassian, or exclusively Laz" but rather Muslim. The community "whose preservation and protection we are trying to secure, does not consist of one element only but of diverse Muslim elements. These elements are compatriots, who respect each other's racial/cultural (ırki), social, and geographic rights."[41] The characterization of the community (millet) inhabiting the rump empire based on religion and the vision of a civic Muslim state concurred with the imperial mindset that abdicated the "preservation and protection" of the non-Muslim groups since the Great War. In this open session, he refrained from identifying the predominantly Arab regions under Franco-British occupation as potential confederate components of a broader political union, a proposition that would have spurred the colonial impulses of Britain and France concurrently deliberating in San Remo.

Even as Kemal stressed the heterogeneity of the Muslim population within the "national boundaries" and enumerated the different Muslim groups, he elided the Arab populations interspersed in the very areas. Unlike other groups, the majority of the broader region's Arab population remained under Franco-British occupation outside the territory Mustafa Kemal delineated. Just as Sharif Husayn had claimed the mixed territories up to the Mersin-Diyarbekir line for a dynastic Arab state, Mustafa Kemal appropriated the same region, down to the self-proclaimed armistice lines, within the realm of the rump empire's sovereignty. He drew a line in the sand that would constrain imperialist ambitions at a time when Britain and France were finalizing the mandates as semi-colonial political constructs, attenuating the prospects of true independence in Syria and Iraq. Kemal foregrounded reason of state as dictated by the strategic circumstances and diplomatic imperatives of the Mudros agreement.

REGIONAL COOPERATION EXPANDS, FRANCE PICKS ITS BATTLES

As the imposition of a French mandate on Syria became imminent, local leaders in the countryside, including some officials and officers of the Damascus government who were stationed in northern Syria, became increasingly more active in organizing the local resistance. Ibrahim Hananu led a militia in Antioch and rallied to the aid of the resistance in Ayntab.[42] Despite assistance from Hananu's militias, the Ayntab resistance would suffer a decisive defeat on May 20 against the French army. This victory notwithstanding, France's overall control over the region deteriorated. To the west of the Amanos range, the militias defeated the enemy forces in Pozantı and forced them to withdraw to Adana. The French negotiated for a temporary twenty-day cease-fire with the Ankara government, which was signed on May 30.[43] The ceasefire with France provided the respite for the Anatolian movement to resume recruitment, propaganda, and collaboration in the broader region. Kamil Polat, who was one of Ankara's liaison officers with the militia forces and most recently had led the resistance against the French in Kilis, continued his efforts around Aleppo.[44] The initiative to collaborate with the Anatolian movement came from local notables, officers, tribal chiefs, and others, and was supported on the basis of perceived communal interests.

The cease-fire applied solely to the conflict in southeastern Anatolia.[45] Nevertheless, it carried significant political and diplomatic implications: for the first time, the French authorities concluded an official agreement with the new Ankara government representing the resistance. After the restitution of Ferid Pasha to the grand vizierate in April, relations between

Ankara and the sultan's government had deteriorated rapidly. The GNA cut all official contact with Istanbul and prohibited the distribution of Istanbul newspapers, which were published under the watchful eye, and many in support, of the government and Allied authorities. As pro-Ankara and pro-Istanbul forces engaged in armed conflict in western Anatolia under the threat of a deepening of the Greek occupation, a court-martial in Istanbul sentenced Mustafa Kemal to death (May 11).[46] At this crucial juncture, the visit of a delegation headed by France's chief political representative in Syria, Robert de Caix, to Ankara in order to negotiate a cease-fire bolstered the legitimacy of the GNA.

The sentiment in favor of cooperating with the Anatolian movement strengthened in Iraq, where pro-independence riots broke out in May. Resistance groups that styled themselves after the defense of rights organizations appeared. In rejecting the British mandate, a group of notables, among them Fattah Pasha, who came from a "Turkified Arab family" and was a lieutenant general in the Ottoman army, held a meeting to demand independence or a "Turkish mandate."[47] British occupation and alliances with tribal groups reconfigured regional balances of power. In June 1920, the shaykh of Muntafik, ʿUjaymi al-Saʿdun, came to Mardin to seek assistance in rallying the Iraqi tribes into the Ottoman fold and obtained money, munitions, and some men. In Mosul, an organization that called itself *Cemiyet-i Hilaliye* (Crescent Society) coordinated contacts with the Anatolian movement. The Society sent a delegation to Ankara and asked for the active support of the army corps based in Diyarbekir. As long as the struggle against French occupation continued to the west of the Euphrates, the Anatolian movement's efforts in northern Iraq remained limited. Upon al-Saʿdun's representation, Ankara approved the dispatch of arms and ammunition to him from the Thirteenth Army Corps in Diyarbekir, including two pieces of artillery and two machine guns, as well as ten thousand gold liras. The leader of the ʿAnaza, Hajim ibn Muhayd, cooperated with al-Saʿdun, who disrupted French communication with Urfa by destroying the railway tracks, forcing the occupation troops to evacuate the town in April.[48]

The cease-fire between the French command in southeastern Anatolia/ northern Syria and Ankara alarmed the Arab government in Damascus, which confronted French demands to yield to the terms of the San Remo agreement and lacked the resources to withstand the pressure. Paradoxically, at a time when the Anatolian resistance disengaged, at least temporarily, from the fight against colonial occupation, the Arab government explored broader cooperation with all elements of the regional resistance. For instance, Taha al-Hashimi, Yasin's brother, who had fought with the Ottoman army in Yemen until 1919, now acted as a liaison between local militia commands and Mustafa Kemal.[49] Wary of the possibility that Ankara would come to a more permanent agreement with France than the recent armistice, a fear that would be substantiated one year later, Faysal sent his defense minister, Yusuf al-'Azma, to Aleppo on June 8 to coordinate joint action with the Anatolian resistance. Faysal followed him one week later in an effort to thwart the Anatolians' agreement with France.[50]

Similar overtures from the Arab government continued. Chief-of-staff Major Mustafa Sabri and Gendarmerie Inspector Hamid separately approached the Ayntab defense forces to negotiate an alliance. A well-documented agreement initiative took place in July 1920 following talks among Kilis Defense of Rights central committee leader Polat Bey, Yasin [al-Hashimi] Pasha, and his brother Taha, who was present as the director of security in the Syrian government, as well as delegates from Iraq. At the meeting held in Kafr Ghan near Kilis, the participants negotiated concerted action against the enemy, a joint war council, and mutual military aid. The president of the Ayntab central committee and, representing the Faysal government, Gendarmerie Inspector Jamil Lutfi drafted the agreement.[51]

The leadership in Ankara did not endorse this agreement, seemingly because of misgivings about Faysal's sincerity, since he had refused to enter into negotiation after a similar initiative earlier in the year, a reference to the agreement Kemal's representatives discussed with Bakdash and Haydar in the winter. The decision suggests caution on the part of the Anatolian resistance to engage in formal agreements with the Damascus government, which would have been tantamount to recognizing Faysal's sovereignty. The Kemalists preferred to support the activities of local guerrilla groups and bands rather than engage in tactical or political alliances with presumptive Syrian national leaders. Ankara instructed the Ayntab committee that these delegations lacked authority and that their main purpose was to seek legitimacy for themselves (i.e., Faysal's government in Damascus) and to preempt the many pro-Ankara groups in and around Aleppo. Indeed, one of the terms of the treaty drafted for submission to Ankara was that brigandage in the region would be suppressed. It was precisely the motley forces in northern Syria, namely the "brigands" the treaty sought to curb, who supported and acted together with the Anatolian movement. In any event, all must have been aware of the imminence of an effort by France to subvert Faysal.

FALL OF THE FAYSALI STATE AND THE FORGING OF THE SÈVRES SCHEME

The contacts were overtaken within days by diplomatic and military developments. After Faysal's rejection of the mandate in Syria, France forced the issue with an ultimatum and backed the threat with troop movements from Beirut and Cilicia into the Syrian interior. The heroic but feeble defense of the Arab army in Khan Maysalun near Damascus on July 24, 1920, resulted in a quick and decisive defeat of the detachments led by Yusuf al-'Azma, who was killed in battle. The debacle forced Faysal to leave Damascus. His political career was henceforth to be closely intertwined with the British mandate of Iraq, where he was crowned the following year with British blessings but no real power, a semblance of what he had come to view as London's contractual obligations to his family.

Faysal had been woefully aware of his military vulnerability in Syria. His better instincts impelled him to forge a compromise with the French or place his hopes in continuing diplomatic processes with Britain's support. He was unable to preempt al-'Azma's patriotic, and equally quixotic, challenge of the French forces in Maysalun. Though Faysal had to leave Damascus in humiliation, the imposition of an overbearing mandate administration sanctified his brief rule and struggle for self-government in Damascus for posterity. All resistance in the region, including that pursued by Syrian groups at cross-purposes with Faysal's political ambitions, came to be folded into the heroic defense of Syria and Syrian rights and cemented Faysal's nationalist credentials.

The collapse of the Faysal government removed the main obstacle to the imposition of the mandates. In the absence of a peace treaty, however, mandates could not be implemented in territories that were legally under Ottoman sovereignty. In August 1920, the Allies invited the Ottoman government to France to sign a draft peace treaty. Damad Ferid Pasha traveled to Sèvres with a small Ottoman delegation and after futile protestations agreed to the punitive treaty on August 10, which formalized the accomplished facts of prior years.[52] The document represented a maximalist fulfillment of European designs in the Ottoman Empire. The Ottoman government recognized the Kingdom of the Hijaz, the territory that Sharif Husayn had claimed as an independent entity in 1917. The treaty earmarked a large swath of land well beyond the Tauruses and into inner Anatolia as a region of prospective Kurdish autonomy under Allied influence and upheld the right of this

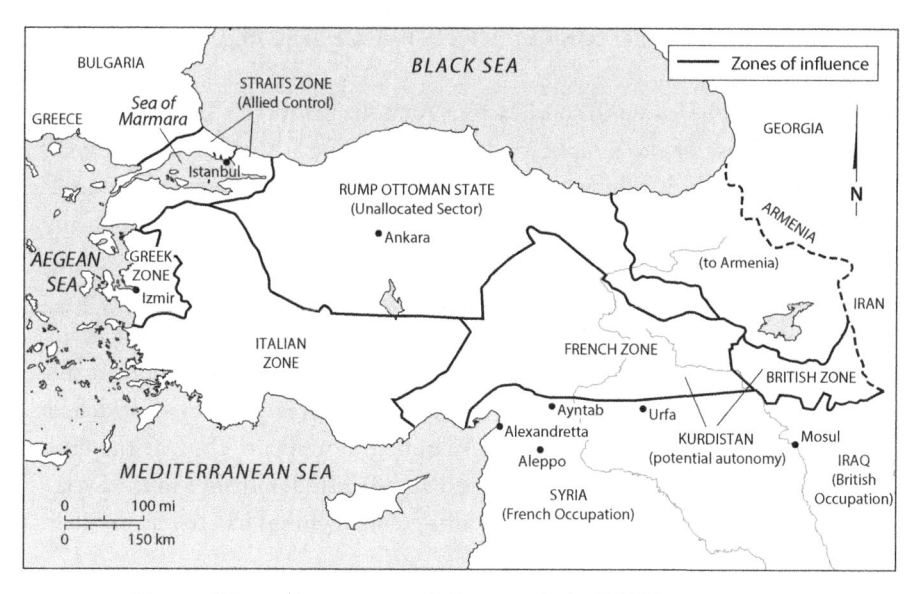

MAP 5. Treaty of Sèvres (August 10, 1920). Cartography by Bill Nelson

region's population to opt for independence. It carved out Mosul as part of the British mandate of Iraq, but it provided for the "voluntary adhesion to ... an independent Kurdish State of the Kurds inhabiting that part of Kurdistan which has hitherto been included in the Mosul vilayet" (Article 64). The boundary between the Ottoman state and the Syria mandate was determined as a line starting from some 30 kilometers to the north of Alexandretta on the Mediterranean coast to Jazirat Ibn Umar (Cezire-i ibn-i Ömer/Cizre) approximately 130 kilometers to the northwest of Mosul. This left Alexandretta, Maraş, Ayntab, Urfa, Mardin, and Dayr al-Zur in Syria and the broad autonomous Kurdish region to the north of these towns under French influence, approximating the contours of the Franco-British agreements finetuned since Sykes-Picot to leave Mosul in British hands. The treaty stipulated an independent Armenia in the east, recognized Greek annexation of Izmir and environs, and rewarded Italy with the control of southwestern Anatolia. It curtailed the Ottoman state to a small region in central and north-central Anatolia with tenuous connection to the capital, presently under Allied occupation, and thus put the state's independent existence as a viable entity in greater peril. The new boundary in the south truncated the territory that the resistance claimed with reference to the Mudros status quo, which it had reified as a categorical, albeit aspirational, border. (See Map 5.)

ANTI-COLONIAL RESISTANCE REGROUPS

Conflict had flared up in southeastern Anatolia before the Treaty of Sèvres with the lapse of the temporary cease-fire in June.[53] The fall of the Faysal government in July followed by the signing of the treaty revamped the anti-colonial resistance in the broader region. The new Ankara government's main preoccupation, however, was in western Anatolia, where the Greek occupation was expanding and rebellions supported by the Istanbul government had broken out (e.g., in Bolu and Düzce) in spring 1920, forcing Ankara to dedicate its attention and any military resources it could summon to the region. The GNA government's rejection of the Treaty of Sèvres widened the rift between Istanbul and the Anatolian movement. Thus, at the crucial juncture of the assertion of French and British dominance in the Syria-Anatolia-Mesopotamia nexus, local anti-colonial groups had to rely on their own devices and mutual assistance.

The ever-itinerant pro-Ankara officer Özdemir took the command of the resistance in Ayntab. Özdemir came from an established Circassian family in Cairo. During World War I, he fled British-occupied Egypt and entered Ottoman service. He had been active in intelligence in Syria and Palestine during the war, most likely with the Teşkilat-ı Mahsusa, the CUP's propaganda and intelligence organ.[54] As an Arabic-speaking militia commander who crisscrossed northern Syria and southeastern Anatolia during the independence struggles, Özdemir epitomized anti-colonial operatives with multilayered identities and allegiances who assumed leadership roles. He emerged and reemerged as one of the pivotal actors of the resistance first in northern Syria and southeastern Anatolia and later northern Mesopotamia (see chapter 5), maintaining loose coordination with the Anatolian resistance that coalesced around Mustafa Kemal.

Faysal remained attentive to the fate of Syria during his brief exile in Italy and early days in Baghdad, as the Hashemites continued their efforts to recuperate British pledges to the family. He extended his support to the Syrian resistance, including to efforts coordinated with the Ankara government, upon the resumption of fighting in Ayntab and elsewhere in the region. In his quest to forge a political space for his own rule after his ouster from Syria, Faysal asked his adviser Satʻi al-Husri to contact the representatives of the Anatolian resistance.[55] Al-Husri had been a prominent Arab-Ottoman official in the bureaucratic hierarchy of Ottoman education and had relocated to Syria to join the Faysali government at the war's end.[56] Al-Husri went to

Istanbul and secretly met with supporters of the Anatolian movement, but there is no evidence of these contacts having led to tangible actions. King Husayn as well assumed a conciliatory stance toward Mustafa Kemal. On September 11, 1920, a British communication from Iraq stated: "It is not surprising... that [King Husayn] has been tempted to listen to the pleading of Mustapha Kemal and that he is endeavoring to give support to the tribesmen of the north in their effort to eject the French troops. In this connection it is noteworthy that he has several times lately announced that it was the Committee of Union and Progress and not the Turkish government against which he revolted."[57] British diplomats confirmed newspaper reports that Mustafa Kemal was in communication with King Husayn.[58]

The sharifs strategized to ensure that the anti-French agitation would continue in Syria and Anatolia, on the one hand, and to prevail upon the British authorities to revive the Hashemite claims, on the other. In a letter written to British premier Lloyd George, Faysal wrote: "I anticipated the trouble in the north, when the French concluded their armistice with Mustapha Kemal, evacuating Jarablus and thereby throwing the door open to Turkish intrigue and propaganda, both in Syria and Mesopotamia. I proposed to Lord Allenby at the time that my Arab troops should hold the frontier, but had no answer to my letter.... If the pledges given to the Arabs through King Hussein are fulfilled, I am confident that things will settle down."[59] Yet Faysal became increasingly irrelevant, even as the indigenous irregular units continued their struggle against the French occupation. Özdemir would report that after Faysal's departure from Damascus public opinion was on the Ottoman side and that the districts of Bab, Manbij, and Raqqa, where the people were prepared to recite the Friday sermon in the Ottoman sultan's name, would separate from Aleppo.[60]

Ayntab's fall to the French in February 1921 enhanced rather than curtailed cross-regional interaction. Özdemir, who had taken part in Ayntab's defense, now received orders to establish an organization in Syria. He carried the title "President of the Council of Syria and Palestine Ottoman Popular Forces" (*Suriye ve Filistin Kuva-yı Milliye-i Osmaniye Heyeti Reisi*).[61] Foreign observers commented on the growing unity between the various resistance forces in the region.[62] The Syrian militias, hampered by the lapse of their contacts with the rest of Syria due to the French military presence, sought financial aid from the Anatolian groups. The army corps in Diyarbekir allocated funds and arms to Özdemir. A quarter of all the ammunition Özdemir received was then given to the Latakia-based militia leader Saleh al-'Ali, who asked for help toward his struggle against the French.⁶³ In May, Major Natiq Bey, who signed his communications with Ankara as "Chief of Staff of the Ottoman National Movement" and alternatively "Chief of Staff of the General Syrian National Organization and Movement" wrote that "Syria today belongs to Turkey more than yesterday. Even the extreme Arabists of Syria accept that it is not possible to survive without Turkey."⁶⁴

The terms of the Treaty of Sèvres pertaining to Mosul (allocated to the British mandate of Iraq) and the adjacent regions in eastern Anatolia (earmarked for Kurdish regional autonomy and Armenian independence) demanded from the resistance a more proactive policy in Mesopotamia. French and British reports warned of troop accumulation in the Diyarbekir-Mardin area as early as the end of 1919 as well as contacts between the "Turkish nationalists" and Arab and Kurdish tribal groups, when a concentration of some one thousand regular soldiers of the Ankara government incited local tribes for a two-pronged assault against Baghdad and Dayr al-Zur.⁶⁵ Greater Syria and Iraq shared historical, geographical, and cultural ties across the Fertile Crescent, long-standing common existence as part of the Ottoman state, and similar vicissitudes during the war and postwar Allied occupation. Iraq's experience during the armistice period also differed from Syria's in important ways. In Syria, the Allied powers were intricately involved in political transactions and outcomes contested by local actors on the ground, which generated discord between Britain and France over issues like the postwar status of Palestine and Mosul; the first originally designated as an area of international administration in the Sykes-Picot agreement, and the second as falling under French indirect influence. Syria, therefore, had remained at the forefront of negotiations on the Middle East in the peace conference. The conference recommended and approved the dispatch of commissions of inquiry to Syria and Anatolia, but not to Iraq. When France agreed to rescind its claim over Mosul in December 1919 in return for a share of oil to be extracted in the region, Franco-British differences in northern Mesopotamia ended.

The British and the French remained on alert in the broader region for "Turkish intrigue." In view of Foreign Secretary Lord Curzon's objections to engaging in diplomacy with Ankara, Churchill argued for allowing "the Arab ruler of Mesopotamia—if and when such a ruler is selected—to enter into direct negotiations with the Angora authorities with the object of protecting Mesopotamia against Turkish nationalist intrigue."⁶⁶ Sharif Abdullah, Husayn's older son, recounted in his memoirs contacts with Mustafa Kemal in the quest for support of his own claims for the crown of Iraq. Abdullah endorsed that "the Arab movement should cooperate with the Turkish movement in order to save both." According to Abdullah, Mustafa Kemal replied affirmatively through an intermediary and asked Kazım Karabekir Pasha to establish contact with Abdullah.[67] Any such collaboration may have been mooted by the British designation of Faysal as ruler of Iraq in March 1921 at the Cairo Conference, a meeting of top British officials involved in Middle Eastern affairs. Faysal arrived in Iraq in June and, following the semblance of a referendum, was crowned on August 23.[68]

Both the resistance in the Anatolia-Syria-Iraq nexus and the Franco-British responses must be viewed against the broader background of anti-colonialism in Asia, which the Allies characterized as a growing pan-Islamic movement. The Soviet Union actively nurtured anti-colonialist mobilization in the Middle East after the signing of the Treaty of Sèvres. In the immediate aftermath of the conference, Moscow sent both gold and arms to the GNA government.[69] In September, the Congress of the Peoples of the East convened in Baku under Moscow's auspices.[70] *Le Temps* gave expression to the fear of an Asian revival spearheaded by the Russians, in which Turco-Arab cooperation could militate against French interests.[71] Yet as late as January 1920, an article in the same paper had pondered whether "Muslim sentiment tied to tradition could not be an ally against Bolshevism, the enemy of tradition."[72] A French information bulletin would hyperbolically report in October 1921, "Today more than ever, all of Islam is fanatically united," exhibiting the familiar and enduring reading of resistance to foreign domination in regions inhabited by Muslims as Islamic fanaticism.[73]

The resistance strove to maintain close relations with the Soviet Union around an anti-imperialist platform, while remaining sensitive to conservative sensibilities about making common cause with the communists. Anti-colonialist ideological affinity and procurement of material help notwithstanding, Ankara's relations with Moscow remained tense over the pursuit of territorial claims in the Caucasus. Kazım Karabekir, who successfully organized troops under his command as the Fifteenth Army Corps, moved against the newly formed Armenia Republic to recover the Ottoman towns of Sarıkamış and Kars. Karabekir signed with Armenia the very first international treaty of the GNA government (Treaty of Alexandropol, December 3, 1920). A month later, the increasingly more coordinated forces of the GNA held off a Greek offensive at İnönü, halfway between the Aegean coast and Ankara. Curzon's reservations about engaging in diplomacy with Ankara notwithstanding, in February 1921, the government of the GNA received recognition from the Allies, who invited its representatives to London along with the delegates of the Istanbul government to participate in a conference aimed at resolving the impasse over the implementation of Sèvres.

While this iteration of the London Conference was inconclusive, the negotiations revealed a loosening in Italy's and France's resolve to press the claims embodied in the Treaty of Sèvres. As the head of the GNA delegation, Foreign Minister Bekir Sami found French interlocutors at the conference prepared to discuss a revision of the Sèvres stipulations that governed the border with the Syria mandate, including access to the Baghdad Railway and transportation rights.[74] Indeed, this conference became the beginning of a process that resulted in a separate peace between the Ankara government and France in the fall of 1921. Successes on the battlefield against the Greek armies buttressed the diplomatic openings. The forces of the GNA halted a second attempt by the Greek army to break through the front at İnönü (April 1, 1921) while it continued the pressure in the Anatolia-Syria frontier through agents and proxies.

The respite that followed the second battle at the western front allowed the dispatch of three divisions of the regular army units to southeastern Anatolia "intimating to [French commander] General Gouraud the right of Turkey to the south of the border, including both Iskenderun [Alexandretta] and Aleppo."[75] At the end of summer 1921, however, the government of the GNA was once again forced to mobilize its forces to counter a Greek push toward Ankara. After a battle on the banks of the Sakarya River, some fifty miles to the west of Ankara, these forces repulsed the attack on September 13 and stopped the Greek advance once and for all. The victory turned the tide against the invading Greek army and achieved a broader psychological effect both on the Kemalists and their vanquished adversaries, which contributed to a diplomatic breakthrough.

ANKARA TREATY WITH FRANCE

The Ankara government struck an accord with France on October 10, 1921, to end the hostilities in the southeastern Anatolia–northern Syria conflict zone. The French government pursued this initiative, concerned about consolidating French rule in the Syria mandate and faced with stiff resistance in Adana, further east in southeastern Anatolia, and northern Syria. The Ankara Treaty (also known as the Franklin-Bouillon Treaty after the French chief negotiator Henry Franklin-Bouillon) entailed a significant modification of French stakes in the Treaty of Sèvres in return for the GNA government's recognition of the French mandatory role in Syria. This significant diplomatic achievement revamped the military field. Even though Ankara did not fully utilize units of the expanding regular army in the south, securing the accord freed the GNA government of logistical preoccupations in the region to capitalize on the victory in Sakarya and push back the Greek occupation in 1922. More important, in addition to increasing the GNA government's prestige, this separate peace strained Franco-British relations, as London still viewed the Istanbul government as the legitimate interlocutor. The Anatolian movement had thus managed to divide the Entente camp as it gained reprieve in the southeast to focus on the Greek occupation forces in the west.

The October 1921 treaty with France, Ankara's first accord with a principal Great Power adversary, represented an important turning point in the international legitimation of the Grand National Assembly in Ankara. The GNA had secured an agreement with Soviet Russia in March 1921, which was consummated in the Treaty of Kars just one week before the Ankara Treaty. The diplomatic feats entailed concessions from Ankara's declared territorial objectives. Even though the March 1921 agreement with Russia had stipulated the recognition of the National Pact, which called for a new plebiscite in the Caucasian Republics in its second article, the Kars treaty in September ignored this clause and left Batum within the Russian sphere. The Ankara Treaty with France partially jettisoned the territorial goals of the National Pact, even as it mooted the French zone of influence in Eastern Anatolia and extended the Sèvres boundary in Ankara's favor as shown on Map 6. Minor adjustments apart, it set the Baghdad Railway (to Nusaybin) and the paved road (to Cizre) as the boundary (Article 8).[76] It thus reclaimed the province of Adana and the northern half of the Aleppo Province for the rump empire but excluded the territories to the south of the railway extending from the north of Alexandretta to Dayr al-Zur, a swath of land that Ankara had claimed on the basis of its interpretation of the "Mudros boundaries." The accord provided tactical advantages for both sides and allowed them to direct their attention elsewhere. France also received concessionary rights over the operations of the railway (Article 10). The Ankara agreement did not resolve France's broader war aims, however, or, in the absence of a multilateral comprehensive peace treaty, disassociate the Anatolian movement from pursuing its interests in Syria and Iraq. The agreement stipulated a special administrative regime for Alexandretta within the French mandate, which the Kemalists

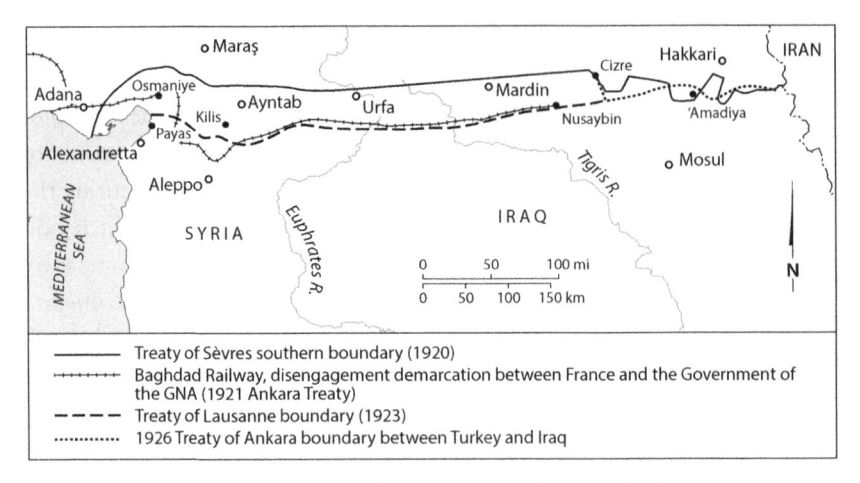

MAP 6. Border making and peace settlement. Cartography by Bill Nelson

unsuccessfully contested with the Wilsonian arrow in their quiver advancing the province's large Turkish-speaking population (Article 7). Otherwise, the treaty did not allude to ethnicity, religion, or nationality in the delimitation of the boundary.

The gradual consolidation of power by Mustafa Kemal and his associates in both the parliament and the centralizing army did not eliminate differences within either institution. The French authorities who monitored the circumstances in Syria and southeastern Anatolia reported that the commander of the Elcezire Army Corps in Diyarbekir, Nihad Pasha, declared that he would not recognize the agreements reached by Mustafa Kemal and would continue the struggle, in the words of General Gouraud, until "Turkey establishes itself in its pre-war borders." According to Gouraud, Nihad created a post in al-Hasakah, about forty miles to the south of the border demarcated in the Treaty, and was engaged in propaganda among the tribes farther south, more than one hundred kilometers from the border, where "Turkish riders" joined the tribes to establish a fortified position in Khsham, southeast of Dayr al-Zur.[77] Sharp differences would surface in the GNA, even as military successes continued and Mustafa Kemal turned to regime consolidation in Ankara.

FIVE

Struggle for Redemption and Imperial Dissolution

DURING THE TWELVE MONTHS THAT FOLLOWED the October 1921 treaties with Soviet Russia and France, the government of the Grand National Assembly in Ankara devoted its resources to reversing the Greek advance in western Anatolia before returning to the pursuit of geopolitical objectives in the Anatolia-Syria-Mesopotamia frontier. Britain and France had expected the Greek forces to vanquish the rebels in Ankara and secure the terms of the Treaty of Sèvres. Within one year of the Sakarya battle, however, Ankara obtained another victory in a decisive battle against the Greek armies at the end of August 1922, which forced the Kingdom of Greece to evacuate Asia Minor and the Allied powers to settle for a cease-fire. Almost four years after the Mudros agreement, which had failed to end armed conflict, Ankara negotiated with the Allies new armistice terms. The Armistice of Mudanya (October 11, 1922) pertained primarily to the state of war in western Anatolia and Thrace and cleared the road to the renegotiation of the Sèvres provisions in renewed talks.

The terms of the agreement prepared the ground for the restoration of the prewar geopolitical status of the Ottoman territories in Europe as negotiated after the Balkan Wars. In the east, the long-standing border with Iran prevailed, while the treaties with Moscow had returned the northeastern provinces of Kars and Ardahan (but not Batum), approximating the pre-Berlin Congress boundary with Russia. In northern Syria and Iraq, the resistance continued the pressure on France and Britain through militia activity, covert action, and proxy warfare alongside the GNA government's diplomatic initiatives. The Ankara Treaty with France and the understanding of the Baghdad Railway as the demarcation of the northern boundary of the Syria mandate had revised the Sèvres boundary stipulations, even as it compromised Ankara's declared territorial goals.

Within weeks of the Mudanya armistice, the Ankara government pronounced the sultan's office and government defunct. Britain and France acquiesced to move forward with the Ottoman settlement by negotiating with the GNA government. Extended talks were held against the backdrop of popular anti-colonial resistance, domestic political exigencies in the Allied states, and the common desire to break the diplomatic impasse after eight years of intermittent warfare. Peace talks in the Swiss town of Lausanne concluded with the signing of a treaty in July 1923. Britain and France relinquished their claims in Anatolia and pressed to secure gains in Syria and Iraq, where they had maintained a military presence since the Great War. Meanwhile, throughout 1922–1923, Mustafa Kemal sought to consolidate his powers in the GNA, buttressed by his military and diplomatic accomplishments, but against growing opposition. His stewardship of the anti-colonial struggle bolstered his quest for power, which shaped the outcomes of the Ottoman settlement in 1923.

RESISTANCE IN NORTHERN IRAQ

In 1922, the Ankara government initiated operations in the Mesopotamian regions that the Treaty of Sèvres had designated as falling within the sphere of a British mandate in Iraq. Broader political, diplomatic, and military developments explain the initiative and its timing. Within weeks of the Sakarya victory, the GNA had approved the Ankara Treaty halting the hostilities with France. By December 1921, the French evacuated the territories under their occupation north of the Baghdad Railway, including Ayntab, where French troops had overcome local resistance. The negotiated French withdrawal made it possible for militia forces freed up in northern Syria and Cilicia to turn to Iraq. A prolonged standoff between the Greek army and the forces of the GNA government following the Sakarya battle allowed Ankara to monitor militia operations in the southeast and to provide a degree of logistical support.

The Treaty of Sèvres had placed within the British sphere of influence districts in eastern Anatolia to the north of Mosul and extending into the Van Province. This area belonged to the broader region that the treaty had earmarked for potential autonomous Kurdish rule. The British government expected that appealing to Kurdish national rights and self-determination in areas under its sphere of influence would bolster British strategic goals. Even as London sought to co-opt the Kurdish population with an autonomous "northern Kurdistan," large areas populated by Kurds in the Mosul Province, where Britain appropriated mandatory rights, would remain outside any autonomous Kurdish entity. The truncated region of Kurdish autonomy would serve as a buffer between Britain's Iraq mandate and an Armenian state, also stipulated in Sèvres and susceptible to fall under Soviet influence.[1]

In contrast to the project for independent Armenia, an agenda for an autonomous or independent Kurdistan as broached by Kurdish organizations in Istanbul or such diaspora Kurdish public figures as Şerif Pasha had not generated a cohesive constituency in the Kurdish regions. Local authorities reporting to Ankara, however, were cognizant of their subversive influences. Colonel Jawdat, the champion of a confederated Ottoman state, wrote from Diyarbekir as early as October 1919 to warn of the "mischief of foreign-supported associations" in Istanbul like the Kürt Teali Cemiyeti (Kurdish Advancement Society), whose members and activities, he argued, served the dissolution of the Ottoman community.[2] He urged against the dispatch of native officials to "Kurdistan" until the conclusion of peace. Local unrest had been endemic in the region. The prolonged Koçgiri rebellion in the Shiite-inhabited region of Dersim adopted the language of Kurdish independence after the Sèvres Treaty.

With diminished preoccupation with the struggle against the French, the GNA government turned its attention to subverting the British claims and agendas in Mesopotamia. Like in Syria and Anatolia, occupation had confronted resistance and revolts in Iraq. Britain had limited military resources and few troops in northern Mesopotamia, where its influence was subject to the vagaries of shifting tribal allegiances and largely dependent on the terror the Royal Air Force could wield. The government of India supplied troops in Iraq but did not always agree with London on the broader objectives to be pursued.[3] British control remained tenuous in most parts of Iraq, and particularly in the Ottoman province of Mosul. Ankara hoped to exploit the perceived British weakness to advance its territorial claims in Mesopotamia, pressure England toward a favorable renegotiation of the Sèvres terms, and gain advantage in the conflict on the western front, where the Allies had left the Greek army to its own devices. The efforts of the Anatolian movement to undermine the British hold in northern Iraq came to a head in 1922.

The influence of the Anatolian resistance extended to the Mosul Province, especially into the mountainous terrain of Sulaymaniya and vicinity near the Iran border. Ankara reconstituted the Thirteenth Army Corps in Diyarbekir as the Elcezire Front Army Command in June 1920 under Nihad Pasha with expanded authority in civilian and military matters, albeit without significant troop reinforcements.[4] The town of Rawanduz, about 150 kilometers north of Sulaymaniya, remained attached to Ankara's Elcezire command and within the sphere of the defense-of-rights organizations. The British tried to establish their authority through alliances with vacillating tribal groups in the broader region in their attempt to undermine the proclivity of large segments of the Kurdish population toward the Muslim-nationalist agenda of the Anatolian movement. The ideological affinity was rooted in sociopolitical organization under chiefs who availed of religious symbols, pedigrees, or charisma in securing their patronage networks. The Ankara government validated this social organization to command the moral and material support of the region's population and to countervail the assiduous enticement of British agents for collaboration. The material interests of Kurdish notables cohered with the agenda of preventing the resettlement of Christian genocide survivors dispossessed and driven out of their lands during the war, including the reinstatement of the displaced Assyrian communities, and above all, the setting up of an Armenian political or administrative entity in eastern Anatolia, as stipulated by the Treaty of Sèvres.

The Ankara government sent religious propagandists to the border regions, among them Shaykh Ahmad al-Sanussi, the Libyan tribal chief who was forced to stay in Istanbul after a visit that coincided with the conclusion of the armistice.[5] French intelligence in Cairo reported in October 1921 that al-Sanussi, who had arrived in Mardin, was destined for Karbala under the direction of Ankara to participate in an Islamic conference.[6] European observers tended to ascribe grander conspiratorial schemes to Islamic propaganda than warranted, but the observation that Sanussi's initiatives would be damaging to British designs was accurate. The majority Shiite population of Iraq mistrusted Faysal and the Hashemite House. Contacts between Sanussi and the leaders in the Shiite holy places had the potential to subvert both British and Hashemite influence.

In December 1921, British troops staged attacks in northeastern Iraq against local groups holding out against mandatory control. The Ankara government resolved to strengthen its hold on Rawanduz and use the town as a forward base in its bid for northern Iraq. It entrusted the militia operative Özdemir, who had distinguished himself in leading the joint Syrian-Anatolian militias against the French, with a forward mission in the Mosul Province. Ankara was hard-pressed to allocate military resources to achieve its territorial and geopolitical desiderata in the south as long as the Greek armies occupied western Anatolia and were poised for further advance. Furthermore, the pursuit of strategic goals in Iraq with overt involvement would have militated against diplomatic efforts with Britain toward ending the Greek occupation. Özdemir's instructions explicitly and emphatically called for the execution of the mission under the guise of an individual initiative "as it is likely that a conference may be about to convene with England to negotiate political matters."[7]

CONFERENCE OF LONDON RECONVENES

The GNA government engaged in a diplomatic offensive armed with the international legitimation that the Ankara Treaty had accorded. Its foreign minister, Yusuf Kemal (Tengirşenk), went to Europe in February 1922 to conduct negotiations in London and Paris toward securing a revised peace treaty.[8] Mustafa Kemal instructed Yusuf Kemal to stop in Istanbul on his way to Europe for an audience with the sultan in an attempt to convince his government to recognize the GNA as an interlocutor at the conference. Yusuf Kemal met with Grand Vizier Tevfik Pasha and Ahmed İzzet Pasha, now foreign minister, but Yusuf Kemal and Ahmed İzzet traveled to England as separate delegations. In his talks with European foreign ministers, Yusuf Kemal addressed the issues at the heart of the peace settlement: the capitulations, the status of the Marmara Sea straits, the border with Greece, and the protection of Greeks and Armenians in Anatolia. His insistence for the complete withdrawal of the Greek forces from Anatolia and eastern Thrace hobbled an agreement in principle.[9] Lord Curzon hoped to reach an understanding with the sultan's delegates first and then present its terms to Yusuf Kemal. The Ankara delegation's preemptory contacts in Istanbul and its proactive discussions with representatives of other governments in London and Paris—complete with an arms sale agreement with France—obviated the strategy, when İzzet Pasha lent support to Ankara's insistence on the terms of the National Pact.[10]

The discussions with Lord Curzon revealed that Ankara's claims in northern Iraq specifically, and border issues in general, were central to the peace settlement. Colonial Secretary Winston Churchill and Secretary of State for India Edwin Montagu feared the spill-over of a possible upheaval in Iraq to India and urged a quick peace settlement.[11] Meanwhile, Curzon's threat that the Allies may demand the relinquishment of Cilicia for an Armenian state in the absence of a territorial concession to the Armenians in the Kars-Ardahan area suggested that Britain regarded the agreement that France and the Ankara government reached in October 1921, which left Cilicia inside the GNA-controlled territory, as unsettled.[12] So did some local notables of Alexandretta, who made a representation in Ankara during the days of the London Conference in March and submitted a petition for attaching their district to Ankara. The British Intelligence Service in Istanbul wrote: "Although the petition ... may be regarded as having been presented in the interests of the Turkish inhabitants of the Alexandretta region, this information tends ... to confirm what is already known of the growing desire of populations in Syria and Palestine to return to Turkish rule."[13]

Some deputies in the GNA viewed the London delegation's actions through the prism of Mustafa Kemal's growing proclivity to enhance his political powers after the military victories. Despite the lull in warfare, Mustafa Kemal asked the Assembly in February for an extension of his prerogatives as commander-in-chief, which had first been granted to him on the eve of the Sakarya battle. The discontented deputies acquiesced, but when a bill for further extension of Kemal's extraordinary powers came back on the floor in May 1922, they opposed it in debates that witnessed the growth of factionalism in the GNA.[14] Suspicious of Mustafa Kemal's contacts with the Allied powers for a renegotiation of the Sèvres Treaty terms, they expected him to focus on the military exigencies of occupation and sought to bar the concentration of executive and military authority in his hands. The authorization of a new campaign in Iraq, at a time when tribal groups friendly to Ankara were becoming the object of British reprisals in northern Iraq, would assuage the dissidents who felt that Mustafa Kemal's political ambitions detracted from the struggle for independence.[15]

THE ÖZDEMIR MISSION

Even as Ankara refrained from an overt provocation, Mustafa Kemal asked his minister of defense to dispatch militia forces to Mosul to consolidate the Anatolian movement's influence in northern Mesopotamia. This would disrupt the British project of unifying Iraq under the nominal kingship of Faysal as a British mandate sanctioned by the League of Nations. Ankara committed only a handful of regular troops to the operation, but Özdemir and his entourage remained in close communication and cooperation with the Elcezire Army Corps in Diyarbekir, more than three hundred kilometers to the northwest of their operation's designated center of gravity in Rawanduz. Located inside the territory that Britain had asked the Ottomans to evacuate after the Mudros Armistice and then claimed for the Iraq mandate, Rawanduz had escaped direct British control. Ankara viewed the town as a base to establish its authority in northern Iraq and had already dispatched a civilian administrator with the title of district governor (*kaymakam*).[16] Özdemir's men received supplies and salaries from the GNA government as well as funds earmarked for distribution in negotiations with tribal groups. A telegraph line was erected from Diyarbekir to Şemdinli just to the north of Rawanduz to facilitate communications.

When Özdemir's contingent reached the Elcezire army headquarters in Diyarbekir, the newly appointed commander Cevad Pasha relayed misgivings to Ankara about Özdemir and his ragtag contingent, consisting of "randomly collected men, career officers, and voluntary officers."[17] He expressed doubts about Özdemir's intelligence, integrity, and ability to discipline his men and indicated that he had heard of his oppressive acts that exasperated and alienated local populations during the Syria campaigns. The report suggests that the local command was not convinced about the likelihood of the militia's success and may have wanted to abort the mission. Ankara rebuffed Cevad's concerns and recommended that Özdemir be warned to punish his men with dismissal for any misconduct. In addition to the funds entrusted to Özdemir, the GNA government allocated an additional amount from the animal tax proceeds of the Cizre district under Ankara's control within the disputed frontier.

The contingent by itself could hardly have posed a credible military challenge to the British forces. Its main mission was therefore to mobilize local groups in this mainly Kurdish-populated region in their opposition to British occupation and Hashemite suzerainty. In turn, British policy was premised on driving a wedge between the Kurds and the Ankara government. Ethnic politics, however, did not prove to be well suited for rallying support, and even less so for determining a territorial settlement. The Treaty of Sèvres had excluded the Mosul Province from the proposed region of Kurdish autonomy but stipulated the "voluntary adhesion" of Mosul to an independent Kurdish state once "Turkey agree[d] . . . to renounce all rights and title over" Kurdish areas (Article 62). As Ankara continued to press its own claims, Britain sought to consolidate the former Mosul Province of the Ottoman Empire as part of the state under the titular rule of Faysal. Local groups in northern Iraq, divided due to the nature of the terrain and segmented social organization, had few stakes in the schemes devised by the European powers in the postwar settlement, including Faysal's investiture. To garner support in the region, both the Anatolian movement and Britain had to establish and maintain mutually beneficial relationships with local leaders. Özdemir's mission was, therefore, as much to carry out propaganda and forge alliances as to establish bases within the territory that Britain claimed for the mandate. Both sides courted powerful local leaders, who were prone to withdraw their support, double-deal, or switch sides.

Özdemir and his retinue arrived in the town in June 1922. The detailed information available about the composition of the detachment reveals the ad hoc organization of the paramilitary units that operated in the Syria-Anatolia-Iraq frontier. The contingent consisted of some thirty low-rank officers, reserve officers, and militia leaders accompanied by an imam, an accountant, and seventy-five volunteers including Algerian soldiers who had changed sides from the French army to Özdemir in Syria or Cilicia.[18] There were as many units already stationed in Rawanduz and 120 soldiers were still expected in June to arrive from Çölemerik (Hakkari) within the region of the Elcezire command.[19] Özdemir soon reported the Algerians in his retinue as useless and faced the task of reconstituting the force.[20] Claiming that the British sent Arab spies to convince some twenty Arab soldiers in his entourage to change sides, he ordered the deserters and the alleged spies to be chased down and executed.[21]

The detachment already stationed in Rawanduz had limited its acts to occasional hit-and-run forays jointly with the tribal armies fighting the British forces. Özdemir argued that once the Çölemerik units arrived, the nucleus of a force capable of sustained backing of local fighters could be created, and he asked for approval to develop an official battlefront in Rawanduz.[22] Chief of Staff Fevzi Pasha (Çakmak) reiterated that the struggle should appear as Özdemir's and the militias' private effort without Ankara's official sanction or the participation of regular units.[23] This recommendation was consistent with the methods of the militia warfare in the Fertile Crescent throughout the period of occupation. Militias acting as surrogates for regular forces could pursue military goals with diffuse accountability. The fragmented, popular, informal, and often spontaneous nature of militia activity created extraordinary challenges for the opponents, in this case the armies and officials of Allied powers (but also for the historian in view of the scarcity of documentation about their activities).

Özdemir brokered agreements with tribal chiefs in northern Iraq around a platform of opposition to the expansion of British presence and control in the region and to the empowerment of Sharif Faysal as a British proxy. The different local groups were motivated by the prospect of the intervention of the GNA government against occupation, time-honored Islamic solidarity symbolized by the caliph in Istanbul, and the custom of unencumbered autonomy under Ottoman governance, as well as material or political advantage anticipated from collaboration. The norms of the kinship-based political configuration of the region, confessional and ethnic segmentation, and the requisites of contestation over scarce resources had to be taken into consideration creatively in cobbling together an alliance that proved to be able to field some five thousand fighters. This predominantly tribal army defeated the British forces at the Derbend Pass in the mountainous terrain between Rawanduz and Erbil on August 30, 1922, and forced the British troops to evacuate Sulaymaniya, auspiciously on the same day that Ankara's regular armies decisively vanquished the Greek army in western Anatolia.[24] The unlikely victory notwithstanding, the alliance did not remain stable in view of regional rivalries, British propaganda, and most formidably, the deployment or threat of the British air power in the plains.

In the hope of reasserting British control in eastern Iraq, within two weeks of the Derbend battle the British brought the local leader of preeminent prestige, Shaykh Mahmud (Barzanji), whom they released from exile, to install his power base in Sulaymaniya with assurances of autonomous rule.[25] The concession of a vaguely defined autonomy in northeastern Iraq would defuse broader resistance and demands for more radical political solutions that could jeopardize the mandate regime. Ankara was similarly eager to advance its influence by co-opting Mahmud, who was more than amenable to collaborating but was frank in impressing on Özdemir that he had bargaining choices in the quest to enhance his standing. He wrote to Özdemir's aide, Fevzi:

> If you have sufficient forces to occupy Kirkuk to Jebel Hamrin, please start your attack immediately. I will be a faithful soldier of the Sultan and will spare no effort in this regard. If you are not ready to come, in order to show goodwill, I am ready to leave Sulaymania for any location you determine. Should you not wish that, please send me ammunition, weapons and money to expel the British. Failing either, please withdraw and re-enter Kurdistan with a better army. Meanwhile, I will avail myself of time and take British money and weapons until you come.[26]

Özdemir appealed to Shaykh Mahmud in the name of religious unity and solidarity, as the British authorities turned to other leaders with influence in the region and with ambiguous relations with Ankara. During the standoff that followed Derbend, the two sides moved to a proxy struggle in northern Iraq by cultivating regional leaders of prestige. Tribal shaykhs were already autonomous in their affairs, but backing from the outside had the potential of creating broader alliances and a semblance of self-rule within the orbit of either Ankara or Baghdad.

Britain displayed a heavy-handed response to the defeat at Derbend with vigorous bombardment of loci of opposition, which increased pro-Ankara sentiment in the region but also weakened the military effectiveness of the Özdemir campaign. In the fall of 1922, Britain gained the upper hand in the contest to control northern Iraq. The GNA government was left to consider the mobilization of regular troops for a campaign, but the diplomatic initiatives in the wake of the defeat of the last Greek armies, which led to the October 1922 armistice, weighed against the initiation of new hostilities. The tussle in Iraq between Ankara and London via proxies on the ground assumed a new dimension in the context of revitalized peace talks between the GNA government and the Allies.[27]

ARMISTICE REDUX TO PEACE TREATY

The defeat of the Greek army in western Anatolia and its expulsion from Izmir swayed the British and French governments to lift the state of war against the Ankara government and initiate armistice talks. The negotiations in the southern Marmara town of Mudanya did not resolve the controversies about the terms and implementation of the Mudros agreement signed by the Ottoman government; but, unlike Mudros, the Mudanya agreement paved the way to a comprehensive peace agreement. The Ankara delegation went to Mudanya to negotiate within the parameters of the National Pact. Mustafa Kemal explicitly advised İsmet Pasha (İnönü), the chief delegate for Ankara, that the government of the GNA would go to war to recover Mosul if necessary.[28] Lord Curzon, in turn, opined in his statement of the British position that the British government could not partake in talks about Thrace "while Kemalist forces are taking hostile action against Kurdistan and Iraq."[29]

The Mudanya negotiations proceeded despite such rhetoric. They revolved around the question of the Allied occupation of eastern Thrace, the Ottoman Empire's European territory demarcated by treaty at the end of the

Balkan Wars in 1913. The final text of the armistice stipulated the evacuation of Greek forces in this region under Allied supervision, before the Allied units themselves would be withdrawn, including from Istanbul, within one month of the Greek evacuation. The negotiation of any borders in the southeastern Anatolia-Syria-Mesopotamia nexus was left to a comprehensive peace treaty, called to convene in the Swiss town of Lausanne the following month. The Allies invited to the talks both the government of the GNA and the sultan's government in Istanbul.

Within the few weeks between the signing of the armistice (October 11, 1922) and the opening of the Lausanne Conference (November 20), the Ankara government moved to end unilaterally the duality in state authority and governance. It carried to the representative assembly a motion providing for the separation of the offices of the sultanate and the caliphate and declaring the Ottoman sultanate defunct (November 1, 1922). The decision to abolish the sultanate effectively nullified the Treaty of Sèvres. The renewed initiative for the Ottoman settlement, unlike the peace talks that decided the fate of all Central Powers in 1919–1920, would not be restricted to the Great War's victors. As the presumptive arbiter of the state's future and availing of its aura deriving from the accomplishments of the independence wars, the government of the GNA adamantly insisted on participating in the talks as the Allies' sole negotiating partner. The resignation of the Istanbul government under the grand vizierate of Tevfik Pasha settled the question of representation in Ankara's favor once and for all.

The abolishment of the sultanate, which had been held by the same dynasty for more than six centuries, was a momentous decision. The military and diplomatic achievements of the Anatolian resistance in over two years had discredited and enfeebled the sultan's authority. Most of the people of the rump empire, including the many deputies in the Assembly, continued to harbor loyalties to the institutions and political traditions of the state that the House of Osman ruled over. The Ankara government had legitimate claims to represent the collective will at this critical juncture of diplomacy after a series of military and diplomatic successes against foreign occupation. The dominant faction around Mustafa Kemal in the Assembly justified the effective coup not in revolutionary terms but as the imperative for the survival of the state. Sultan Vahideddin's subservience to the Allied dictates provided grist for this contention. The retention of the office of the caliphate, even as the sultanate (monarchy) was being abrogated, ensured the passage of the historic measure in the Assembly with only moderate dissent.

The restoration of the constitutional order in 1908, almost a decade and a half earlier, had curtailed the effective power of the monarch, even though Sultan Vahideddin reclaimed some of the political prerogatives of the office after the death of Sultan Reşad in July 1918 and the collapse of the wartime government three months later. On the Assembly floor, Mustafa Kemal provided justification for the separation (and abolition) of the sultanate and proffered assurances for the Ottoman House's rightful claims to the Islamic caliphate. Sultan Vahideddin left Istanbul on a British warship for Malta, and his cousin Abdülmecid was appointed caliph on November 17. Opponents of the abrogation worried as much about the demise of a time-honored institution as Mustafa Kemal's unmistaken bid to enhance his own political standing and power. The retention of an Ottoman caliph in office tempered the objections of both Ottoman loyalists in the contested domains of the Ottoman Empire and among external Muslims.

The Anatolian resistance, and Mustafa Kemal as its leader, commanded the admiration and goodwill of peoples under colonial domination for its successful struggle against the European powers, especially after the implementation of the mandates. The mandate regime attested to the disjuncture between the professed principles of the Allied powers about self-determination and liberal governance and their neo-imperialist agendas. This incongruity had first become apparent in Egypt. Forty years of colonial rule had engendered a nationalist movement in the country. Britain allowed the further development of institutions of self-rule that had their beginnings in the period before the British occupation (1882), but when the war broke out in 1914, Britain declared Egypt a protectorate and suspended the legislature. The resources Egypt provided for the British war effort were crucial for Britain's Middle Eastern campaigns. Egyptians had little choice but to acquiesce in this role, appeased with the promise of independence at the end of the hostilities. The movement for self-determination that coalesced around the populist member of parliament and former minister Sa'ad Zaghlul at the war's end was suppressed at home and ignored in the peace conference.[30] The Anatolian resistance became an inspiration to both those nationalists who favored full independence and the groups that saw for Egypt a future with strong connections to the Ottoman state and the caliphate.[31]

At the beginning of 1922, religious scholars in Cairo's prestigious al-Azhar University published prayers in support of the Ottomans, the caliph-sultan, and the Kemalist troops for redemption "from the misfortunes caused them by the imperialists (colonizers) . . . and [for the] return to the Nile Valley its usurped rights in full."[32] British consideration of the possible implications of the Anatolian struggle for Egypt was in the background of the nominal independence that Egypt obtained in the same year. The failure of Zaghlul's bid to participate in the Paris Peace Conference in 1919 had triggered mass demonstrations, remembered today as the Egyptian Revolution of 1919. The vociferous demand of Egypt's self-styled nationalists for the implementation of the Wilsonian principles in their country led to the granting of partial independence in 1922 but did not secure for Egypt representation at the Lausanne Conference. There was no Arab representation at Lausanne.

In the days leading to the opening of the conference on November 20, Ankara selected a delegation and identified its aims. İsmet Pasha, the former chief of staff of the Ottoman army, the commander of the western front, the principal negotiator of the Mudanya Armistice, and now foreign minister, was appointed as the head of the delegation. The conference convened against the background of military tensions in Iraq. Anticipating that Mosul would be a main issue of contention at the conference, Ankara considered initiating an offensive in Iraq at this juncture with an eye to achieve a *fait accompli* and expand control in northern Iraq, in the event the talks failed, or to obtain a favorable bargaining position at the conference table.[33]

LAUSANNE CONFERENCE: NEGOTIATING MOSUL

The conference invited the government of the Grand National Assembly to represent Turkey as an independent legatee of the Ottoman state and the sole stakeholder from the post-1914 Ottoman political geography. The parties to the talks proceeded to define Turkey's territory, rights, and obligations.[34] In the early rounds of the Paris Peace Conference in 1919, the Allies had given a semblance of recognition to Hashemite interests. Faysal then spoke in the name of the Arabs and upheld broad Arab independence under the stewardship of his family. Lausanne, however, did not provide for the representation of Arab constituencies, who might have argued for a plebiscitary process. By virtue of having co-opted Faysal to mandatory rule, Britain arrogated to itself the prerogative to speak on behalf of Faysal and the Iraqis. France negotiated for Syria without so much as a similar pretense in the absence of a titular indigenous ruler. King Husayn of the independent state of the Hijaz "did not ask for representation," according to the British authorities, but seems to have offered advice by vehemently urging against concessions on Mosul, "an integral part of the Arab state of Iraq."[35]

İsmet Pasha's delegation left the capital with a set of directives drafted by the government, now presided over by Rauf (Orbay). Foremost was the imperative to secure the southern borders along the detailed demarcations that Mustafa Kemal had articulated in December 1919 and that were subsequently identified as the National Pact boundaries.[36] The boundary with the Syria mandate agreed upon in October 1921 had fallen short of the National Pact borders by some one hundred kilometers in its eastern reaches and thirty kilometers at its western end on the Mediterranean. In the case of the Iraq border, the government charged the delegation with safeguarding Mosul, Kirkuk, and Sulaymaniya. The western borders in Thrace had been largely prefigured by the Mudanya Armistice. The northeastern borders that the GNA government had negotiated with Russia and the long-standing and stable Ottoman border with Iran were not contested at Lausanne. The negotiations about the southern borders quickly revealed that Ankara had overestimated its bargaining power to retain the areas that the resistance movement had declared as having remained under Ottoman control in October 1918, or to secure a plebiscite to determine their status.

In contrast to Britain and France's indifference to the letter and the spirit of the Wilsonian principles and their obligations as mandatories, Ankara's representatives gravitated toward Wilsonian arguments and a defense of territorial rights based on self-determination. In his opening speech at the conference, Ismet Pasha broached the revived claim that the Mudros agreement was predicated upon the Wilsonian principles, a premise that, notably, had not been acknowledged by the Allies at the signing of the agreement or since. At the same time, Ankara defended its territorial goals in a contrived appropriation of the Wilsonian benchmark of ethnicity/nationality and coupling it with the disengagement agreed upon at Mudros. Ismet maintained that the population of Mosul consisted primarily of Turks and Kurds and resorted to dubious demographic and ethnological arguments. Possibly with a degree of conviction reflecting his mixed Turkish and Kurdish parentage, he claimed that the two were one and the same people by ancestral origin. Lord Curzon vehemently rejected the notion of ethno-national commonality between Turks and Kurds, insisting on the Indo-European origins of the Kurds and the Kurdish language.[37] The British delegation produced population statistics that supported the predominantly Arab and Kurdish composition of the northern regions. İsmet Pasha alleged that to the north of Baghdad, the number of Turks exceeded Arabs. Rather than denying this proposition, in view of large Turkmen communities in this region, the British side dismissed the argument by asserting that those Turkmen speak a very different kind of Turkish. In addition to the rhetorical battle of specious demographic and ethnological claims and counterclaims not grounded in sound statistics or any established yardsticks of exclusion and inclusion, the sides vied for the economic potential of northern Iraqi territories. Indeed, the preliminary sessions of the conference had taken up arrangements for the sharing of revenues from the exploitation of the oil resource held by the Turkish Petroleum Company.

In Ankara, where the GNA monitored the proceedings of the conference, the deputies voiced views more radical than those put forward by their delegation. Prime Minister Rauf Bey took the floor in the GNA on December 16 to question the validity of the Mudros agreement itself, suggesting that territorial allocations should not be predicated on its explicit or implicit provisions. He argued that the Allies rendered the agreement null and void by violating its every clause and, strikingly, that "we have never considered it an agreement in force."[38] Hinting thus at maximalist territorial demands not pegged to military circumstances at the time of the armistice's signing, Rauf chose his words to create pressure on the Allies. As the specifics of the Lausanne negotiations came to be known and debated in Ankara, the deputies appealed for territorial borders beyond what Ismet Pasha could sue for and secure at the negotiating table. All viewed the Mosul Province as belonging to Turkey.

The San Remo treaty had included Mosul in the envisaged British mandate of Iraq, and Sèvres had endorsed a border some one hundred kilometers to the town's north, incorporating into the mandate territory most of the Ottoman Mosul Province. Since Sèvres had not been ratified by Ankara, disagreement between the Ottoman and British delegates about the border in Mesopotamia emerged as the main obstacle to the progress of the talks. Calibrating its negotiating position again along Wilsonian precepts, İsmet Pasha demanded the determination of the boundary based on a plebiscite. In the Franco-British negotiations leading to the San Remo Treaty in 1920, the French Foreign Minister Berthelot had shown reservations about the utility of consulting popular opinion, while Lord Curzon, British foreign minister and chief negotiator at Lausanne, had advocated the determination of Syria's borders on the basis of a referendum.[39] At Lausanne, however, Curzon rejected a plebiscite comprising northern Iraq early in the discussions.

Boundary determination came to a head at the conference in the last week of January 1923. At the meeting of the Territorial and Military Commission,

Lord Curzon proposed to bring the border disagreement before the Council of the League of Nations for arbitration.[40] İsmet had no reason to have faith in any arbitration in the councils of the League, widely perceived as a club under the sway of the western European powers, despite assurances from Curzon that Turkey would receive "perfectly equal treatment" at the League Council. Curzon had expected that the Turkish delegation would accept League arbitration in its desire to gain membership to the new international body. İsmet, however, frustrated Curzon by insisting on a plebiscite. Curzon displayed unmitigated colonialist scorn for the Turkish proposal in his report to Prime Minister Balfour. He resorted to time-honored Orientalist tropes, the hallmark of Western abdication of moral responsibility for the peoples of the region, in rejecting the notion "that we should submit the decision as to this frontier to that most futile and pernicious of all forms of tribunal, namely, a plebiscite among tribes and communities sundered by centuries of racial and religious difference."[41] Separately, he wrote to Assistant Under Secretary Ronald Lindsay, "How futile and dangerous an instrument a plebiscite must be in a country with a partially nomadic population, presenting no unity of descent or interest, largely illiterate possessing strong racial or religious prejudices, and suddenly called upon to pronounce by their votes, not upon a single defined issue, but upon such a question as the tracing of a disputed frontier in areas inhabited by turbulent and hostile tribes."[42] Ismet held steadfast, which elicited the threat that London would then apply to the League unilaterally.[43]

A divergence of opinion between Mustafa Kemal and İsmet on the one hand and the government led by Rauf on the other crystallized around the Mosul question and reflected a parallel divide within the GNA. As the talks in Lausanne progressed, Mustafa Kemal gravitated toward compromise rather than driving hard bargains.[44] Being in the position to negotiate an agreement as an equal of the Great Powers, and with a recognized claim to independent existence in a significantly larger part of the Ottoman Empire than the war's victors had conceded at Sèvres, constituted an achievement unimaginable even a few months earlier. These accomplishments secured Mustafa Kemal favorable prospects for the consolidation of his powers, but he would have to navigate the Mosul crisis and obtain a final peace settlement.

During the days of critical negotiations in Lausanne, Mustafa Kemal traveled to northwestern Anatolia. In a town meeting in Eskişehir, he extolled the virtues of peace for the sake of "our own interests and those of the world" and declared that the people (*millet*), the government, and the representative assembly all favor peace.⁴⁵ Such was the importance of priming public opinion toward the acceptance of what might be considered concessions at the conference table that Kemal did not interrupt his tour when he received word in Eskişehir that his mother had passed away in Izmir. The next day, in Arifiye, a small town on the railway line to the north of Eskişehir, he noted, "Our history is replete with shining victories, but our forefathers neglected reaping the fruits of victories." Continuing to nearby İzmid, just to the east of Istanbul, he met with the representatives of the Istanbul press with the agenda of cementing the support of the pro-Ankara press in the capital.⁴⁶ He concluded his conversation with the journalists by stating that peace may or may not be in the offing and opined that the foundation of foreign policy is a robust domestic policy, auguring the heavy-handed policies he would turn to in order to marshal support behind continued engagement in Lausanne.⁴⁷

Kemal's unmistakable message was that Ankara could capitalize on its military victories by moderation and commitment to peace. Toward the end of the month, he went to Izmir to marry Latife (Uşaklıgil), whom he had met during his stay in that city following the expulsion of the Greek armies. In a letter he penned to Prime Minister Rauf he wrote: "We must compare very carefully the results any military operations [in Mosul] might bring with the cost of rejecting [the British offer]. If we are bound to accept the offer, it is important that we do so now, before the talks are suspended and İsmet Pasha returns to Ankara. Should İsmet Pasha return, there is only one decision left to make, which is to start military operations."⁴⁸

Britain was already stepping up its military actions in northern Iraq in anticipation of an escalation but also to strengthen its hand in diplomacy toward securing its objectives. The air force engaged in renewed bombardment of northern regions to break the impasse in Lausanne. Referring to Turkish propaganda in the "turbulent region," the French representative in Baghdad, [Jacques-Roger?] Maigret, wrote: "The British air force is bombing the Turkish-Iraqi border. The measures taken abruptly by the English seem to be correlated with the delivery of the conditions of peace to the Turks, because, locally, the situation is stable. . . . The pro-Turkish sentiments are obvious, but the country is rather calm, at least in appearance. In the event of hostilities between England and Turkey, a mutiny of certain members of the Arab army seems possible."⁴⁹ As the bombs were falling, according to Maigret, the Mosul population was preparing a declaration to affirm pro-Turkish sentiments and to protest Lord Curzon's memorandum at Lausanne.⁵⁰

On January 31, the British delegation in Lausanne presented its Turkish counterpart with a draft treaty that ignored Ankara's objection to bringing the matter of Mosul before the League of Nations. İsmet attempted to break the impasse by proposing the exclusion of the Mosul question from the treaty and its settlement bilaterally between Britain and Turkey within one year. The British refusal resulted in the collapse of the Lausanne talks. While Mosul was the main sticking point, the Turkish delegation was also unable to agree to proposed economic concessions without consulting the representative assembly. Even though Mustafa Kemal had surmised that a breakdown of the talks would lead to war, Ankara refrained from engaging Britain in military operations in northern Iraq.[51]

Soon after İsmet returned home in February, he reported on the Lausanne negotiations to the GNA (February 21), which deliberated on the progress of the talks in several successive sessions. There was palpable concern in the Assembly that the government would concede to British demands on Mosul, and some deputies exhibited a strident stance. On February 27, following İsmet Pasha's presentation, several deputies took issue with the conference outcomes, which they argued contravened the National Pact, not only in relation to the border determination in northern Iraq but also the endorsement of the Ankara Treaty boundary with the Syria mandate. Mustafa Kemal presented a revisionist view of the misak that contradicted the prior interpretations upon which he had predicated the geopolitical objectives of the resistance movement. He stated that the manifesto did not specify "this line or that line" or draw a map. Indeed, the document specified the areas that had not been seized at the time of the armistice. Kemal's assertion was tantamount to acknowledging that neither the Mudros agreement nor the misak, which invoked Mudros, outline territorial delimitations that could be considered boundaries, in spite of his previous (and repeated) representations of a precise demarcation inherent in these documents. Addressing the charge that the government was "scrapping and sacrificing" the misak, he declared that it is the interests of the millet and the discretion of the government that determine the borders.[52]

Mustafa Kemal favored the suspension of the settlement of the Mosul question for one year to remove it as a bottleneck at the talks and argued that this would not mean giving up on Mosul. "We can easily take Mosul today, but that would prolong the war," he said.[53] A few days later, opposition deputy Hüseyin Avni implored Mustafa Kemal to return to the command of the army and "press [his] flag and bayonet against the throat" of the enemy at our border.[54] "Were you able to get back Egypt from the English? Were you able to get back Cyprus? Why should someone who does not give Mosul today do so tomorrow?" he implored. The next day, a deputy asked for a vote of confidence for the government.[55] This was averted with the narrow passing of a resolution to authorize the Lausanne delegation to return to the negotiating table.[56]

During the controversy over Mosul, neither the delegation at Lausanne nor the Ankara government maintained stable communications with Özdemir. Faced with the British and Hashemite efforts to build a tribal alliance favorable to the mandate, Özdemir took countervailing independent action in cooperation with Shaykh Mahmud by mobilizing the vestiges of the defense-of-rights organization still extant in northern Iraq, especially in Kirkuk. Instead of organizing the resistance by co-opting individual tribal chiefs in the region, Özdemir set out to revive and reinforce the organizational structure of the Anatolian movement, which would create horizontal linkages among varied groups under the auspices of a representative council. Mahmud would preside over the representative council, which would speak for an autonomous entity that would accommodate familial, ethnic, and sectarian groupings and confederate with the GNA.[57]

The initiative led to the Sulaymaniya Congress, which convened on January 29, 1923, during the crucial days of the Mosul negotiations in Lausanne. The congress issued a declaration asserting preference for decentralized rule under the auspices of the legitimate government (*hükümet-i şeriyye*) in Ankara over independence that might be proffered by Britain.[58] Mahmud designated a committee of three consisting of a deputy for Sulaymaniya in the 1914 parliament, Ahmed Bey, and one civil and another military officer, both affiliated with Özdemir and the Ankara government, to draft the congress resolutions for dispatch to Ankara.

The resulting document heralded the creation of Southern Kurdistan General National Operations Command, which Shaykh Mahmud would assume as the president of the Southern Kurdistan representative council. Ankara would finance and arm the command and attach to it the regular forces in Rawanduz while retaining the authority for general defense and foreign affairs, which would include giving an ultimatum to London for the evacuation of the region from the Iranian border to the Tigris River up to Şemdinli in the north and Jabal Hamrin in the south, situated on the Tigris half way between Mosul and Baghdad.[59] In Southern Kurdistan, Özdemir was fashioning a defense organization consistent with the various formations that surfaced in the Anatolia-Syria-Iraq nexus and negotiated tactical and political alliances during the course of the resistance movement. As a close observer of the military and political events in this region since the beginning of the resistance, Özdemir was abreast of earlier confederative initiatives and steered the Southern Kurdistan project in this direction. However, the initiative invited reprisals from the British forces and no timely support from Ankara. Özdemir resisted with the forces he could summon, but after a two-week battle, the British forces took Rawanduz and forced Özdemir to flee on April 22, the day before the Lausanne Conference reconvened.[60]

The Ankara delegation was able to return to Lausanne under continued military pressure from British forces in Mosul. Political maneuvers that were aimed not only at manufacturing consent in the representative assembly for the draft treaty but also at manipulating the structures of power made this breakthrough possible. On April 1, 1923, the GNA dissolved itself amid controversy and opposition.[61] Kemal announced the formation of a political faction, which isolated the emerging opposition that had found its voice during the deliberations on the draft Lausanne Treaty, in particular, the Mosul question. The loyalist faction became the nucleus of the single party that monopolized power in the new Turkey until 1950, Halk Fırkası (People's Party) (later Cumhuriyet Halk Partisi [Republican People's Party]).[62] Mustafa Kemal secured amendments to the Treason Law of 1921 that further narrowed the scope of open dissent. Any significant opposition could be characterized as advocacy for the sultanate and tried in the extraordinary "independence courts." These measures opened the way for the talks that resumed in Lausanne on April 23, the third anniversary of the opening of the Ankara assembly, which was now suspended until the conduct of new elections. Mustafa Kemal would manage the elections in June to exclude opposing voices in the legislature.

The political maneuvers cleared the way in April for the signing of a concessionary economic agreement with an American concern, Ottoman-American Development Company represented by retired Rear Admiral Colby M. Chester. The agreement was at odds with the Ankara government's quest for economic independence and almost certainly would have been disputed in the Assembly. The country was economically debilitated, however, and lacked the financial and technological means to fortify its infrastructure independently. Further, the agreement could potentially drive a wedge between the United States and the European allies, in particular as it pertained to northern Iraq, and secure American support for the Ankara government as its delegation returned to the peace talks.[63] The Chester Railway Project entailed the construction of several railroads linking eastern Anatolia with the Black Sea and the Mediterranean, with another line stretching to Mosul and Sulaymaniya in Iraq. The Chester Company would receive the rights for oil exploration and exploitation of mineral resources along the railway. In the spring of April, and on the eve of the conclusive negotiations at Lausanne, the Chester concession served the Ankara government to advance its claims over northern Iraq. The agreement met with French and British opposition and soon lapsed.[64]

In the final draft of the Lausanne Treaty, the status of the border between the British mandate of Iraq and Turkey remained unresolved, with the stipulation of a settlement within nine months in bilateral negotiations. In the event of disagreement, the Turkish delegation consented to the submission of the border dispute to the Council of the League of Nations.[65] Britain in turn agreed to ask the League not to act on it for twelve months, during which the two sides would continue to try and forge a negotiated solution without third-party arbitration. This was the outcome that London had favored: it left Britain in a strong position to dictate its will subsequently in the League of Nations, an instrument of the Great War's victors.

The supervisory role of the League in the mandate regime had already compromised self-determination in Syria. The rhetoric of benevolent guidance toward independent statehood stymied resistance on the ground. The popular movement that coalesced in Anatolia, on the other hand, had registered success in warding off colonial incursion and redeemed some of the territorial losses sustained since the beginning of the Long War. At the Lausanne settlement, the GNA government made a bid to pick up more pieces, as the struggle over northern Iraq demonstrated. It further aimed to revise the Ankara Treaty borders with Syria, which strategic and military considerations had dictated in October 1921, before France's claims on Syria obtained international legal sanction.

SYRIA AND THE LAUSANNE CONFERENCE

As the anti-French sentiment increased in Syria with the imposition of semi-colonial rule, segments of the Syrian population, particularly in northern Syria, looked to Ankara and the Lausanne talks in the hope of invalidating French rule. Turkey's ability to ward off occupation with military success and engage in peace negotiations with the Great Powers made a deep impression in Syria. Placards posted in the streets of Aleppo declared that the mandate of no country other than Turkey could be accepted.[66] The French police rounded up the agitators and, fearful of violent protest, collected arms in districts like al-Bab to the north of Aleppo.[67] The call for a "Turkish mandate" signified the popular proclivity for a reconstructed common political framework that would provide for political or administrative autonomy for its constituent parts. Confronted with the requirement to adopt a legal nationality, some groups within the French mandate territory declared that they would not recognize a nationality other than Turkish, while at the same time resisting the French authorities' attempts to relocate them across the border.[68]

In northern Syria, tribal groups exhibited strong allegiance to the Anatolian movement. Their influence and pastoral mobility cut across the border that the Ankara Treaty had determined. The 'Anaza tribe inhabiting the Anatolian-Syrian-Mesopotamian frontier was caught up in the turmoil of the apportionment of territories during the postwar years. Ankara accorded to its leader Hajim ibn Muhayd the honorific rank of *mirliva* (major general) and the title President of the Patriotic Movement of Elcezire (*Elcezire Hareket-i Vataniye Reisi*). In a letter Hajim sent to the GNA as early as 1921 during the London Conference, he stressed his influence over both the Kurdish and Arab inhabitants between the Euphrates and Tigris Rivers in northeastern Syria. He conveyed the insistent protestations of the people of the Elcezire region against European states' reported demands to carve up Arab and Kurdish entities within the Ottoman domains. Hajim maintained that the idea of the independence of Muslim elements served nothing more than Europe's goal of shattering the Ottoman Empire and expanding European influence and that it exposed a hypocrisy: He argued that the European states should first liberate the Muslim peoples under their own rule.[69]

Hajim was headquartered in the Raqqa district near Dayr al-Zur, a region that the Ankara Treaty left in French hands, but his following spread to the north over areas that were within the sphere of the Anatolian resistance. In February 1923, the French authorities in Aleppo summoned him and his cousin Mujham and presented them with a cash reward in an apparent attempt to co-opt them into subservience, in case Ankara's objective to revise the Syrian boundary at Lausanne led to conflict.[70] Fully aware that his acceptance of France's good graces was known in Ankara, Hajim penned a letter to Mustafa Kemal.[71] He alluded to his past services in the name of Islam and the salvation of the homelands in accordance with the duty of jihad. Asserting his wish not to separate from the Muslims' struggle, and "its guardian, the glorious Turkey," he explained that he was bound to reside to the south of the border where the villages that provide his livelihood as well as the grazing lands needed for his followers' animals were situated. He continued: "It may have appeared as if I were separating from Turkey. I will never separate. Despite French reprisal I do not refrain from expressing that I will never turn against Turkey. I will comply with orders to participate in the struggle on behalf of Turkey both in the Jazira, where I am, but also in Aleppo, Dayr al-Zur, even Baghdad." The sentiments were taken seriously enough that the Elcezire command in Diyarbekir recommended financial assistance to Hajim in May 1923 to preclude his co-optation by the mandatory power.[72]

The relations between France and Turkey showed strains over Syria when the conference talks reconvened in April and brought the bilateral Ankara Treaty between the GNA government and France within the framework of the broader peace settlement. Mustafa Kemal's tour of Anatolia had taken him to Adana in mid-March. According to one observer, in a speech, Kemal singled out and referred to Alexandretta as "Turkish soil since four thousand years ago."[73] In June, the army command in Adana prepared for an incursion into Syria, which would entail a three-pronged attack by regular troops, militias, and the fighters anticipated to join these forces after the capture of their districts. The averred objective was to incite a general popular movement aimed at ending the French administration and supplanting it with one in the name of the government of the GNA. The regional commander in Adana in charge of the plans, Colonel Mehmed Kenan, envisaged the destruction of railroads, telegraph lines, and bridges to disrupt French communications and the defection of the North African Muslim troops in the French army "who are looking for an opportunity to attach themselves to us." He recommended forceful action against any Syrians collaborating with the French forces. The chief of staff approved the proposed plan of action, but the initiative was overtaken by the peace treaty in July.[74]

A report that the militia leader Shakir Ni'mat, now in residence in Ayntab, received from a contact in Aleppo described the mood and circumstances in the city on the eve of the conclusion of the conference. According to the informant, the news that the peace agreement would be signed at Lausanne on July 18 had caused sadness and hopelessness. On Bastille Day, the French contingents in town staged a triumphant parade with the participation of fifteen hundred infantry from Algeria, Tunisia, and Indochina, eight hundred Algerian cavalry, and seven hundred militia men, Circassians, and gendarmes, accompanied by tanks, armored cars, and military motorcycles. While the Aleppines evinced little enthusiasm for the show of force, the report said,

French authorities were benefitting from local informants, who provided information about forces stationed to the north of the border. Those Aleppines in communication with Anatolian groups had become subjects of investigation, and Hajim was believed to have defected.[75] The former mutasarrıf of Ayntab, the publisher of a Turkish newspaper in Aleppo, collaborated with the French authorities by leaking secret communications between Aleppo and Ayntab across the border.[76] Najib al-'Uwayyid, a resistance leader in northern Syria, continued his opposition to France and was sentenced by a French court-martial to twenty years in prison.[77]

The signing of the peace treaty enfeebled the resistance in Syria and the Anatolian-Syrian frontier. Ankara's regional commander Mehmed Kenan argued in favor of sustaining the anti-colonial organizational network on both sides of the border, as the French efforts to bring local administration under control was meeting with militia resistance and tribal opposition.[78] Well aware of the consolidation of French rule under the circumstances of the treaty, the chief of staff deemed continued support of the opposition costly and did not endorse Kenan's suggestion to maintain the organizational framework among the Turks.[79] Twelve weeks later, on October 5, Kenan informed the chief of staff that "political propaganda within Syria is called off per your instructions. Organizations and individuals working on this have been told to stop their operations."[80]

IMPLICATIONS OF THE PEACE TREATY FOR THE OTTOMAN PATRIMONY

The Lausanne Treaty delineated the territories of the rump empire except the border with the British mandate of Iraq and reconstituted these territories as internationally recognized sovereign Turkey.[81] It invoked and certified borders that the Istanbul government or the GNA had acceded to in previous accords with other states, including the line that marked the northern boundary of the Syria mandate, which was determined in the Ankara Treaty as largely corresponding to the railway. Ankara signed the Lausanne Treaty with the ill-fated caveat about the determination of the Iraq border in direct talks between Turkey and Britain within nine months. Apart from leaving this border unsettled, the Lausanne Treaty formally dismantled the Ottoman Empire by acknowledging the political status of the Arab provinces of the empire as incorporated into separate states within the mandate structure under the League of Nations oversight or pursuant to agreements struck between Britain and local actors in the Arabian Peninsula. Britain and France thus upheld the imprimatur that the League of Nations had given to the mandatory arrangement as the keystone of the Lausanne agreement, to which Turkey consented in return for the Allies' validation of its sovereignty within the prescribed borders.

Lausanne addressed Egypt insofar as to deny Turkey any claims in this territory that Britain had declared a protectorate in 1914 (Article 17) and to rule out any Egyptian initiatives to claim organic ties with Ankara. Just as there was strong Egyptian sentiment in favor of the Anatolian movement for independence and Mustafa Kemal's military successes against imperialist designs, interest in the Lausanne talks also remained high in Egypt. A French diplomat reported from Cairo as late as May 1923 that the very same "Turkish agents" who were active in Damascus and southern Syria were acting as intermediaries in contact with Syrian exiles in Egypt and the Azharite ulama, spreading the propaganda that the Ankara government aimed at the liberation of Muslim peoples.[82]

The Treaty of Lausanne resolved the disputes of the new Turkey with its Balkan neighbors and addressed the status of non-Muslims who remained within the boundaries of the state.[83] By elaborating special safeguards for non-Muslim minorities, the treaty recognized Turkey's core political community as consisting of Muslims, consonant with the premise of the resistance movement as a struggle by the Muslims for the Muslims. A preamble to the treaty negotiated at the outset of the talks approved the relocation of the Greek Orthodox population of Anatolia to Greece and the Muslims of Greece to Anatolia.[84] Non-Muslims in the new Turkey would primarily consist of the Jews, the remainder of the Armenian population, and the Greeks of Istanbul (who were exempted from the population transfer, as were the Muslims in western Thrace on the Greek side). The rights of the non-Muslim communities had to be protected with distinct guarantees by international treaty much like those of foreign individuals and concerns. The general stipulations that addressed the status of the non-Muslims in the new state, such as the right to choose one's legal nationality, applied to those members of Muslim communities who inhabited the new state but had distinctive communal or heritage bonds beyond the new borders. Article 39 of Lausanne stipulated the free use "by any Turkish national of any language in private intercourse, in commerce, religion, in the press, or in publications of any kind or at public meetings." Unlike in the case of non-Muslims, the treaty did not comprise guidance for an institutional framework that would ensure communal rights for such linguistic/cultural Muslim groups as Kurds and Arabs unassimilated to the state language.

The territorial reconfiguration and the political transformations that laid the foundations of a new state occurred against the background of a demographic sea change in Anatolia and Thrace. These areas lost more than four million, or approximately one-third, of their population within one decade to the destruction and deprivations of the war, massacres, and emigration.[85] Depopulation altered the social fabric of the society, particularly because of the disproportionate number of male deaths. About one million Muslims who immigrated into these areas during the Long War decade offset only a portion of the population loss but contributed to the thorough demographic Islamization of the new Turkey. The Turkish nation-state was founded in a struggle against Western imperialism within newly created and internationally agreed boundaries and upon unification around the common communal bonds of Islam. Both fundaments were to be turned on their head after independence with the Kemalist project of a self-consciously secular nationalism and the methodical embrace of Western culture and institutions by the Republican elites.

As the international accord that ultimately resolved the boundaries of a sovereign Ottoman successor state based in Anatolia and Thrace, the Treaty of Lausanne created modern Turkey. The new state comprised more than three times as much territory that the signatories of the Treaty of Sèvres were prepared to grant to a sovereign enclave three years earlier, and Lausanne thus affirmed the achievements of armed resistance that had lasted as many years. The new Turkey assumed two-thirds of the Ottoman debt to European states, with repayment scheduled to start in 1929. Just as full sovereignty had been compromised in economic affairs, Turkey agreed to demilitarize the Straits of Marmara (Bosporus and Dardanelles) and allow international supervision. Against the immediate background of the wartime military defeats, postwar occupation, and the terms of Sèvres tantamount to extinction, Turkish histories celebrate Lausanne as the foundational charter of the state and a national triumph.

At the same time, the treaty affirmed the demise of a world empire. If the territorial settlement of Lausanne is appraised against the Ottoman Empire's patrimony before it entered the Great War, the treaty ratified the dismemberment of the Ottoman state's Syrian, Mesopotamian (with the status of Mosul Province in abeyance), and Arabian provinces. Even as the Ottomans reincorporated the northeastern districts of Kars and Ardahan lost to Russia in 1878, approximately half the territories and more than one-third of the population over which the Ottomans exercised jurisdiction in 1914 separated from the state to be reconstituted as the mandatory states of Iraq (with disputed boundaries in the north), Syria (including Lebanon), Palestine, and Jordan, in addition to the Kingdom of the Hijaz, which Sharif Husayn had secured as independent entity during the Great War.

The resistance movement could not reclaim the territories lost on the battle fronts of the Great War but strived to retain under its control all parts that remained to the empire at the time the government entered into obligations of military surrender as decided at Mudros. The structures of empire (e.g., administrative organization, constitutional institutions, residual army, and leadership cadres) upheld the popular movement in these regions, modulated by the exigencies of renewed warfare that inevitably engendered novel geopolitical visions.[86] The vision of a reorganized Ottoman state had survived the Great War. The prospects of a federative or confederative reconstruction remained against the background of the implementation of the mandates. The Treaty of Lausanne certified the forfeiture of these geopolitical projects and presaged further territorial concessions with the pending resolution of the boundary in upper Mesopotamia. The consent of the Ankara government to reconcile to borders proposed at Lausanne met with the vehement objections of lawmakers. Only the authoritarian measures that Mustafa Kemal implemented, including the purge of the Assembly and the establishment of party discipline, prevented the collapse of the Lausanne negotiations.

When the GNA abrogated the constitutional monarchy at the end of 1922, it was poised to transform into a constituent body. By tightly managing the elections of 1923, Mustafa Kemal ensured the election of loyalists. The party organization he presided over further enhanced his powers. Lausanne provided the geopolitical and international-legal framework for the new state, which Mustafa Kemal and his associates proceeded to christen as a republic on October 29, 1923. The declaration of the republic and the elimination of the office of the caliph some three months later witnessed heated discussion, even in the reconstituted Assembly consisting of loyalists, with repercussions beyond the borders of the new Turkey among Muslims.

LAUSANNE'S AFTERMATH

Mosul and Alexandretta had emerged as the most immediately and resolutely contested Ottoman districts in the post-armistice scramble to extend

Allied occupation. Dispute about their status continued beyond the Treaty of Lausanne.

The Ankara Treaty of October 1921 identified Alexandretta as a district with a special administration within the French sphere in Syria. Lausanne incorporated the region into the French mandate of Syria as such without delineating the particulars of the special status. Though legally settled at Lausanne, the border with Syria remained unstable and porous. Critics in France took exception to the provisions of the treaty. In the words of one, "The border remains precarious, subject to all sorts of disputes, poorly defended, poorly supervised."[87] In particular, Turkey continued to contest the ill-defined special status of Alexandretta. In 1936, the ratification of a Franco-Syrian treaty would present Turkey with an opportunity to successfully press demands for the province's separation from Syria as an autonomous state. No sooner was a republic declared in this splinter state in 1938 than Turkey maneuvered to stage a controversial election with French assent and against the objections of Damascus. The election produced an assembly favoring annexation with Turkey, which was ratified on June 29, 1939.[88]

Turkish ambitions in Mosul were thwarted at Lausanne when the resolution of the status of northern Iraq was tabled to be renegotiated the following year. The talks would not be scheduled until May 1924. In the interim, Britain continued to prop up Faysal and the semblance of an indigenous independent government in Iraq. Faysal's rule continued to meet with the opposition of some Kurdish and Shiite groups. The Shiite ulama in Najaf and Karbala boycotted the preparations to elect a constituent assembly and threatened punishment for anyone who participated in the elections. The French Ministry of War ascribed the resistance to Turkish instigation.[89]

Britain's and Turkey's delegations met in May in Istanbul (*Haliç Konferansı*, or the Golden Horn Conference) to renegotiate the status of Mosul.[90] The British delegates exhibited a hard-line stance on the border, extending the demands as far north as to include the Hakkari district, ostensibly in order to extend protection to the Christian Assyrian community in this region. The disagreement defaulted to the submission of the Mosul question to the League of Nations Council. London expected to be able to secure its desiderata within the League, where Turkey was not a member. The League approached the task of adjudicating the dispute with thoroughness and the appearance of rectitude in a drawn-out effort that contrasted with the determination of the Syria border in 1921, which was the outcome of a tactical imperative to bring an end to the hostilities between the GNA government and France in one arena of conflict. The confirmation of this border arrangement at Lausanne had given Ankara a territorial advantage over the Sèvres delimitation but comprised a significant territorial concession from the misak. In northern Mesopotamia, the Turkish government advanced the misak as the basis of its demands as late as 1924.

The League set up a commission led by delegates representing member countries disinterested in the dispute. The commission conducted a painstaking and prolonged investigation on the ground into discrete facets of the conflict and listened to arguments from both sides: demographic composition, geography, economic connections, historical factors, and stakes in the region's oil. It became apparent that none of these factors on their own or in combination provided compelling criteria for division. Ethnic and sectarian population figures presented to the commission were starkly divergent, as had been the case during the Lausanne talks. Ankara once more insisted on a plebiscite, against British opposition. The commission chose instead to conduct interviews with several hundred informants. In December 1925, the League decided in favor of a provisional border that had been discussed at a League meeting in Belgium in Turkey's absence before the commission started its work. The "Brussels Line" incorporated the Mosul Province into the Kingdom of Iraq under the British mandate with minor adjustments in the north and the allocation of one-tenth of the future oil revenues from the region to the Republic of Turkey. A major uprising in predominantly Kurdish eastern Anatolia prompted by a spate of secular policies that the government legislated and implemented, including the abolition of the caliphate on March 3, 1924, exposed the region to British intrigue from Iraq, highlighting for Turkey the urgency of settling the Iraq border. The government signed off on the proposed line in June 1926 with a second Treaty of Ankara, which finalized the borders of the Turkish Republic until the annexation of Alexandretta in 1939. (See Map 6.)

Conclusion

IN OCTOBER 1918, the Ottomans succumbed to the European armies, adding another devastating defeat to the reverses the empire had suffered since the 1870s. In 1878, the European states cobbled together the Congress of Berlin within months of the Ottoman surrender to Russian forces at the outskirts of Istanbul. The Ottoman state was able to cut its territorial losses at Berlin owing to Western European countries' concerns about Russia's extension of power to the Aegean and the imminent danger of it sweeping over the Ottoman capital, which portended seismic shifts in the European balances of power. The treaty averted a vital threat to the Ottoman state, yet it also sanctioned secessions in the Balkans and paved the way for the colonization of other provinces, resulting in vast losses in the Ottomans' domains spread over three continents. Thirty-five years later, the recently independent Balkan states vied for the empire's remaining European territories in Macedonia and Thrace with unified military action. The empire confronted another threat to its survival with Bulgarian armies advancing within miles of Istanbul; yet a dispute over the spoils among the Balkan allies resulted in a less ruinous settlement than anticipated, even as it divested the Ottoman state of most of its territories in Europe. Five years later in 1918, the Ottomans once again surrendered vast lands, this time in Asia, to the armies of the rival Entente Powers. Ottoman response to defeat was similar in 1878, 1913, and 1918. It focused on minimizing territorial loss, securing an internationally sanctioned agreement with the least disadvantageous terms, and reconsolidating the empire by reasserting state authority. At the Great War's end, unlike in 1878 and 1913, the belligerents did not reconfigure the postwar geopolitical status quo in the Middle East by treaty. This contrasted with the experience of the other Central Powers, who signed peace treaties within a year. A settlement in the Middle East remained in abeyance.

The fruition of the Triple Entente between Britain, France, and Russia in 1907 had upended the balance of power system in Europe, which had been destabilized upon German unification in the 1870s and militarization in subsequent decades. The alliance, motivated by the desire to contain Germany, signified Anglo-French acquiescence in Russia's time-honored geostrategic ambitions in the Straits and eastern Anatolia. As tensions grew in Europe during the decade before the Great War and culminated in the June Crisis of 1914, Ottoman statesmen scrambled in vain to come to a diplomatic agreement with one or more Entente powers. The fear of predation convinced the CUP government that neutrality could not be an option as war camps took shape.[1] Istanbul's eventual alliance with the Central Powers further crystallized the Triple Entente's war aims in the Middle East. The start of the hostilities legitimized formal understandings within the Triple Entente about prospective divisions of Ottoman territories, which were first delineated in the Constantinople Agreement of 1915, an understanding reached in an exchange of notes. The accord's moniker conveys the momentous concession of the Ottoman capital to Russia as a reward for its commitment to the Entente war effort. The agreement recognized in return British claims for Mesopotamia and French claims for Syria. In 1916, the Sazonov-Sykes-Picot agreement further elaborated on a precise apportionment of the empire's Arab provinces as war aims.

Throughout the Great War, the Ottoman government devoted an extraordinary effort to the defense, retention, and regeneration of the Arab provinces, most notably in Greater Syria governed by Cemal Pasha. At the core of these efforts was the restoration of the authority and legitimacy of the empire. Ottoman policy in Syria during the war, informed by the oppressive stringency of Cemal's enactments, signified a reversion of the center's post-1913 proclivity to accommodate demands for decentralizing reform. Under the strains of the violence that Syria confronted on both the battlefronts and the home front and the destitution that permeated the society owing to exactions, deprivation, and pestilence, the objective to bolster the legitimacy of the state became unmoored from the increasingly dire realities on the ground and was severely challenged by Sharif Husayn's revolt in Mecca in 1916. Toward the end of the war, the Ottoman government strove to redeem its authority and explored federative initiatives to reintegrate the empire with the Arab provinces intact. Expanding Allied occupation at the end and in the immediate aftermath of the Great War both complicated these efforts and, paradoxically, revived them as a platform upon which anti-colonial resistance was articulated across the empire by both elite and popular groups motivated by Muslim nationalism.

Just as the accommodation of long-standing Russian aspirations set the stage for the parceling out of the Ottoman imperium, Bolshevik Russia's precipitate withdrawal from the war after the October Revolution in 1917 muddled the very project. The truce with Russia was followed by the Brest-Litovsk Treaty with its favorable terms for the Ottoman Empire, including the restitution of large swaths of occupied territory in eastern Anatolia and the abandonment of the Russian quest for Istanbul. Peace with Bolshevik Russia gave a new lease on life to the Ottomans in the last year of the war and strengthened the prospects for the state's survival in tandem with a rejuvenation of the Central Powers' war effort in Europe. By the fall of 1918, however, the tide had turned against the Central Powers everywhere and forced them to negotiate for peace.

The path to the relinquishment of arms in October and November 1918, the "pre-Armistice agreement" and the armistices themselves, was paved by rhetoric to uphold the Wilsonian principles, which both resonated and vied with Lenin's formal denunciation of imperialism. Istanbul's appeals to the Wilsonian imperatives in its quest for peace would not find a sympathetic ear among the victors of the war. The Armistice of Mudros, negotiated and signed at the end of October 1918, was not predicated on the letter or the spirit of the Fourteen Points. It validated Allied military control of Ottoman territories that Britain and France had partitioned by secret treaty. Its provisions also included loopholes to expand the occupation and ensure the pursuit of territorial war aims not achieved in their entirety at the time of the signing. The Allies immediately took action to achieve these objectives, effectively nullifying the agreement and undermining the sovereignty of the Ottoman state. Their actions plunged the Middle East into renewed armed conflict, extending the warfare and mobilizing the Ottomans into a new phase of the struggle aimed at salvaging the state and redeeming territorial losses. In subsequent years, histories erroneously consecrated the Mudros cease-fire as having deliberately effected a separation of Turkish and Arab ethnonational populations.

Armed conflict remained endemic in the Middle East in the absence of a formal peace agreement. Allied military occupation expanded into different regions throughout the empire, the armistice notwithstanding. The resistance to occupation forces was local and isolated at first but became increasingly coordinated. Sequestered contingents of Ottoman forces continued the fighting in the Arabian periphery in Medina and Yemen. Once the utility of wartime alliances with local powerholders became moot, Britain left the Arabian Peninsula to the vagaries of internecine contestation, most significantly between Ibn Sa'ud in Najd and the Hashemites. As a more unified political and military movement consolidated in Ankara, communal groups, including Circassians, Kurds, and Albanians, incited rebellions, jostling for power and influence in the wake of the seismic changes brought about by the events of 1914–1918. In the Caucasus, remnants of the Ottoman army under the command of Kazım Karabekir Pasha skirmished with forces of the Armenian Republic over contested Kars and its vicinity. Popular groups in Syria challenged Faysal's attempt in Damascus to consolidate his authority under British auspices.

What is today known as the Turkish national movement (or the Turkish struggle for independence) developed as a series of local militia movements driven by the imperative to preserve the political rights of the Muslims. The "societies for the defense of rights," which directed the local resistance movements, grew directly out of the local branches of the CUP. After the Greek occupation of Izmir and its environs in May 1919, these organizations coalesced on the regional level in a series of congresses. Even though the top leaders of the CUP had gone into exile, the secondary cadres of the Committee took the helm of the resistance movements availing of existing organizational structures in the provinces. As the local committees of defense became coordinated regionally, they articulated broader objectives for the resistance movement.

At the time of the formal end of the hostilities in the fall of 1918, European colonial ambitions in the Middle East had trumped Wilsonian notions such as self-determination, state sovereignty, rejection of right of force, and denunciation of secret agreements. The Principles' Twelfth Point pertaining to the Middle East, a region where the United States was not directly involved in wartime hostilities, displayed ambiguities that were not meaningfully clarified by the president's later pronouncements. If the principles were not meant to give a free hand to the American allies in the Ottoman Empire, they nevertheless had this effect. Yet the Ottoman statesmen, civic groups, and militias selectively deployed Wilsonian idioms as an anti-colonial defensive platform and a template against which to formulate political desiderata. The

Istanbul government, the provincial resistance, the Syrian Congress, and the literati and opinion makers advanced political agendas in the idiom of Wilsonian ideals, sometimes at cross-purposes. The imprecision of the Twelfth Point provided latitude in the formulation of the demand to preserve the state by minimizing loss of territory. The Istanbul government touted caliphal sovereignty and, barring the restoration of the status quo ante, it proposed a federative structure that would accommodate the occupied provinces within the Ottoman fold. The leadership of the resistance based its claims for a political solution on its interpretation of Wilson's principles and the moral force of the armistice agreement. It asserted rights over territories it defined as lying "within armistice lines," which included portions of the mandates of Syria and Iraq as agreed upon by Britain and France. It conceded the fate of the Ottoman territories to the south of this line to the vote of the inhabitants. The Faysal administration touted self-determination for Syria "within its natural boundaries," which adhered to expansive territorial limits that his father, Sharif Husayn, had expounded to High Commissioner McMahon.

During the Paris Peace Conference in 1919, Wilson was confronted with the intricacies of the conflicting wartime assurances proffered to the Hashemites and Zionists as well as differences between the principal American allies, Britain and France, pertaining to spheres of control in the Middle East. Wilson's advocacy for the dispatch of a fact-finding mission to Syria was tantamount to support for Syrians' self-determination. The attenuation of this initiative owing to lack of cooperation from America's allies and Washington's lapse into isolationism jettisoned the King-Crane commission's recommendations and mooted the effort to appraise self-determination in Syria. A parallel initiative spawned in Paris and aimed at restoring Armenian rights in Anatolia met with a similar fate when the resistance in Anatolia rejected the notion of an American mandate in Armenia or more broadly in the region.

Clusters of resistance in the Anatolia-Syria-Mesopotamia nexus subscribed to a reconceptualized Ottomanism, namely a Muslim civic ideal. The resonance of an Ottomanism that accommodated the empire's diverse religious groups had progressively weakened with the diminution of the numerical strength of the Christians. It received a fatal blow with the Armenian Genocide in the early years of the war. The understanding of the Ottoman political community as a civic Muslim one informed the re-integrationist policy of the CUP during the Great War. This concept of state and community prevailed in the immediate wake of the war, even as new governmental structures that impinged on the sultan-caliph's sovereignty came into existence. The post-defeat vulnerability of the empire and the Allies' support of the Armenians who survived the war to reclaim their domiciles and property further hardened the attitudes against the Christians. The Greek occupation of Izmir in 1919 in a manifestation of a clientage relationship between enemy powers and Ottoman Christians only exacerbated the anti-Christian sentiments. The project of setting up ethno-religious political entities at the Treaty of Sèvres heightened the existential concerns of the majority Muslims. The anticolonial forces in Anatolia, northern Syria, and northern Mesopotamia maintained contact, collaborated, and kept alive the possibility of confederation.

The discovery, recovery, accumulation, and publicization of facts that resonated with the Wilsonian principles became an end within the empire to secure redemption in the peace process and to mitigate the consequences of defeat and occupation. Mustafa Kemal, the Istanbul government, the Hashemites, and popular groups utilized Wilsonian language instrumentally. In relating his memoirs in 1926, Mustafa Kemal said: "I have to confess that I somewhat endeavored to formulate the national border in accordance with the humanitarian purposes of the Wilsonian principles." Betraying skepticism about the principle of nationality rights, he mused, "Poor Wilson. He failed to understand that no principle can defend boundaries that are not defended with bayonets, force, honor, and dignity."[2] Wilsonianism resonated with and reinforced Arabist and Turkist sentiment and spawned Kurdist agendas abetted by Britain. The resistance groups appealed first and foremost to religious sentiment, however, and elevated Muslim commonality in opposing colonial schemes to ensure sovereign existence.

The Kemalist leadership was motivated by the same consideration that had motivated Ottoman governments since the onset of military reverses, namely the preservation of the maximum extent of the empire's territory. Wielding military force and motivated by state patriotism, the Kemalists reversed the dictates of the Treaty of Sèvres with military victories and diplomatic acts to preserve a geopolitically and economically viable state that included some of the contested territories at the Anatolia-Syria frontier. The territorial gains were demarcated in the south by the railway line that had been built by the Germans, was now shared with France, and would subsequently be touted as circumscribing lands inhabited by Turks. The determination of the new border in northern Mesopotamia proved to be more protracted and contested. A swath of land that Mustafa Kemal identified in 1919 as inalienable, reaching deep into the Euphrates basin down to Dayr al-Zur and east to Sulaymaniya, remained within the Syria and Iraq mandates. This region and the lands to its south, the political future of which the Kemalists had declared to be contingent on the will of the inhabitants as to be determined by their free vote, came to be included in the mandates without plebiscitary procedures, except spurious exercises in Iraq in 1919 and 1921.

Each time a crisis erupts in the Middle East, observers invoke the arbitrary nature of political boundaries that ignore geographical, historical, cultural, and economic realities on the ground. During the Republican period in Turkey, nationalist indoctrination and accompanying historical revisionism have postulated Turkey's border with Syria as a "natural" ethno-national boundary, marking the domicile of a primordial Turkish collectivity. The delimitation of the territory of the modern Turkish nation-state has thus come to be viewed as an exception to the contingent determination of boundaries in the region. As acute an observer of modern Turkey as Dankwart Rustow, for instance, has written that "throughout most of the Third World, the present borders of would-be nation states were drawn up by European colonial rulers and do not coincide with any sense of national identity. . . . Except for the lingering Kurdish intransigence in the southeast and the relatively less significant Sunni-Alevi cleavage, Turkey represents the exceptional phenomenon of an almost complete coincidence of national and state identities."[3] The caveat about Kurdish resistance to the Turkish national project as "intransigence" implies that Turkish national identity was the product of a discursive and sociopolitical construction rather than the manifestation of an auspicious correspondence of state and the essential nation.

The territorial boundaries of the rump Ottoman state remained fluid and subject to the contestations of international diplomacy. The Kemalist quest to reintegrate the domains of the imperial state continued until the consummation of the two armistice agreements with a peace treaty at Lausanne in 1923—considered an honorable settlement in that it reversed the disastrous terms of the rejected Treaty of Sèvres. The Treaty of Lausanne solidified the southeastern boundary that had been agreed upon in the Ankara accord with France in 1921 as a tactical concession. The resolution of the state borders and the consolidation of political power in the hands of Mustafa Kemal and his associates were mutually dependent. Having acquired authority and prestige owing to successes on the battlefield and the conference table, Kemal avoided further military entanglements as he sought to institutionalize his powers. The borders in the Anatolia-Syria-Mesopotamia nexus ensued from the vagaries of war, diplomacy, and contestation for economic advantage, with scant regard to geography or ethno-national identity. They unfolded as accomplished facts or remained as unfinished projects with a destabilizing effect in the region for decades to come.

For the Kemalists, Turkey as it emerged from the Lausanne Treaty became the vessel in which Mustafa Kemal and the leadership of the resistance movement would build the new nation and further consolidate their power. The self-view of the Turk as a citizen of the new Turkey was that of a Muslim who had shared the ideal of ridding the homeland of foreign occupation and securing a defensible portion of the Ottoman patrimony with internationally recognized boundaries. The success of the struggle had imparted prestige and legitimacy to the leadership. Mustafa Kemal and his followers in Ankara rode the wave of military victory to challenge and destroy the bastions of the old regime. The leadership itself was divided about the wisdom and extent of the transformations, as factionalism within the vanguard of the resistance movement would reveal and make it all the more important for the Kemalists to strengthen their hold on power.

In the former domains of the Ottoman Empire, popular attitudes favoring regional cooperation and solidarity persisted after the signing of the Lausanne treaty. Ottomanist papers in Syria reflected this pro-Turkish sentiment.[4] The Ankara government's ability to sign a peace treaty on equal footing with the Allied Powers reverberated in the region and enhanced its regional prestige. The declaration of a republic in Turkey in October 1923, the full implementation of the mandates in Greater Syria and Iraq, and the abrogation of the caliphate in March 1924 brought a practical and theoretical end to confederative schemes in the region, while a combination of events cut a larger-than-life figure of Mustafa Kemal among the Arab peoples. In Palestine, for instance, there was a sentiment for recognizing Mustafa Kemal as caliph. As late as 1929, participants in religious holiday celebrations invoked his name and proclaimed blessings to him.[5] A Lebanese American author and activist for Arab unity, who acted as intermediary between King 'Ali of the Hijaz and Ibn Sa'ud of Najd in 1925 reported that both Ibn Sa'ud and Imam Yahya of Yemen were seeking treaties with Mustafa Kemal. "The Turks are fast getting back into Nejd and Yemen, and sentiment in both these sections is decidedly pro-Turkish: Neither with Turkey as a ruler, but both consider her a powerful ally when necessary." In transmitting the report, British consul in Damascus, C. E. S. Palmer advised: "It will be remembered that I always, while at Damascus, did my utmost to keep track of possible Kemalist agents, and there will seem to be great need of similar precautions again at present."[6]

Two distinctive facets of the Turkish Republic under Mustafa Kemal have resulted in the underestimation of mutual attitudes and synergy between Turkey and Arab countries: the evolution of Turkish nationalism in an ethnicist direction in the 1930s and the repudiation of traditional institutions identified with Islam, now branded as an Arab religion.[7] In the early years of the Republic, Turkishness denoted a civic communality commensurate with Ottomanness in the previous period. A civics textbook published under Mustafa Kemal's auspices and the name of his twenty-two-year-old adopted daughter, Afet İnan, represents the inflection point between the early Republic's civic idea of nationhood and an ethnonationalism that foregrounded and glorified a putative primordial Turkish identity.[8] The book defines the "Turkish millet" as "those people who established the Republic of Turkey," and asserts: "Within this Turkish political and social community, there are compatriots and co-nationals who have been subjected to propaganda that instills notions of being Kurdish, Circassian, even Bosniak and Laz." Ascribing these influences to mindless reactionaries, and asserting that they have not had any effect other than causing sorrow, the author turns to the Arabs: "One wonders if the Arabs, who have refused to unite with the Turks to form a millet—even though we accepted their religion—are pleased with their servitude today?" The book evinces a continued consciousness of bonds with Arabs as natural but ill-fated members of the sociopolitical community. In the 1930s, the growth of racialist Turkish nationalism denied other Muslim identities and fashioned the Turkish-Arab alterity, yet it did not eviscerate cross-regional interactions or historical connections.[9]

Assumptions about Turkish secularism, which suggest indifference to Muslim neighbors, and the latter-day narrative of a peace-loving and passive foreign policy by an inward-looking Turkey in Kemal's republic have obscured Turkey's relationship with the Arab world. Interrogating the notion of Turkey's detachment from the Arab world and its Middle Eastern neighbors, Amit Bein has concluded that Republican Turkey has purposefully vied for influence in the Arab world.[10] With the important exception of Turkey's irredentist annexation of Alexandretta, its conflictual relationship with the Arab countries was a product of the Cold War era when Turkey positioned itself against the dominant ideological and political currents in the Arab Middle East. The resurgence of cooperative relations between Turkey and its southern neighbors during the last three decades, an aspect of what is identified as neo-Ottomanism, points to the resilience of ties grounded in historical and cultural commonalities a century after the Ottoman Empire's political fragmentation.[11]

NOTES

PREFACE

1. Kayalı, *Arabs and Young Turks: Ottomanism, Arabism, and Islamism in the Ottoman Empire, 1908–1918* (Berkeley: University of California Press, 1997).

2. While the Arabic term for Mesopotamia is *al-Jazira* ("the island," by virtue of being between the two rivers), in some contexts *al-Jazira* (*Elcezire*) refers more specifically to northern Mesopotamia, while *al-'Iraq* connotes central Mesopotamia. Iraq and Mesopotamia will be used interchangeably here as geographical terms.

INTRODUCTION

1. See Hobsbawm, "The End of Empires," 12; Esherick et al., *Empire to Nation*, 21–22.

2. Beyond the instrumentalist fabrications of ancient bonds, scholars have explored the potency of elements of nationness in ancient history in modern nationalist ideologies. See, Roshwald, *The Endurance of Nationalism*; Goodblatt, *Elements of Ancient Jewish Nationalism*.

3. The notion of the ancient (pre-Islamic) roots of the nation has had appeal to secular elements in these societies to counter the abiding centrality of Islam in collective consciousness. See, for instance, Baram, "Territorial Nationalism in the Middle East."

4. The term *Middle East*, contested because of its vague contours and relatively recent and Eurocentric coinage, refers here to the general region where Ottoman sovereignty (or suzerainty) persisted on the eve of the world war, spanning from Thrace to Iran, from the Caucasus to the southern Arabian Peninsula, and in parts of North Africa.

5. Gülalp, "The Eurocentrism of Dependency Theory and the Question of 'Authenticity.'"

6. On historical studies, see, for instance, Duara, *Rescuing History from the Nation*, especially his Conclusion, 229–36. On general social studies, see Wimmer and Schiller, "Methodological Nationalism and Beyond," 302–8.

7. Notably, Chatterjee, *The Nation and Its Fragments*.

8. Suny, "Religion, Ethnicity, and Nationalism," 23.

9. Early in the twentieth century Britain, France, and Russia aligned diplomatically as the Triple Entente, which with the outbreak of World War I in 1914 became a military pact. This alliance, joined by Italy in 1915, will be referred to here as the "Entente." In 1917, when the United States and Greece joined the war on the side of the Entente as "associated powers" and Russia left the same pact, the new configuration of "Allied and Associated Powers" emerged, which will be referred to as the "Allies."

10. See chapter 2 on Mudros and chapter 5 on Mudanya.

11. In 1926 the Turkish government deliberated on how to characterize and inscribe this period in the registers of the new state. The choice fell on "*İstiklal Harbi*" (War of Independence). Başbakanlık Devlet Arşivleri, *İstiklal Harbi ile İlgili Telgraflar*, 301–2.

12. The prevalent translation as "national struggle" carries anachronistic overtones. See below for a discussion of the context-bound connotations of the term *milli* in Ottoman/Turkish usage.

13. *Innsbrucker Nachrichten* (25 May 1919), cited by Gerwarth, *The Vanquished*, 5. On the theme of "war in peace," see also Gerwarth and Manela, *Empires at War*.

14. For a corrective to this view, see Brown, *Imperial Legacy*.

15. Hitti, *History of the Arabs*. For an early revisionist interpretation of the Ottoman past see Kawtharani, *Al-ittijahat al-ijtimaʿiyah al-siyasiyah*.

16. A similar tendency in Western scholarship to compartmentalize Arab and Ottoman history has more recently been addressed in both specialized monographs and chronologically broad surveys. See, for instance, Hathaway and Barbir, *The Arab Lands under Ottoman Rule, 1516–1800*, and Masters, *The Arabs of the Ottoman Empire, 1516–1918*.

17. For the dilemmas of Republican nationalist historiography, see Ersanlı, "The Ottoman Empire in the Historiography of the Kemalist Era," 120–23.

18. For instance, Lewis, *The Emergence of Modern Turkey*, and Berkes, *The Development of Secularism in Turkey*.

19. The ebb-and-flow of political events in recent decades has influenced segments of the academic establishment throughout the Middle East to revive the Ottoman past with a tinge of nostalgia. The ascendance of the conservative religious right in Turkey and positive responses to its early initiatives of opening up to Arab countries, a departure from past policy sometimes characterized as "neo-Ottomanism," have been accompanied by long-neglected cultural and academic contacts throughout the region, even if at times they have been beholden to the political impulse and sponsorship that facilitated them.

20. Zürcher, *The Unionist Factor*, and "The Ottoman Legacy of the Turkish Republic." Indeed, in his later concise history of Turkey, Zürcher examines the

entire period from 1908, when the so-called Young Turk modernists restored the constitutional monarchy, to 1950 under the rubric of "the Young Turk era." Zürcher, *Turkey: A Modern History*.

21. See, for instance, Ahmad, "Politics and Political Parties in Republican Turkey," 4:226.

22. Kasaba, "Dreams of Empire, Dreams of Nations," 216–21.

23. Kansu, *The Revolution of 1908 in Turkey*, chapter 1.

24. Üngör, "Seeing Like a Nation-State."

25. See Avedian, "State Identity, Continuity, and Responsibility"; Levene, "Creating a Modern Zone of Genocide:" Levene traces a "genocidal sequence" from the late Ottoman Empire to the successor states as manifested in "near-genocidal" violence against the Kurds and Assyrians in Turkey and, more recently, in Iraq (394–97).

26. General Kazım Karabekir's memoirs, which take issue with aspects of Kemalist policy, were destroyed once printed, while the memoirs of Rıza Nur, prominent politician and statesman, could not be published in Turkey until recent years. See, "Young Turk Memoirs as a Historical Source: Kazım Karabekir's *İstiklal Harbimiz*" in Zürcher, *The Young Turk Legacy and Nation Building*, 17–25. For intrinsic features and pitfalls of memoirs as historical sources in general and on wartime Syria in particular, see Deringil, *The Ottoman Twilight in the Arab Lands*, x–lxviii.

27. *Nutuk* was first published in 1927 with a companion volume of documents. A more recent edition in three volumes, in which the third volume comprises the documents, is used in this study. Atatürk, *Nutuk*.

28. Morin and Lee, "Constitutive Discourse of Turkish Nationalism"; Alaranta, "Mustafa Kemal Atatürk's Six-Day Speech of 1927."

29. "Atatürk'ün nutku ile (1927) bu mücadelenin tarihi resmi ve en selahiyettar ağzından hakiki ifadesini buldu." Gökbilgin, *Milli Mücadele Başlarken*, 1:vii.

30. Since Mustafa Kemal christened the town of Antep ('Ayntab) with the appellation Gazi-Antep (Antep, the valorous warrior), similar modifications of towns' names hearken back to their anti-colonial struggle circa 1920. Neighboring Maraş has secured a name change as Kahraman-Maraş (Heroic Maraş), and more recently, the town of Urfa as Şanlı-Urfa (Glorious Urfa).

31. Manning, *Navigating World History*, 15.

32. Kayalı, "The Ottoman Experience of World War I," 882–83.

33. See, for example, Sakallı, *Milli Mücadele'nin Sosyal Tarihi*.

34. Erik Zürcher has led the way in this line of inquiry. Many of his articles have been compiled in Zürcher, *The Young Turk Legacy and Nation Building*.

35. al-Qasimiyya, *Al-hukuma al-'arabiyya fi dimashq*; Russell, *The First Modern Arab State*; Gelvin, *Divided Loyalties*; Thompson, *How the West Stole Democracy from the Arabs*.

36. Khoury, *Syria and the French Mandate*, and *Urban Notables and Arab Nationalism*; Watenpaugh, *Being Modern in the Middle East*; Provence, *The Last Ottoman Generation and the Making of the Modern Middle East*; Méouchy, "From the Great War to the Syrian Armed Resistance Movement (1919–1921)."

37. Middle East scholars have written about terminological/conceptual issues and identified thorny problems of varied meanings and translation. See, for instance, Lewis, *The Political Language of Islam*.

38. Hendrich, *Milla, millet*.

39. The Armenian, Greek Orthodox, and Jewish millets became institutionalized in the nineteenth century not only around their clergy but also a constitutional charter and representative body. Even as the Armenian, Greek Orthodox, and Jewish millets were partially secularized starting in the 1850s, they emerged as reconstituted religion-based institutions and part of the Ottoman administrative system, much more so, revisionist scrutiny has held, than they did earlier. See Benjamin Braude, "Foundation Myths of the Millet System," 1:69–88.

40. M. Şükrü Hanioğlu, *A Brief History of the Late Ottoman Empire*, 165.

41. *Cemaat* replaced *millet* in reference to non-Muslim communities as well as distinctive Muslim groups, such as the followers of a Sufi order.

42. The evolution of cognate terms in European languages has followed similar trajectories (and similarly varied meanings from one language domain to the other). In grappling with the vague and shifting terminology of "nation," theoreticians of nationalism have explored the etymology of the word and its various historical connotations and semantic transformations. See Hobsbawm, *Nations and Nationalism since 1780*, 15–35 and Greenfeld, *Nationalism: Five Roads to Modernity*, 4–10.

43. See chapter 3.

44. Sami, *Kamus-ül Alam*, 1:389–97.

45. *Sancak* (in the English language, *sanjak*) was a subdivision of the province in the late Ottoman administrative system, also called "*mutasarrıflık*."

46. Özkan, "Making a National Vatan in Turkey," 4.

47. The sharifs of Mecca enjoyed recognition and prestige as descendants of Prophet Muhammad belonging to the Hashim clan and hence were known as the Hashemites. They commanded prestige as the superintendents of the Muslim holy sites in Mecca and Medina.

48. For an argument on Turkey's continued involvement in the Middle East after 1923, see Bein, *Kemalist Turkey and the Middle East*.

CHAPTER 1. UNFOLDING OF AN OTTOMAN PROJECT

1. For a relational and diachronic survey of national movements and state transformations in the Ottoman Empire, see Anscombe, *State, Faith, and Nation in Ottoman and Post-Ottoman Lands*.

2. For an account of Greek independence movement that is sensitive to the Ottoman context, see Gallant, *The Edinburgh History of the Greeks, 1768 to 1913*, chapter 3.

3. Morris and Ze'evi, *The Thirty-Year Genocide*. For sober appraisals of the genocide of the Armenians, see Suny et al., eds., *A Question of Genocide*. For demographic engineering policies after 1913, see Dündar, *Modern Türkiye'nin Şifresi*.

4. A notable exception was Lebanon, where the French mandatory drew the borders to ensure a Christian majority in the new state.
5. Smith, *The Ethnic Origins of Nations*, 91.
6. Tezcan, *The Second Ottoman Empire*.
7. For a comprehensive history of the Ottoman Empire in the long nineteenth century, see Hanioğlu, *A Brief History of the Ottoman Empire*; for an economic history, see Pamuk, *Uneven Centuries*, chapters 1–7.
8. Davison, *Reform in the Ottoman Empire, 1856–1876*.
9. Salzman, "Citizens in Search of a State," 39–51.
10. This was akin to the "empire nationalism" that Germany (*Reichsnationalismus*) and Austria-Hungary sought to cultivate. Ortaylı, *İmparatorluğun En Uzun Yüzyılı*, 90.
11. Hanley, "What Ottoman Nationality Was and Was Not."
12. The Electoral Law that this parliament passed governed five general elections, the last in 1919.
13. Ahmad, *The Young Turks: The Committee of Union and Progress*; Birinci, *Hürriyet ve İtilâf Fırkası*.
14. Geiss, "The Civilian Dimension of the War," 16–17.
15. Blumi, *Reinstating the Ottomans*, 189.
16. For Instance, İsmail Kemal (Ismail Qemali), the architect of the Albanian state, was a deputy in the Ottoman parliament for Berat (Albania) and had held the governorship of Beirut to Trablusgarb (Tripolitania). Kemal and Story, *The Memoirs of Ismail Kemal Bey*, 17; Gawrych, *The Crescent and the Eagle*, 200.
17. Clayer, "Albanian Students of the Mekteb-i Mülkiye, 295–98." The leadership of Albanian independence offered the presidency of the newly established state in 1913 to Ahmed İzzet Pasha, renowned general and Minister of War in 1913 of Albanian heritage, who perceived this post as "a step down" and chose to remain in Ottoman state service. He became grand vizier in 1918. Mango, *From the Sultan to Atatürk*, 27.
18. Özoğlu, *Kurdish Notables and the Ottoman State*, 69–85.
19. Reynolds, *Shattering Empires*, 56–72; Busch, *Mudros to Lausanne*, 181–92.
20. For a brief review of historical precedents and early nineteenth century trends, see Kayalı, *Arabs and Young Turks*, 5–9. For a critical appraisal of this scholarship, see Gelvin, "'Arab Nationalism.'"
21. See, for instance, Dawn, *From Ottomanism to Arabism*, and Khoury, *Urban Notables and Arab Nationalism*.
22. Saab, *The Arab Federalists of the Ottoman Empire*, 225–50.
23. Fuhrmann, "Zwei Völker in Waffen," 239.
24. Landau, *Pan-Turkism in Turkey*, 47–48.
25. For assessments of this view with respect to the Arab population of the empire see Kayalı, *Arabs and Young Turks*, 127–32. For the Kurds, Özoğlu, *Kurdish Notables and the Ottoman State*, 83–84, 117–18. See also Öztan, "Point of No Return?"
26. Zürcher, "The Vocabulary of Muslim Nationalism," 81–92, and *Young Turk Legacy*, 276–77.

27. The invocation of Islam on the public level and on the level of individual psyche and communal consciousness did not reverse the course of secularization in the Ottoman society since the nineteenth century. The Ottoman government passed measures during the war years that curtailed the influence of the Muslim religious establishment. For instance, the office of the şeyhülislam (chief mufti) was attached to the cabinet. In 1917, the government promulgated the Family Law, which brought aspects of sharia law, including marriage and inheritance, under civil jurisdiction. Thus, even as Muslim commonality and solidarity upheld Ottomanist strategies of imperial integration and self-preservation, the increasing prominence of Muslim collective identity did not impinge on the secularizing thrust of the late empire, contrary to what the cognate designation "Islamic nationalism" might suggest. See Cleveland, *Islam against the West*.

28. Alkan, "Modernization from Empire to Republic and Education in the Process of Nationalism," 110.

29. One Turkist, Şevket Süreyya (Aydemir), influential author of the Republican era, famously put to the test the identification of his rank-and-file soldiers while serving as a young officer in Anatolia during the Great War. When he asked his men the simple but weighty question, "What millet do we belong to?" he received a cacophony of different and confused responses. "Aren't we Turks?" he followed up. The men retorted unanimously: "Allah forbid (*Estağfurullah*)." Their demurral was not so much to the word's familiar connotation of a boorish person as to its narrower use to refer to the Shiite "heretics" of eastern Anatolia. Aydemir, *Suyu Arayan Adam*, 104; Aktar, "Yüzbaşı Torosyan'ın Adı Yok," 39.

30. Adıvar, *Conflict of East and West in Turkey*, 13.

31. Adıvar, 31.

32. Suny, "Religion, Ethnicity, and Nationalism," 25.

33. For a discussion of the "emotional and intellectual climate" in post-Balkan War Istanbul, including Anatolianism, see Aksakal, *The Ottoman Road to War in 1914*, 21–41. See also Ginio, *The Ottoman Culture of Defeat*.

34. Kayalı, *Arabs and Young Turks*, 136.

35. Zürcher, "The Young Turks—Children of the Borderlands?," 275–86.

36. Atay, *Batış Yılları*, 73. The reference to "tens of thousands of lives" refers to Anatolia as the main base for conscription.

37. Özkan, "Making a National *Vatan* in Turkey," 466. A geography textbook published in 1891 divided Ottoman lands in Asia into six parts: Aegean islands, Anatolia, Kurdistan, Cezire (al-Jazira)-Iraq-al-Hasa, Syria-Palestine, Hijaz-Yemen. Noteworthy in this division is the occurrence of Kurdistan as the only ethnologically designated region, especially in the light of the inclusion of the empire's most densely Kurdish areas, Cezire, in a different geographical category. Ahmed Cemal, *Coğrafya-ı Umumi* (Istanbul: Harbiye-i Şahane Matbaası, 1891), cited in Özkan, "Making a National Vatan in Turkey," 461.

38. Beşikçi, *The Ottoman Mobilization of Manpower in the First World War*, 77.

39. Anscombe, *State, Faith, and Nation*, 126.

40. Scholarship on the Armenian Genocide has proliferated in recent years. See bibliographic essay ("Historians Look at the Armenian Genocide") in Suny, "They Can Live in the Desert but Nowhere Else," 367–74.

41. Compared to the number of lives lost, the conversions were numerically insignificant but tellingly emblematic of the sociopolitical underpinnings of the persecution of Christians.

42. On Armenians, see Kaligian, *Armenian Organization and Ideology under Ottoman Rule: 1908–1914*, chapter 5; on Greeks, Kechriotis, "Greek-Orthodox, Ottoman Greeks or Just Greeks?"; and on Arabs, Kayalı, *Arabs and Young Turks*, 116–43. Also, Ahmad, *The Young Turks and the Ottoman Nationalities*.

43. Cemal Pasha wrote an account and vindication of his role in the Ottoman government during the years of the Long War, which was published in 1922, the year of his death (*Hatırat, 1913–1922*), and translated into Western languages (*Memories of a Turkish Statesman, 1913–1919*, and *Erinnerungen eines türkischen Staatsmannes*). The references I cite in in this book will be to an edition published by his son: Cemal Paşa, *Hatıralar*, in 1977. Talha Çiçek's monograph is the most comprehensive account of Cemal's tenure in Syria: Çiçek, *War and State Formation in Syria*. For a broader biographical study, see Artuç, *Cemal Paşa: Askeri ve Siyasi Hayatı*.

44. At the end of 1911, Cemal crippled the new Liberty and Entente Party's organizational efforts in Iraq as governor of Baghdad by intimidating its founders and implicating them with breaking the law. During the general elections of Spring 1912, similar measures assured the CUP a victory in Baghdad and other Iraqi provinces, as frenzied complaints were voiced about the vali's interventions. Başbakanlık Osmanlı Arşivi (BBA) [Ottoman Prime Ministry Archives]/Dahiliye Nezareti Siyasi Kısım [Ministry of the Interior Political Section] (DH-SYS) 83-1/2-42, March 20, 1912. In 1913, Cemal consolidated the CUP's position in the capital by suppressing the Liberty and Entente opposition and sending its leaders to the gallows. Kayalı, *Arabs and Young Turks*, 193.

45. For a recent comprehensive analysis of Syria's war experience that integrates firsthand accounts and is sensitive to the war's broader context see Fawaz, *A Land of Aching Hearts*. See also, Al-Qattan, "Safarbarlik"; her "When Mothers Ate Their Children; and Tanielian, *The Charity of War*.

46. After the devastating explosion in Beirut's port in August 2020, mass antiregime protests in Martyrs' Square set up mock gallows inverting the symbolism of the square. "Lebanon Protesters Storm Ministries as Violent Protests Grip Beirut." See www.cnn.com/2020/08/08/middleeast/beirut-judgment-day-protests-intl/index.html (accessed August 30, 2020).

47. Ortak, *Osmanlı'nın Son Manevralarından Suriye ve Garbi Arabistan Tehciri*, 92–106.

48. *Âliye Divan-ı Harbisinde Tedkik Olunan Mesele-i Siyasiye Hakkında İzahat / La vérité sur la question Syrienne* (Istanbul: Tanin, 1916).

49. Cemal, *Hatıralar*, 49.

50. Pointing to the many problems in the determination of the number and percentage of Arab soldiers (or recruits from the "Arab provinces") at any given point during the Great War, Mehmet Beşikçi estimates the number to be between one-third and one-fourth of the entire army. Beşikçi, *The Ottoman Mobilization of Manpower*, 252–54. According to Alexander Aaronsohn of the Zionist community in Palestine, who was naturalized and served in the Ottoman army, only some twenty thousand of the one hundred fifty thousand troops mobilized to the Suez front were Anatolian (Aaronsohn, *With the Turks in Palestine*, 29). Zürcher estimates that just under half of the troops in Palestine were Arabs. Zürcher, *The Young Turk Legacy*, 174. In contrast, the official Turkish military history of the Palestine campaign places the number of Arab soldiers at a few thousand (Beşikçi, 253). Ömer Kürkçüoğlu cites British intelligence that the number of Arab soldiers in the Ottoman army was around one hundred thousand; six divisions consisted entirely and five partially of Syrian soldiers in 1915 (Kürkçüoğlu, *Osmanlı Devletine Karşı Arap Bağımsızlık Hareketi*, 90).

51. Zürcher, *The Young Turk Legacy*, 186–87.

52. Cemal enumerates his reform projects in his memoirs, *Hatıralar*, 370–403. For contemporary observations of the same, see Erden, *Birinci Dünya Harbinde Suriye Hatıraları*, 65–92; Wiegand et al., *Halbmond im Letzten Viertel*. See also Kayalı, "Wartime Regional and Imperial Integration of Greater Syria during World War I"; "Jamal basha fi suriya"; and "Ottoman and German Imperial Objectives in Syria during World War I"; Çiçek, *War and State Formation in Syria*; Hudson, *Transforming Damascus*, 121–26; and Theunissen, "War, Propaganda and Architecture."

53. Bennett, *The Birth of the Museum*, 21.

54. Bennett, 225; Tibawi, *A Modern History of Syria*, 247.

55. Weber, *Zeugnisse Kulturellen Wandels*, 119; Strauss, "The Disintegration of Ottoman Rule in the Syrian Territories," 317.

56. Cemal had a propaganda film produced before the Suez campaign in 1915. Tamari, *Year of the Locust*, 94; Strohmeier, *Al-Kulliya as-Salahiya in Jerusalem*, 62. The prominent proponent in Syria of Ottoman patriotism and Islamic bonds and member of the Ottoman parliament for Acre, mufti Shaykh As'ad al-Shuqayri, gave an address in the Damascus theater named Çanakkale (Chanaq Qal'a) after the 1915 battle of Gallipoli in the Çanakkale district in front of an audience that included Cemal Pasha, Sharif Faysal, and the governors of Syria, Jerusalem, and Mt. Lebanon. Tamari, "A 'Scientific' Expedition to Gallipoli," 18.

57. Tamari, *The Great War and the Remaking of Palestine*, 1–3.

58. Bahjat and al-Tamimi, *Wilayat Beirut*.

59. *Lubnan: mubahis 'ilmiyya wa ijtima'iya* (Scientific and Social Research), cited in Deringil, *The Ottoman Twilight in the Arab Lands*, xxiii–xxiv. Noting that the book was published in August 1918 and that the Ottomans had already lost territory to British armies in Mesopotamia and Palestine at the time the book was commissioned eight months earlier, Deringil asks, "Were the Ottomans hoping that

they would be able to keep Lebanon as part of the Empire after the peace treaty?" See chapter 2 on the political and military circumstances in the first half of 1918 to consider this a plausible assumption.

60. Shaw, *Possessors and Possessed*, 28.

61. Çelik, "Defining Empire's Patrimony," 469. For a close analysis of this effort, see Theunissen, "War, Propaganda and Architecture."

62. Anderson, *Imagined Communities*, xiv; Kayalı, "Jamal basha fi suriya," 214.

63. Gencer, *Jöntürk Modernizmi ve "Alman Ruhu,"* 220.

64. Wiegand, *Halbmond im Letzten Viertel*; Roth, *Preussens Gloria im heiligen Land*, 282.

65. Wiegand and Djemal Pascha, *Alte Denkmäler aus Syrien, Palästina und Westarabien*.

66. Wiegand and Kress von Kressenstein, *Sinai*.

67. Kayalı, "Jamal basha fi suriya," 213–14, and "Ottoman and German Imperial Objectives in Syria," 1128–29.

68. The reference appears to be to al-Barghouti and Tutah, *Tarikh Filastin*, 248–52.

69. Tamari, *Year of the Locust*, 10.

70. Some sancaks, among them Jerusalem (Kudüs/al-Quds), were not attached to a province and classified as "independent sancak."

71. BBA/Başbakanlık Evrak Odası [Sublime Porte Records Office] (BEO) 324853, no. 143, January 14, 1915.

72. Bahadır, "Bir Şehir Kurma Teşebbüsü (1900–1917)."

73. Roth, *Preussens Gloria im Heiligen Land*, 273.

74. Strohmeier, *Al-Kulliya as-Salahiya in Jerusalem*, 63–64; Bahadır, "Bir Şehir Kurma," 67–68.

75. Strauss, "The Disintegration of Ottoman Rule," 317, quotes Hedin, *Till Jerusalem*, 551.

76. Uebelhör, *Syrien im Kriege*, 17.

77. Tamari, *Year of the Locust*, 59.

78. Cemal Paşa, *Hatıralar*, 403.

79. Aaronsohn, *With the Turks in Palestine*, 50.

80. Fortna, *Imperial Classroom*.

81. Adıvar, *House with Wisteria*, 355–87; Atay, *Zeytindağı*, 48–49; Çiçek, *War and State Formation in Syria*, 181–90.

82. Cemal Paşa, *Hatıralar*, 399–403; Kayalı, "Wartime Regional Integration of Greater Syria," 302–3; Bahadır, "Bir Şehir Kurma," 68.

83. Mitchell, *Colonising Egypt*, 35.

84. Strohmeier, *Al-Kulliya as-Salahiya in Jerusalem*, 23.

85. Tibawi, *A Modern History of Syria*, 229–30.

86. Wiegand, *Halbmond im Letzten Viertel*, 248. For the efforts to renovate Islamic sites, including Salah al-Din's tomb, see Theunissen, "War, Propaganda and Architecture," especially 244–51.

87. Khalidi, "The Press as a Source for Modern Arab Political History."

88. Genel Kurmay Askeri Tarih ve Stratejik Etüt Başkanlığı Arşivi (General Staff Military History and Strategic Studies Directorate) (ATASE), World War I (WWI) 531/843-2078, no. 1 (May 29, 1915).

89. Hülagü, *Pan-Islâmist Faaliyetler*, 76–77.

90. Thus, *al-Muqtabas* received L (liras) 22.5, *Ra'y al-'Am* L19, *Balagh* L15, Iqbal L12.5, *Ittihad al-Islam* L10.

91. ATASE WWI 531/843, nos. 2-9, 2-10. While Cemal coordinated broader policy with Istanbul, he availed of his emergency powers in day-to-day decisions, including in the indictment and execution of presumed dissidents. See, Tauber, *The Arab Movements in World War I*, 50–51.

92. Çiçek, *War and State Formation in Syria*, 46–47. Cemal Pasha chose Kurd 'Ali over Shakib Arslan, a Druze by faith. See also Çiçek, "Visions of Islamic Unity," 466–67.

93. Commins, *Islamic Reform*, 143.

94. Saab, *The Arab Federalists of the Ottoman Empire*, 225–41.

95. Samir Seikaly, "Ali, Muḥammad Kurd," in 1914–1918–Online: International Encyclopedia of the First World War, ed. Ute Daniel, Peter Gatrell, Oliver Janz, Heather Jones, Jennifer Keene, Alan Kramer, and Bill Nasson, issued by Freie Universität Berlin, Berlin, 2015. DOI: 10.15463/ie1418.10580 (accessed December 30, 2020). Kurd 'Ali's own retrospection vindicates his latter-day Arab nationalist detractors. "Various passages in Kurd 'Ali's 'Memoirs' deal with the deliberate and repeated denigration of Turkish culture. In a chapter called 'Turkish dislike for the Arabs' the author blames the Ottoman authorities for monopolizing the key-positions in the government, for forbidding that Arabic be spoken, and for keeping the Arabs in ignorance and cultural backwardness." Havemann, "Between Ottoman Loyalty and Arab 'Independence'," 349.

96. Tamari, "A 'Scientific Expedition' to Gallipoli," 8, and his "Muhammad Kurd Ali and the Syrian-Palestinian Intelligentsia," 37–39.

97. Falih Rıfkı devotes his (Atay)*Zeytindağı* to his Syria experiences. For Halide Edib's memoirs of her stay in Syria, see Adıvar, *House with Wisteria*, 321–87.

98. Rasim, *Muharrir Bu Ya*, 109–15.

99. Fortna, *The Circassian*, 174–75.

100. For a close examination of desertion in the Ottoman army during World War I, see Beşikçi, *The Ottoman Mobilization of Manpower in the First World War*, 247–309.

101. Aktar, "A Propaganda Tour Organized by Djemal Pasha," 61–86.

102. Tamari, "A 'Scientific Expedition' to Gallipoli." (This article is an early version of Tamari's "Muhammad Kurd Ali and the Syrian-Palestinian Intelligentsia in the Ottoman Campaign against Arab Separatism.")

103. *Meclis-i Mebusan Zabıt Cerideleri* (MMZC) (Proceedings of the Ottoman Chamber of Deputies), Term III, Year 1, Session 46 (III/1/46). November 8, 1915.

104. See, for instance, Allawi, *Faisal I of Iraq*, 63.

105. Yalman, *Turkey in the World War*, 88; Liman von Sanders, *Five Years in Turkey*, 28.

106. BBA/BEO 328076, no. 8, September 8, 1915.

107. According to Hilmar Kaiser, the CUP coordinated the deportation of some two hundred fifty thousand Ottoman Greeks and one hundred thousand Bulgarians to Greece, Bulgaria, or inland Anatolian provinces. Three hundred forty thousand Muslims from the relinquished Balkan provinces were forced to leave and immigrated to the Ottoman Empire. See Kaiser, "Genocide at the Twilight of the Ottoman Empire," 369–70.

108. Kaiser, "Regional Resistance to Central Government Policies."

109. Kurt, "A Rescuer, an Enigma and a Genocidaire"; Panian, *Goodbye, Antoura*; Deringil, "'Your Religion Is Worn and Outdated.'"

110. Yalman, *Die Türkei*, 8–9; Strauss, "The Disintegration of Ottoman Rule," 307.

111. Antonius, *The Arab Awakening*, 151.

112. Mehmetefendioğlu, "Rahmi Bey'in İzmir Valiliği," 355–58.

113. Liman von Sanders, *Five Years in Turkey*, 146.

114. Çiçek, "Myth of the Unionist Triumvirate," in his *Syria in World War I*, 18, quotes Kaiser, *The Extermination of Armenians in the Diarbekir Region*, 421–22; Üngör, "How Armenian Was the 1915 Genocide?"

115. Akın, *When the War Came Home*, for instance, 82–85.

116. Scott, *Seeing Like a State*, 6.

117. Lewis, *The Emergence of Modern Turkey*, 223; Bozdoğan, *Modernism and Nation Building*, 20.

118. Çelik, "Defining Empire's Patrimony," 459.

119. For an overview of the Mesopotamia campaign from the Ottoman vantage, see Erickson, *Ottoman Army Effectiveness in World War I*, 61–89.

120. Kayalı, "A Glimpse from the Periphery."

121. Commenting on an ice production plant that Cemal Pasha had built, Naci Kaşif Kıcıman, who was an officer in the units stationed in the town, later wrote about the new lease on life that ice gave to the men and the indescribable pleasure of eating ice and date ice cream in the extreme heat of Medina. Kıcıman, *Medine Müdafaası*, 123; Wasti, "The Defence of Medina, 1916–19," 645.

122. Liman von Sanders, *Five Years in Turkey*, 208.

123. Liman von Sanders, 207.

124. Hülagü, *Pan-Islâmist Faaliyetler*, 113.

125. "The greatest foe to the Turks has been Imam Yahya. This Sayyid's attitude has been misunderstood. You cannot judge a man fairly by a short spell of his career, and ignore his history as a whole. This has been done in this war, and King Hussein has been lauded as the prominent foe of the Turks. He has been a foe only in recent years. We chose him because of his prospective value to us, as keeper of the two sacred shrines in lieu of the Turks. He is accessible by sea and so we rightly put the money on him." The British National Archives (NA). Foreign Office (FO)

141/776/70. Report on the future of Yemen by Lieut. Colonel H.F. Jacob, Cairo, March 30, 1919.
126. Hanioğlu, *Preparation for a Revolution*, 317.
127. Hanioğlu, *A Brief History of the Late Ottoman Empire*, 178–79. Hadramawt lies along the northern Indian Ocean (Arabian Sea) coast of the Arabian Peninsula.
128. Atay, *Batış Yılları*, 86; Çiçek, *War and State Formation in Syria*, 26.
129. Artuç, *İttihatçı-Senûsi İlişkileri (1908–1918)*, 136.
130. For early Ottoman-Sanussi relations see Minawi, *The Ottoman Scramble for Africa*.
131. Genel Kurmay Başkanlığı, *Türk İstiklal Harbi*, I: 18.
132. Saab, *The Arab Federalists of the Ottoman Empire*, 242–45; Kayalı, *Arabs and Young Turks*, 136–37. Alp Yenen's recent article on the Austria-Hungary model in Ottoman imagination reached me too late to fully benefit from it. Yenen, "Envisioning Turco-Arab Co-Existence between Empire and Nationalism."
133. Kayalı, *Arabs and Young Turks*, 126–130, 137–40.
134. Karabekir, *İstiklal Harbimizin Esasları*, 17.
135. Kreiser, *Atatürk*, 114.

CHAPTER 2. REVERSALS OF FORTUNE AND RESILIENCE

1. https://www.marxists.org/archive/lenin/works/1917/oct/25-26/26b.htm (accessed December 30, 2020).
2. This agreement was hammered out in the winter of 1915–16 in negotiations between Mark Sykes, diplomat and Middle East advisor to the British cabinet, and François Georges-Picot, a French diplomat. It entailed a detailed division of Greater Syria, Mesopotamia, and parts of eastern Anatolia, which had been agreed upon in its general lines in the Constantinople Agreement between Britain, France, and Russia in May 1915. The accord is also known as the Sazonov-Sykes-Picot Treaty because Russia acceded to the formal signing of its terms in May 1916, which reaffirmed Russian war aims in northeastern Anatolia and the Straits as stipulated in the Constantinople Agreement. When revolutionary Russia renounced the treaty, its implementation became a Franco-British project. Sykes-Picot has since become an emblem of duplicitous foreign intervention and influence in anti-imperialist rhetoric, especially in the Arab countries. As the Islamic State group expanded its control in Iraq and Syria in 2014, it issued a propaganda film titled *The End of Sykes-Picot*. https://www.belfasttelegraph.co.uk/video-news/video-islamic-state-media-branch-releases-the-end-of-sykespicot-30397575.html (accessed December 30, 2020).
3. Tibawi, *A Modern History of Syria*, 259–60.
4. Zeine, *The Struggle for Arab Independence*, 21; Çiçek, *War and State Formation in Syria*, 63–65; Tauber, *The Arab Movements in World War I*, 153; Allawi, *Faisal I of Iraq*, 109.
5. Tauber, *The Arab Movements in World War I*, 154; Rogan, *The Fall of the Ottomans*, 358–59; Allawi, *Faisal I of Iraq*, 108–9.

6. Allawi, *Faisal I of Iraq*, 110; Çiçek, *War and State Formation in Syria*, 64.
7. On al-ʿAskari and other Arab officers who switched sides only after being recruited by British intelligence in prison camps, see Provence, *The Last Ottoman Generation*, 44–45.
8. Allawi, *Faisal I of Iraq*, 110, quotes Musa, *Al-murasalat*, 156; Tauber, *The Arab Movements in World War I*, 154–55.
9. Çiçek, *War and State Formation in Syria*, 64, 75.
10. MMZC III/4/13; Bayur, *Türk İnkılabı Tarihi*, 3:104–8.
11. Reynolds, *Shattering Empires*, 171.
12. "Not for the King of Prussia," a French expression, patently incomprehensible even to the more cosmopolitan members of the parliament, suggesting misplaced or futile goals.
13. https://wwi.lib.byu.edu/index.php/Prime_Minister_Lloyd_George_on_the_British_War_Aims (accessed December 30, 2020) https://wwi.lib.byu.edu/index.php/President_Wilson%27s_Fourteen_Points (accessed December 30, 2020).
14. Manela, *The Wilsonian Moment*.
15. Helmreich, *From Paris to Sèvres*, 2 ; Evans, *United States Policy and the Partition of Turkey*, 71–85.
16. "Open covenants of peace must be arrived at, after which there will surely be no private international action or rulings of any kind, but diplomacy shall proceed always frankly and in the public view."
17. "The Russian representatives have insisted, very justly, very wisely, and in the true spirit of modern democracy, that the conferences they have been holding with the Teutonic and Turkish statesmen should be held within open, not closed, doors, and all the world has been audience."
18. Article 9: "A readjustment of the frontiers of Italy should be effected along clearly recognizable lines of nationality."
19. In large part, owing to the widely disseminated account of Henry Morgenthau, US ambassador to Istanbul until 1916. Morgenthau, *Ambassador Morgenthau's Story*.
20. Baker, *Woodrow Wilson and World Settlement*, 1:74; Ziemke, *Die Türkei*, 73.
21. February 11, 1918. Helmreich, *From Paris to Sèvres*, 8; https://wwi.lib.byu.edu/index.php/President_Wilson%27s_Address_to_Congress,_Analyzing_German_and_Austrian_Peace_Utterances (accessed December 30, 2020).
22. Yerasimos, *Milliyetler ve Sınırlar*, 156; Reynolds, *Shattering Empires*, 159.
23. Genel Kurmay Başkanlığı, *Türk İstiklal Harbi*, 1:14.
24. Maurice, *The Armistices of 1918*, 1.
25. Jacob Landau, for instance, argues for Enver's Turkic irredentism in *Pan-Turkism in Turkey*, 54–56. For a critique of this argument, see Reynolds, "Buffers, Not Brethren"; and Aksakal, *The Ottoman Road to War in 1914*, 16.
26. Reynolds, "Buffers, Not Brethren," 139.
27. Article 4. https://wwi.lib.byu.edu/index.php/The_Peace_Treaty_of_Brest-Litovsk (accessed December 30, 2020); Wambaugh, *Plebiscites since the World War*, 9.

28. https://www.mountvernon.org/preservation/mount-vernon-ladies-association/mount-vernon-through-time/mount-vernon-during-world-war-i/woodrow-wilsons-july-4-1918-mount-vernon-speech/ (accessed December 30, 2020).

29. Dyer, "The Turkish Armistice of 1918: 1," 145, 170.

30. According to a German observer, the plebiscite was held "under the force of the Turkish bayonets." Ziemke, *Die Neue Türkei*, 51. On objections to the referendum, see Kılıç, *Türk-Sovyet İlişkilerinin Doğuşu*, 414–15.

31. Shaw, *From Empire to Republic*, 1:67.

32. Hille, *State Building and Conflict Resolution in the Caucasus*, 107.

33. Liman von Sanders, *Five Years in Turkey*, 231.

34. For the Mosul governor's telegram informing Istanbul of the restoration of Ottoman authority in Kirkuk, see Hakan, *Türkiye Kurulurken Kürtler (1916–1920)*, 67.

35. Erickson, *Gallipoli and the Middle East, 1914–1918*, 206.

36. Görgülü, *On Yıllık Harbin Kadrosu, 1912–1922*, 264.

37. For instance, on June 11, 1918, press censorship was lifted. Köroğlu, *Ottoman Propaganda and Turkish Identity*, 14; Feroz Ahmad, *The Young Turks: Struggle for the Ottoman Empire*, 181.

38. Ortak, *Osmanlı'nın Son Manevralarından Suriye ve Garbi Arabistan Tehciri*, 134–48; Çiçek, *War and State Formation in Syria*, 62–63.

39. Allawi, *Faisal I of Iraq*, 113.

40. Özkan, *From the Abode of Islam to the Turkish Vatan*, 62.

41. Saab, *Arab Federalists of the Ottoman Empire*, 237; Tauber, *The Arab Movements in World War I*, 155; Çiçek, *War and State Formation in Syria*, 65; Yenen, "Envisioning Turco-Arab Co-existence," 18.

42. Antonius, *Arab Awakening*, 270–74; Tauber, *The Formation of Modern Syria and Iraq*, 8.

43. https://en.wikisource.org/wiki/Declaration_to_the_Seven (accessed January 24, 2021); Antonius, *The Arab Awakening*, 433–34.

44. Grainger, *The Battle for Syria, 1918–1920*, 47–50.

45. Tauber, *The Arab Movements in World War I*, 116.

46. https://arabrevolt.jo/en/heros-list/fuad-al-khatib/ (accessed December 30, 2020); NA FO 141/654; G. S. Symes [to the Arab Bureau], Ramleh, June 13, 1918. D. G. Hogarth (Arab Bureau) reporting on same conversation with Dr. Faris Nimr, June 13, 1918.

47. Tauber, *The Arab Movements in World War I*, 116.

48. Genel Kurmay Başkanlığı, *Türk İstiklal Harbi*, 1:15.

49. Russell, *The First Modern Arab State*, 9–16; Rafeq, "Gesellschaft, Wirtschaft und Politische Macht in Syrien, 1918–1925," 441.

50. Shaw, *From Empire to Republic*, 1:68–69, quotes NA FO 371/3448/165564, Rumbold to Foreign Office, no. 1840, October 4, 1918; Dyer, "The Turkish Armistice of 1918," 153–54.

51. *New York Times*, "The President Speaks," September 28, 1918.

52. In the United States, a less charitable armistice had strong proponents. "Let [the Allies] impose their common will on the nations responsible for this hideous

disaster which has almost wrecked mankind," opined former president Theodore Roosevelt. House and Seymour, *The Intimate Papers of Colonel House*, 4:148–52.

53. Genel Kurmay Başkanlığı, *Türk İstiklal Harbi*, 1:27–28; Fromkin, *A Peace to End All Peace*, 367.

54. MMZC III/5/4, October 19, 1918; Tansel, *Mondros'tan Mudanya'ya Kadar*, 1:16.

55. Türkgeldi, *Moudros ve Mudanya Mütarekelerinin Tarihi*, 29.

56. OETA-East, comprising the area of Faysal's administration, and OETA-South, Palestine, would be under British supervision.

57. Cebesoy, *Milli Mücadele Hatıraları*, 14. Extending to the town of A'zaz, these hills allowed in 2012 the Free Syrian Army to repulse the government forces during the Syrian civil war.

58. Ahmad, *The Young Turks: Struggle for the Ottoman Empire*, 190.

59. Ahmet İzzet, *Feryadım*, 2:286.

60. House and Seymour, *The Intimate Papers of Colonel House*, 4:199.

61. Ahmet İzzet, *Feryadım*, 2:206.

62. Ahmet İzzet, *Feryadım*, 2:20–21.

63. Türkgeldi, *Moudros ve Mudanya Mütarekelerinin Tarihi*, 69–73.

64. Ziemke, *Die Neue Türkei*, 131. "The Mudros Treaty did not draw an actual line of demarcation, but it was clear from its content that the enemy troops should in principle not advance beyond the points reached at the time of the cessation of hostilities" except as stipulated in special clauses. Cited in Hendrich, *Milla, millet*, 68n252.

65. Méouchy, "From the Great War to the Syrian Armed Resistance Movement," 513–14.

66. Nişanyan, *Yanlış Cumhuriyet*, 379.

67. In his letter dated July 14, 1915, Sharif Husayn asked that Britain "recognises the independence of the Arab countries, which are bounded: on the north, by the line Mersin-Adana to parallel 37N and thence along the line Birejik-Urfa-Mardin-Midiat-Jazirat (Ibn 'Umar)-Amadia, to the Persian frontier; on the east, by the Persian frontier down to the Persian Gulf; on the south by the Indian Ocean (with the exclusion of Aden whose status will remain as at present); on the west, by the Red Sea and the Mediterranean Sea back to Mersin." On October 24, 1915, McMahon responded, "The districts of Mersin and Alexandretta, and portions of Syria lying to the west of the districts of Damascus, Homs, Hama and Aleppo, cannot be said to be purely Arab, and must on that account be excepted from the proposed delimitation." Antonius, *The Arab Awakening*, 414, 419.

68. Russell, *The First Modern Arab State*, 20–21.

69. See chapter 3.

70. For the complexity of allegiances, identities, and political outlooks in the northern Syria–southeastern Anatolia frontier and their essentialization as a result of territorial settlements see Shields, *Fezzes in the River*, especially 17–26.

71. For this correspondence between November 3 and November 5, see *Harp Tarihi Vesikaları Dergisi*, 28 (1959), Documents 715, 728, 735; Genel Kurmay

Başkanlığı, *Türk İstiklal Harbi*, 1:51–53; *Atatürk'ün Tamim, Telgraf ve Beyannameleri*, 4:14–17.

72. Genel Kurmay Başkanlığı, *Türk İstiklal Harbi*, 1:79.

73. See note 67.

74. The British forces also entered and occupied Batum, the Caucasian town that had returned to the Ottoman Empire in July following a plebiscite.

75. Kocatürk, *Atatürk ve Türkiye Cumhuriyeti Tarihi Kronolojisi*, 6, 8.

76. NA FO 141/654. Bassett to Arbur (Cairo), no. 356/272, Jeddah, October 27, 1918.

77. Kandemir, *Peygamberimizin Gölgesinde Son Türkler*; Kıcıman, *Medine Müdafaası*.

78. Nuri al-Sa'id would serve as prime minister of Iraq intermittently from 1930 to 1958.

79. Sina Akşin, "Turkish-Syrian Relations in the Time of Faysal (1918–1920)," 3; Kayalı "Bağımsızlık Mücadelesi İçinde Anadolu-Suriye İlişkileri," 359–65; Umar, *Türkiye-Suriye İlişkileri, 1918–1940*, 42–44; Çiçek, "Osmanlı Hâkimiyeti Sonrası Türk-Arap İlişkilerinde Değişim ve Süreklilik," 78–79.

80. ATASE WWI 396/894-1564, no. 1, November 14, 1918.

81. ATASE WWI 396/894-1564, November 12, 1918.

82. See note 59.

83. ATASE WWI 396/894-1564, November 18, 1918.

84. Cebesoy, *Millî Mücadele Hatıraları*, 28–29; Akşin, "Turkish-Syrian Relations in the Time of Faysal (1918–1920)," 3.

85. Lewis, *Emergence of Modern Turkey*, 204.

86. Saab, *The Arab Federalists of the Ottoman Empire*, 224–26.

87. Zeine, *The Struggle for Arab Independence*, 47.

88. BBA. Dahiliye Nezareti Şifre Kalemi [Ministry of the Interior Cipher Office] (DH-ŞFR) 93/315, November 27, 1918.

89. In 1918, 166 of the 256 members of the Chamber of Deputies elected in 1914 had remained, and 30 of the 48 elected to the Chamber of Notables. Gökbilgin, *Milli Mücadele Başlarken*, 1:12.

90. MMZC III/5/11, November 4, 1918. Gökbilgin, *Milli Mücadele Başlarken*, 1:8–9.

91. Karaca, *Meclis-i Mebusan'dan Türkiye Büyük Millet Meclisi'ne Geçiş Sürecinde son Osmanlı Meclis-i Mebusan Seçimleri*, 18–19; Gökbilgin, *Mili Mücadele Başlarken*, 21. On January 4, 1919, a decree was issued postponing the elections. Shaw, *From Empire to Republic*, 1:106.

CHAPTER 3. ANTI-COLONIAL RESISTANCE

1. Ergil, *Milli Mücadelenin Sosyal Tarihi*, 63–88; Sakallı, *Milli Mücadele'nin Sosyal Tarihi*, 288–363.

2. Zürcher, *The Unionist Factor*, 68–93.

3. Zürcher, *The Unionist Factor*, 84; Méouchy, "From the Great War to the Syrian Armed Resistance Movement," 503–5.

4. Antonius, *The Arab Awakening*, 274, 435–36; Russell, *The First Modern Arab State*, 27.

5. Thompson, *How the West Stole Democracy from the Arabs*, 16.

6. Fortna, *The Circassian*, 59.

7. Morris and Ze'evi, 321-22. As early as January 1918, the rumor that the Armenian émigrés would undertake a surprise attack caused alarm in Ayntab. BBA.DH-ŞFR 94/226. January 23, 1918.

8. Aktar, "Debating the Armenian Massacres in the Last Ottoman Parliament, November–December 1918," 253–59; Kocaoğlu, "Mütareke Meclisinde Ermeni Meselesi Tartışmaları," 170–71.

9. Arıkan, *Mütareke ve İşgal Dönemi İzmir Basını, 30 Ekim 1918-8 Eylül 1922*, 62–63.

10. Robert Zeidner describes them as "inveterate bands of Muslim brigands [who] gained a measure of popular approval among their co-religionists." Zeidner, *The Tricolor over the Taurus*, 80.

11. Tanör, *Türkiye'de Kongre İktidarları, 1918–1920*, 115–17; Budak, *İdealden Gerçeğe*, 47–56.

12. Manela, *The Wilsonian Moment*.

13. Gökbilgin, *Milli Mücadele Başlarken*, 1:12.

14. November 13, 1918. Quoted in Arıkan, *Mütareke ve İşgal Dönemi İzmir Basını*, 15, 180.

15. Arıkan, 21.

16. Gökbilgin, *Milli Mücadele Başlarken*, 1:28–29.

17. Beyoğlu, "Türk-Arap İlişkilerinin Son Kırılma Noktası," 455–57.

18. Abdullah, *Memoirs of King Abdullah of Transjordan*, 179–80.

19. FO 608/82/8. A. Calthorpe, High Commissioner to Lord Balfour, no. 72/1031 (fol. 494-8), Constantinople, January 18, 1919. Troops belonging to the Ottoman army fought with Imam Yahya against the British into the spring of 1919. Ziemke, *Die Neue Türkei*, 68.

20. Horne et al., *Source Records of the Great War*, 7:40.

21. Helmreich, *From Paris to Sèvres*, 54–55.

22. Horne et al., *Source Records of the Great War*, 7:134.

23. Zeine, *The Struggle for Arab Independence*, 63, 219; Russell, *The First Modern Arab State*, 33.

24. Helmreich, *From Paris to Sèvres*, 53.

25. Helmreich, 40; Aydın, *The Politics of Anti-Westernism in Asia*, 130.

26. Akşin, *İstanbul Hükümetleri ve Milli Mücadele*, 1:166; Budak, *İdealden Gerçeğe*, 59.

27. Genel Kurmay Başkanlığı, *Türk İstiklal Harbi*, 1:100–101.

28. Gökbilgin, *Milli Mücadele Başlarken*, 1:43–44.

29. See for instance the purpose statement of the *Trakya-Paşaeli Müdafaa-ı Hukuk Cemiyeti*, which declared commitment to Ottoman bonds and territorial

integrity, in Gökbilgin, 1:75. Wilson's Article 13 pertaining to the Balkans acclaimed "historically established lines of allegiance and nationality."
30. Gökbilgin, 1:26, 66–67.
31. February 1919. Gökbilgin, 1:27.
32. Budak, *İdealden Gerçeğe*, 37, 47.
33. Gökbilgin, *Milli Mücadele Başlarken*, 1:118.
34. Rudin, *Armistice, 1918*, 318–22; Helmreich, *From Paris to Sèvres*, 21.
35. Evans, *United States Policy and the Partition of Turkey, 1914–1924*, 106.
36. The Trabzon Congress (held "before April 9") communicated its resolutions to the British representative. NA FO 608/82/8. "Extracts from Weekly Situation Report of Captain Crawford," no. J.C. 66, April 19, 1919. Attached to Richard Webb (for High Commissioner) to Secretary of State for Foreign Affairs, no. 733/M. 1939, May 14, 1919; Tanör, *Türkiye'de Kongre İktidarları*, 114.
37. Tanör, *Türkiye'de Kongre İktidarları*, 110.
38. Tauber, *The Formation of Modern Syria and Iraq*, 16–18; Thompson, *How the West Stole Democracy from the Arabs*, 109–12. According to Tauber, a "Congress of the Societies" was set up consisting of the representatives of a wide range of political groupings and other associations to coordinate a petition campaign. This is analogous to the National Congress in Istanbul.
39. Hence the moniker "Damad," or son-in-law. Ferid Pasha served as grand vizier March–October 1919 and again April 1920–October 1920 (see below).
40. Gökbilgin, *Milli Mücadele Başlarken*, 1:119–20; Budak, *İdealden Gerçeğe*, 71.
41. Ahmet İzzet, *Feryadım*, 2:315–16; Budak, *İdealden Gerçeğe*, 74. According to Akşin, Ferid's remarks amounted to a "thoughtless" admission of the Tauruses as an ethno-linguistic dividing line. Akşin, *İstanbul Hükümetleri ve Milli Mücadele*, 1:399.
42. Damad Ferid to M. Clemenceau, June 23, 1919, in Woodward and Butler, *Documents on British Foreign Policy, 1919–1939*, 4:648; Akşin, *İstanbul Hükümetleri ve Milli Mücadele*, 1:400.
43. For the full text of this memorandum and commentary on the variant renderings in primary and secondary sources see Budak, *İdealden Gerçeğe*, 75–85.
44. Zürcher, *Young Turk Legacy*, 6–16; Parla, *Türkiye'de Siyasal Kültürün Resmî Kaynakları*, vol. 1.
45. Davison, *Essays in Ottoman and Turkish History, 1774–1923*, 209.
46. https://www.inkilaptarihi.gen.tr/amasya-genelgesi-22-haziran-1919-2/ (accessed December 30, 2020).
47. NA FO 608/82/8. The Greeks of Black Sea to Lloyd George, no. 5609, Paris [?], April 3, 1919. Toynbee's note dated April 4.
48. Gologlu, *Milli Mücadele Tarihi I*, 119–20.
49. Preamble of declaration dated August 7, 1919. See also Article 3: "All interventions and occupation will be considered as aiming at the institution of a Greek or Armenian presence and will be defended and resisted in unanimity." Gologlu, *Milli Mücadele Tarihi I*, 227–29.
50. Article 6 insisted on the "cultural and economic superiority" of Muslims in these provinces. Gologlu, 120. For an argument on durable implications of

Armenian dispossession on state formation, see Üngör and Polatel, *Confiscation and Destruction*.

51. Levene, "Creating a Modern Zone of Genocide," 408.
52. Thompson, *How the West Stole Democracy from the Arabs*, 27, 33.
53. Şimşir, *İngiliz Belgelerinde Atatürk, 1919–1938*, 1:78–80. (FO 371/4233/119322. Mr. Balfour in Paris to Earl Curzon. No: 1656 385/3/7/18095 [August 20, 1919]); Sonyel, *Mustafa Kemal (Atatürk) ve Kurtuluş Savaşı*, 1:352–54; Sonyel, *Turkish Diplomacy 1918–1923*, 22; Rafeq, "Arabism, Society and Economy in Syria, 1918–1920," 7–10; Akşin, "Turkish-Syrian Relations in the Time of Faysal (1918–1920)," 3–6; Naramoto, "An Introductory Note on Military Alliance between the Arab and Turkish Nationalists 1919–1920," 238, 251.
54. For example, Akşin comments on the rendering of Husayn's title as "Pasha" and not "King," the title he held at this time in the Hijaz. Less convincing is the contention that the reference to the "Turkish Empire" suggests that the document may have been fabricated by the Turks to create suspicion between the Entente Powers and the Hashemites. Akşin, "Turkish-Syrian Relations in the Time of Faysal (1918–1920)," 4–5.
55. Akşin, "Turkish-Syrian Relations in the Time of Faysal (1918–1920)," 3.
56. Ministère de la Défense (MD). 5N 199. (Cabinet du Ministre / Renseignements sur messages téléphones et télégrammes / Orient Balkans / Juillet 1919–Janvier 1920) Constantinople, no. 3434, parvenu au Ministère [de la guerre] 12.12.1919, December 8, 1919.
57. Helmreich, *From Mudros to Sèvres*, 145–46.
58. Russell, *The First Modern Arab State*, 89–90.
59. According to French reports, British agents recruited for the "Sharifian army" in Kilis, Ayntab, and Antioch. (MD 7N 1640. Service des Informations de la Marine dans le Levant, Service Central, La situation en Syrie, en Cilicie et en Egypte, no. 8, October 24, 1919). They distributed bribes to inhabitants of areas as far north as Diyarbekir to convince them to enter the fold of the Arab government. The Kurds in Diyarbekir robbed the British agents and sent them back south toward Mardin. (MD 7N 1640. Ministère de la Guerre, Etat-Major de l'Armée, Section d'Afrique, no. 9.233 9/11. Bulletin de Renseignements des Questions Musulmans, October 30, 1919.)
60. Gologlu, *Milli Mücadele Tarihi II: Sivas Kongresi*, 259–61.
61. Akgün, "The General Harbord Commission and the American Mandate Question."
62. For a detailed analysis of factionalism between the loyalists and resistance groups, as well as shifting alliances, in the South Marmara region, see Gingeras, *Sorrowful Shores*, especially chapters 3–5.
63. Shaw, *From Empire to Republic*, 2:703–4; Özer, "Ali Galip Olayı."
64. The commission found that Syrians overwhelmingly rejected "any help from France." (Sections II/2 and III/3). https://wwi.lib.byu.edu/index.php/The_King-Crane_Report (accessed December 30, 2020).
65. Akşin, "Turkish-Syrian Relations in the Time of Faysal (1918–1920)," 7, quotes NA FO 371/4160, 151996.

66. Kemal Atatürk, *Nutuk* 3:1102–5; document no. 156c. October 16/17, 1919.

67. MD 7N 1640. (Ministère de la Guerre, État-Major de l'Armée, Section d'Afrique, no. 9.233 9/11. Bulletin de Renseignements des Questions Musulmans, October 30, 1919.

68. NA FO 141/654. Meinertzhagen to Prodrome, London, no. 49305, November 6, 1919. Also see, NA FO 141/654. EGYPFORCE to DIRMILINT, no. I.660/S, November 8, 1919; Şimşir, *İngiliz Belgelerinde Atatürk*, 1:192–93.

69. The name occurs as "Jasim Pasha" in the text.

70. MD 7N 1640. Georges-Picot to A.E. (Telg.), no. 1499, Beyrouth, November 12, 1919. This is likely a reference to the controversial document dated June 16, 1919, discussed above. "Absolute independence" refers to independence from France.

71. MD 7N 1640. Le General Chef de Mission, de la Panouse [?], No. 1587 WOR, December 6 [1919]. Michael Provence dates Yasin al-Hashimi's arrest in January 1920 and his release in March 1920. Provence, *Last Ottoman Generation*, 113–14.

72. "Turkish influence is gradually creeping back, and signs are not wanting of a rejuvenated popularity of Turkish rule with all its forgotten disadvantages." Zeine, *The Struggle for Arab Independence*, 114 quotes FO 406/41, no. 173. Colonel Meinertzhagen to Earl Curzon, General Headquarters Egyptian Expeditionary Force, Cairo, November 10, 1919.

73. Mikusch, *Mustapha Kemal*, 28.

74. "It follows from the lamentations I received from Adana that the whole Muslim population is extremely agitated and indignant about this violation of rights. We protest strongly against this process in the name of the Ottoman national unity and we ask for reparation. Au nom du Comité Central de la Défense des droits de la nation, Moustafa Kemal (28 Nov 1919)." MD 7N 1640 No. 582/3, December 8, 1919; FO 406/41, no. 196/1, quoted in Şimşir, *İngiliz Belgelerinde Atatürk*, 1:277–78; Jäschke, "Ein scherifisches Bündnisangebot an Mustafa Kemal," 387.

75. Major J. N. Clayton to G.H.Q., Cairo, Damascus, October 15, 1919. Document 98, Report no. 37, in Bidwell et al., *British Documents on Foreign Affairs*, Part II, Series B 1:164; Lawson, "The Northern Syrian Revolts of 1919–1921," 260; Zeine, *The Struggle for Arab Independence*, 113; Provence, *The Last Ottoman Generation*, 111–12. According to Khoury, Ni'mat was a former Ottoman colonel, who "vehemently opposed the Arab Revolt and Hashimite claims to Syria." He formed the Democratic Party of Aleppo, which "appealed mainly to former Ottoman senior officials ignored by the nationalist regime in Damascus." Khoury, *Syria and the French Mandate*, 113.

76. Üzel, *Gaziantep Savaşının İç Yüzü*, 103–5; Jäschke, "Ein scherifisches Bündnisangebot an Mustafa Kemal," 387; Akşin, "Turkish-Syrian Relations in the Time of Faysal," 7.

77. MD 7N 1640 Service des Informations de la Marine dans le Levant, Service Central, La situation en Syrie, en Cilicie et en Egypte, . . . , no. 8, October 24, 1919.

78. Lawson, "The Northern Syrian Revolts of 1919–1921," 259, quotes United States National Archives (USNA) RG 165, box 1498, 2558-38.

79. Zeine, *The Struggle for Arab Independence*, 114; Şimşir, *İngiliz Belgelerinde Atatürk, 1919–1938*, 1:192.

80. According to Rafeq, many former officers of the Ottoman army belonged to this anti-Hashemite organization. Rafeq, "Gesellschaft, Wirtschaft und Politische Macht in Syrien," 456; Üzel, *Gaziantep Savaşının İç Yüzü*, 36.

81. See Debus, *Sebilürreşad: Eine vergleichende Untersuchung zur islamischen Opposition*. The journal was published under the name *Sırat-ı Müstakim* until 1912.

82. Kayalı, "Islam in the Thought and Politics of Two Late Ottoman Intellectuals," 329. Akif was proud of his Albanian heritage. According to Gingeras, "Despite being the author of [Turkey's] national anthem, [Akif] was by no means a 'pure' Turk. The son of an Albanian father and a mother born in the Russian Empire, he was raised in Ottoman Istanbul. Although he grew into a man devoted to the empire and its survival, his patriotism was rooted in his belief in Islam." Gingeras, *Eternal Dawn*, vii.

The Ministry of Education solicited independence marches that would "reflect the spirit of our recent struggle." TBMMZC I/2/1 (March 1, 1921). The Assembly voted to adopt Akif's submission on March 12, 1921 (TBMMZC I/2/6).

83. Philip Khoury has pointed out that "on the popular level, the Syrian masses applauded and supported the Turkish independence struggle, and the northern Syrian resistance movement was far more influenced by the Turkish nationalist movement than it was by the Arab nationalist movement," and that "religious solidarity with the Turks, at least in northern Syria, was especially strong. "Khoury, *Syria and the French Mandate*, 105–7. See also, Lawson, "The Northern Syrian Revolts of 1919–1921," 257.

84. Woodward, *Documents on British Foreign Policy*, 403–4; Zeine, *The Struggle for Arab Independence*, 103.

85. Moubayed, *Steel and Silk*, 376; Khoury, *Syria and the French Mandate, 1920–1945*, 105–10; Watenpaugh, *Being Modern in the Middle East*, 174–82.

86. Moubayed, *Steel and Silk*, 363–64.

87. Russell, *The First Modern Arab State, 1918–1920*, 21.

88. Moubayed, *Steel and Silk*, 200–201.

89. Provence, *The Last Ottoman Generation*, 113; See also, Naramoto, 224–25. Like Hananu, Shallash was a graduate of the Ottoman military academy. He had served the Ottoman army in the Libyan war.

90. BBA. Dahiliye Nezareti Kalem-i Mahsus [Ministry of the Interior Office of the Private Secretary] (DH-KMS) 57-2/23. December 23, 1919.

CHAPTER 4. STATE TRANSFORMATIONS

1. Like the Ottoman Empire, France had postponed elections due in 1918 for one year. Maier, *Recasting Bourgeois Europe*, 89.

2. Sonyel, *Mustafa Kemal (Atatürk) ve Kurtuluş Savaşı*, 331–32, quotes FO 371/4227/108842, July 27, 1919.

3. Akşin, *İstanbul Hükümetleri ve Milli Mücadele*, vol. 2. Mahmut Goloğlu, in turn, identifies as the "Third Constitutional Period" the era initiated with the establishment of the Grand National Assembly in Ankara on April 23, 1920, following the closure of the Istanbul parliament under Allied pressure. (Goloğlu, *Üçüncü Meşrutiyet*). In his early work, Sina Akşin also subscribed to Goloğlu's characterization. He later concluded that the term, "though accurate analytically and historically, is not appropriate because it does not take notice of the revolutionary attributes or potential" of the Ankara assembly (2:5). For an analysis of the merits and demerits of the Third Constitutional Period designation, see Bülent Tanör, *Osmanlı-Türk Anayasal Gelişmeleri (1789–1980)*, 245.

4. Karaca, *Meclis-i Mebusan'dan Türkiye Büyük Millet Meclisi'ne*, 291–92. Elections were mandated for Mosul but could not be held because of British occupation.

5. Karaca, 341.

6. The only non-Muslim deputy-elect was Mişon Ventura, a Jewish professor at the Faculty of Law at the imperial academy. Segments of Ottoman and Greek populations boycotted the elections. Some harbored hopes of political frameworks outside the Ottoman system emerging in the peace settlements. Others advocated for a proportional system that that would ensure seats to their communities (whose numerical and proportional presence had diminished in most provinces) even in the case of individual candidates' failure at the electoral district level. Karaca, 316–29.

7. Atatürk, *Nutuk*, 3:1178–90; document no. 220.

8. Atatürk, 3:1186.

9. Gökbilgin, *Milli Mücadele Başlarken*, 1:189; 2:389–92; Akşin, "Turkish-Syrian Relations in the Time of Faysal," 8.

10. Atatürk, *Nutuk*, 3:1186.

11. Atatürk, 3:1184–85.

12. Saral and Saral, *Vatan Nasıl Kurtarıldı*, 170–71.

13. Both the minister of the interior and some deputies raised the question of the determination of a quorum, specifically whether the quotas of districts where elections could not be held because of occupation would need to be factored in to determine the quorum mandated by the constitution. Karaca, *Meclis-i Mebusan'dan Türkiye Büyük Millet Meclisi'ne*, 343–44.

14. The translations are based on the text of the National Pact as rendered in Toynbee and Kirkwood, *Turkey*, 85.

15. Eissenstat, "Metaphors of Race and Discourse of Nation"; Çağaptay, *Islam, Secularism, and Nationalism in Modern Turkey*, 245–54.

16. Zürcher, "The Borders of the Republic Reconsidered," 54, 59. Some readings of the original text render the word as *örf* (custom, tradition), which has even greater similarity to *ırk* in Arabic/Ottoman-script longhand (عرف).

17. *Milli Egemenlik Belgeleri* (Ankara: TBMM, 2015).

18. The "Wilsonian moment" is the rubric Erez Manela uses in his examination of the international and transnational adumbration of Wilsonianism during the negotiations at the Versailles Peace Conference in 1919. Manela, *The Wilsonian Moment*.

19. Özbudun, "Milli Mücadele ve Cumhuriyetin Resmi Belgelerinde Yurttaşlık ve Kimlik Sorunu," 64–65.

20. See, for instance, a book on the First Parliament by one of the most prominent legal scholars of the Turkish Republic, for this very elision. Velidedeoğlu, *İlk Meclis ve Milli Mücadele'de Anadolu*, 10. A textbook assigned in the mandatory History of the Revolution classes at the university level renders the misak's Article 1 by further modifying the original phrase "the parts inhabited by an Ottoman Muslim majority" as "Turkish and Muslim majority." Akyüz et al., *Atatürk İlkeleri ve İnkılap Tarihi I*, 82.

21. For a critical assessment of this view, see Bein, *Kemalist Turkey and the Middle East*.

22. See Turan, *Türk Devrim Tarihi*, 2:82–91, for an analysis of the process by which the draft resolution progressed to its final form.

23. Zeine, *The Struggle for Arab Independence*, 134–35.

24. Akşin, "Turkish-Syrian Relations in the Time of Faysal," 11; Mango, *Atatürk*, 270.

25. Saral, *Vatan Nasıl Kurtarıldı*, 172, 193.

26. Zeine, *The Struggle for Arab Independence*, 135. Zeine provides ample information on this mission based on his interview with Haydar; Çiçek, "Türk-Arap İlişkilerinde Değişiklik ve Süreklilik," 182–83.

27. *Atatürk'ün Tamim, Telgraf ve Beyannameleri*, 4:181–82.

28. Zeine, *Struggle for Arab Independence*, 134–35, cites NA FO 371/5032. India Office to Foreign Office, London. E21/2/44, February 10, 1920.

29. *Atatürk'ün Tamim, Telgraf ve Beyannameleri*, 4:213–15, cites *Harp Tarihi Vesikaları Dergisi* 15 (1956), document no. 402; Jäschke, "Ein scherifisches Bündnisangebot an Mustafa Kemal," 390.

30. Jäschke, "Ein scherifisches Bündnisangebot an Mustafa Kemal," 390.

31. Akşin, "Turkish-Syrian Relations in the Time of Faysal," 9, cites the records of the Ottoman Council of Ministers (BBA. "Meclis-i Vükela Mazbataları, v. 218.")

32. Akyüz, *Türk Kurtuluş Savaşı ve Fransız Kamuoyu*, 98; Shaw and Shaw, *History of the Ottoman Empire and Modern Turkey*, 2:349.

33. Zeine, *The Struggle for Arab Independence*, 136, cites *Parliamentary Debates, House of Commons*, v. 127, Fifth Ser., 1920, 186.

34. March 29, 1920. Akyüz, *Türk Kurtuluş Savaşı ve Fransız Kamuoyu, 1919–1922*, 62.

35. Gelvin, *Divided Loyalties*, 248–49; Sluglett, *Britain in Iraq, 1914–1932*, 39.

36. *The New York Times*, April 20, 1919.

37. Yerasimos, *Milliyetler ve Sınırlar*, 167–70; Zeine, *The Struggle for Arab Independence*, 138.

38. *The New York Times*, April 20, 1919.

39. *The New York Times*, April 26, 1919.

40. Türkiye Büyük Millet Meclisi Zabıt Cerideleri (hereafter TBMMZC) (Proceedings of the Grand National Assembly of Turkey), Term I, Year 1, Session 2 (I/1/2) (closed 4th sitting). April 24, 1920.

41. TBMMZC I/1/8, May 1, 1920.
42. Zeidner, *The Tricolor over the Taurus*, 207, 225.
43. Shaw, *From Empire to Republic*, 3:1403–4.
44. Lawson, "The Northern Syrian Revolts of 1919–1921," 258–59.
45. A French push on the Black Sea coast resulted in fresh occupation of coal-rich northern Anatolian districts during the cease-fire period. Shaw, *From Empire to Republic*, 2:601–2.
46. Shaw, *From Empire to Republic*, 2:845–50.
47. On Fattah Pasha, see Batatu, *The Old Social Classes and the Revolutionary Movements of Iraq*, 316. The meeting was held in the home of Fu'ad Daftari. Öke, *Belgelerle Türk İngiliz İlişkilerinde Musul ve Kürdistan Sorunu, 1918–1926*, 80.
48. Genel Kurmay Başkanlığı, *Türk İstiklal Harbi Güney Cephesi*, 4:18; Türkmen, *Musul Meselesi*, 24.
49. On Taha al-Hashimi, see Provence, *The Last Ottoman Generation and the Making of the Modern Middle East*, 137.
50. Khoury, *Syria and the French Mandate*, 97–98; Rafeq, "Arabism, Society, and Economy in Syria, 1918–20," 10. According to Rafeq, "Faysal kept supporting the Turks against the French till the very last day of his rule in Syria and even later on." Jäschke, on the other hand, maintains that Faysal opposed an accord with the Anatolians because he wanted to remain loyal to his father. Jäschke, "Ein scherifisches Bündnisangebot an Mustafa Kemal," 390. Further contacts in July support Rafeq's argument.
51. ATASE İstiklal Harbi (İH) (War of Independence) 756/21-13 (no. 2) (July 19, 1920). Jäschke, "Ein scherifisches Bündnisangebot an Mustafa Kemal," 392; Üzel, *Gaziantep Savaşının İç Yüzü*, 100; Akşin, "Turkish-Syrian Relations in the Time of Faysal," 13.
52. For the text of the Treaty of Sèvres, see https://wwi.lib.byu.edu/index.php/Section_I,_Articles_1_-_260 (accessed December 30, 2020).
53. Jäschke, "Ein scherifisches Bündnisangebot an Mustafa Kemal," 396.
54. Ali, "The Career of Ozdemir," 980; Adil, *Hayat Mücadeleleri*, 342; Türkmen, *Musul Meselesi*, 37, 86–89.
55. Allawi, *Faisal I of Iraq*, 302; Rafeq, "Arabism, Society, and Economy in Syria, 1918–20," 11; Naramoto, "An Introductory Note on Military Alliance between the Arab and Turkish Nationalists," 237–38.
56. Cleveland, *The Making of an Arab Nationalist*.
57. NA FO 141/776/70. Acting High Commissioner to Curzon, Ramleh, no. 1110, September 30, 1920.
58. NA FO 141/430/3. High Commissioner [?] to FO no. 5411/68, September 10, 1920.
59. NA FO 141/776/70. Faisal to Lloyd George, Cernobbio, September 11, 1920.
60. ATASE İH 1168/25-2, April 4, 1921. The ritual mention of the sovereign's name in the mosque sermon signified political allegiance.
61. Umar, *Türkiye-Suriye İlişkileri*, 30–34.
62. Lawson, "The Northern Syrian Revolts of 1919–1921," 261.

63. Umar, *Türkiye-Suriye İlişkileri*, 36–37.
64. ATASE İH 1168/25-2 (May 16, 1921); ATASE İH 1168/52-3 (June 4, 1921).
65. MD 7N 1640. Tel. 2133 et 2134 du Général de la Panouse, December 6, [1919].
66. Rush and Priestland, *Records of Iraq, 1914–1966*, 2:769.
67. Abdullah, *Memoirs of King Abdullah of Transjordan*, 192.
68. Allawi, *Faisal I of Iraq*, 361–81; Sluglett, *Britain in Iraq*, 69–70.
69. Shaw, *From Empire to Republic*, 3:1473–80.
70. Shaw, 3:1506–38.
71. December 13, 1920. Akyüz, *Türk Kurtuluş Savaşı ve Fransız Kamuoyu*, 132.
72. January 14, 1920. Akyüz, *Türk Kurtuluş Savaşı ve Fransız Kamuoyu*, 59.
73. MD 7N 2201. Bulletin d'informations politiques, no. 21, Port Said, October 21, 1921.
74. Sonyel, *Turkish Diplomacy 1918–1923*, 103.
75. Sonyel, 119
76. For the French text and official English translation of the Ankara Treaty, see "Despatch from His Majesty's Ambassador at Paris, enclosing the Franco-Turkish Agreement signed at Angora on October 20, 1921," London, His Majesty's Stationery Office, 1921." http://www.hri.org/docs/FT1921/Franco-Turkish_Pact_1921.pdf (accessed December 30, 2020).
77. MD 7N 2200. Gouraud, no. 670–71, November 26, 1921. Analyse des Documents, État-Major de l'Armée, 3rd Bureau Section d'Orient, November 29, 1921.

CHAPTER 5. STRUGGLE FOR REDEMPTION

1. Helmreich, *From Mudros to Sèvres*, 27.
2. Kemal Atatürk, *Nutuk*, 3:1103; document no. 156c. October 16–17, 1919.
3. See, for instance, House, *The Intimate Papers of Colonel House*, 4:467; Sonyel, *Turkish Diplomacy 1918–1923*, 149.
4. Erdaş, "Nihad (Anılmış) Paşa'nın Elcezire Cephe Komutanlığı ve Yargılanması Meselesi," 9.
5. Artuç, *İttihatçı-Senusi İlişkileri (1908–1918)*, 177–78.
6. MD 7N 2201. Gaillard to Ministère des Affaires Étrangères, Cairo, October 1, 1921.
7. Türkmen, *Musul Meselesi*, 36–40.
8. Turan, *Türk Devrim Tarihi*, 2:261–62; Mango, *Atatürk*, 336.
9. MD 7N 2200 (E.M.A. Section d'Afrique, 1920–1922). "Orient / Conference des Ministres des Affaires Étrangères, Paris 23–26 Mars 1922 / Questions Militaires" "Draft Terms of an Armistice between the Greek and Turkish Armies in Anatolia."
10. Shaw, *From Empire to Republic*, 3:1599–609.
11. House, *The Intimate Papers of Colonel House*, 4:467.
12. Shaw, *From Empire to Republic*, 3:1606.
13. NA FO 371/7861. No. 621, March 16, 1922. Şimşir, *İngiliz Belgelerinde Atatürk*, 1919–1938, 4:225–26.

14. Demirel, *Birinci Meclis'te Muhalefet*, 260–302; Turan, *Türk Devrim Tarihi*, 259–60.
15. Türkmen, *Musul Meselesi*, 37.
16. Jwaideh, *The Kurdish National Movement*, 188.
17. ATASE İH 1687/15-452. Cevad to Chief of Staff (#1094), April 30, 1922; Chief of Staff Fawzi to Ministry of Defense, n.d., nos. 13-1, 13-2, 13-3; Cevad to Chief of Staff (#1149), May 4, 1923.
18. ATASE İH 1687/15-452. Cevad to Chief of Staff (#1595), June 19, 1922.
19. The mission reported to the regional command in Diyarbekir at the beginning and later to the Eastern Army under General Kazım Karabekir's command.
20. ATASE İH 1687/15-452. Cevad to Chief of Staff (#1643), June 24, 1922.
21. ATASE İH 1687/15-452. Deputy [Elcezire Corps] commander Hasan Basri to Chief of Staff, July 21, 1922.
22. ATASE İH 1687/15-452. Cevad to Chief of Staff Fevzi Pasha (#1643), June 24, 1922.
23. ATASE İH 1687/15-452. Fevzi to Cevad, June 26 (?), 1922.
24. Güztoklusu, *Özdemir Bey'in Filistin-Suriye Kuvva-ı Milliyesi ve Elcezire Konfederasyonu*, 12; Genel Kurmay Başkanlığı, *Türk İstiklal Harbi Güney Cephesi*, 4:305–9.
25. Othman Ali, "The Career of Ozdemir," 973. The British authorities in Iraq had a checkered relationship with Mahmud. In the days leading to the Mudros agreement, Britain looked for an ally in the Kurdish regions it occupied, where Ottoman loyalties, dynastic ambitions, and linkages with Iranian Kurds were strong. The British patronized Mahmud, who within six months of the armistice, revolted against his patrons and was exiled to India. McDowall, *A Modern History of the Kurds*, 121–23.
26. Ali, "The Career of Ozdemir," 974, cites Rafiq Hilmi, *Yadasht* (memoirs) (Baghdad, 1958), 6:72–74.
27. Türkmen, *Musul Meselesi*, 65.
28. Shaw, *From Empire to Republic*, 4:1789.
29. Statement dated October 1, 1922. Shaw, 4:1792.
30. Manela, *The Wilsonian Moment*, 63–76.
31. Sa'id and Thabit, *Gazi Mustafa Kemal Paşa'nın Hayatı*.
32. NA FO 141/680/7. A.W.K.B., no. 408/35, February 4, 1922.
33. Genel Kurmay Başkanlığı, *Türk İstiklal Harbi Güney Cephesi*, 4:312–13. An operation by the regular army remained as a possibility throughout the talks but was not carried out.
34. The treaty's signatories were "L'Empire Britannique, la France, l'Italie, le Japon, la Bulgare, la Gréce, la Roumanie, la Russe, l'état Serbe-Croate-Slovéne et la Turquie." http://www.mfa.gov.tr/data/Kutuphane/Kurucu_Anlasmalar/lozan-anlasmasi.pdf (accessed December 30, 2020).
35. NA FO 839/16. Naji al-Assil, Ministre Plènipotentiaire de Sa Majesté Hachimite to Monsieur Le Secrétaire-Générale de la Conférence de la Paix, Lausanne, January 29, 1923.

36. Genel Kurmay Başkanlığı, *Türk İstiklal Harbi Batı Cephesi*, 2:117.
37. Shaw, *From Empire to Republic*, 4:1921.
38. TBMMZC I/3/157. December 16, 1922; Genel Kurmay Başkanlığı, *Türk İstiklal Harbi Batı Cephesi*, 157.
39. Olcay, *Sevres Andlaşmasına Doğru*, 55.
40. The proceedings are summarized in the following document: File F. c. XIV / Docket IX. Advisory Opinion No. 12. November 21, 1925. Permanent Court of International Justice Ninth (Extraordinary) Session. Article 3, Paragraph 2, of the Treaty of Lausanne (Frontier between Turkey and Iraq). http://www.worldcourts.com/pcij/eng/decisions/1925.11.21_lausanne.htm (accessed September 26, 2020).
41. NA FO 839/16. Curzon to Balfour, January 25, 1923.
42. NA FO 371/E961/1/44. Curzon to Lindsay, no. 224, January 23, 1923. In *Documents on British Foreign Policy*. First series. XVIII, 360; Shaw, *From Empire to Republic*, 4:1925.
43. NA FO 839/16. H.R. [Horace Rumbold?] to Mr. Henderson (Constantinople), no. 75, Lausanne, January 25, 1923.
44. Fahir Armaoglu, "Lozan Konferansı ve Musul Sorunu," 129–35.
45. Atatürk Günlüğü [Atatürk Today], January 15, https://www.ataturktoday.com/AtaturkGunlugu/OcakJanuary/15.htm (accessed December 30, 2020), quotes Kocatürk, *Atatürk ve Türkiye Cumhuriyeti Tarihi Kronolojisi*.
46. Atatürk Günlüğü, January 16, https://www.ataturktoday.com/AtaturkGunlugu/OcakJanuary/16.htm (accessed December 30, 2020). Arar, *Atatürk'ün İzmit Basın Toplantısı*. Mustafa Kemal would not visit Istanbul until 1927, even after Allied occupation ended at the end of 1922. Some Istanbul papers opposed Mustafa Kemal and the Ankara government virulently.
47. Arar, *Atatürk'ün İzmit Basın Toplantısı*, 60–61.
48. Commander-in-Chief Gazi Mustafa Kemal to Prime Minister Rauf Bey, No. 346. January 28, 1923. *Atatürk'ün Bütün Eserleri*, 15:26, quotes Şimşir, *Atatürk ile Yazışmalar (1920–1923)*, 466.
49. MD 7N 2201. Maigret to Ministère des Affaires Étrangères, Baghdad [?], January 25, 1923.
50. MD 7N 2201. Maigret to Ministère des Affaires Étrangères, [Baghdad, par?] Beirut, January 26, 1923.
51. Ali, "The Career of Ozdemir," 976.
52. TBMMZC I/3/200, February 27, 1923 (closed session); Turan, "Misak-ı Milli ve Atatürk'ün Lozan Sonrası Hedefleri," 53.
53. TBMMZC I/3/200, February 27, 1923; Armaoğlu, "Lozan Konferansı ve Musul Sorunu," 139.
54. TBMMZC I/3/4, March 4, 1923 (closed session); Murat Güztoklusu, *Elcezire ve Özdemir Harekâtı*, 124; Türkmen, *Musul Meselesi*, 74.
55. TBMMZC I/3/5, March 5, 1923.
56. TBMMZC I/3/6, March 6, 1923.
57. Güztoklusu, *Elcezire ve Özdemir Harekâtı*, 152–55.
58. Güztoklusu, *Elcezire ve Özdemir Harekâtı*, 159.

59. The leading historian of Ankara's initiatives in northern Iraq in the years 1922–1923, Murat Güztoklusu, refers to the proposed entity as the "Özdemir Project," suggesting that it was Özdemir's brainchild.

60. Türkmen, *Musul Meselesi*, 81–84.

61. For factionalism in the GNA see Ahmet Demirel, *Birinci Meclis'te Muhalefet*, and Akın, *TBMM Devleti, 1920–1923*, 398–407.

62. Turan, *Türk Devrim Tarihi*, 2:259.

63. Anonymous, "Lausanne and the Chester Concession," *Advocate of Peace through Justice* 85 (1923):5, 195–96.

64. On French sentiment regarding the Chester concession, see MD 20N 1239. Bulletin de Renseignements des Questions Musulmanes, Ministère de la Guerre, État-Major de l'armée, Section d'Afrique et d'Orient, no. 1.590 9/11, Paris, May 17, 1923.

65. Article 33: The Turkish and British Governments reciprocally undertake that, pending the decision to be reached on the subject of the frontier, no military or other movement shall take place which might modify in any way the present state of the territories of which the final fate will depend upon that decision.

66. On enthusiasm regarding a Turkish mandate in Palestine, see Halabi, "Liminal Loyalties: Ottomanism and Palestinian Responses to the Turkish War of Independence, 1919–22," 31–32. ATASE İH 858/13-20.

67. ATASE İH 1690/239-462. Chief of Staff to the Foreign Ministry, no. 3-1. January 15, 1923.

68. ATASE İH 1690/239-462. Cevad Pasha to the Chief of Staff, no. 18. April 2, 1923.

69. TBMMZC I/2/17, April 7, 1921.

70. ATASE İH 1690/239-462. Cevad Pasha to the Chief of Staff, no. 26-3. February 26, 1923.

71. ATASE İH 1690/239-462, no. 26-1. April 5, 1923.

72. ATASE İH 1690/239-462. Cevad Pasha (?) to the Supreme Command, no. 26. May 9, 1923.

73. Kemal claimed that the area was first inhabited by Turks coming from Central Asia, advancing the notion that would be the mainstay of the racialist Turkish ideology in the 1930s, and adding to the many ethnographic claims the different parties advanced in disputes during the course of the peace talks. Yerasimos, *Milliyetler ve Sınırlar*, 187, quotes, Sökmen, *Hatay'ın Kurtuluşu İçin Harcanan Çabalar*, 70.

74. ATASE İH 1693/250-474. Mehmed Kenan to the Chief of Staff, no. 4895. June 26, 1923.

75. ATASE İH 1693/250-474, August 7, 1923.

76. ATASE İH 1690/239-462, August 7, 1923. In 1924, Celal Kadri was placed on a list of 150 personae non gratae (*Yüzellilikler*) expelled from Turkey and barred from reentry. His case was discussed in a closed session in the Assembly on April 16, 1924. TBMMZC II/2/39 (closed second sitting).

77. 'Uwayyid was forced to seek asylum in Turkey. Rafeq, "Arabism, Society and Economy in Syria, 1918–1920," 19–20.

78. ATASE İH 1690/239-462. Kenan to the Chief of Staff, nos. 6-2, 6-3. August 4, 1923.

79. ATASE İH 1693/250-474. 6 August 1923.

80. ATASE İH 1693/250-474, October 5, 1923.

81. Treaty of Lausanne, Section I: Territorial Clauses, https://wwi.lib.byu.edu/index.php/Treaty_of_Lausanne.

82. MD 7N 2201. Gaillard to Ministère des Affaires Étrangères, Cairo, May 11, 1923.

83. Treaty of Lausanne, Section III: Protection of Minorities, https://wwi.lib.byu.edu/index.php/Treaty_of_Lausanne (accessed December 30, 2020).

84. Initiatives in 1913–14 between the Ottoman Empire, Bulgaria, and Greece for formal transfers had not come to fruition owing to the outbreak of the war, but they provided antecedents to the 1923 agreement. Özsu, *Formalizing Displacement*, 51–59.

85. According to Owen and Pamuk, the number of civilian and military Muslim casualties of the war was 2 million; 1.4 million Armenians perished or left; and 1.2 million Greeks left after Lausanne only. Turkey's population in 1924 was 13 million. Owen and Pamuk, *A History of Middle East Economies in the Twentieth Century*, 11. Population figures for the tumultuous decade are rough estimates. According to Zürcher, Anatolia's population decreased by one-fifth from 1914 to 1918. Zürcher, *The Young Turk Legacy*, 139.

86. "Turkey inherited its governmental tradition, including sizeable cadres of a civilian and military bureaucracy, from the Ottoman Empire; indeed, when that empire collapsed in 1918, over half of the civilian bureaucrats and 90 percent of the trained military staff officers continued their service in the Turkish Republic, with only a small minority serving in other successor states such as Syria, Iraq, or Libya." Rustow, "Turkish Democracy in Historical and Comparative Perspective," 6.

87. Gontaut-Biron and Le Révérend, *D'Angora à Lausanne*, 34.

88. Sanjian, "The Sanjak of Alexandretta (Hatay)," 191–205.

89. MD 20N 1239. Ministère de la Guerre, État-Major de l'Armée, Section d'Afrique et d'Orient, No. 2955 9/11, Paris, Sept 4, 1923.

90. Öke, *Belgelerle Türk-İngiliz İlişkilerinde Musul ve Kürdistan Sorunu, 1918–1926*, 129–76.

CONCLUSION

1. Aksakal, *The Ottoman Road to War in 1914*, 90–92.

2. Atatürk, *Atatürk'ün Bütün Eserleri*, 3:55; Atay, *Atatürkün Bana Anlattıkları*, 61.

3. Rustow, "Turkish Democracy in Historical and Comparative Perspective," 6.

4. According to Picard, *Taqaddum* and *Ray al-'Am* were pro-Ottoman and later pro-Turkish, but only until 1924. Picard, "Die arabischen Nationalisten im Fruchtbaren Halbmond und der Kemalismus," 382.

5. Halabi, "Liminal Loyalties: Ottomanism and Palestinian Responses to the Turkish War of Independence, 1919–22," 32–33.

6. C. E. S. Palmer to First Secretary, the Residency Cairo, February 16 (statement minutes) and 17 (cover letter), 1925. FO 141/776/70 "Statement by Amin Rihani as the result of his efforts to make peace between Ibn Saud and King Ali of the Hedjaz."

7. Deringil, *The Ottoman Twilight in the Arab Lands*, xv.

8. İnan, *Vatandaş için Medeni Bilgiler*, 28–29.

9. Büke, "Arabs in Visual Rhetoric and the Emergence of Turkish National Identity, 1908–1939."

10. Bein, *Kemalist Turkey and the Middle East*.

11. Yavuz, *Nostalgia for the Empire*.

BIBLIOGRAPHY

Aaronsohn, Alexander. *With the Turks in Palestine*. Boston: Houghton Mifflin Company, 1916.
Abdullah. *Memoirs of King Abdullah of Transjordan*. London: Cape, 1950.
Adil, Selahattin. *Hayat Mücadeleleri: Selahattin Adil Paşanın Hatıraları*. Istanbul: Zafer Matbaası, 1982.
Adıvar, Halide Edib. *Conflict of East and West in Turkey*. Lahore: S.M. Ashraf, 1935.
———. *House with Wisteria: Memoirs of Turkey Old and New*. New Brunswick, NJ: Transaction Publishers, 2009.
Ahmad, Feroz. "Politics and Political Parties in Republican Turkey." In *Cambridge History of Turkey*, vol. 4: *Turkey in the Modern World*, edited by Reşat Kasaba. Cambridge: Cambridge University Press, 2008.
———. *The Young Turks and the Ottoman Nationalities: Armenians, Greeks, Albanians, Jews, and Arabs, 1908–1918*. Salt Lake City: University of Utah Press, 2014.
———. *The Young Turks: The Committee of Union and Progress in Turkish Politics, 1908–1914*. Oxford: Clarendon Press, 1969.
———. *The Young Turks: Struggle for the Ottoman Empire, 1914–1918*. Istanbul: Bilgi University Press, 2019.
Ahmet İzzet, Paşa. *Feryadım*, edited by Süheyl İzzet Furgaç and Yüksel Kanar. 2 vols. Istanbul: Nehir Yayınları, 1992.
Akgün, Seçil Karal. "The General Harbord Commission and the American Mandate Question." In *Studies in Atatürk's Turkey: The American Dimension*, edited by George S. Harris and Bilge Criss. Leiden, Netherlands: Brill, 2009.
Akın, Rıdvan. *TBMM Devleti, 1920–1923: Birinci Meclis Döneminde Devlet Erkleri ve İdare*. Istanbul: İletişim, 2001.
Akın, Yiğit. *When the War Came Home: The Ottomans' Great War and the Devastation of an Empire*. Stanford, CA: Stanford University Press, 2018.
Aksakal, Mustafa. *The Ottoman Road to War in 1914: The Ottoman Empire and the First World War*. Cambridge: Cambridge University Press, 2010.
Akşin, Sina. *İstanbul Hükümetleri ve Milli Mücadele*. 2 vols. Istanbul: Cem Yayınevi, 1976.

———. "Turkish-Syrian Relations in the Time of Faysal (1918–1920)." In *Milletlerarası Münasebetler Türk Yıllığı*, vol 20. Ankara: Ankara Üniversitesi Siyasal Bilgiler Fakültesi Yayınları, 1980–1981.

Aktar, Ayhan. "Debating the Armenian Massacres in the Last Ottoman Parliament, November–December 1918." *History Workshop Journal* 64, no. 1 (2019): 240–70.

———. "A Propaganda Tour Organized by Djemal Pasha." In *Syria in World War I: Politics, Economy and Society*, edited by M. Talha Çiçek. London: Routledge, Taylor & Francis Group, 2016.

———. "Yüzbaşı Torosyan'ın Adı Yok," introduction to Yüzbaşı Sarkis Torosyan, *Çanakkale'den Filistin Cephesine*, trans. Gizem Şakar. Istanbul: İletişim Publications, 2012.

Akyüz, Yahya. *Türk Kurtuluş Savaşı ve Fransız Kamuoyu, 1919–1922*. Ankara: Türk Tarih Kurumu Basımevi, 1988.

Akyüz, Yahya, et al. *Atatürk İlkeleri ve İnkılap Tarihi I*. 2 vols. Ankara: Yüksek Öğretim Kurulu Yayınları, 1997.

Alaranta, Toni. "Mustafa Kemal Atatürk's Six-Day Speech of 1927: Defining the Official Historical View of the Foundation of the Turkish Republic." *Turkish Studies* 9, no. 1 (2008): 115–29.

Ali, Othman. "The Career of Ozdemir: A Turkish Bid for Northern Iraq, 1921–1923." *Middle Eastern Studies* 53, no. 6 (2017): 966–85.

Alkan, Mehmet Ö. "Modernization from Empire to Republic and Education in the Process of Nationalism." In *Ottoman Past and Today's Turkey*, edited by Kemal Karpat. Leiden: Brill, 2000.

Allawi, Ali A. *Faisal I of Iraq*. New Haven, CT: Yale University Press, 2014.

Anderson, Benedict R. *Imagined Communities: Reflections on the Origin and Spread of Nationalism*. London: Verso, 1991.

Anscombe, Frederick F. *State, Faith, and Nation in Ottoman and Post-Ottoman Lands*. New York: Cambridge University Press, 2014.

Antonius, George. *The Arab Awakening*. London: H. Hamilton, 1938.

Arar, İsmail. *Atatürk'ün İzmit Basın Toplantısı, 16–17 Ocak 1923*. Istanbul: Burçak Yayınevi, 1969.

Arıkan, Zeki. *Mütareke ve İşgal Dönemi İzmir Basını, 30 Ekim 1918–8 Eylül 1922*. Ankara: Atatürk Kültür, Dil ve Tarih Kurumu, Atatürk Araştırma Merkezi, 1989.

Armaoğlu, Fahir. "Lozan Konferansi ve Musul Sorunu." In *Misak-ı Milli ve Türk Dış Politikasında Musul, Kerkük ve Erbil Meselesi Sempozyumu*. Ankara: Atatürk Kültür, Dil ve Tarih Yüksek Kurumu, Atatürk Araştırma Merkezi, 1998

Artuç, Nevzat. *Cemal Paşa: Askeri ve Siyasi Hayatı*. Ankara: Türk Tarih Kurumu, 2008.

———. *İttihatçı-Senusi İlişkileri (1908–1918): İttihat ve Terakki'nin İttihad-ı İslam Siyaseti Çerçevesinde*. Istanbul: Bilge Kültür Sanat, 2013.

Atatürk, Kemal. *Atatürk'ün Bütün Eserleri*. 30 vols. Istanbul: Kaynak Yayınları, 1998–2011.

———. *Nutuk*. 3 vols. Istanbul: Milli Eğitim Basımevi, 1971.

Atatürk'ün Tamim, Telgraf ve Beyannameleri. 4 vols. Ankara: Türk Tarih Kurumu Basımevi, 1991.

Atay, Falih Rıfkı. *Atatürkün Bana Anlattıkları.* Istanbul: Sel Yayınları, 1955.

———. *Batış Yılları.* Istanbul: Dünya Yayınları, 1963.

———. *Zeytindağı.* Istanbul: Remzi Kitabevi, 1943.

Avedian, Vahagn. "State Identity, Continuity, and Responsibility: The Ottoman Empire, the Republic of Turkey and the Armenian Genocide." *European Journal of International Law* 23, no. 3 (2020): 797–820.

Aydemir, Şevket Süreyya. *Suyu Arayan Adam.* Istanbul: Remzi Kitabevi, 1997.

Aydın, Cemil. *The Politics of Anti-Westernism in Asia: Visions of World Order in Pan-Islamic and Pan-Asian Thought.* New York: Columbia University Press, 2007.

Bahadır, Elif Fatma. "Bir Şehir Kurma Teşebbüsü (1900–1917)." MA thesis, Fatih Sultan Mehmet Vakıf Üniversitesi, 2018.

Bahjat, Muhammad, and Rafiq al-Tamimi, *Wilayat Beirut.* 2 vols. Beirut: Matbaʿat al-iqbal, 1916.

Bahrani, Zainab, Zeynep Çelik, and Edhem Eldem, eds. *Scramble for the Past: A Story of Archaeology in the Ottoman Empire, 1753–1914.* Istanbul: SALT, 2011.

Baker, Ray Stannard. *Woodrow Wilson and World Settlement.* 3 vols. Garden City, NY: Doubleday, Page & Co., 1922.

Baram, Amatzia. "Territorial Nationalism in the Middle East." *Middle Eastern Studies* 26, no. 4 (1990): 425–48.

al-Barghouti, Omar Saleh, and Khalil Tutah. *Tarikh Filastin.* Jerusalem: Matbaʿa Bayt al-Maqdis, 1923.

Barkey, Karen, and Mark Von Hagen, eds. *After Empire: Multiethnic Societies and Nation-Building: The Soviet Union and the Russian, Ottoman, and Habsburg Empires.* Boulder, CO: Westview Press, 1997.

Bartov, Omer, and Phyllis Mack, eds. *In God's Name: Genocide and Religion in the Twentieth Century.* Studies on War and Genocide. New York: Berghahn Books, 2001.

Başbakanlık Devlet Arşivleri Genel Müdürlüğü. *İstiklal Harbi ile İlgili Telgraflar* (Ankara: T.C. Başbakanlık Devlet Arşivleri Genel Müdürlüğü, Cumhuriyet Arşivi Daire Başkanlığı, 1994)

Batatu, Hanna. *The Old Social Classes and the Revolutionary Movements of Iraq: A Study of Iraq's Old Landed and Commercial Classes and of Its Communists, Baʿthists, and Free Officers.* Princeton, NJ: Princeton University Press, 1978.

Bayur, Yusuf Hikmet. *Türk İnkılabı Tarihi.* 3 vols. Ankara: Türk Tarih Kurumu, 1983.

Bein, Amit. *Kemalist Turkey and the Middle East: International Relations in the Inter-War Period.* Cambridge: Cambridge University Press, 2018.

Bennett, Tony. *The Birth of the Museum: History, Theory, Politics.* London: Routledge, 1995.

Berkes, Niyazi. *The Development of Secularism in Turkey.* Montreal: McGill University Press, 1964.

Beşikçi, Mehmet. *The Ottoman Mobilization of Manpower in the First World War: Between Voluntarism and Resistance.* Leiden: Brill, 2012.

Beyoğlu, Süleyman. "Türk-Arap İlişkilerinin Son Kırılma Noktası: Medine'nin Tahliyesi." *Atatürk Araştırma Merkezi Dergisi* 26 (2010): 425–60.
Bidwell, Robin Leonard, et al. *British Documents on Foreign Affairs*, Part II, Series B. Lanham, MD: University Publications of America, 1985.
Bilgin, Nuri, ed. *Cumhuriyet, Demokrasi ve Kimlik*. Istanbul: Bağlam, 1997.
Birinci, Ali. *Hürriyet ve İtilâf Fırkası: II. Meşrutiyet Devrinde İttihat ve Terakki'ye Karşı Çıkanlar*. Istanbul: Dergâh Yayınları, 1990.
Bloxham, Donald, and Dirk A. Moses, eds. *The Oxford Handbook of Genocide Studies*. Oxford: Oxford University Press, 2010.
Blumi, Isa. *Reinstating the Ottomans: Alternative Balkan Modernities, 1800–1912*. New York: Palgrave Macmillan, 2011.
Bozdoğan, Sibel. *Modernism and Nation Building: Turkish Architectural Culture in the Early Republic*. Seattle: University of Washington Press, 2001.
Braude, Benjamin. "Foundation Myths of the Millet System." In *Christians and Jews in the Ottoman Empire: The Functioning of a Plural Society*, edited by Benjamin Braude and Bernard Lewis. 2 vols. New York: Holmes & Meier Publishers, 1982.
Braude, Benjamin, and Bernard Lewis, eds. *Christians and Jews in the Ottoman Empire: The Functioning of a Plural Society*. 2 vols. New York: Holmes & Meier Publishers, 1982.
Brown, L. Carl, ed. *Imperial Legacy: The Ottoman Imprint on the Balkans and the Middle East*. New York: Columbia University Press, 1996.
Budak, Mustafa. *İdealden Gerçeğe: Misâk-ı Millî'den Lozan'a Dış Politika*. Istanbul: Küre Yayınları, 2002.
Büke, İlkim. "Arabs in Visual Rhetoric and the Emergence of Turkish National Identity, 1908–1939." PhD diss. Ben Gurion University of the Negev, 2015.
Busch, Briton Cooper. *Mudros to Lausanne: Britain's Frontier in West Asia, 1918–1923*. Albany: State University of New York Press, 1976.
Çağaptay, Soner. *Islam, Secularism, and Nationalism in Modern Turkey: Who Is a Turk?* London: Routledge, 2006.
Cebesoy, Ali Fuat. *Milli Mücadele Hatıraları*. Istanbul: Vatan Neşriyatı, 1953.
Çelik, Zeynep. "Defining Empire's Patrimony: Late Ottoman Perception of Antiquities." In *Scramble for the Past: A Story of Archaeology in the Ottoman Empire, 1753–1914*, edited by Zainab Bahrani, Zeynep Çelik, and Edhem Eldem. Istanbul: SALT, 2011.
Cemal (Djemal), Ahmad. *Memories of a Turkish Statesman, 1913–1919*. New York: Doran, 1922.
Cemal Paşa, *Erinnerungen eines türkischen Staatsmannes*. Munich: Drei Masken Verlag, 1922.
———. *Hatırat, 1913–1922*. S.n.: Dersaadet, 1922.
Cemal Paşa and Behçet Cemal. *Hatıralar: İttihat ve Terakki, I. Dünya Savaşı Anıları*. Istanbul: Çağdaş Yayınları, 1977.
Chatterjee, Partha. *The Nation and Its Fragments: Colonial and Postcolonial Histories*. Princeton, NJ: Princeton University Press, 1993.

Çiçek, M. Talha. "Osmanlı Hâkimiyeti Sonrası Türk-Arap İlişkilerinde Değişim ve Süreklilik." *Divan: Disiplinlerarası Çalışmalar Dergisi* 17 (2012): 173–92.

———, ed. *Syria in World War I: Politics, Economy and Society.* London: Routledge, Taylor & Francis Group, 2016.

———. "Visions of Islamic Unity: A Comparison of Djemal Pasha's *al-Sharq* and Sharif Husayn's *al-Qibla* Periodicals." *Die Welt des Islams* 54 (2014): 46–82.

———. *War and State Formation in Syria: Cemal Pasha's Governorate during World War I, 1914–1917.* London: Routledge/Taylor & Francis Group, 2014.

Clayer, Nathalie. "Albanian Students of the Mekteb-i Mülkiye: Social Networks and Trends of Thought." In *Late Ottoman Society: The Intellectual Legacy*, edited by Elisabeth Özdalga. London: RoutledgeCurzon, 2005.

Cleveland, William L. *Islam against the West: Shakib Arslan and the Campaign for Islamic Nationalism.* Austin: University of Texas Press, 1985.

———. *The Making of an Arab Nationalist: Ottomanism and Arabism in the Life and Thought of Sati' Al-Husri.* Princeton, NJ: Princeton University Press, 1971.

Commins, David Dean. *Islamic Reform: Politics and Social Change in Late Ottoman Syria.* New York: Oxford University Press, 1990.

Davison, Roderic H. *Essays in Ottoman and Turkish History, 1774–1923: The Impact of the West.* Austin: University of Texas Press, 1990.

———. *Reform in the Ottoman Empire, 1856–1876.* Princeton, NJ: Princeton University Press, 1963.

Dawn, C. Ernest. *From Ottomanism to Arabism: Essays on the Origins of Arab Nationalism.* Urbana: University of Illinois Press, 1973.

Debus, Esther. *Sebilürreşad: Eine vergleichende Untersuchung zur islamischen Opposition der vor- und nachkemalistischen Ära.* Frankfurt am Main: Peter Lang, 1991.

Demirel, Ahmet. *Birinci Meclis'te Muhalefet: İkinci Grup.* Istanbul: İletişim, 1994.

Deringil, Selim. *The Ottoman Twilight in the Arab Lands: Turkish Testimonies and Memories of the Great War.* Brighton, MA: Academic Studies Press, 2018.

———. "'Your Religion Is Worn and Outdated': Orphans, Orphanages and Halide Edib during the Armenian Genocide: The Case of Antoura." *Études arméniennes contemporaines*, no. 12 (2019): 33–65.

Duara, Prasenjit. *Rescuing History from the Nation: Questioning Narratives of Modern China.* Chicago: University of Chicago Press, 1995.

Dündar, Fuat. *İttihat ve Terakki'nin Müslümanları İskân Politikası, 1913–1918.* Istanbul: İletişim, 2001.

———. *Modern Türkiye'nin Şifresi: İttihat ve Terakki'nin Etnisite Mühendisliği, 1913–1918.* Istanbul: İletişim, 2008.

Dyer, Gwynne. "The Turkish Armistice of 1918: 1—The Turkish Decision for a Separate Peace, Autumn 1918." *Middle Eastern Studies* 8, no. 2 (1972): 143–78.

Eissenstat, Howard. "Metaphors of Race and Discourse of Nation: Racial Theory and State Nationalism in the First Decades of the Turkish Republic." In *Race and Nation: Ethnic Systems in the Modern World*, edited by Paul Spickard. New York: Routledge, 2004.

Erdaş, Sadık. "Nihad (Anılmış) Paşa'nın Elcezire Cephe Komutanlığı ve Yargılanması Meselesi." *Cumhuriyet Tarihi Araştırmaları Dergisi* 14, no. *28* (2018): 3–36.
Erden, Ali Fuad. *Birinci Dünya Harbinde Suriye Hatıraları*. Istanbul, 1954.
Ergil, Doğu. *Milli Mücadelenin Sosyal Tarihi*. Ankara: Turhan Kitabevi, 1981.
Erickson, Edward J. *Gallipoli and the Middle East, 1914–1918: From the Dardanelles to Mesopotamia*. London: Amber Books, 2008.
———. *Ottoman Army Effectiveness in World War I: A Comparative Study*. London: Routledge, 2007.
Ersanlı, Büşra. "The Ottoman Empire in the Historiography of the Kemalist Era: A Theory of Fatal Decline." In *The Ottomans and the Balkans: A Discussion of Historiography*, edited by Fikret Adanır and Soraiya Faroqhi. Leiden, The Netherlands: Brill, 2002.
Esherick, Joseph, Hasan Kayalı, and Eric Van Young, eds. *Empire to Nation: Historical Perspectives on the Making of the Modern World*. Lanham, MD: Rowman & Littlefield, 2006.
Evans, Laurence. *United States Policy and the Partition of Turkey, 1914–1924*. Baltimore: Johns Hopkins University Press, 1965.
Fawaz, Leila Tarazi. *A Land of Aching Hearts: The Middle East in the Great War*. Cambridge, MA: Harvard University Press, 2014.
Fortna, Benjamin C. *The Circassian: A Life of Eşref Bey: Late Ottoman Insurgent and Special Agent*. Oxford: Oxford University Press, 2016.
———. *Imperial Classroom: Islam, the State, and Education in the Late Ottoman Empire*. Oxford: Oxford University Press, 2002.
Fromkin, David. *A Peace to End All Peace: The Fall of the Ottoman Empire and the Creation of the Modern Middle East*. New York: Avon Books, 1990.
Gallant, Thomas W. *The Edinburgh History of the Greeks, 1768 to 1913: The Long Nineteenth Century*. Edinburgh: Edinburgh University Press, 2015.
Gawrych, George W. *The Crescent and the Eagle: Ottoman Rule, Islam and the Albanians, 1874–1913*. London: I.B. Tauris, 2006.
Geiss, Imanuel. "The Civilian Dimension of the War." In *Facing Armageddon: The First World War Experienced*, edited by Hugh Cecil and Peter Liddle. London: Cooper, 1996.
Gelvin, James. "'Arab Nationalism': Has a New Framework Emerged?" *International Journal of Middle East Studies* 41, no. 1 (2009): 10–12.
———. *Divided Loyalties: Nationalism and Mass Politics in Syria at the Close of Empire*. Berkeley: University of California Press, 1998.
Gencer, Mustafa. *Jöntürk Modernizmi ve "Alman Ruhu."* Istanbul: İletişim, 2003.
Genel Kurmay Başkanlığı. *Türk İstiklal Harbi*, vol. 1. *Mondros Mütarekesi ve Tatbikatı*. Ankara: Genel Kurmay Basımevi, 1962.
———. *Türk İstiklal Harbi Batı Cephesi: İstiklal Harbinin Son Safhası*. Edited by Abidin Tüzel. Ankara: Genel Kurmay Basımevi, 1969.
———. *Türk İstiklal Harbi Güney Cephesi*, vol. 4. Ankara: Genel Kurmay Basımevi, 2009.

Gerwarth, Robert. *The Vanquished: Why the First World War Failed to End*. New York: Farrar, Straus and Giroux, 2016.

Gerwarth, Robert, and Erez Manela. *Empires at War, 1911–1923*. Oxford: Oxford University Press, 2014.

Gingeras, Ryan. *Eternal Dawn: Turkey in the Age of Atatürk*. New York: Oxford University Press, 2019.

———. *Sorrowful Shores: Violence, Ethnicity, and the End of the Ottoman Empire, 1912–1923*. Oxford: Oxford University Press, 2009.

Ginio, Eyal. *The Ottoman Culture of Defeat: The Balkan Wars and Their Aftermath*. New York: Oxford University Press, 2016.

Gökbilgin, M. Tayyib. *Milli Mücadele Başlarken*. 2 vols. Ankara: Türk Tarih Kurumu, 1959.

Gologlu, Mahmut. *Milli Mücadele Tarihi I: Erzurum Kongresi*. Istanbul: Türkiye İş Bankası Kültür Yayınları, 2006 (first published 1968).

———. *Milli Mücadele Tarihi II: Sivas Kongresi*. Istanbul: Türkiye İş Banakası Kültür Yayınları, 2008 (first published 1969).

———. *Üçüncü Meşrutiyet 1920*. Ankara: Başnur Matbaası, 1970.

Gontaut-Biron, Roger, and L. Le Révérend. *D'Angora à Lausanne*. Paris: Plon-Nourrit et Cie, 1924.

Goodblatt, David M. *Elements of Ancient Jewish Nationalism*. Cambridge: Cambridge University Press, 2006.

Görgülü, İsmet. *On Yıllık Harbin Kadrosu, 1912–1922: Balkan-Birinci Dünya ve İstiklâl Harbi*. Ankara: Türk Tarih Kurumu Basımevi, 1993.

Grainger, John D. *The Battle for Syria, 1918–1920*. Woodbridge, UK: Boydell Press, 2013.

Greenfeld, Liah. *Nationalism: Five Roads to Modernity*. Cambridge, MA: Harvard University Press, 1992.

Gülalp, Haldun. "The Eurocentrism of Dependency Theory and the Question of 'Authenticity.'" *Third World Quarterly* 19, no. 5 (1998): 951–61.

Güztoklusu, Murat. *Elcezire ve Özdemir Harekatı: Kurtuluş Savaşı'nın Son Cephesi*. Ankara: Ümit Yayıncılık, 2006.

———. *Özdemir Bey'in Filistin-Suriye Kuvva-ı Milliyesi ve Elcezire Konfederasyonu*. Istanbul: Bengi Yayınları, 2010.

Hakan, Sinan. *Türkiye Kurulurken Kürtler (1916–1920)*. Istanbul: İletişim, 2013.

Halabi, Awad. "Liminal Loyalties: Ottomanism and Palestinian Responses to the Turkish War of Independence, 1919–22." *Journal of Palestine Studies* 41, no. 3 (2012): 19–37.

Hanioğlu, M. Şükrü. *A Brief History of the Late Ottoman Empire*. Princeton, NJ: Princeton University Press, 2008.

———. *Preparation for a Revolution: The Young Turks, 1902–1908*. Oxford: Oxford University Press, 2001.

Hanley, Will. "What Ottoman Nationality Was and Was Not." *Journal of Ottoman and Turkish Studies Association* 3, no. 2 (2016): 277–98.

Harris, George S., and Bilge Criss, eds. *Studies in Atatürk's Turkey: The American Dimension*. Leiden, Netherlands: Brill, 2009.
Hathaway, Jane, and Karl K. Barbir. *The Arab Lands under Ottoman Rule, 1516–1800*. Harlow, UK: Pearson Longman, 2008.
Havemann, Axel. "Between Ottoman Loyalty and Arab 'Independence': Muhammad Kurd 'Ali, Girgi Zaydan, and Shakib Arslan." *Quaderni di Studi Arabi* 5–6 (1987): 347–56.
Hedin, Sven. *Till Jerusalem*. Stockholm: A. Bonnier, 1917.
Helmreich, Paul C. *From Paris to Sèvres: The Partition of the Ottoman Empire at the Peace Conference of 1919–1920*. Columbus: Ohio State University Press, 1974.
Hendrich, Béatrice. *Milla, millet, Nation: von der Religionsgemeinschaft zur Nation? Über die Veränderung eines Wortes und die Wandlung eines Staates*, PhD dissertation, University of Giessen, 2002. Frankfurt: Peter Lang, 2003.
Hille, Charlotte Mathilde Louise. *State Building and Conflict Resolution in the Caucasus*. Leiden, The Netherlands: Brill, 2010.
Hitti, Philip Khuri. *History of the Arabs*. London: Macmillan, 1943.
Hobsbawm, E. J. "The End of Empires." In *After Empire: Multiethnic Societies and Nation-Building: The Soviet Union and the Russian, Ottoman, and Habsburg Empires*, edited by Karen Barkey and Mark Von Hagen. Boulder, CO: Westview Press, 1997.
———. *Nations and Nationalism since 1780: Programme, Myth, Reality*. Cambridge: Cambridge University Press, 1991.
Horne, Charles F., Walter F. Austin, and Leonard Porter Ayres. *Source Records of the Great War: A Comprehensive and Readable Source Record of the World's Great War*, vol. 7. Indianapolis: The American Legion, 1931.
House, Edward Mandell, and Charles Seymour. *The Intimate Papers of Colonel House*, vol. 4. Boston: Houghton Mifflin Company, 1926.
Hudson, Leila. *Transforming Damascus: Space and Modernity in an Islamic City*. London: Tauris Academic Studies, 2008.
Hülagü, M. Metin. *Pan-Islamist Faaliyetler: 1914–1918*. Istanbul: Boğaziçi, 1994.
İnan, Afet. *Vatandaş İçin Medeni Bilgiler*. Istanbul, 1930.
Jäschke, Gotthard. "Ein scherifisches Bündnisangebot an Mustafa Kemal." In *Der Orient in der Forschung, Festschrift für Otto Spies zum 5. April 1966*, edited by Wilhelm Hoenerbach. Wiesbaden: Harrassowitz, 1967.
Jwaideh, Wadie. *The Kurdish National Movement: Its Origins and Development*. Syracuse, NY: Syracuse University Press, 2006.
Kaiser, Hilmar. *The Extermination of Armenians in the Diarbekir Region*. Istanbul Bilgi University Press, 2014.
———. "Genocide at the Twilight of the Ottoman Empire." In *The Oxford Handbook of Genocide Studies*, edited by Donald Bloxham and Dirk A. Moses. Oxford: Oxford University Press, 2010.
———. "Regional Resistance to Central Government Policies: Ahmed Djemal Pasha, the Governors of Aleppo, and Armenian Deportees in the Spring and Summer of 1915." *Journal of Genocide Research* 12, nos. 3–4 (2010): 173–218.

Kaligian, Dikran Mesrob. *Armenian Organization and Ideology under Ottoman Rule: 1908–1914*. New Brunswick, NJ: Transaction Publishers, 2009.
Kandemir, Feridun. *Peygamberimizin Gölgesinde Son Türkler: Medine Müdafaası*. Istanbul: Yağmur Yayınevi, 1974.
Kansu, Aykut. *The Revolution of 1908 in Turkey*. Leiden, The Netherlands: Brill, 1997.
Karabekir, Kazım. *İstiklal Harbimizin Esasları*. Istanbul: Emre, 1995.
Karaca, Taha Niyazi. *Meclis-i Mebusan'dan Türkiye Büyük Millet Meclisi'ne Geçiş Sürecinde Son Osmanlı Meclis-i Mebusan Seçimleri*. Ankara: Türk Tarih Kurumu, 2004.
Kasaba, Reşat. "Dreams of Empire, Dreams of Nations." In *Empire to Nation: Historical Perspectives on the Making of the Modern World*, edited by Joseph Esherick, Hasan Kayalı, and Eric Van Young. Lanham, MD: Rowman & Littlefield, 2006.
Kawtharani, Wajih. *Al-ittijahat al-ijtimaʿiyah al-siyasiyah fi jabal lubnan wa-al-mashriq al-ʿarabi, 1860–1920*. Beirut: Maʿhad al-Inmaʾ al-ʿArabi, 1976.
Kayalı, Hasan. *Arabs and Young Turks: Ottomanism, Arabism, and Islamism in the Ottoman Empire, 1908–1918*. Berkeley: University of California Press, 1997.
———. "Bağımsızlık Mücadelesi İçinde Anadolu-Suriye İlişkileri." In *Bilanço 1923–1938*, edited by Zeynep Rona. Istanbul: Tarih Vakfı Yurt Yayınları, 1999.
———. "A Glimpse from the Periphery: Medina in the Young Turk Era." In *Istanbul as Seen from a Distance: Centre and Provinces in the Ottoman Empire*, edited by Elisabeth Özdalga, M. Sait Özervarlı, and Feryal Tansuğ, 139–54. Istanbul: Swedish Research Institute in Istanbul, 2011.
———. "Islam in the Thought and Politics of Two Late Ottoman Intellectuals: Mehmed Akif and Said Halim." *Archivum Ottomanicum* 19 (2001): 307–33.
———. "Jamal basha fi suriya: Hal huwa kawmi am infisali am ittihadi." *Al-Ijtihad* 11 (2000): 189–216.
———. "Ottoman and German Imperial Objectives in Syria During World War I: Synergies and Strains Behind the Front Lines." In *War and Collapse: World War I and the Ottoman State*, edited by Hakan Yavuz and Feroz Ahmad. Salt Lake City: University of Utah Press, 2015.
———. "The Ottoman Experience of World War I: Historiographical Problems and Trends." *Journal of Modern History* 89, no. 4 (2017): 875–907.
———. "Wartime Regional and Imperial Integration of Greater Syria during World War I." In *The Syrian Land: Processes of Integration and Fragmentation: Bilad Al-Sham from the 18th to the 20th Century*, edited by Thomas Philipp and Birgit Schäbler. Stuttgart: F. Steiner, 1998.
Kechriotis, Vangelis. "Greek-Orthodox, Ottoman Greeks or Just Greeks? Theories of Coexistence in the Aftermath of the Young Turk Revolution." *Études balkaniques*, no. 1 (2020): 51–71.
Kemal, Ismail, and Sommerville Story, *The Memoirs of Ismail Kemal Bey*. London: Constable, 1920.
Khalidi, Rashid. "The Press as a Source for Modern Arab Political History: ʿAbd Al-Ghani Al-ʿUraisi and Al-Mufid." *Arab Studies Quarterly* 3, no. 1 (1981): 22–42.

Khoury, Philip S. *Syria and the French Mandate: The Politics of Arab Nationalism, 1920–1945*. Princeton, NJ: Princeton University Press, 1987.

———. *Urban Notables and Arab Nationalism: The Politics of Damascus, 1860–1920*. Cambridge: Cambridge University Press, 1983.

Kıcıman, Naci Kaşif. *Medine Müdafaası Yahut Hicaz Bizden Nasıl Ayrıldı?* Istanbul: Sebil Yayınevi, 1971.

Kılıç, Selami. *Türk-Sovyet İlişkilerinin Doğuşu: Brest-Litovsk Barışı ve Müzakereleri, 22 Aralık 1917–3 Mart 1918*. Istanbul: Dergah Yayınları, 1998.

Kocaoğlu, Bünyamin. "Mütareke Meclisinde Ermeni Meselesi Tartışmaları." *Journal of Social Sciences Institute* (Balıkesir University), 16 (2013): 167–83.

Kocatürk, Utkan. *Atatürk ve Türkiye Cumhuriyeti Tarihi Kronolojisi: 1918–1938*. Ankara: Türk Tarih Kurumu, 1983.

Köroğlu, Erol. *Ottoman Propaganda and Turkish Identity: Literature in Turkey during World War I*. London: Tauris Academic, 2007.

Kreiser, Klaus. *Atatürk: Eine Biographie*. Munich: C.H. Beck, 2008.

Kürkçüoğlu, Ömer. *Osmanlı Devletine Karşı Arap Bağımsızlık Hareketi (1908–1918)*. Ankara: A.Ü.S.B.F. Basın ve Yayın Yüksek Okulu Basımevi, 1982.

Kurt, Ümit. "A Rescuer, an Enigma and a Genocidaire: Cemal Pasha." In *End of the Ottomans: The Genocide of 1915 and the Politics of Turkish Nationalism*, edited by Hans-Lukas Kieser et al. London: I.B. Tauris, 2019.

Landau, Jacob M. *Pan-Turkism in Turkey: A Study of Irredentism*. Hamden, CT: Archon Books, 1981.

Lawson, Fred. "The Northern Syrian Revolts of 1919–1921." In *From the Syrian Land to the States of Syria and Lebanon*, edited by Thomas Philipp and Christoph Schumann. Würzburg: Ergon in Kommission, 2004.

Levene, Mark. "Creating a Modern Zone of Genocide: The Impact of Nation-State-Formation on Eastern Anatolia, 1878–1923." *Holocaust and Genocide Studies* 12, no. 3 (1998): 393–433.

Lewis, Bernard. *The Emergence of Modern Turkey*. London: Oxford University Press, 1961.

———. *The Political Language of Islam*. Chicago: University of Chicago Press, 1988.

Liman von Sanders, Otto Viktor Karl. *Five Years in Turkey*. Translated by Carl Reichmann. Annapolis, MD: United States Naval Institute, 1927.

Maier, Charles S. *Recasting Bourgeois Europe: Stabilization in France, Germany, and Italy in the Decade after World War I*. Princeton, NJ: Princeton University Press, 1975.

Manela, Erez. *The Wilsonian Moment: Self-Determination and the International Origins of Anticolonial Nationalism*. Oxford: Oxford University Press, 2007.

Mango, Andrew. *Atatürk*. London: John Murray, 1999.

———. *From the Sultan to Atatürk: Turkey*. London: Haus Pub., 2009.

Manning, Patrick. *Navigating World History: Historians Create a Global Past*. New York: Palgrave Macmillan, 2003.

Masters, Bruce Alan. *The Arabs of the Ottoman Empire, 1516–1918: A Social and Cultural History*. Cambridge: Cambridge University Press, 2013.
Maurice, Frederick. *The Armistices of 1918*. London: Oxford University Press, 1943.
McDowall, David. *A Modern History of the Kurds*. London: I.B. Tauris, 2004.
Mehmetefendioğlu, Ahmet. "Rahmi Bey'in İzmir Valiliği," *Çağdaş Türkiye Tarihi Araştırmaları Dergisi* 1 (1993): 347–70.
Méouchy, Nadine. "From the Great War to the Syrian Armed Resistance Movement (1919–1921): The Military and the Mujahidin in Action." In *The World in World Wars: Experiences, Perceptions, and Perspectives from Africa and Asia*, edited by Heike Liebau, Katrin Bromber, Katharina Lange, Dyalah Hamzah, Ravi Ahuja. Leiden, Netherlands: Brill, 2010.
Mikusch, Dagobert von. *Mustapha Kemal: Between Europe and Asia: A Biography*. New York: Doubleday, 1931.
Minawi, Mostafa. *The Ottoman Scramble for Africa: Empire and Diplomacy in the Sahara and the Hijaz*. Stanford, CA: Stanford University Press, 2016.
Misak-ı Milli ve Türk Dış Politikasında Musul, Kerkük ve Erbil Meselesi Sempozyumu. Ankara: Atatürk Kültür, Dil ve Tarih Yüksek Kurumu, Atatürk Araştırma Merkezi, 1998.
Mitchell, Timothy. *Colonising Egypt*. Cambridge: Cambridge University Press, 1988.
Morgenthau, Henry. *Ambassador Morgenthau's Story*. Garden City, NY: Doubleday, 1918.
Morin, Aysel, and Ronald Lee. "Constitutive Discourse of Turkish Nationalism: Atatürk's Nutuk and the Rhetorical Construction of the 'Turkish People.'" *Communication Studies* 61, no. 5 (2010): 485–506.
Morris, Benny, and Dror Ze'evi. *The Thirty-Year Genocide: Turkey's Destruction of Its Christian Minorities, 1894–1924*. Cambridge, MA: Harvard University Press, 2019.
Moubayed, Sami M. *Steel and Silk: Men and Women Who Shaped Syria 1900–2000*. Seattle, WA: Cune, 2006.
Musa, Sulayman. *Al-murasalat al-tarikhiyah: Al-thawra al-'arabiyah al-kubra*. Amman: al-Mu'allif, 1973.
Naramoto, Eisuke. "An Introductory Note on Military Alliance between the Arab and Turkish Nationalists 1919–1920: Dayr Az-Zur Raid and the Cilicia Campaign." *Annals of Japan Association for Middle East Studies* 1 (1986): 217–52.
Nişanyan, Sevan. *Yanlış Cumhuriyet: Atatürk ve Kemalizm üzerine 51 Soru*. Istanbul: Kırmızı Yayınları, 2008.
Öke, Kemal. *Belgelerle Türk-İngiliz İlişkilerinde Musul ve Kürdistan Sorunu, 1918–1926*. Ankara: Türk Kültürünü Araştırma Enstitüsü, 1992.
Olcay, Osman. *Sevres Andlaşmasına Doğru: Çeşitli Konferans ve Toplantıların Tutanakları ve Bunlara İlişkin Belgeler*. Ankara: S.B.F. Basın ve Yayın Yüksek Okulu Basımevi, 1981.
Ortak, Şaban. *Osmanlı'nın Son Manevralarından Suriye ve Garbi Arabistan Tehciri*. Ankara: Pegem Akademi, 2011.
Ortaylı, İlber. *İmparatorluğun En Uzun Yüzyılı*. Istanbul: Hil Yayın, 1983.

Owen, Roger, and Şevket Pamuk. *A History of Middle East Economies in the Twentieth Century*. Cambridge, MA: Harvard University Press, 1998.

Özbudun, Ergun. "Milli Mücadele ve Cumhuriyetin Resmi Belgelerinde Yurttaşlık ve Kimlik Sorunu." In *Cumhuriyet, Demokrasi ve Kimlik*, edited by Nuri Bilgin. Istanbul: Bağlam, 1997.

Özdalga, Elisabeth, ed. *Late Ottoman Society: The Intellectual Legacy*. London: RoutledgeCurzon, 2005.

Özdalga, Elisabeth, M. Sait Özervarlı, and Feryal Tansuğ, eds. *Istanbul as Seen from a Distance: Centre and Provinces in the Ottoman Empire*. Istanbul: Swedish Research Institute in Istanbul, 2011.

Özer, Sevilay. "Ali Galip Olayı." *Stratejik ve Sosyal Araştırmalar Dergisi*, 1, no. 2 (2017): 1–12.

Özkan, Behlül. "Making a National Vatan in Turkey: Geography Education in the Late Ottoman and Early Republican Periods." *Middle Eastern Studies* 50, no. 3 (2014): 457–81.

Özoğlu, Hakan. *Kurdish Notables and the Ottoman State: Evolving Identities, Competing Loyalties, and Shifting Boundaries*. Albany: State University of New York Press, 2004.

Özsu, Umut. *Formalizing Displacement: International Law and Population Transfers*. Oxford: Oxford University Press, 2015.

Öztan, Ramazan. "Point of No Return? Prospects of Empire after the Ottoman Defeat in the Balkan Wars (1912–1913)." *International Journal of Middle Eastern Studies* 50, no. 1 (2018): 65–84.

Pamuk, Şevket. *Uneven Centuries: Economic Development of Turkey since 1820*. Princeton, NJ: Princeton University Press, 2018.

Panian, Karnik. *Goodbye, Antoura: A Memoir of the Armenian Genocide*. Stanford, CA: Stanford University Press, 2015.

Parla, Taha. *Türkiye'de Siyasal Kültürün Resmi Kaynakları*. Istanbul: İletişim Yayınları, 1991.

Philipp, Thomas, and Birgit Schäbler, eds. *The Syrian Land: Processes of Integration and Fragmentation: Bilad Al-Sham from the 18th to the 20th Century*. Stuttgart: F. Steiner, 1998.

Philipp, Thomas, and Christoph Schumann, eds. *From the Syrian Land to the States of Syria and Lebanon*. Würzburg: Ergon in Kommission, 2004.

Picard, Elizabeth. "Die arabischen Nationalisten im Fruchtbaren Halbmond und der Kemalismus." In *Der Nahe Osten in der Zwischenkriegszeit, 1919–1939: Die Interdependenz von Politik, Wirtschaft und Ideologie*, edited by Linda Schatkowski Schilcher and Claus Scharf. Stuttgart: F. Steiner, 1989.

Provence, Michael. *The Last Ottoman Generation and the Making of the Modern Middle East*. Cambridge: Cambridge University Press, 2017.

al-Qasimiyya, Khayriyya. *Al-hukuma al-'arabiyya fi dimashq*. Cairo, 1971.

al-Qattan, Najwa. "Safarbarlik: Ottoman Syria and the Great War." In *From the Syrian Land to the States of Syria and Lebanon*, edited by Thomas Philipp and Christoph Schumann. Würzburg: Ergon in Kommission, 2004.

———. "When Mothers Ate Their Children: Wartime Memory and the Language of Food in Syria and Lebanon." *International Journal of Middle East Studies* 46, no. 4 (2014): 719–36.

Rafeq, Abdul-Karim. "Arabism, Society and Economy in Syria, 1918–1920." In *State and Society in Syria and Lebanon*, edited by Youssef M. Choueiri. New York: St. Martin's Press, 1994.

———. "Gesellschaft, Wirtschaft und Politische Macht in Syrien, 1918–1925." In *Der Nahe Osten in der Zwischenkriegszeit, 1919–1939: Die Interdependenz von Politik, Wirtschaft und Ideologie*, edited by Linda Schatkowski Schilcher and Claus Scharf. Stuttgart: F. Steiner, 1989.

Rasim, Ahmet. *Muharrir Bu Ya*. Ankara: M. E. B. Devlet Kitapları, 1969.

Reynolds, Michael A. "Buffers, Not Brethren: Young Turk Military Policy in the First World War and the Myth of Panturanism." *Past & Present* 203, no. 1 (2020): 137–79.

———. *Shattering Empires: The Clash and Collapse of the Ottoman and Russian Empires 1908–1918*. Cambridge: Cambridge University Press, 2011.

Rogan, Eugene L. *The Fall of the Ottomans: The Great War in the Middle East*. New York: Basic Books, 2015.

Roshwald, Aviel. *The Endurance of Nationalism: Ancient Roots and Modern Dilemmas*. Cambridge: Cambridge University Press, 2006.

Roth, Erwin. *Preussens Gloria im heiligen Land: Die Deutschen und Jerusalem*. Munich: G.D.W. Callwey, 1973.

Rudin, Harry Rudolph. *Armistice, 1918*. New Haven, CT: Yale University Press, 1944.

Rush, Alan de Lacy, and Jane Priestland. *Records of Iraq, 1914–1966*. 15 vols. Cambridge, UK: Archive Editions, 2001.

Russell, Malcolm B. *The First Modern Arab State: Syria under Faysal, 1918–1920*. Minneapolis: Bibliotheca Islamica, 1985.

Rustow, Dankwart, "Turkish Democracy in Historical and Comparative Perspective." In *Politics in the Third Turkish Republic*, edited by Metin Heper and Ahmet Evin. Boulder, CO: Westview Press, 1994.

Saab, Hassan. *The Arab Federalists of the Ottoman Empire*. Amsterdam: Djambatan, 1958.

Saʻid, Amin, and Karim Khalil Thabit. *Gazi Mustafa Kemal Paşa'nın Hayatı: Anadolu'da Türk Milli Mücadelesi*. Translated by Zekeriya Kurşun. Istanbul: Doğan Kitap, 2010.

Sakallı, Bayram. *Milli Mücadele'nin Sosyal Tarihi: Müdafaa-ı Hukuk Cemiyetleri*. Istanbul: İz, 1997.

Salzman, Ariel. "Citizens in Search of a State: The Limits of Political Participation in the Late Ottoman Empire." In *Extending Citizenship, Reconfiguring States*, edited by Michael Hanagan and Charles Tilly. Lanham, MD: Rowman & Littlefield, 1999.

Sanjian, Avedis. K. "The Sanjak of Alexandretta (Hatay): A Study in Franco-Turco-Syrian Relations." PhD diss., University of Michigan, 1956.

Saral, Ahmet Hulki, and Tosun Saral. *Vatan Nasıl Kurtarıldı: Nur Dağları (Amanoslar), Toroslar, Adana, Maraş, Gaziantep ve Urfa'da Yapılan Kuvayı Milliye Savaşları*. Ankara: Türkiye İş Bankası Kültür Yayınları, 1970.

Schilcher, Linda Schatkowski and Claus Scharf, eds. *Der Nahe Osten in der Zwischenkriegszeit, 1919–1939: Die Interdependenz von Politik, Wirtschaft und Ideologie*. Stuttgart: F. Steiner, 1989.

Scott, James C. *Seeing Like a State: How Certain Schemes to Improve the Human Condition Have Failed*. New Haven, CT: Yale University Press, 1998.

Şemseddin, Sami. *Kamus-ül Alam*, vol. 1. Istanbul: Mihran Matbaası, 1889.

Shaw, Stanford J. *From Empire to Republic: The Turkish War of National Liberation, 1918–1923: A Documentary Study*. 5 vols. Ankara: Türk Tarih Kurumu Basımevi, 2000.

Shaw, Stanford J., and Ezel Kural Shaw. *History of the Ottoman Empire and Modern Turkey*. 2 vols. Cambridge: Cambridge University Press, 1976.

Shaw, Wendy M. K. *Possessors and Possessed: Museums, Archaeology, and the Visualization of History in the Late Ottoman Empire*. Berkeley, CA.: University of California Press, 2003.

Shields, Sarah D. *Fezzes in the River: Identity Politics and European Diplomacy in the Middle East on the Eve of World War II*. New York: Oxford University Press, 2011.

Şimşir, Bilâl N. *Atatürk ile Yazışmalar (1920–1923)*. Ankara: Kültür Bakanlığı, 1981.

———. *İngiliz Belgelerinde Atatürk*, 1919–1938. 4 vols. Ankara: Türk Tarih Kurumu Basımevi, 1973.

Sluglett, Peter. *Britain in Iraq, 1914–1932*. London: Ithaca Press for the Middle East Centre, St. Antony's College, Oxford, 1976.

Smith, Anthony D. *The Ethnic Origins of Nations*. Oxford: Blackwell, 1986.

Sökmen, Tayfur. *Hatay'ın Kurtuluşu İçin Harcanan Çabalar*. Ankara: Türk Tarih Kurumu Basımevi, 1978.

Sonyel, Salahi Ramadan. *Mustafa Kemal (Atatürk) ve Kurtuluş Savaşı: Yeni Belgelerle, 1918–1923*. 3 vols. Ankara: Türk Tarih Kurumu, 2008.

———. *Turkish Diplomacy 1918–1923: Mustafa Kemal and the Turkish National Movement*. London: Sage, 1975.

Strauss, Johann. "The Disintegration of Ottoman Rule in the Syrian Territories as Viewed by German Observers." In *The Syrian Land: Processes of Integration and Fragmentation: Bilad Al-Sham from the 18th to the 20th Century*, edited by Thomas Philipp and Birgit Schäbler. Stuttgart: F. Steiner, 1998.

Strohmeier, Martin. *Al-Kulliya as-Salahiya in Jerusalem: Arabismus, Osmanismus und Panislamismus im Ersten Weltkrieg*. Stuttgart: F. Steiner, 1991.

Sundhaussen, Holm, Ulf Brunnbauer, Andreas Helmedach, and Stefan Troebst, eds. *Schnittstellen: Gesellschaft, Nation, Konflikt und Erinnerung in Südosteuropa: Festschrift für Holm Sundhaussen zum 65. Geburtstag*. Südosteuropäische Arbeiten. Munich: R. Oldenbourg, 2007.

Suny, Ronald G. "Religion, Ethnicity, and Nationalism" In *In God's Name: Genocide and Religion in the Twentieth Century*, edited by Omer Bartov and Phyllis Mack. New York: Berghahn Books, 2001.

———. *"They Can Live in the Desert but Nowhere Else": A History of the Armenian Genocide*. Princeton, NJ: Princeton University Press, 2015.

Suny, Ronald G., Fatma Müge Göçek, and Norman M. Naimark, eds. *A Question of Genocide: Armenians and Turks at the End of the Ottoman Empire*. New York: Oxford University Press, 2011.

Tamari, Salim. *The Great War and the Remaking of Palestine*. Oakland: University of California Press, 2017.

———. "Muhammad Kurd Ali and the Syrian-Palestinian Intelligentsia in the Ottoman Campaign against Arab Separatism." In *Syria in World War I: Politics, Economy and Society*, edited by M. Talha Çiçek. London: Routledge, Taylor & Francis Group, 2016.

———. "A 'Scientific Expedition' to Gallipoli: The Syrian-Palestinian Intelligentsia and the Ottoman Campaign against Arab Separatism." *Jerusalem Quarterly* 56–57 (2013): 6–28.

———. *Year of the Locust: A Soldier's Diary and the Erasure of Palestine's Ottoman Past*. Berkeley: University of California Press, 2011.

Tanielian, Melanie S. *The Charity of War: Famine, Humanitarian Aid, and World War I in the Middle East*. Stanford, CA: Stanford University Press, 2018.

Tanör, Bülent. *Osmanlı-Türk Anayasal Gelişmeleri (1789–1980)*. Istanbul: Yapı Kredi Kültür Sanat Yayıncılık, 1998.

———. *Türkiye'de Kongre İktidarları, 1918–1920*. Istanbul: Yapı Kredi Kültür Sanat Yayıncılık, 1998.

Tansel, Selahattin. *Mondros'tan Mudanya'ya Kadar*. 4 vols. Ankara: Başbakanlık Basımevi, 1973.

Tauber, Eliezer. *The Arab Movements in World War I*. London: Frank Cass, 1993.

———. *The Formation of Modern Syria and Iraq*. Ilford, UK: Frank Cass, 1995.

Tezcan, Baki. *The Second Ottoman Empire: Political and Social Transformation in the Early Modern World*. New York: Cambridge University Press, 2010.

Theunissen, Hans. "War, Propaganda and Architecture: Cemal Pasha's Restoration of Islamic Architecture in Damascus During World War I." In *Jihad and Islam in World War I: Studies on the Ottoman Jihad on the Centenary of Snouck Hurgronje's "Holy War Made in Germany,"* edited by Erik Jan Zürcher. Leiden: Leiden University Press, 2016.

Thompson, Elizabeth F. *How the West Stole Democracy from the Arabs: The Syrian Arab Congress of 1920 and the Destruction of Its Historic Liberal-Islamic Alliance*. New York: Atlantic Monthly Press, 2020.

Tibawi, Abdul Latif. *A Modern History of Syria, Including Lebanon and Palestine*. London: Macmillan/St. Martin's, 1969.

Torosyan, Yüzbaşı Sarkis. *Çanakkale'den Filistin Cephesine*. Translated by Gizem Şakar. Istanbul: İletişim Publications, 2012.

Toynbee, Arnold Joseph, and Kenneth P. Kirkwood. *Turkey*. New York: Scribner, 1927.

Türkgeldi, Ali Fuat. *Moudros ve Mudanya Mütarekelerinin Tarihi*. Ankara: Güney Matbaacılık ve Gazetecilik, 1948.

Turan, Refik. "Misak-ı Milli ve Atatürk'ün Lozan Sonrası Hedefleri." In *Misak-ı Milli ve Türk Dış Politikasında Musul, Kerkük ve Erbil Meselesi Sempozyumu*. Ankara: Atatürk Kültür, Dil ve Tarih Yüksek Kurumu, Atatürk Araştırma Merkezi, 1998.

Turan, Şerafettin. *Türk Devrim Tarihi*. Istanbul: Bilgi Yayınevi, 1991.

Türkmen, Zekeriya. *Musul Meselesi: Askeri Yönden Çözüm Arayışları, 1922–1925*. Ankara: Atatürk Araştırma Merkezi, 2003.

Uebelhör, Max. *Syrien im Kriege*. Stuttgart: Deutsche Verlags-Anstalt, 1917.

Umar, Ömer Osman. *Türkiye-Suriye İlişkileri, 1918–1940*. Elazığ: T.C. Fırat Üniversitesi Orta-Doğu Araştırmaları Merkezi, 2003.

Üngör, Uğur Ümit. "How Armenian Was the 1915 Genocide?" In *Let Them Not Return: Sayfo: The Genocide against the Assyrian, Syriac and Chaldean Christians in the Ottoman Empire*, ed. David Gaunt et al. New York: Berghahn, 2017.

———. "Seeing Like a Nation-State: Young Turk Social Engineering in Eastern Turkey, 1913–50." *Journal of Genocide Research* 10, no. 1 (2008): 15–39.

Üngör, Uğur Ümit, and Mehmet Polatel. *Confiscation and Destruction: The Young Turk Seizure of Armenian Property*. London: Continuum, 2011.

Üzel, Sahir. *Gaziantep Savaşının İç Yüzü*. Ankara: Doğuş Matbaası, 1952.

Velidedeoğlu, Hıfzı Veldet. *İlk Meclis ve Milli Mücadele'de Anadolu*. Istanbul: Çağdaş, 1990.

Wambaugh, Sarah. *Plebiscites since the World War*, vol. 1. Washington: Carnegie Endowment for International Peace, 1933.

Wasti, S. Tanvir. "The Defence of Medina, 1916–19," *Middle Eastern Studies* 27, no. 4 (1991): 642–53.

Watenpaugh, Keith David. *Being Modern in the Middle East: Revolution, Nationalism, Colonialism, and the Arab Middle Class*. Princeton, NJ: Princeton University Press, 2006.

Weber, Stefan. "Zeugnisse Kulturellen Wandels: Stadt, Architektur und Gesellschaft des osmanischen Damaskus im 19. und frühen 20. Jahrhundert." PhD diss, Freie Universität Berlin, 2001.

Wiegand, Theodor, and Djemal Pascha. *Alte Denkmäler aus Syrien, Palästina und Westarabien*. Berlin: G. Reimer, 1918.

Wiegand, Theodor, and Friedrich Anton Karl Kress von Kressenstein. *Sinai*. Berlin and Leipzig: Vereinigung Wissenschaftlicher Verleger, 1920.

Wiegand, Theodor, Marie Wiegand, and Gerhard Wiegand. *Halbmond im Letzten Viertel: Briefe und Reiseberichte aus der Alten Türkei von Theodor und Marie Wiegand, 1895 bis 1918*. Munich: Bruckmann, 1970.

Wimmer, Andreas, and Nina Glick Schiller. "Methodological Nationalism and Beyond: Nation-State Building, Migration and the Social Sciences." *Global Networks* 2, no. 4 (2002): 301–34.

Woodward, E. L., and R. Butler, eds. *Documents on British Foreign Policy, 1919–1939*. First Series, v. 4. London: Her Majesty's Stationary Office, 1952.

Yalman, Ahmet Emin. *Die Türkei*. Gotha: F.A. Perthes, 1918.

———. *Turkey in the World War*. New Haven, CT: Yale University Press, 1930.

Yavuz, M. Hakan. *Nostalgia for the Empire: The Politics of Neo-Ottomanism.* New York: Oxford University Press, 2020.

Yenen, Alp. "Envisioning Turco-Arab Co-existence between Empire and Nationalism." *Die Welt des Islams* 61, no. 1 (2021): 72–112

Yerasimos, Stefanos. *Milliyetler ve Sınırlar: Balkanlar, Kafkasya ve Orta-Doğu.* Istanbul: İletişim, 2000.

Zeidner, Robert F. *The Tricolor over the Taurus: The French in Cilicia and Vicinity, 1918–1922.* Ankara: Atatürk Supreme Council for Culture, Language and History, 2005.

Zeine, Zeine N. *The Struggle for Arab Independence: Western Diplomacy and the Rise and Fall of Faisal's Kingdom in Syria.* Delmar, NY: Caravan Books, 1977.

Ziemke, Kurt. *Die Neue Türkei: Politische Entwicklung, 1914–1929.* Stuttgart: Deutsche Verlags-anstalt, 1930.

Zürcher, Erik Jan. "The Borders of the Republic Reconsidered." In *Bilanço 1923–1938*, edited by Zeynep Rona. Istanbul: Tarih Vakfı Yurt Yayınları, 1999.

———. *Jihad and Islam in World War I: Studies on the Ottoman Jihad on the Centenary of Snouck Hurgronje's "Holy War Made in Germany."* Leiden: Leiden University Press, 2016.

———. "The Ottoman Legacy of the Turkish Republic: An Attempt at a New Periodization." *Die Welt des Islams* 32, no. 2 (1992): 237–53.

———. *Turkey: A Modern History.* London: I.B. Tauris: 1997.

———. *The Unionist Factor: The Rôle of the Committee of Union and Progress in the Turkish National Movement, 1905–1926.* Leiden: E.J. Brill, 1984.

———. "The Vocabulary of Muslim Nationalism." *International Journal of the Sociology of Language*, no. 137 (1999): 81–92.

———. *The Young Turk Legacy and Nation Building: From the Ottoman Empire to Atatürk's Turkey.* London: I.B. Tauris, 2010.

INDEX

Abdulhamid II (r. 1876–1909), 26–27, 35, 39, 44, 52, 82
Abdullah, Sharif, 91, 130, 140–41
Abu Tulul, 68
Adana, xiii*map*, 80, 88, 197n67, 202n74; Ankara Treaty (Franklin-Bouillon Treaty) (1921), 143–44, 144*map*, 167; appropriating Wilsonian principles, 95; postwar occupation and resistance, 89, 111–12, 133, 142
Aden, xiii*map*, 51, 197n67
Aegean islands, 73, 93, 188n37
Africa: Islamic ideology as resistance to colonialism, 27; Paris Peace Conference (1919), 92–94. *See also* specific country names
Ahmad, Feroz, 9
Ahmed (Sulaymaniya deputy), 163
Ahmed Emin, 47–48
Ahmed İzzet Pasha. See İzzet Pasha
Ahmet Rasim, 45
Akşin, Sina, 117–18, 204n3
Albanianism, Muslim groups and collective identity, 29–31
Albanians/Albania: Ahmed İzzet Pasha, 70–71; local power structures, 107, 177; Muslim groups and collective identity, 14, 29–31, 107; Mehmed Akif, 203n82
Aleppo, 71; Aleppo Province as Syria/Anatolia frontier, 16, 78; Aleppo Province regiment in Gallipoli front, 45-47; Anatolian movement, territorial objectives, 119–21, 120*map*; Armistice of Mudros (1918), 74, 75, 76, 77*map*, 78, 79; Lausanne Conference, negotiating Syria, 165–68; Paris Peace Conference (1919), 99–100; postwar occupation and resistance, 88; resistance to French occupation, 133; war and mobility of troops, 45–47. *See also* Syria
Aleppo National / Popular Organization *(Halep Teşkilat-ı Milliye Riyaseti)*, 128
Alexandretta, 77*map*, 78, 79, 80; Ankara Treaty (Franklin-Bouillon Treaty) (1921), 143–44, 144*map*; desire to return to Turkish rule, 150; postwar occupation and resistance, 88; Treaty of Lausanne (1923), aftermath of, 171–73
Aleyh, Syria, 38
Algeria, 23, 152, 167
Ali Fuad (Cebesoy) Pasha, 81, 100
'Ali Haydar (Asir deputy), 83
Ali İhsan (Sabis) Pasha, 79
Ali, Kılıç, 127
Ali Rıza Pasha, 117
al-'Ali, Saleh, 114, 139–40
al-Jam'iya al-Islamiya (İslam Cemiyeti), 112–13
al-Jazira, xiii*map*, 99–100, 183n2, 188n37. See also Elcezire
Allawi, Ali, 67
Allenby, Edmund, 54, 69, 93–94, 111
Allied and Associated Powers (Allies), 55, 184n9; Allied Supreme Council at San Remo (1920), 131; Anatolian-Syrian collaboration and, 104–5, 111, 127,

Allied and Associated Powers (*continued*) 141–42; Armistice of Mudanya (1922), 145–46; Armistice of Mudros (1918), 73–80, 77*map*, 86, 89, 91; Greece and, 93, 96–97, 100, 147; London Conference (1922), 149–50; November 1917, 55–56; Treaty of Sèvres (1920), 136–37, 137*map*; Wilsonian principles, acceptance of, 95. *See also* Entente alliance; specific treaty names

Amanos Mountains: Armistice of Mudros (1918), 74

Anatolia: Anatolian-Syrian collaboration, summer 1919, 103–6; appropriating Wilsonianism, 94–100; Anatolianism, 32–33; armistice and the opening of the Lausanne Conference, 154–57; battle in Sarıkamış (December 1914), 55; Erzurum Congress on, 101–2; Fertile Crescent territory boundaries, xvii; Fourteen Points, Article 12 clarification on postwar status, 72; the French threat and collaboration in the Anatolia-Syria frontier, 109–15; demographic upheaval, 26–28; Paris Peace Conference (1919), 93; postwar occupation and resistance, 86–88, 176–79; Syrian exiles in, 38; terminology, 14–15; Treaty of Lausanne (1923), 146. *See also* Anatolian movement (1920–1922)

Anatolia and Rumelia Defense of Rights Society (ARDRS), 106–7, 111–12, 118, 128–33

Anatolian movement, 116; abolishment of Ottoman sultanate, 155–56; Ankara Treaty (1921), 142–44, 144*map*; Armistice of Mudanya (1922), 145; blueprint for liberation, 119–21, 120*map*; cooperation in resistance to French occupation, 127–30, 133–35; expansion of colonial resistance after Treaty of Sèvres (1920), 138–42, 176–79; London Conference (1922), 149–50; Grand National Assembly, formation of, 130–33; Greek army defeat (August 1922), 153; Kemalist efforts to maintain Ottoman territories, 179–82; Lausanne Conference, opening of, 154–57; National Pact (misak-ı milli), 121–27; resistance in northern Iraq, 146–49; Third Constitutional Period, 117–18; Treaty of Sèvres (1920), xviii, 136–137, 137*map*. *See also* Anatolian movement; Grand National Assembly (GNA)

'Anaza tribe, 166–68

Anderson, Benedict, 40

Ankara government: adoption of Independence March poem, 113; Ankara Treaty (1921), 142–44, 144*map*, 145; Armistice of Mudanya (1922), 154–57; Lausanne Conference, armistice and the opening of, 154–57; Lausanne Conference, negotiating Mosul, 157–65; Lausanne Conference, negotiating Syria, 142, 165–68; London Conference (1922), 149–50; Northern Iraq, support for resistance, 140, 146–49, 151; Syria, support for resistance, 138. *See also* Anatolian movement; Grand National Assembly (GNA)

Ankara Treaty (1921), 142–44, 144*map*, 145. *See also* Franklin-Bouillon Treaty

Ankara Treaty (Treaty of Ankara) (1926), 114*map*, 173

Antalya, 96

Antioch, 77*map*, 78, 119–21, 120*map*, 133

Antonius, George, 48

Arab Congress (1913), 30, 44–45, 53

Arabism, Muslim groups and collective identity, 29–31

Arab provinces: Anatolian movement joint resistance with local militia forces, 127–30; Anatolian movement (1920–1922), territorial objectives, 119–21, 120*map*; Anatolian-Syrian collaboration, summer 1919, 103–6; Armistice of Mudros (1918), 73–80, 77*map*, 176; Declaration to the Seven, 67–68; early paths to statehood, 21, 167; efforts to create Arab-Turkish federation, post World War I, 80–85; expansion of anti-colonial resistance after Treaty of Sèvres (1920), 138–42, 176–79; Fourteen Points, Article 12 clarification on postwar status, 72; the French threat and collaboration in the Anatolia-Syria frontier, 110–15; Grand National

Assembly, Kemal's call for Muslim unity, 131–33; Kemalist efforts to maintain Ottoman territories, 179–82; Lausanne Conference, negotiating Mosul, 157–65; Lausanne Conference, negotiating Syria, 166–68; Lloyd George and Woodrow Wilson's statements on war aims, 59–64; misak-ı milli (National Pact) on self-determination of Arab majorities, 125–27; negotiations with Ottoman state and Great Britain (1918), 67–68; normality of nation and the Ottoman past, historiography and sources, 7–12; November 1917 as pivotal month in World War I, 56–57; Ottoman government acknowledgment of injustices toward, 83; Ottoman state compulsory enlistment practices, 38; Ottoman surrender in, 91; Ottoman war effort in, overview of, 49–53, 175–76; Paris Peace Conference (1919), 92–94; terminology and geographical designations, 14; Treaty of Lausanne (1923), implications for the Ottoman patrimony, 168–71; Umur-u Şarkiye Dairesi (Office of Eastern Affairs), 87. *See also* specific location names; Occupied Enemy Territory Administration (OETA)

Arab provinces, use of term, 14, 15*map*

Arab Revolt (1916), 30–31, 50, 82

Ardahan, 22–23, 55, 58; Brest-Litovsk Treaty (1918), 64–66; decision to remain in Ottoman Empire (July 1918), 65–66; London Conference (1922), discussions on Armenia state, 149–50; Treaty of Lausanne (1923), implications for the Ottoman patrimony, 170–71. *See also* Three Provinces

ARDRS. *See* Anatolia and Rumelia Defense of Rights Society (ARDRS)

Armenians: Fourteen Points, Article 12 clarification on postwar status, 72; Fourteen Points on non-Muslim nationalities, 62; genocide of, 35, 47, 64, 87, 178–79; Lloyd George and Woodrow Wilson's statements on war aims, 59–64; London Conference (1922), discussion on Armenian state, 149–50; Muslim groups' fear of Christian intentions, 88–90, 93-94, 101–3, 178–79; acknowledgment of injustices toward Christians, 83, 89; pursuit of national rights in Paris (1918), 69–70, 178; resettlement of displaced Christian populations, 93-94, 148; secessionism from Ottoman Empire, 23; Sivas Congress on, 107; territorial claims between Ankara and Russia, 141–42; Transcaucasian Democratic Federative Republic, 64–65; Treaty of Lausanne (1923), implications for non-Muslim minorities, 169–70; Treaty of Sèvres (1920), 137, 137*map*

Armistice of Mudanya (1922), 5, 145, 154–57, 158

Armistice of Mudros (1918), 5, 73–80, 77*map*, 95, 99, 102, 106, 151, 159, 176; basis of political settlement, 125, 133, 162, 178; violation of, 89, 91, 108, 115

Armistice Period (1918–1923), 5

Arslan, Shakib, 44, 128

Asia Minor: Fertile Crescent territory boundaries, xvii, 16; Fourteen Points, Article 12 clarification on postwar status, 72; Lloyd George and Woodrow Wilson's statements on war aims, 59–64; London Conference (1920) and, 130–33; Paris Peace Conference (1919), 93, 99–100. *See also* Anatolia

Asir, 50, 73–74, 77*map*, 98

al-'Askari, Ja'far, 56–57

Assyrians, 23, 148, 172

Austro-Hungarian Empire, 59–62, 67, 70, 82, 87, 103, 127. *See also* Habsburg Empire

Hüseyin Avni (deputy), 162–63

Ayntab, 80, 133, 135; expansion of anticolonial resistance after Treaty of Sèvres (1920), 138–39; postwar occupation and resistance, 88; Treaty of Sèvres (1920), 137, 137*map*

Azerbaijan, 64–65, 69

al-'Azma, Yusuf, 110, 135-36

Azmi (Beirut governor), 39

Baalbek, 128–29

Baghdad, xiii*map*, 15*map*; British population statistics for, 158–59; Declaration to

INDEX · 233

Baghdad (*continued*)
the Seven, 67–68; expansion of anticolonial resistance after Treaty of Sèvres (1920), 140; Fourteen Points and, 62; Ottoman war effort in Arab provinces, 49–50, 58, 140. *See also* Iraq
Baghdad Railway, 76, 142, 146; Ankara Treaty (Franklin-Bouillon Treaty) (1921), 143–44, 144*map*
Bahjat, Muhammad, 39
Bahrein, 51
Bakdash, Badiʿ, 127
Baku, 65, 69
Balfour, Arthur, 103
Balfour Declaration, 54
Balkan Peninsula: Congress of Berlin (1878), 174; defeat of Central Powers, 69; demographic upheaval, 26–28; secessions from Ottoman Empire, 21–23, 29–30. *See also* specific country names
Balkan Wars (1912–1913), 4, 23, 84; immigration and Muslim nationalism, 31–35, 52–53
Batum, 22–23, 55, 58, 64–66. *See also* Three Provinces
Bein, Amit, 182
Beirut, xiii*map*, 15*map*; Cemal's influence on local journalism, 44; collective identity, Arab consciousness in, 36, 39; execution of Arab opponents, 38; Ottoman state infrastructure projects in, 42; resistance to French occupation and, 127–29; 39, 75, 82
Bekir Sami, 142
Belgium, 63, 173
Benghazi, 23
Berlin-Baghdad Railway, 76, 77*map*, 141, 143, 144*map*, 145, 146, 168, 179,
Berlin Congress (Congress of Berlin) (1878), 10, 22, 26-27, 145, 174.
Biʾr al-Sabʿ, xiii*map*, xix, 39, 41–42, 54
Birecik-Urfa-Mardin line (37th parallel), 77*map*, 80, 93, 197n67
Bolshevik Revolution (1917), 6, 54–56
Bosnians, 22, 182
Bosporus, 55, 83, 170
Bozdoğan, Sibel, 49

Brest-Litovsk Treaty (1918): early discussions, 62–64; signing of, 64–66, 176
Bulgaria, 117; defeat of Central Powers and pursuit of ceasefire, 69; Balkan Wars, 4, 28; secessionism from Ottoman Empire, 22–23
Büyük Millet Meclisi. *See* Grand National Assembly (GNA)

Cairo Conference (1921), 141
Caix, Robert de, 134
caliphate: Abdulhamid II (r. 1876–1909), self-proclaimed caliph, 26–27; abolishment of the office, 171; İzzet Pasha's pledge of continued allegiance to caliphate, 71–72, 81; separation of Ottoman sultanate and caliphate, 155–56; Mustafa Kemal, notion as possible caliph, 181; National Pact (1920) on security of the caliphate, 122; Sivas Congress on continued existence of caliphate, 106–7
Calthorpe, Somerset, 91, 116
Caucasus region: armistice with Russia (1917), 58; Brest-Litovsk Treaty (1918), 64–66; Anatolia territory boundaries, xvii, 14; Northern Caucasus Republic, 65; Ottoman pan-Turkist agenda, 65; postwar occupation and resistance, 88–90, 176; Russian annexation of Kars, Ardahan, and Batum (1878), 55; separation from Ottoman Empire, 22; territorial claims between Ankara and Russia, 141–42; Treaty of Kars (1921), 143. *See also* specific location names
Çelik, Zeynep, 40, 49
Cemal Pasha: departure from Syria, 50; as governor and commander in Syria in World War I, 36–50, 175; November 1917 as pivotal month in World War I, 56–57; Syria, mobilizing support amid war's violence, 43–45; treatment of Armenians, 47
Cemiyet-i Hilaliye (Crescent Society), 134
Central Powers: Armistice of Mudros (1918), 6, 73; Brest-Litovsk Treaty (1918), 58, 63–65; British-controlled Egypt, 23, 36; Ottoman entry into alliance, 175;

Ottoman experience as different from other, viii, 59, 70, 84–85, 87, 95, 115, 155, 174–75; Paris Peace Conference (1919), exclusion from, 92; World War I defeat 68–69, 84–85, 176
Cevad Pasha, 151
Chester, Colby M., 164–65
Chester Railway Project, 164–65
Christians: Balkan Wars (1912–1913), immigration, Muslim nationalism, and Turkism, 31–32; demographic upheaval, 26–28; Faysal's Syria, 102–3; 107, 109; identity production and ideology, 40–41; Muslim groups fear of Christian demands, 88–90, 101–3, 178–79; postwar parliament, lack of representation in, 118; purge of Christian populations, 31, 34–35, 47, 48–49, 178–79; religious patriotism in wartime mobilization of Ottoman Muslims, 34–35; resettlement of displaced populations, 148; secessionism from Ottoman Empire, religious motivations for, 22–23; Treaty of Lausanne (1923), implications for non-Muslim minorities, 169–70
Churchill, Winston, 129, 140, 149–50
Church of the Nativity, Bethlehem, 41
Çiçek, Talha, 56–57
Cilicia, 74, 77*map*, 78, 136, 146, 149–50
Cimcoz, Salah (Istanbul deputy), 57–58
Circassians/Circassia, 14, 65, 107, 177, 181
Cobbe, Alexander, 71
collective identity: al-Jam'iya al-Islamiya (İslam Cemiyeti), 112–13; anti-colonial movements and Wilsonian principles, 90–91; appropriating Wilsonianism, 94–100; Grand National Assembly, Kemal's call for Muslim unity, 131–33; Kemalist efforts to maintain Ottoman territories (1919–1930s), 179–82; Lausanne Conference, negotiating Mosul, 157–65; militia groups motivation of Islamic solidarity, 153; misak-ı milli (National Pact), 121–27; Muslim groups and, 28–31, 52–53; Sivas Congress, 105–9; Treaty of Lausanne (1923), implications for the Ottoman patrimony, 169–71. *See also* Islam

colonialism: anti-colonial movements, religious motivations for, 113–15; anti-colonial movements, Wilsonian principles and, 90–91; appropriating Wilsonianism, 94–100; Egypt's self-determination movement, 156–57; expansion of anti-colonial resistance after Treaty of Sèvres (1920), 138–42, 176–79; Four Principles, Woodrow Wilson, 64; Fourteen Points, Woodrow Wilson, 60–61; Islamic ideology as resistance to colonialism, 27; London Conference (1920) and, 130–33; postwar ambitions of France and Great Britain, 116, 117, 121, 126–27; prior to World War I, 23; Soviet support for anti-colonial movements, 141; Syrian resistance to French occupation, 127–30, 133–35
Committee of Union and Progress (CUP), 27–28, 30, 47, 48; Balkan Wars (1912–1913), immigration, Muslim nationalism, and Turkism, 31–35, 52–53; collapse of wartime government, 83–84; Janus face of Ottoman State practices in Syria, 37–43; June Crisis (1914), response to, 175; postwar decline in power and influence, 86–87; Teşkilat-ı Mahsusa (Special Organization), 87
Concert of Europe, 22–23
Conference of London (London Conference), (1920) 130–31; (1921) 141–42, 150, 166; (1922) 149–50
Constantinople Agreement (1915), 175
Constitution of 1876, 26; (1909) revised, 27
Crescent Society (Cemiyet-i Hilaliye), 134
cultural identities: cultivating historical memory for identity production and ideology, 40–41; misak-ı milli (National Pact), 121–27; Muslim groups and collective identity, 28–31, 52–53; "race," use of terms related to, 123–25; terminology, as evidence of shifting meanings of community, 13–16. *See also* collective identity; religion
CUP. *See* Committee of Union and Progress (CUP)

Curzon, George, 116, 141–42, 149–50; armistice and the opening of the Lausanne Conference, 154–57; Lausanne Conference, negotiating Mosul, 157–65

Damascus, xiii*map*, 36, 102, 128, 169, 181; Armistice of Mudros (1918), 76, 77*map*; Cemal Pasha's governorate, 39, 43–44; execution of Arab opponents, 38; Faysal's government in, 17–19, 69–71, 81–82, 86–88, 90, 110, 115, 127, 130, 133, 177; Syria, resistance to French occupation and, 128–29, 133–35

Dardanelles, 170

Dayr al-Zur, xiii*map*, 79, 114; Anatolian movement (1920–1922), territorial objectives, 119–21, 120*map*; Ankara Treaty (Franklin-Bouillon Treaty) (1921), 143–44, 144*map*; Armistice of Mudros (1918), 75, 77*map*; Treaty of Sèvres (1920), 137, 137*map*

Declaration to the Seven, 67–68

Demolins, Edmond, 82

Derbend Pass, 153

Diyarbekir, xiii*map*16, 93, 99, 105*map*, 120*map*, 133–134, 139; Anatolian resistance in northern Iraq (1921–1922), 147–49, 150–54; expansion of anti-colonial resistance after Treaty of Sèvres (1920), 140

Economic circumstances: American economic interests in Middle East, 61–62; Ottoman-American Development Company and, 164–65; Treaty of Lausanne (1923), deliberation on Iraqi oil, 159.

Edirne, xii*map*; 4

education: salafi movement, 44–45; in Syria under Cemal Pasha, 42–43

Egypt: 70, 163. British invasion of (1882), 23; Declaration to the Seven, 67–68; Ottoman war effort in Arab provinces, 51–52; self-determination movement, 156–57; Treaty of Lausanne (1923), implications for the Ottoman patrimony, 169

Egyptian Expeditionary Force, 54–55

Elcezire, 99–100, 144, 166–67, 183n2, 188n37. *See also* al-Jazira

Elcezire Front Army Command, 148, 150–54

Emin Bey (Lieutenant Colonel), 128

empire-to-nation transition: nation-state as the predominant sociopolitical frame, 1–4; normality of nation and the Ottoman past, 7–12; periodization and, 4–7

Entente alliance, 184n9; Armistice of Mudros (1918), 5, 73–80, 77*map*, 176; Brest-Litovsk Treaty (1918), effects of, 65-66; fall of 1918, defeat of Central Powers and pursuit of ceasefire, 69–73; June Crisis (1914) and, 175; Lloyd George and Woodrow Wilson's statements on war aims, 59–64; November 1917 as pivotal month in conflict, 54; Paris Peace Conference (1919), 92–94, 95–100. *See also* Allied and Associated Powers (Allies); specific treaty names

Enver Pasha, 43–44, 46, 50, 52, 65-66, 87

epidemics, 37, 42, 48

Erbil, 153

Erzurum Congress, 101–3, 106–7, 117, 121, 123

ethno-linguistic communities: anti-colonial opposition and, 94, 99; Armistice of Mudros (1918), 76–77, 77*map*, 176; Muslim groups and collective identity, 28–31, 38, 46, 52–53, 124, 126, 182

Euphrates: xiii*map*; Anatolian movement (1920–1922), territorial objectives, 119–21, 120*map*

Fahreddin Pasha (Türkkan), 50, 80

Falih Rıfkı (Atay), 33–34, 45

al-Fatat, 127

Fattah Pasha, 134

Fawzi al-'Azm, Muhammad, 96–97

Faysal, Sharif, 17, 18, 19, 46, 76–77; Anatolian resistance in northern Iraq (1921–1922), 151–53; Anatolian-Syrian collaboration, 103–6, 135; claim of leadership of an Arab state, 88; efforts to create Arab-Turkish federation, post World War I, 81–85; expansion of anti-colonial resistance after Treaty of Sèvres (1920), 138–39; fall of 1918; defeat of Central Powers and pursuit of ceasefire, 69, 71–72; fall of the Faysali state, 133–39, 177; the French threat and collaboration in the Anatolia-Syria frontier, 113–14; negotiations with Ottoman government, 67–68; November 1917 as pivotal month in World War I, 56–57; Paris Peace Conference (1919), 92–94; Syrian Congress (al-mu'tamar al-suri), 96–97, 102–3; Treaty of Lausanne (1923), aftermath of, 172–73

Ferid Pasha, Damad, 97, 99–100, 107, 117, 119–20, 133–34, 136

Fertile Crescent, use of term, xvi–xvii

Fevzi (Çakmak) Pasha, 152

Four Ends, Woodrow Wilson, 66, 71

Fourteen Points, 59–64; appropriating Wilsonianism, 94–100; Armistice of Mudros (1918), interpretations of, 77*map*, 78–79; Article 5, 62–63; Article 6, 62–63; Article 12, ambiguities of, 61, 63, 72, 94, 178; Article 12, Kemal's invocation of, 119, 121; "Commentary" by Colonel House, 72; Four Ends, 66, 71; Four Principles, 64; League of Nations, 92; use by anti-colonial movements, 90–91

Fourth Army Corps, 36, 50

France: Ankara Treaty (Franklin-Bouillon Treaty) (1921), 142–44, 144*map*, 145, 146; Armenian support of forces, 88–89; Armistice of Mudros (1918), 73–80, 176; Brest-Litovsk Treaty (1918), effects of, 65; Constantinople Agreement (1915), 175; expansion of colonial resistance after Treaty of Sèvres (1920), 138–42, 176–79; fall of the Faysali state and forging of Sèvres scheme, 136–37; Fourteen Points on French territories, 63; the French threat and collaboration in the Anatolia-Syria frontier, 109–15; June Crisis (1914), 175; Lausanne Conference, negotiating Syria, 165–68; London Conference and, 130–33; Occupied Enemy Territory Administration (OETA), French control in Syria, 71; Ottoman Empire, warfare during 1911-1922, 4; Paris Peace Conference (1919), 92–94, 95–100; postwar colonial ambitions, 116, 117, 121, 126–27; postwar occupation and resistance, 88, 107–9; secessionism from Ottoman Empire, support for, 22–23; Sykes-Picot accord, 55, 109–10; Syrian resistance to French occupation, 127–30, 133–35; Treaty of Lausanne (1923), 146; Treaty of Lausanne (1923), aftermath of, 171–73; Treaty of Lausanne (1923), implications for the Ottoman patrimony, 168–71

Franklin-Bouillon Treaty (Ankara Treaty) (1921), 142–46, 144*map*, 149, 162, 165–68, 172

Fraşeri, Şemseddin Sami, 14

Galib, Ali, 107

Georges-Picot, François, 111, 194n2

Georgia, 64–65

Germany, 17, 44, 50–51, 57–58, 67, 70, 73, 81, 95, 113, 115, 175; Brest-Litovsk talks, 62–64; Brest-Litovsk Treaty (1918), effects of, 65; cultural endeavors and power in Syria, 40–41; model for federal state, 67, 81; Paris Peace Conference (1919), 92–94; secessionism from Ottoman Empire, support for, 22–23; Syria, geographical importance of, 36; war in Mesopotamia, 49–53; Wilson's Four Principles and, 64

Ghanem, Chekri, 92

Gouraud, Henri, 144

Grand National Assembly (GNA), 130–33; abolishment of Ottoman sultanate, 155–57; Anatolian resistance in northern Iraq (1921–1922), 150–54; Armistice of Mudanya (1922), 145; differences within, 144, 146, 150; diplomatic achievements (1921), 143–46, 144*map*, (1922) 149, 154–55, 159–60, 164; Lausanne Conference, negotiating Mosul, 157–65; Lausanne Conference, negotiating Syria, 166–68; rejection of the Treaty of Sèvres, 138; resistance to French occupation, 133–34; Soviet support for anti-colonial movements,

Grand National Assembly (*continued*) 141; Treason Law (1921), 164; Treaty of Lausanne (1923), 146; Treaty of Lausanne (1923), aftermath of, 172–73; Treaty of Lausanne (1923), implications for the Ottoman patrimony, 168–71. *See also* Ankara government; Anatolian movement

Great Britain: Anatolian resistance in northern Iraq (1921–1922), 150–54; Ankara Treaty (Franklin-Bouillon Treaty) (1921) and, 143–44, 145; armistice and the opening of the Lausanne Conference, 154–57; Armistice of Mudros (1918), 73–80, 77*map*, 176; battle of Turmus 'Ayya, 66; Brest-Litovsk Treaty (1918), effects of, 65; Constantinople Agreement (1915), 175; Declaration to the Seven, 67–68; defense of Suez Canal, 36; Egypt, invasion of (1882), 23; Egypt, self-determination movement in, 156–57; expansion of anti-colonial resistance after Treaty of Sèvres (1920), 138–42, 176–79; fall of 1918, defeat of Central Powers and pursuit of ceasefire, 69–73; Faysal, in Iraq, 136; Faysal, support for (1919), 103–5, 110; fomenting of Kurdish uprisings by, 30; Fourteen Points, Article 12 clarification on postwar status, 72; Fourteen Points on British territories, 63; Iraq, resistance to occupation, 134; June Crisis (1914), 175; Kurdish identity, cultivation of, 60, 146–49; Lausanne Conference, negotiating Mosul, 157–65; Lloyd George's statement on war aims (January 5, 1918), 59–64; London Conference (1922), 149–50; negotiations with Faysal, 67–68; November 1917 as pivotal month in World War I, 54–57; Paris Peace Conference (1919), 92–100; postwar colonial ambitions, 116, 117, 121; postwar occupation and resistance, 88, 107–9; resistance to occupation in Iraq (1921–1922), 146–49; secessions from Ottoman Empire, support for, 22–23; Suez Canal campaigns, 51–52; support for revival of CUP (1919), 116; Sykes-Picot accord, 55–56, 109; Syria, geographical importance of, 35–36; Syria, handing over to French (1919), 109, 111; Syria, military campaigns in, 67–68; Treaty of Lausanne (1923), 146; Treaty of Lausanne (1923), aftermath of, 172–73; Treaty of Lausanne (1923), implications for the Ottoman patrimony, 168–71; war in Mesopotamia, 49–53

Great War. *See* World War I (1914–1918)

Greeks/Greece: Ankara Treaty (Franklin-Bouillon Treaty) (1921) and, 143–44; appropriating Wilsonianism, 94–100; Armistice of Mudanya (1922), 145; Balkan Wars (1912–1913), immigration and Muslim nationalism, 31; Erzurum Congress on Greek intentions, 101–2; expansion of anti-colonial resistance after Treaty of Sèvres (1920), 141–42; Fourteen Points, Article 12 clarification on postwar status, 72; London Conference (1922), discussion of Greece border, 149–50; Muslim groups fear of Christian expansionism, 88–90, 101–3; occupation of Izmir, 97; Ottoman Empire, warfare (1911–1922), 4–7, 28; Ottoman government acknowledgment of injustices toward Greeks, 83; secessionism from Ottoman Empire, 21–23; Sivas Congress on, 107; Treaty of Lausanne (1923), implications for non-Muslim minorities, 169–70; Treaty of Sèvres (1920), 137, 137*map*

Greek Revolt, 22–23

Gulf of Alexandretta: Anatolian movement (1920–1922), territorial objectives, 119–21, 120*map*, 129.

Habsburg Empire, 6, 59–62, 72. *See also* Austria-Hungary
Hadramawt, 51
Hajim ibn Muhayd, 166–68
hakimiyet-i milliye (popular sovereignty): use of term, 13
Halide Edib (Adıvar), 32, 42, 45, 47
Halil Pasha, 66
Halk Fırkası (People's Party), 164

Hama, 76, 77*map*
Hammam al-'Alil, 77*map*, 79
Hananu, Ibrahim, 114, 133
Hanioğlu, Şükrü, 51
Harbord, James, 107, 108
Hasan Fehmi (Sinop deputy), 58
Hashemites, 7, 56, 63, 72, 76, 77*map*, 82, 102, 110, 113, 115, 119, 148, 151, 157, 163, 177–79, 186n47; Anatolian-Syrian collaboration, summer 1919, 104–6; expansion of colonial resistance after Treaty of Sèvres (1920), 138–39; resistance to French occupation, 129–30
al-Hashimi, Taha, 135, 206n49
al-Hashimi, Yasin Pasha, 111, 114, 135
Hawran, 128–29
Hijaz, 36, 52, 61*map*, 67, 68, 70, 72, 80, 91, 98–100, 136; Armistice of Mudros (1918), 73–74, 77*map*; Ottoman surrender in, 91; Ottoman war effort in Arab provinces, 50-51, 58; Treaty of Lausanne (1923), implications for the Ottoman patrimony, 171. *See also* Hijaz Railway; Kingdom of the Hijaz
Hijaz Railway, 42, 50, 80
Homs, 76, 77*map*, 129
House, Edward, 60, 72
Hürriyet ve İtilaf (Liberty and Entente) Party, 28, 118
Husayn, Sharif, 17, 50, 56, 80; communication with Mustafa Kemal, 139; Sharif Husayn-McMahon correspondence (July 1915–January 1916), 76, 79, 197n67. *See also* Hashemites; Kingdom of the Hijaz
Hüseyin Kazım (Aleppo governor), 39
al-Husri, Sat'i, 138–39

Ibn Sa'ud, 177
Imam Yahya Hamid al-Din, 50–51
immigration: Balkan Wars (1912–1913), immigration, Muslim nationalism, and Turkism, 31–35, 52–53, 170
infrastructure: improvements between Syria and Anatolia, 46–47; improvements in Syria, 39–42; Ottoman-American Development Company and, 164–65
İnönü (battle sites), 141–42, 162

Iraq: Anatolian movement (1920–1922), territorial objectives, 119–21, 120*map*; Anatolian resistance in northern Iraq (1921–1922), 150–54; Ankara Treaty (Franklin-Bouillon Treaty) (1921), 143–44, 144*map*, 145; anti-colonial movement, 5–6; armistice and the opening of the Lausanne Conference, 154–57; British offensive fall of 1918, 71; Constantinople Agreement (1915), 175; expansion of colonial resistance after Treaty of Sèvres (1920), 138–42, 176–79; Faysal mandate in, 136; Fertile Crescent territory boundaries, xvi–xvii; Grand National Assembly, Kemal's call for Muslim unity, 132–33; Kemalist efforts to maintain Ottoman territories, 179–82; Lausanne Conference, negotiating Mosul, 157–65; Ottoman war effort in, 66–68; Paris Peace Conference (1919), 98–100; postwar occupation and resistance, 88, 105, 107–9, 134, 146–49; Treaty of Lausanne (1923), 146; Treaty of Lausanne (1923), aftermath of, 172–73; Treaty of Lausanne (1923), implications for the Ottoman patrimony, 168–71. *See also* Mesopotamia; Elcezire; al-Jazira
Islahiye, 129
Islam: al-Jam'iya al-Islamiya (Islam Cemiyeti), 112–13; Anatolian movement (1920–1922), territorial objectives, 119–21; Anatolian-Syrian collaboration, summer 1919, 103–6; anti-colonial movements and religious motivations, 113–15; appropriating Wilsonianism, 94–100; Balkan Wars (1912–1913), immigration, Muslim nationalism, 31–35; the French threat and collaboration in the Anatolia-Syria frontier, 109–15; Grand National Assembly, Kemal's call for Muslim unity, 131–33; Kemalist efforts to maintain Ottoman territories, 179–82; militia group motivations for Islamic solidarity, 153; misak-ı milli (National Pact), 121–27; Muslim groups and collective identity, 28–31, 52–53; Muslim groups fear of Christian collaboration with European states and expansionism, 88–90, 101–3,

Islam (*continued*)
178–79; normality of nation and the Ottoman past, historiography and sources, 8; Ottomanism association with Muslims under Abdulhamid II (r. 1876–1909), 26–28; patronage of history for identity production and ideology, 40–41; postwar increase in provincial religious-based movements, 86–87; postwar parliament, absence of non-Muslims in, 118; religious education in Syria, 42–43; religious patriotism in mobilization of Ottoman Muslims, 34–35, 188n27; salafi movement, 44–45; secessionism from Ottoman Empire, religious motivations for, 22–23; Sivas Congress, 105–9; Syria, mobilizing support amid war's violence, 43–45; terminology, challenges with, 12–13; Treaty of Lausanne (1923), implications for the Ottoman patrimony, 169–71; Turkish, as synonym for Muslim, 62; Umum Alem-i İslam İhtilal Teşkilatı (Revolutionary Organization of the Islamic World), 87; Umur-u Şarkiye Dairesi (Office of Eastern Affairs), 87. *See also* caliphate

Islamic Caucasus Army, 65

Islamism: 45, 52, 112; Ottoman policy, spring of 1918, 66–68. *See also* Turks, Turkism, pan-Turkism

İsmet (İnönü) Pasha: armistice and the opening of the Lausanne Conference, 154; Lausanne Conference, negotiating Mosul, 157–62; Mudanya Armistice, negotiation of, 157

Istanbul, xii*map*; Armistice Period (1918–1923), 5–6; Balkan Wars and Bulgarian advance toward (1912–13), 4; control of popular press, 43–45; documentary evidence, keeping of, 10; Faysal, relations with, 17; growing salience of Anatolianism, 32–33; historical relationship with Arab provinces, 7–8; June Crisis (1914), response to, 175; Kurdish organizations in, 30; Lausanne Conference, abolishment of Ottoman sultanate, 155–57; Ottoman-Russian War and Russian advance to (1878), 174; Paris Peace Conference (1919), 18, 19; Treaty of Sèvres (1920), 19. *See also* Ottoman Empire / Ottoman State

Italy: Antalya, forces in, 96; Armistice of Mudros (1918), 74, 77*map*; Fourteen Points and, 62; Libya, colonization of, 23; Ottoman war effort in Arab provinces, 52; Paris Peace Conference (1919), 92–94; Treaty of Ouchy (1912), 4; Treaty of Sèvres (1920), 137, 137*map*

Izmir, 89, 97, 137, 137*map*

Izmir Society for the Defense of Ottoman Rights (*İzmir Müdafaa-ı Hukuk-u Osmaniye Cemiyeti*), 89

İzzet Pasha, Ahmed, 71–73, 81, 83, 149

Jabal Sam'an, 77*map*, 78
Jawdat, Ahmad (Colonel), 110–11, 147
al-Jaza'iri, Sa'id, 69
Jericho, 68
Jerusalem: xii*map*, 15map, 42–43; Armistice of Mudros (1918), 75; Declaration to the Seven, 67–68; Great Britain capture of (1917), 17, 36, 43, 54–55
Jews: British support of Jewish home in Palestine, 55–56; Jewish millet, 13, 186n39; Jewish sites in Syria, preservation efforts, 40; Treaty of Lausanne (1923), implications for non-Muslim minorities, 169–70; Treaty of Lausanne (1923), on Jewish populations in Turkey, 169. *See also* Zionists
jihad: Anatolian-Syrian collaboration, summer 1919, 104–6; Ottomanist war propaganda and, 34, 44, 45, 51–52, 166
journalism: Istanbul's control of popular press in Syria, 43–46; official history and, 11; press censorship, 112, 134, 196n37; propaganda, 119, 161; Treaty of Lausanne (1923) on use of language in, 169
Jubur tribe, 119
June Crisis (1914), 175

Kafr Ghan, 135
Kansu, Aykut, 9
Kars, 22–23, 55, 58, 177; Brest-Litovsk Treaty (1918), 64–66; decision to remain in Ottoman Empire (July 1918), 65–66;

Kars Muslims' Congress *(Kars İslam Şurası)*, 89–90; London Conference (1922), discussion on Armenian state, 149–50; Treaty of Lausanne (1923), implications for the Ottoman patrimony, 170–71. *See also* Three Provinces

Kars Muslims' Congress *(Kars İslam Şurası)*, 89–90

Kasaba, Reşat, 9

Kazım Karabekir Pasha, 53, 100, 141–42, 177

Kemal, Mustafa (Atatürk): abolishment of Ottoman sultanate, 155–57; Ankara speech (December 1919) and territorial objectives, 119–21, 120*map*; Anatolian resistance in northern Iraq (1921–1922), 150–54; Anatolian-Syrian collaboration, summer 1919, 103–6; armistice and the opening of the Lausanne Conference, 154–57; Armistice of Mudros (1918), implications of, 77–78, 77*map*; bias in memoir literature during presidency (1923–1938), 10; consolidation of power (1921), 144, 146; court-martial of, 134; at the Erzurum Congress, 101–2; extension of extraordinary powers (May 1922), 150; the French threat and collaboration in the Anatolia-Syria frontier, 111–12; Grand National Assembly calls for Muslim unity, 131–33; historiography and sources, 8; Sharif Husayn, contact with Kemal, 139; Kemalist efforts to maintain Ottoman territories, 179–82; Lausanne Conference, negotiating Mosul, 160–65; Lausanne Conference, negotiating Syria, 166–68; *Nutuk (Speech)* (1927), 10–11, 100–101; parliament elections of 1919, 117–18; retreat from Aleppo, 79–80; rise to power, 100–103; Sivas Congress and, 105–9; Syrian resistance to French occupation and, 127–30, 133–35; Third Constitutional Period, 117–18; Treason Law (1921), 164; Treaty of Lausanne (1923), 146; Treaty of Lausanne (1923), implications for the Ottoman patrimony, 169–71; on Wilsonian principles, 179

Yusuf Kemal (Tengirşenk), 149–50

Mehmed Kenan (Colonel), 167, 168

al-Khatib, Fu'ad, 68

Kilis, 77*map*, 78, 133, 135

King-Crane Commission, 93, 96–97, 103, 105, 108, 109, 125, 178

Kingdom of the Hijaz, 73, 136, 157, 171, 181

Kirkuk, 66; Anatolian movement, territorial objectives, 119–21, 120*map*; Lausanne Conference, negotiating Mosul, 157–65; Paris Peace Conference (1919), 99–100

Kurd 'Ali, Muhammad, 44–45, 46

Kurdism, 60, 179; Muslim groups and collective identity, 30

Kurds, 80; Anatolian movement, territorial objectives, 119–21, 120*map*; Anatolian resistance in northern Iraq (1921–1922), 151–52; Anatolian-Syrian collaboration, summer 1919, 105–6; British appeals to Kurdish populations following Treaty of Sèvres (1920), 146–49, 151–52; British patronage of local power-holders, 60, 107, 153, 208n25; in contested armistice frontier regions, 90–91; expansion of anti-colonial resistance after Treaty of Sèvres (1920), 140, 177; Kürt Teali Cemiyeti (Kurdish Advancement Society), 147; Lausanne Conference, negotiating Mosul, 157–65; Muslim groups and collective identity, 29–31; Ottoman state enlistment practices, 38; Paris Peace Conference (1919), 99–100; Southern Kurdistan General National Operations Command, 163–64; Treaty of Lausanne (1923), aftermath of, 172–73; Treaty of Sèvres (1920), 136–37, 137*map*

Kürt Teali Cemiyeti (Kurdish Advancement Society), 147

Kut al-Amara, 50

Kuwait, 51

language: use of Turkish by Ottoman elites, 24–28. *See also* ethno-linguistic communities

language choices in text, xviii–xix, 183n4

Latakia, 77*map*, 78, 99, 139–141

Lausanne Conference, xviii, 146; implications for the Ottoman patrimony, 20, 168–71; Mudanya Armistice and

Lausanne Conference (*continued*)
lead-up to conference, 154–57; Mosul negotiations, 157–65; Syria negotiations, 165–68; *See also* Treaty of Lausanne (1923)
Law of Nationality (1869), 25
Lawrence, T. E., 68
League of Nations, 92, 95–96, 99–100, 109, 116; Lausanne Conference, negotiating Mosul, 160, 165; Treaty of Lausanne (1923), determination of Turkey-Iraq border, 172–73; Treaty of Lausanne (1923), implications for the Ottoman patrimony, 168–71
Lebanon: Fertile Crescent territory boundaries, xvii; Treaty of Lausanne (1923), implications for the Ottoman patrimony, 171. *See also* Beirut; Mount Lebanon
Lenin, Vladimir: "Decree on Peace" (1917), 55–56, 59–60, 62, 65, 176
Lewis, Bernard, 49, 82
Liberty and Entente Party. *See* Hürriyet ve İtilaf
Libya, 4; al-Sanussi, Ahmad, 148; Armistice of Mudros (1918), 74, 77*map*; Italy's colonization of, 23; Ottoman war effort in Arab provinces, 51–52
Liman von Sanders, Otto, 50, 66, 71.
linguistic communities. *See* ethno-linguistic communities
linguistic conquerors, 14–15
Lloyd George, David, 59–64, 111, 139
London Conference (Conference of London), (1920) 130–31; (1921) 141–42, 150, 166; (1922) 149–50
Lutfi, Jamil, 135

Macedonia, xii*map*, 4–7, 22–23, 28, 29, 174
Mahmud (Barzanji), Shaykh, 153–54, 163–65, 208n25
Mamuret-ül-Aziz province, 107
Maraş, xii*map*, 88, 96, 110, 112, 118, 121, 127–30, 137, 137*map*, 144*map*
Mardin, 137, 137*map*, 140, 144*map*
Maronite, 23, 102, 109
Martyrs' Square, Beirut and Damascus, 38
Mash'al, 119

McMahon, Henry, 76, 77, 77*map*, 79, 80, 92, 197n67
Mecca, xiii*map*, 50, 80, 175
media; Syria, mobilizing support amid war's violence, 43–46
Medina, xiii*map*; Cemal, Faysal, and Enver Pasha's trip (1916), Islamic-Ottoman allegiance and, 46; Cemal's infrastructure projects in, 50; Ottoman forces refusal to surrender, 80, 91; Ottoman war effort in Arab provinces, 50–51, 80, 91, 177
Mehmed Akif (Ersoy), 45, 113, 203n82
Mehmed Reşid (Şahingiray) (Diyarbekir governor), 48–49
Mersin, xiii*map*, 80, 88, 108, 133, 197n67
Mersinli Cemal Pasha, 56–57, 69, 80
Mesopotamia: Anatolian movement, territorial objectives, 119–21, 120*map*; Anatolian resistance in northern Iraq (1921–1922), 150–54; Armistice of Mudros (1918), 79, 176; Constantinople Agreement (1915), 175; Declaration to the Seven, 67–68; expansion of colonial resistance after Treaty of Sèvres (1920), 138–42, 176–79; Fertile Crescent territory boundaries, xvii; Fourteen Points, Article 12 clarification on postwar status, 72; GNA, Kemal's call for Muslim unity, 132–33; GNA efforts to subvert British claims in, 147–49; Kemalist efforts to maintain Ottoman territories, 179–82; Kirkuk, British forces in (1918), 66; Lausanne Conference, armistice and the opening of talks, 154–57; Lausanne Conference, negotiating Mosul, 157–65; Lloyd George and Woodrow Wilson's statements on war aims, 59–64; London Conference and, 130–33; Ottoman war effort in, 49–53, 66–68; Paris Peace Conference (1919), 92–94, 99–100; postwar occupation and resistance, 105, 107–9; resistance to occupation, 134; Treaty of Lausanne (1923), aftermath of, 172–73; Treaty of Lausanne (1923), implications for the Ottoman patrimony, 170–71. *See also* Iraq; Elcezire; al-Jazira

Middle East: American economic interest in, 61–62; Armistice of Mudros (1918), 73–80, 77*map*, 176; Constantinople Agreement (1915) and, 175; Kemalist efforts to maintain Ottoman territories, 179–82; Lloyd George and Woodrow Wilson's statements on war aims, 59–64; Paris Peace Conference (1919), 92–94; postwar occupation and resistance, 88, 107–9, 176–79; use of term, 183n4. *See also* specific locations

military service, Ottoman: number and percentage of Arab soldiers, 190n50; Ottoman state enlistment practices, 38; postwar demobilization, 86–87; war and mobility, 45–47

militia groups: diffuse accountability of, 152–53; early anti-colonial mobilization, 18, 107–9; local resistance to British occupation of Iraq, 20, 145, 146, 148–52; local resistance to French occupation of Syria, 18, 109, 114, 127–29, 130, 133, 135, 139–40, 145, 167–68; motivation of Islamic solidarity, 88, 153, 177–79

millet: shifting meanings of, 12–13, 186n39, 186n41; use in misak-ı milli (National Pact), 122–27

Milli Mücadele (popular struggle), 6

Misak-ı milli (National Pact), 121–27, 149–50; Lausanne Conference, negotiating Mosul, 158–65

al-Misri, Shafiq. See Özdemir.

modernity, practices of, 49

Montagu, Edwin, 149–50

Montenegro: Balkan Wars (1912–1913) 4, 28–31; secessions from Ottoman Empire, 22–23

Mosul, 66, 71; Anatolian movement, territorial objectives, 119–21, 120*map*; Anatolian resistance in northern Iraq (1921–1922), 147–49; Ankara Treaty (1926), 144*map*, 173; Armistice of Mudros (1918), 74, 77*map*, 79; expansion of anti-colonial resistance after Treaty of Sèvres (1920), 140; Kurds in, 146–47; Lausanne Conference, negotiating Mosul, 157–65; Paris Peace Conference (1919), 99–100; postwar occupation and resistance, 88, 107–9, 134; Treaty of Lausanne (1923), aftermath of, 171–73; Treaty of Sèvres (1920), 137, 137*map*

Mount Lebanon: Armistice of Mudros (1918), 75; Ottoman war effort in Arab provinces, 51; secessionism from Ottoman Empire, 23

Mudanya. *See* Armistice of Mudanya (1922)

Muhayd, Hajim ibn, 134, 166, 168

Murad V (r. May–August 1876), 52

Muslims. *See* Islam

Nablus, 66, 69

Najd, 51, 177, 181

names, spelling and transliteration, xviii–xix, 12–16

Nasser, Jamal, 110

Natiq (Major), 140

nationalism: appropriating Wilsonianism, 94–100; Muslim nationalism, 11, 31-35, 176; Fourteen Points, on political allegiance and nationality, 11, 62, 157; Kemalist efforts to maintain Ottoman territories, 179–82; Lausanne Conference, negotiating Mosul, 157–65; misak-ı milli (National Pact), 121–27; Muslim groups and collective identity, 28–31, 52–53; North Africa, movements in, 23, 156; Ottoman government response to secessionist movements, 23–28; religious patriotism in mobilization of Ottoman Muslims, 34–35; Sivas Congress and, 105–9; *Speech (Nutuk)* (Kemal, 1927), 10–11, 100–101; Treaty of Lausanne (1923), implications for the Ottoman patrimony, 169–70; warfare, effect on political identity and ideology, 5; in historiography, 2–5, 7–9, 11, 36–37; as post-Ottoman project, 2, 3, 10, 30, 33, 180–82. *See also* collective identity

National Pact (misak-ı milli), 121–27, 149–50; Lausanne Conference, negotiating Mosul, 158–65

nation-building: Armistice of Mudros (1918), 7 5, 77*map*; practices of modernity and, 49

nation-states: nationness, xv, xvi–xvii; nation-state as the predominant

INDEX · 243

nation-states (*continued*)
    sociopolitical frame, 1–4; normality of nation and the Ottoman past, 7–12; periodization and, 4–7
Nesimi, Ahmed, 57
New imperialism, 27
newspapers. *See* journalism
Nihad Pasha, 144, 148
Niʻmat al-Shaʻbani, Shakir (Lieutenant Colonel), 112, 128, 129
Noel, E. W. C., 107
North Africa: French colonization, 23; nationalist movements in, 23; Ottoman Empire, warfare during 1911-1922, 4–7; Treaty of Ouchy (1912), 4. *See also* specific locations
Northern Caucasus Republic, 65
Nubar Pasha, 69–70
Nuri Pasha, 52, 65
Nutuk (Speech) (Kemal, 1927), 10–11, 100–101

Occupied Enemy Territory Administration (OETA), 71, 111, 197n56
Oman, 51
Ömer Halis (Bıyıktay), 81
Orthodox Church: institutionalization of millets, 186n39; Paris Conference, Greek territorial demands, 93, 96; secessionism from Ottoman Empire, religious motivations for, 22–23; Treaty of Lausanne (1923), relocation of populations, 169
Osman Fuad (Prince), 52, 130
Osmaniye, 129
Osmanlılık (Ottomanness), 24–28. *See also* Ottomanism
Ottoman Africa Groups, 52
Ottoman-American Development Company, 164–65
Ottoman caliphate. *See* caliphate
Ottoman Corps of Army Engineers, 41–42
Ottoman Council for the Defense of Thrace (Trakya-Paşaeli Müdafaa Heyet-i Osmaniyesi), 89–90
Ottoman Empire / Ottoman State: after Balkan Wars (1913), xii–xiii*map*; appropriating Wilsonianism at Paris Peace Conference (1919), 97–100; Arab provinces, 14–16, 15*map*; Armistice of Mudros (1918), 73–80, 77*map*, 176; Armistice Period (1918–1923), 4–7; armistice with Russia (1917), 57–58; Balkan Wars (1912–1913), immigration, Muslim nationalism, and Turkism, 31–35, 52–53; Brest-Litovsk Treaty (1918) and, 64–66, 176; efforts to create Arab-Turkish federation, post World War I, 80–85; fall (1918), debacle in Syria, pursuit of ceasefire, and new government, 69–73; Fourteen Points, Article 12 clarification on postwar status, 72; June Crisis (1914), 175; Kemalist efforts to maintain Ottoman territories, 179–82; language of ruling elites, 24; Lloyd George and Woodrow Wilson's statements on war aims, 59–64; misak-ı milli (National Pact), 121–27; normality of nation and the Ottoman past, historiography and sources, 7–12; official records after 1918, historiography and sources, 10; parliament, challenges with resuming after Great War, 82–85; parliamentary elections, postwar (1919), 117–18; periodization, effects of warfare during 1911-1922, 4–7; postwar foreign occupation and local resistance movements, 86–91, 107–9, 176–79; secessionist movements, early paths to statehood and nationhood, 21–23; secessionist movements, Ottoman response to, 23–28; Second Constitutional Era, 82–84; surrender to Russia (1878), 174; Syria, mobilizing support amid war's violence, 43–45; Syria, Ottoman state practices in, 37–43, 47–49; Third Constitutional Period, 117–18; Treaty of Lausanne (1923), implications for the Ottoman patrimony, 168–71; Treaty of London (1913), 4; war and mobility, 45–47. *See also* Anatolian movement; Istanbul; specific treaty agreements
Ottoman Forces General Council Defending Syria and Palestine (Suriye ve Filistin Müdafii Kuva-yı Osmaniye Heyet-i Umumiyesi), 128
Ottomanism, 25–26, 45, 48, 66, 178, 182

Ottoman Turkish, 25–28. *See also* Turks, Turkism, pan-Turkism
Özdemir (Shafiq al-Misri), 128, 138, 139, 148–54, 163–65

Palestine: desire to return to Turkish rule, 150; fall of 1918, battles of, 69; Fertile Crescent territory boundaries, xvii; Fourteen Points, Article 12 clarification on postwar status, 72; Lloyd George and Woodrow Wilson's statements on war aims, 59–64; London Conference (1920) and, 130–31; November 1917 as pivotal month in World War I, 54–57; Ottoman Corps of Army Engineers modernization efforts, 41–42; Paris Peace Conference (1919), 92–94, 98–100; Treaty of Lausanne (1923), implications for the Ottoman patrimony, 171
pan-Turkism. *See* Turks, Turkism, pan-Turkism
Paris Peace Conference (1919), 92–94, 130, 149, 157, 178; Anatolian-Syrian collaboration, summer 1919, 103–6; appropriating Wilsonianism, 94–100; League of Nations, establishment of, 95–96
Peloponnese Peninsula: secessionism from Ottoman Empire, 22–23
Persian Gulf, xiii*map*, 15*map*, 197n67; Declaration to the Seven, 67–68; Ottoman war effort in Arab provinces, 49–50
Polat, Kamil (Captain), 127, 133, 135
political identity: effects of war and, 5; in the Hamidian period (1878–1908), 26–28; ruling elites, Osmanlılık, 24–28. *See also* Anatolian movement
popular/national will (milli irade), 102
Pozantı, 133
pre-national identities: Muslim groups and collective identity, 28–31, 52–53
press. *See* journalism
propaganda: Ankara's efforts in Iraq, 152, 161; Ankara's efforts in Syria, 168, 169; claims of Turkishness in Paris Conference negotiations, 94–95; films for, 39; Kemalist propaganda on Ottoman caliphate and Arab bonds, 110–11, 112; Ottoman support for Libya, 67; race as essence of Turkish identity, 123–24, 182; Syria, mobilizing support amid war's violence, 43–45, 47; teaching of history for identity production and ideology, 40–41; Teşkilat-ı Mahsusa (Special Organization), 87, 138; on validity of the caliphate, 84–85
proto-national identities: Muslim groups and collective identity, 28–31, 52–53
Provence, Michael, 114
Provisional Government of the Southwestern Caucasus, 89–90
public health, 39, 49; wartime disease, 37, 42, 48

Qatar, 51
Qatma, 77*map*, 78, 81, 119, 120*map*
qawm (people/kinship group), 13, 90

"race," use of terms related to, 123–25
Rahmi (Evrenoszade) (Aydın governor), 48–49
Raqqa, 77*map*, 79, 114, 139, 166
Ra's al-'Ayn, 77*map*, 99–100
Rauf (Orbay), 73, 158–61
Rawanduz, 120*map*, 148, 151–54
religion: al-Jam'iya al-Islamiya (Islam Cemiyeti), 112–13; Anatolian resistance in northern Iraq (1921–1922) and, 148–49; Anatolian-Syrian collaboration, summer 1919, 103–6; appropriating Wilsonianism, 94–100; Balkan Wars (1912–1913), immigration, Muslim nationalism, 31–35, 52–53; British capture of Jerusalem (1917), impact of, 54–55; the French threat and collaboration in the Anatolia-Syria frontier, 109–15; Grand National Assembly, Kemal's call for Muslim unity, 131–33; militia group motivations for Islamic solidarity, 153; misak-ı milli (National Pact), 121–27; Muslim groups and collective identity, 28–31; Muslim groups fear of Christian demands and expansionism, 88–90, 101–3; postwar increase in provincial religious-based movements, 86–87; postwar parliament, lack of Christian representation,

religion (*continued*)
118; purge of Christian populations, 31, 34–35, 47, 48–49, 83, 178–79; religious patriotism as tool to mobilize Ottoman Muslims, 34–35, 188n27; resettlement of displaced Christian populations, 148, 178–79; salafi movement, 44–45; secessionism from Ottoman Empire, motivations for, 22–23; Sivas Congress, 69, 105–9; as source of anti-colonial movement, 113–15; state patronage of religious traditions, 40–41; Turkish, as synonym for Muslim, 62; Umum Alem-i İslam İhtilal Teşkilatı (Revolutionary Organization of the Islamic World), 87; Umur-u Şarkiye Dairesi (Office of Eastern Affairs), 87

Republic of Turkey, 20, 122, 126, 164, 170, 172, 173, 181–82; normality of nation and the Ottoman past, historiography and sources, 7–12

Reşad (Mehmed V, r. 1909–18), 52, 69, 84, 156

Reynolds, Michael, 65

al-Rikabi, 'Ali Rida Pasha, 68, 69

Romania, 22–23

Romanov Empire, 6, 56, 58

Rumbold, Horace, 70

Russian Turks: Muslim groups and collective identity, 29

Russia / Soviet Russia, 6; armistice with Ottoman state (1917), 57–58; Bolshevik revolution, 6, 54–56, 176; Brest-Litovsk Treaty (1918), 64–66, 176; Congress of Berlin (1878), European concerns about Russia, 174; Constantinople Agreement (1915), 175; "Decree on Peace" (1917), 55; denunciation of Sykes-Picot accord, 55–56; fomenting of Kurdish uprisings by, 30; Fourteen Points on, 62–63; June Crisis (1914), 175; secessionism from Ottoman Empire, support for, 22–23; support for anti-colonial movements, 141; Treaty of Kars (1921), 143–44, 144*map*, 145; Wilson's Four Principles and, 64

Sabri, Mustafa, 135
al-Sa'dun, 'Ujaymi, 134

Sa'id al-Jaza'iri, Amir, 127
al-Sa'id, Nuri, 81
salafi movement, 44–45
San Remo Treaty (1920), 131–32, 134, 159
al-Sanussi, Ahmad, 23, 51–52, 148
Sazonov-Sykes-Picot Agreement (1916), 175, 194n2. See Sykes-Picot accord
Second Constitutional Period, 82–84
seferberlik, use of term, 37, 49
Serbia, 4, 22, 28, 29
Sharqat, 77*map*, 80
Sidon, 129
Sinjar, 77*map*, 79
Sivas Congress, 101, 105–9, 121, 123
Southern Kurdistan General National Operations Command, 163–64
Soviet Russia. *See* Russia / Soviet Russia
Speech (Nutuk) (Kemal, 1927), 10–11, 100–101
spelling and transliteration in text, xviii–xix, 12–16, 185n27
Sudan, 51–52
Suez Canal, 36, 51–52
Sulaymaniya, 79; Anatolian movement, territorial objectives, 119–21, 120*map*; Anatolian resistance in northern Iraq (1921–1922), 147–48, 153–54; Lausanne Conference, negotiating Mosul, 157–65
Sulaymaniya Congress (1923), 163
Suny, Ronald, 3, 32
Sykes-Picot accord, 194n2; Fourteen Points and, 60–61, 63; the French threat and collaboration in the Anatolia-Syria frontier, 109–10; Mosul, control over, 79, 105; Occupied Enemy Territory Administration (OETA), 71; Russian denunciation of, 55–56; Wilson's Four Ends as a repudiation of, 71
Symes, G. E., 68
Syria: Anatolian movement, territorial objectives, 119–21, 120*map*; Anatolian-Syrian collaboration, summer 1919, 103–6; Ankara Treaty (Franklin-Bouillon Treaty) (1921), 142–44, 144*map*, 145; anti-colonial movement, 5–6; antiquities, protection of, 40–41; armistice and the opening of the Lausanne Conference, 154–57; Armistice of

Mudros (1918), 73–74, 75, 77*map*; Cemal Pasha as governor in World War I, 36–50, 175; Constantinople Agreement (1915), 175; Declaration to the Seven, 67–68; desire to return to Turkish rule, 150; education system under Cemal Pasha, 42–43; efforts to create Arab-Turkish federation, post World War I, 81–85; expansion of anti-colonial resistance after Treaty of Sèvres (1920), 138–42, 176–79; fall of 1918, defeat of Central Powers and pursuit of ceasefire, 69–73; fall of the Faysali state and Treaty of Sèvres (1920), 136–37; Faysal's negotiations with Ottoman government, 67–68; Faysal's postwar claim of leadership in, 88; Fertile Crescent territory boundaries, xvi–xvii; Fourteen Points, Article 12 clarification on postwar status, 72; the French threat and collaboration in the Anatolia-Syria frontier, 109–15; geographical importance of, 35–36; Grand National Assembly, Kemal's call for Muslim unity, 132–33; Kemalist efforts to maintain Ottoman territories, 179–82; Lausanne Conference, negotiating Syria, 165–68; Lloyd George and Woodrow Wilson's statements on war aims, 59–64; London Conference and, 130–33; Martyrs' Square, 38; as microcosm of war and Ottoman integration, 35–37; mobilizing support amid war's violence, 43–45; nahda (cultural awakening), 29–31; Occupied Enemy Territory Administration (OETA) division of Syria, 71; Ottoman state practices in, 37–43, 47–49; Ottoman war effort in, 66–68; Paris Peace Conference (1919), 92–94, 98–100, 178; postwar British evacuation (Fall 1919), 86–87; postwar occupation and resistance, 88, 107–9; resistance to French occupation, 127–30, 133–35; Syrian Congress (al-mu'tamar al-suri), 96–97; Treaty of Lausanne (1923), 146; Treaty of Lausanne (1923), aftermath of, 171–73; Treaty of Lausanne (1923), implications for the Ottoman patrimony, 168–71; war and mobility, 45–47; wartime disease in, 42
Syrian Congress (al-mu'tamar al-suri), 19, 96, 102–3, 105, 108, 114, 130

Tal 'Afar, 77*map*, 79
Talat Pasha, 45, 70–71
Tamari, Salim, 41, 45
al-Tamimi, Rafiq, 39
Tanzimat (reorganization), 25
Taqtaq, 77*map*, 79
Tarsus, 95
Taurus Mountains: Anatolian movement, territorial objectives, 119–21, 120*map*; Armistice of Mudros (1918), 74, 77*map*; postwar occupation and resistance, 88, 107–9; as Syria-Anatolia physical dividing line, 14–15
terminology, challenges with, xviii–xix, 12–16; "race," use of terms related to, 123–25; "nation," use of terms related to, 12-13, 19, 122
Teşkilat-ı Mahsusa (Special Organization), 87, 138
Tevfik Pasha, 83, 90–91, 93, 116, 149
Third Battle of Gaza (November 7, 1917), 54–55
Thirteenth Army Corps, 147–48
Thrace: Armistice of Mudanya (1922), 145; Balkan Wars, 4, 28; Lloyd George and Woodrow Wilson's statements on war aims, 59–60; London Conference (1922), evacuation of Allied forces in, 149–50; Paris Peace Conference (1919), 93; secessions from Ottoman Empire, 22–23
Three Provinces (Elviye-i Selase), 22–23, 58, 65, 89. *See also* Kars; Ardahan; Batum
Trablusgarp (Tripolitania), 23. *See also* Libya
Trabzon Society for the Protection of National Rights (Trabzon Muhafaza-ı Hukuk-u Milliye Cemiyeti), 95
Transcaucasian Democratic Federative Republic, 64–65
Transjordan (Jordan): British promises to Faysal, 67–68; Fertile Crescent territory boundaries, xvii; Treaty of Lausanne (1923), implications for the Ottoman patrimony, 171

Treason Law (1921), 164
Treaty at Neuilly-sur-Seine (1919), 116
Treaty of Kars (1921), 143–44, 144*map*
Treaty of Lausanne (1923), 20, 122, 144*map*, 164; aftermath of, 171–73, 181; balance sheet in relation to the Treaty of Sèvres, 170, 173; implications for the Ottoman patrimony, 168–71; Kemalist efforts to maintain Ottoman territories, 180–81; Mosul's status in, 165. *See also* Lausanne Conference
Treaty of London (1913), 4
Treaty of Ouchy (1912), 4
Treaty of Saint-Germain (1919), 116
Treaty of Sèvres (1920), xviii, 136–38, 137*map*, 144*map*, 145, 179–80; British appeals to Kurdish populations following treaty, 146–47; expansion of colonial resistance after Treaty of Sèvres (1920), 138–42, 176–79;
Treaty of Versailles (1919), 95, 116
tribal groups: Anatolian resistance in northern Iraq (1921–1922), 151–54, 177–79; assistance with British and Hashemite troops in Syria, 76–77; assistance with British in Iraq, 147, 148, 163; Kurdish groups, 30, 107, 140; Lausanne Conference, negotiating Syria, 166–68; Lausanne Conference border disputes, Özdemir efforts to build alliances, 163–65; Lausanne Conference border disputes, plebiscite in tribal areas, 160; in Libya, 51–52, 148; militia group motivations for Islamic solidarity, 104, 153; qawm (kinship group), 13; resistance to British in Iraq, 119, 134, 140, 147, 150, 151, 152–54, 163; resistance to French in Syria, 133, 166, 168; Treaty of Lausanne (1923), aftermath of, 172–73; Treaty of Lausanne (1923), implications for the Ottoman patrimony, 169–71
Triple Entente. *See* Entente alliance
Tripoli, xii*map*, 23, 129
Tunisia, 23, 167
Turkey: anti-colonial movement, 5–6; appropriating Wilsonianism, 94–100; Fertile Crescent territory boundaries, xvii; Kemalist efforts to maintain Ottoman territories, 179–82; Lloyd George and Woodrow Wilson's statements on war aims, 59–64; misak-ı milli (National Pact) as foundational charter, 122–27; normality of nation and the Ottoman past, historiography and sources, 7–12; Paris Peace Conference (1919), 92–94; Treaty of Lausanne (1923), aftermath of, 171–73; Treaty of Lausanne (1923), implications for the Ottoman patrimony, 168–71; varied meanings of the word, xvii, 16, 47, 94, 125, 159. *See also* Anatolia
Turkish Petroleum Company, 159
Turks, Turkism, pan-Turkism: al-Jam'iya al-Islamiya (İslam Cemiyeti), 112–13; Anatolian movement, territorial objectives, 119–21, 120*map*; anti-colonial movements and Wilsonian principles, 90–91; appropriating Wilsonianism, 94–100, 179–80; Armistice of Mudros (1918), implications of, 75–76, 77*map*, 78, 176; Balkan Wars (1912–1913), immigration, Muslim nationalism, and Turkism, 31–35, 52–53; Kemalist efforts to maintain Ottoman territories, 179–82; Lausanne Conference, negotiating Mosul, 157–65; Lausanne Conference, negotiating Syria, 166–68; Lloyd George and Woodrow Wilson's statements on war aims, 59–64; misak-ı milli (National Pact), 121–27; Muslim groups and collective identity, 29–31; myths of Turkic origins, 33; Ottoman pan-Turkist agenda, Caucasus and, 65–68; saving the empire and constraints of Turkism, 51; Sivas Congress and, 105–9; *Speech (Nutuk)* (Kemal, 1927), 10–11, 100–101; Treaty of Lausanne (1923), implications for the Ottoman patrimony, 169–71; Turkish, as synonym for Muslim, 62
Turmus 'Ayya, 66

ummah (religious community), 13
Umum Alem-i İslam İhtilal Teşkilatı (Revolutionary Organization of the Islamic World), 87

Umur-u Şarkiye Dairesi (Office of Eastern Affairs), 87
United States: Armistice of Mudros (1918), 73–80; disinvestment in peace process, 109; failure to join League of Nations, 116; Harbord Commission, 107–8; November 1917 as pivotal month in World War I, 54–57; Ottoman-American Development Company, 164–65; Ottoman appeal to broker a ceasefire, fall of 1918, 70–73; Paris Peace Conference (1919), 92–94; Wilson's Fourteen Points declaration, 59–64. *See also* King-Crane Commission
Urfa, 80, 88, 96, 134, 137, 137*map*

Vahideddin (Mehmed VI, r. 1918–1922), 69, 70, 84–86, 101; abolishment of Ottoman sultanate, 155–57; Anatolian-Syrian collaboration, summer 1919, 104–6
Veli (Aydın deputy), 57–58
Venizelos, Eleftherios, 93, 101
von Falkenhayn, Erich, 36, 50, 66
von Sanders, Liman, 50, 66, 71

War of Independence (İstiklal Harbi), 6
War of Salvation (Kurtuluş Savaşı), 6
Wiegand, Theodor, 41
Wilson, Woodrow: disdain for Sykes-Picot agreement, 63, 178; disengagement from peace talks, 95, 109, 116; Four Ends, 66, 71; Four Principles, 64; Fourteen Points declaration, 59–64; Ottoman appeal to broker a ceasefire, fall of 1918, 70–73, 78; Paris Peace Conference (1919), 92–94
Wilsonian principles, 11, 13, 18, 30, 60–64, 66, 71, 78, 84, 87, 97, 99, 117, 144; Egypt's self-determination movement and, 156–57; Lausanne Conference, negotiating Mosul, 157–65; misak-ı milli (National Pact) use of Wilsonian ideas, 121, 125; Mustafa Kemal on, 119, 121, 179; in Sivas Congress, 105–9; use by anti-colonial movements, 90–91, 95, 176, 177–79
World War I (Great War, 1914–1918): Muslim religious patriotism in Ottoman war effort, 34–35; November 1917 as pivotal month in conflict, 54–57; Ottoman war effort in Arab provinces beyond Syria, 49–53; purge of Christian populations, 34–35, 47, 62, 64, 87, 211n85; Syria, as microcosm of war and Ottoman integration, 35–37; Syria, geographical importance of, 35–36; Syria, mobilizing support amid war's violence, 43–45; war and mobility in the Ottoman Empire, 45–47. *See also* Armistice of Mudros (1918); Paris Peace Conference (1919)

Yemen, 73; Anatolian movement (1920–1922), territorial objectives, 120; Armistice of Mudros (1918), 73–74, 75, 77*map*; Ottoman surrender in, 91; Ottoman war effort in Arab provinces, 50–51; Paris Peace Conference (1919), 98–100
Yıldırım (Thunderbolt) Army, 50, 66, 71, 78
al-Yusuf, 'Abd al-Rahman, 96–97
Yusuf Kemal (Tengirşenk), 149

Zaydi, 50, 73
Zionists: Armistice of Mudros (1918), 76; November 1917 as pivotal month in World War I, 54–57; Paris Peace Conference (1919), conflicting priorities at, 178; Sykes-Picot accord, 55–56, 64, 76; Syrian Congress on, 105. *See also* Jews
Ziya Gökalp, 67–68
Zürcher, Erik, 9

Founded in 1893,
UNIVERSITY OF CALIFORNIA PRESS
publishes bold, progressive books and journals
on topics in the arts, humanities, social sciences,
and natural sciences—with a focus on social
justice issues—that inspire thought and action
among readers worldwide.

The UC PRESS FOUNDATION
raises funds to uphold the press's vital role
as an independent, nonprofit publisher, and
receives philanthropic support from a wide
range of individuals and institutions—and from
committed readers like you. To learn more, visit
ucpress.edu/supportus.

Made in the USA
Monee, IL
17 May 2023